Psychoanalysis and the Patriarchal Tradition

Also by Peter L. Rudnytsky

Mutual Analysis: Ferenczi: Severn, and the Origins of Trauma Theory (2022)

Formulated Experiences: Hidden Realities and Emergent Meanings from Shakespeare to Fromm (2019)

ed., *The Discovery of the Self: A Study in Psychological Cure,* by Elizabeth Severn (2017)

Rescuing Psychoanalysis from Freud and Other Essays in Re-Vision (2011)

ed., *Her Hour Come Round at Last: A Garland for Nina Coltart* (with Gillian Preston) (2011)

ed., *Psychoanalysis and Narrative Medicine* (with Rita Charon) (2009)

Reading Psychoanalysis: Freud, Rank, Ferenczi, Groddeck (2002)

ed., *Psychoanalyses/Feminisms* (with Andrew M. Gordon) (2000)

Psychoanalytic Conversations: Interviews with Clinicians, Commentators, and Critics (2000)

ed., *Ferenczi's Turn in Psychoanalysis* (with Antal Bókay and Patrizia Giampieri-Deutsch) (1996)

ed., *Freud and Forbidden Knowledge* (with Ellen Handler Spitz) (1994)

ed., *Transitional Objects and Potential Spaces: Literary Uses of D. W. Winnicott* (1993)

The Psychoanalytic Vocation: Rank, Winnicott, and the Legacy of Freud (1991)

ed., *Contending Kingdoms: Historical, Psychological, and Feminist Approaches to the Literature of Sixteenth-Century England and France* (with Marie-Rose Logan) (1990)

ed., *The Persistence of Myth: Psychoanalytic and Structuralist Perspectives* (1988)

ed., Ivan L. Rudnytsky, *Essays in Modern Ukrainian History* (1987)

Freud and Oedipus (1987)

Psychoanalysis and the Patriarchal Tradition

Augustine to Milton

Peter L. Rudnytsky

BLOOMSBURY ACADEMIC

NEW YORK · LONDON · OXFORD · NEW DELHI · SYDNEY

BLOOMSBURY ACADEMIC
Bloomsbury Publishing Inc
1385 Broadway, New York, NY 10018, USA
50 Bedford Square, London, WC1B 3DP, UK
29 Earlsfort Terrace, Dublin 2, Ireland

BLOOMSBURY, BLOOMSBURY ACADEMIC and the Diana logo
are trademarks of Bloomsbury Publishing Plc

First published in the United States of America, 2026

Copyright © Peter L. Rudnytsky, 2026

For legal purposes the Acknowledgments on p. x constitute an
extension of this copyright page.

Series design by Daniel Benneworth-Gray |
Cover image: Bronze and copper alloy aquamanile in the form of Aristotle and
Phyllis, late 14th or early 15th century, South Netherlandish © Robert Lehman
Collection, 1975, The Met, NY

Library of Congress Cataloging-in-Publication Data

Names: Rudnytsky, Peter L., author.
Title: Psychoanalysis and the patriarchal tradition :
Augustine to Milton / Peter L. Rudnytsky.
Description: New York : Bloomsbury Academic, 2025. | Series: Psychoanalytic
horizons | Includes bibliographical references and index.
Identifiers: LCCN 2024050960 (print) | LCCN 2024050961 (ebook) |
ISBN 9798765131145 (paperback) | ISBN 9798765131138 (hardback) |
ISBN 9798765131152 (epub) | ISBN 9798765131169 (ebook)
Subjects: LCSH: Psychoanalysis and literature. | Patriarchy in literature. |
Feminist theory. | LCGFT: Literary criticism.
Classification: LCC PN98.P75 R83 2025 (print) | LCC PN98.P75 (ebook) |
DDC 809.001/9–dc23/eng/20241231
LC record available at https://lccn.loc.gov/2024050960
LC ebook record available at https://lccn.loc.gov/2024050961

ISBN: HB: 979-8-7651-3113-8
          PB: 979-8-7651-3114-5
        ePDF: 979-8-7651-3116-9
       eBook: 979-8-7651-3115-2

Series: Psychoanalytic Horizons

Typeset by Integra Software Services Pvt. Ltd.
Printed and bound in the United States of America

To find out more about our authors and books visit www.bloomsbury.com
and sign up for our newsletters.

For Cheryl, again,

whose firmness makes my circle just

Contents

Acknowledgments

My thanks go to my coeditors of the Psychoanalytic Horizons series, Hilary Neroni and Esther Rashkin, who have been ideal collaborators; to Haaris Naqvi, who gave our series a home at Bloomsbury Academic; and to Amy Martin, who is now at the helm. We mourn the loss of our shining light, Mari Ruti. And "evermore thanks, the exchequer of the poor," must repay "the debt immense of endless gratitude" I owe in this book to Margaret Ferguson, Stephen Greenblatt, A. C. Spearing, Madelon Spregnether, and Mitchell Wilson.

Earlier versions of the following chapters have been previously published: Chapter 1, in *Freud and Forbidden Knowledge*, ed. Peter L. Rudnytsky and Ellen Handler Spitz (New York: New York University Press, 1994), pp. 128–52; Chapter 3, in *American Imago*, 40(1983):371–83; Chapter 4, in *Contending Kingdoms: Historical, Psychological and Feminist Approaches to the Literature of Sixteenth-Century England and France*, ed. Marie-Rose Logan and Peter L. Rudnytsky (Detroit: Wayne State University Press, 1990), pp. 149–72; Chapter 5, in *The Psychoanalytic Study of Literature*, ed. Joseph Reppen and Maurice Charney (Hillsdale, NJ: Analytic Press, 1985), pp. 169–90; Chapter 6, in *Modern Philology*, 96(1999):291–311; Chapter 7, in *Trauma and Transformation: The Political Progress of John Bunyan*, ed. Vera J. Camden (Stanford: Stanford University Press, 2007), pp. 14–35; and Chapter 8, in *The Persistence of Myth: Psychoanalytic and Structuralist Perspectives*, ed. Peter L. Rudnytsky (New York: Guilford Press, 1988), pp. 153–76. All have been more or less drastically revised to bring them in line with my current thinking.

I have excluded essays that appear in my previous authored books. Readers interested in my further psychoanalytic explorations of Shakespeare and Milton are referred to: "Rethinking *King Lear*: From Incestuous Fantasy to Primitive Anxieties," in *Rescuing Psychoanalysis from Freud and Other Essays in Re-Vision* (London: Karnac Books, 2011), pp. 123–49; "Freud as Milton's God: Mapping the Patriarchal Cosmos in Psychoanalysis and *Paradise Lost*," *American Imago*, 71(2014):253–87; rpt. in *Formulated Experiences: Hidden Realities and Emergent Meanings from Shakespeare to Fromm* (New York: Routledge, 2019), pp. 39–69; "*Othello* and *Macbeth*: Complementary Borderline Pathologies at the Basic Fault," in *Formulated Experiences*, pp. 167–86; and "'I Am Not What I Am': Iago and Negative Transcendence," *Fromm Forum*, 22(2018):21–37; rpt. in *Formulated Experiences*, pp. 187–204.

Note on Texts

All quotations from Shakespeare are to *The Riverside Shakespeare* (Evans et al., 1974); all quotations of Milton's poetry are to the edition of Merritt Y. Hughes (1957). Donne is quoted from the edition of Grierson (1912), and Marvell from the third edition of Margoliouth (1988). Quotations from St. Augustine's *City of God* are to the translation by Dods. References to Sophocles and Euripides are to the translations by Grene. For Lucretius I have relied on the edition of Martin Ferguson Smith. All quotations from the Bible are to the King James Version. Unless otherwise noted, all italics and brackets that appear in quotations are in the original texts, while all ellipses have been added.

Introduction

This palimpsest has been decades in the making. A proposal in my files for a book with the same title dates back to 1994, while fifteen years earlier my doctoral dissertation at Yale, *Siege of Contraries: An Essay in Psychoanalytic Criticism*, brought together Freud, Sophocles, and Milton to explore why the myths of Oedipus and the Fall have exerted so profound an influence on the Western imagination through the ages. The answer I proposed had to do with their unrivaled claims to explain the human condition in universal terms, and this, in turn, opened the possibility of tracing the often-intertwined genealogies of these hegemonic narratives of the Hellenic and Hebraic traditions.

Throughout my career, I have tried to sustain my identity as a scholar trained in Renaissance literature while pursuing my passion for psychoanalysis, not simply as a mode of literary criticism but as a field of intellectual history in its own right. The fact that the sections of my dissertation that focused on Freud and Sophocles resulted in *Freud and Oedipus* (1987), while the Milton section became an article, was prophetic of how all my subsequent authored books and all but one of my edited books—not counting my father's *Essays on Modern Ukrainian History*—have centered on the history and theory of psychoanalysis, while my literary forays have been the labors of my "left hand." *Psychoanalysis and the Patriarchal Tradition* is my attempt at least partially to redress this imbalance.

While my commitment to psychoanalysis has been unwavering—and I have since 2010 not only obtained a license in social work but also graduated from the Chicago Psychoanalytic Institute to be able to "tend the homely slighted Shepherd's trade"—my theoretical views have evolved to the point where my outlook today is very different from what it was forty-five years ago. In this process, the Independent tradition of British object relations theory, of which Winnicott is the foremost representative, and the courageous examples of Ferenczi and Fromm, have had the greatest influence on my thinking. I have come to see Freud's principal flaws as having been his minimizing of the importance of environmental factors in his drive theory and the phallocentric attitudes toward gender that warp his entire system. I also regard him as an authoritarian character whose placing of personal loyalty above the search for truth bequeathed a tragic legacy to psychoanalysis. Analogously, I now consider both Augustine's interpretation of the Fall story in Genesis and Freud's shibboleth of the Oedipus complex to be based on untenable assumptions about human nature. Both, I would argue, are largely attempts to blame the victims— whether individual children or the human race as a whole—by imputing to them an inherent sinfulness that is in reality a result of the traumas inflicted on them by the parental figures (including God) who supposedly have their best interests at heart.

Paradoxically, however, when it comes to literature, I remain captivated by the enduring power of these master myths despite my intellectual reservations about them; and one of my leitmotifs in the ensuing chapters is how the incest taboo functions as the "latent content" of the Fall story. Similarly, when the concepts of Klein or Lacan have seemed to illuminate a text, I have not hesitated to draw on them, even though I am neither a Kleinian nor a Lacanian. The deconstruction to which I was exposed as a graduate student and the new historicism that transformed Renaissance studies early in my career have likewise left their marks, although I am by no means a postmodernist or social constructivist. My longstanding interest in the subjective roots of creativity draws me to psychobiography, which, when done judiciously, enhances rather than reduces our understanding of the works that enthrall us; and I reject the aspersion that it is naive or illegitimate to look upon literary characters as "imagined human beings" (Paris, 1997) that can, when there is sufficient evidence, be analyzed accordingly. Above all, I prize close reading as much as I do open-minded listening in clinical practice, and I hope in this book to have exhibited the diversity of psychoanalytic approaches to literature.

By my title, *Psychoanalysis and the Patriarchal Tradition*, I mean to take up the challenge posed by Gayle Rubin's (1975) observation that "psychoanalysis is a feminist theory *manqué*" (p. 185). In so doing, my project stands in a dialectical relation to that of my *Doktorvater* Harold Bloom, who in *The Western Canon* (1994) defines the canon as "a choice of texts struggling among one another for survival"—a choice that he maintains should be made "by late-coming authors who feel themselves chosen by particular ancestral figures," rather than by "the composite god of historical process" (p. 20). But when I look at the ancestral figures who have chosen me in this book and recognize that they are all the proverbial Dead White Males, how can I deny the role of the historical process in my rounding up of the Usual Suspects?

Thus, while I am an unrepentant humanist, I am also a partisan of the opposing forces that Bloom brands the School of Resentment. Even truths that we hold to be self-evident can be only imperfectly discerned—let alone lived up to—at any given historical moment, and the greatest artistic masterpieces should not be exempt from ideological critique. And while I hope that my embrace of feminism as a complement to psychoanalysis has permitted me to go some way toward dismantling the patriarchy from within, I have tried to be cognizant of the limitations in my perspective. If, as Rubin (1984) points out in a later essay, "feminism is the theory of gender oppression" (p. 32), and this insight is one of my mainstays, I have less to say about other dimensions of sexuality, or issues of race and class, though I have tried to be mindful of these as well. And because of my own formation in an era when the idea of Great Books could be taken for granted, and the composition of the "canon" was consequently much more stable than it is today, my reach does not extend to the "sisters" of Shakespeare and Milton, whose works have gained increased recognition in recent decades and are now integral to the collective enterprise of "rewriting the Renaissance" (Ferguson, Quilligan, and Vickers, 1986).

As to what I mean by "patriarchy," I cannot agree with Rubin (1975) that it "ought to be confined to the Old Testament-type pastoral nomads from whom the term derives, or groups like them" (p. 168). In my more capacious definition, which goes back not only to Adam but also to Oedipus, the term encompasses any form of the "sex/gender system" that results in "the oppression of women, of sexual minorities, and of certain aspects of human personality within individuals" (p. 159). Notwithstanding the obvious differences between cultures, which must also be taken into account, there are also remarkably tenacious bulwarks of male privilege that Rubin herself— drawing on Freud and the structuralist anthropology of Lévi-Strauss—sums up as the "traffic in women." These, she acknowledges, constitute "a long tradition in which women do not inherit, in which women do not lead, and in which women do not talk to god" (p. 164).

In Stephen Greenblatt's (2017) estimation, not only is *Paradise Lost* "the greatest poem in the English language," it is also "an unprecedented, even shocking fulfillment of Augustine's injunction to interpret Genesis literally" (p. 163). There is thus an intrinsic logic to where I begin and end my story, and every way station on my journey fits Frank Kermode's (1975) conception of a classic as a text that survives "by being patient of interpretation" (p. 134), and because it "must always signify more than is needed by any one interpreter or any one generation of interpreters" (p. 140). In psychoanalysis, the indispensable classic remains Freud, concerning whom I take as my watchword Luce Irigaray's (1974) commentary on the Janus-like nature of his work: "By exhibiting this 'symptom,' this crisis point in metaphysics where we find exposed that sexual 'indifference' that had assured metaphysical coherence and 'closure,' Freud offers it up for our analysis. With his text offering itself to be understood, to be read, as doubtless the most relevant re-mark of an ancient dream of self ... one that had never been interpreted" (p. 28; ellipses in original).

The patriarchal tradition is still too much with us, but I hope to have unsettled it with my interpretations and provided a provisional closure with my parentheses.

Chapter 1

Augustine's Family Romance

"What difference does it make whether it is in a wife or in a mother, provided that we nonetheless avoid Eve in any woman? For this shadow of a son's love for his mother comes from the leaves of that tree with which our parents first clothed themselves in that damnable nakedness."

—St. Augustine, Epistle 243

1

In the first modern psychological study of St. Augustine's *Confessions*, E. R. Dodds (1928) proposed that the book should be envisaged, "on the one hand, as the earliest example of a well-defined and curious literary genre, the introspective autobiography; on the other, as the intimate record of a neurotic conflict." The origins of the "permanent disharmony" in Augustine's soul, continues the great classicist, "lie deeper than anything we commonly call religious experience" (p. 460). Dodds thus invites us simultaneously to read the *Confessions* as a psychoanalytic case study and to see it as inaugurating a tradition of self-analysis that culminates in Freud's *Interpretation of Dreams* (1900). Reinforcing this conjunction, Carl E. Schorske (1973) has observed that in his masterwork Freud combines the "visible structure of the scientific treatise" with an "invisible personal narrative" that takes us into "the underground recesses of his own buried self," as if one were to imagine St. Augustine "weaving his *Confessions* into *The City of God*" (p. 330).

That the *Confessions* lends itself to a psychoanalytic reading is, however, by no means a universally accepted proposition. Deriding the efforts of "modern psychiatrists" to interpret Augustine's text, Garry Wills (1999) takes exception to the notions that the saint might have harbored "incestuous feelings for his mother or homosexual feelings for his friend" (p. xvii). With respect to Augustine's mother, Wills contends that "too much is often made of her role in Augustine's life" (p. 57). Similarly, James O'Donnell (1985) insists that the *Confessions* "is emphatically not 'the first modern autobiography,' for the autobiographical narrative that takes up part of the work is incidental content while prayer is the significant form" (p. 83).

The hyperbole in the rhetoric of Wills and O'Donnell exposes the dogmatism of their objections to psychological readings of the *Confessions*. To recognize the centrality of prayer to the form of the work need not entail reducing Augustine's gripping account of his life to "incidental content." Peter Brown offers a more nuanced assessment in his biography, *Augustine of Hippo* (1967). Brown points out that "Augustine takes up a position analogous to that of Freud" not only in postulating that "a dislocation in human consciousness" (p. 261) makes language opaque and in need of interpretation, but also in discerning "unconscious consent to the 'desires of sin' as betraying itself in a slip of the tongue" (p. 366). Quoting the passage where Augustine declares that his mother, Monica, a devout Christian—unlike her husband Patricius, who did not convert until he was on his deathbed—"did all that she could to see that you, my God, should be a Father to me rather than he" (1.11),[1] Brown remarks that "Augustine has deservedly brought down upon his head the attentions of modern psychological interpreters" (p. 31). Brown preemptively rebuts both Wills's minimizing of Monica's importance to Augustine and O'Donnell's denial of Augustine's modernity when he writes, "What Augustine remembered in the *Confessions* was his inner life; and this inner life is dominated by one figure—his mother" (p. 29).

Nevertheless, despite being favorably disposed to psychoanalysis, Brown (1967) remains hesitant about its utility as a method of interpretation. "It is," he remarks, "one thing to take due note of a blatant childhood tension that was still very much in Augustine's mind as he wrote the *Confessions* in middle age; and it is quite another to follow the tension through, from its roots in Augustine's childhood, throughout a long and variegated life" (p. 31). Of "the unexpected combinations, ramifications and resolutions that a properly sophisticated knowledge of modern psychology would lead one to expect," Brown maintains that these "escape the historian" (p. 31).

Despite his doubts, however, Brown has furnished the roadmap for a "properly sophisticated" psychoanalytic reading of the *Confessions*. What is needed is precisely to "take due note" of Augustine's "childhood tension" and then to "follow the tension through" by tracing its "ramifications" in his "long and variegated life." In so doing, I shall contend that Augustine's narrative conforms to the blueprint delineated by Freud (1909) of a "family romance," in which the hero seeks out substitutes for parental figures—especially the father—and asserts a bond with the mother from which both his paternal and sibling rivals are excluded. Augustine's theft of the pears in Book 2 marks the point of convergence between his Oedipus complex and

---

[1] Quotations from the *Confessions* (*c.* 397) are to the translation by R. S. Pine-Coffin, with book and section numbers given parenthetically.

his reenactment of the Fall. Since, as John Freccero (1986) has commented, Augustine invents the genre of autobiography in a work that provides "the first literary expression" of "a pattern named after Oedipus since Freud" (p. 19), Augustine is the precursor of Freud above all in distilling out of his "intimate record of a neurotic conflict" a doctrine of primordial guilt that attempts to explain the human condition by means of a master-myth of all-embracing explanatory power.

2

Nowhere are both Augustine's psychological acuity and his affinity with Freud more clearly in evidence than in Book 1 of the *Confessions*, where he contemplates infancy. Indeed, he even wonders whether there was anything that preceded "the stage of life that I spent in my mother's womb" (1.6). Seeking to substantiate his hypothesis that "no man is free from sin, not even a child who has lived only one day on earth" (1.7), Augustine presents a recognizably "Freudian" view of human nature.[2] A cornerstone of Freud's outlook is his conviction that the psyche is governed by the pleasure principle, a drive to fulfill wishes through tension-reduction. Augustine likewise emphasizes how, as an infant, he strove "to make my wishes known to others, who might satisfy them" (1.6). But, he continues, "because my wishes were inside me, while other people were outside," adults often failed to understand him, "so I would toss my arms and legs about and make noises, hoping that such few signs as I could make would show my meaning, though they were quite unlike what they were meant to mime" (1.6). In this analysis of preverbal communication, Augustine anticipates not only Freud's thesis concerning the primacy of endogenous drives but also his elaboration of the "two principles of mental functioning" (1911), according to which the reality principle achieves by indirect means the aims of the pleasure principle.

Augustine utilizes direct observation—presumably of his son Adeodatus, born of his union with the mistress with whom he cohabited for thirteen years—to corroborate conclusions reached by introspection: "By watching babies I have learnt that this is how they behave, and they, quite unconsciously, have done more than those who brought me up to convince

---

[2]　Augustine's insistence that infants are tainted by original sin is likewise integral to the psychoanalytic vision of Klein. As Winnicott (1971) points out, "the concept of the death instinct" that Klein adopted from Freud "could be described as a reassertion of the principle of original sin." What this outlook ignores, Winnicott continues, is "the full implication of dependence and therefore of the environmental factor" (pp. 70–1).

me that I behaved in just the same way myself" (1.6). Turning to the theme of sibling rivalry, Augustine affirms that he has witnessed "jealousy in a baby," citing the example of an infant who, "whenever he saw his foster-brother at the breast, … would go pale with envy. Mothers and nurses," Augustine adds, "say that they can work such things out of the system by one means or another, but surely it cannot be called innocence, when the milk flows in such abundance from its source, to object to a rival desperately in need and depending for its life on this one form of nourishment" (1.7).

Beyond their shared ideas about infancy, Augustine resembles Freud in endorsing the premise that early experience provides a template for later stages of the life cycle: "commanders and kings may take the place of tutors and schoolmasters, nuts and balls and pet birds may give way to money and estates and servants, but these same passions remain with us while one stage of life follows another" (1.19). He notes the hypocrisy with which adults judge the activities of children: "grown-up games are called 'business,' and even though boys games are much the same, they are punished for them by their elders" (1.9). The paradigm of the infant at the mother's breast reverberates throughout the *Confessions*. Equating God's mercy with "the comfort of woman's milk" (1.25), Augustine anchors his proclamation of Christian faith in an appeal to the reader's archaic memories, "Let us scent your fragrance and taste your sweetness" (8.4).

Augustine's commitment to the genetic principle of explanation is evident in the portraits he draws of Monica and Patricius, which enable us to follow the process whereby Augustine projects internalized images—or imagos— of his parents onto people he meets throughout his life. These dynamics of transference stand out in the case of male figures, who outnumber and—with the exception of his mother—overshadow female ones in the *Confessions*. Augustine's characterization of his father is marked by a combination of affection and criticism. He was unfaithful to his wife and had a "hot temper," but could also be "remarkably kind" (9.9). Despite being, in Rebecca West's (1933) phrase, "a country gentleman of very narrow acres" (p. 18), Patricius "was ready to provide his son with all that was needed" for travel and study, but "took no trouble at all to see how I was growing in your sight or whether I was chaste or not" (2.3). When Patricius one day in the public baths chanced to see "the signs of active virility coming to life" in Augustine, he responded affirmatively to his son's burgeoning sexuality, though Augustine adds that his delight in the thought of grandchildren "was due to the intoxication that causes the world to forget you, its Creator" (2.3).

Augustine subsequently encounters two contrasting father figures, Faustus and Ambrose. As a young man in Carthage, Augustine awaits Faustus, the Manichean sage, with "keenest expectation" (5.6), and is at first impressed by his polished manner. Upon seeking to know his teacher better, however, Augustine is disappointed by the poverty of his scholarship. Faustus's inability to resolve Augustine's intellectual doubts causes the young seeker to begin questioning Manichean doctrines. But though his final judgment is negative, Augustine lauds Faustus for recognizing his limitations because "modesty and candour are finer equipment for the mind than scientific knowledge of the kind I wished to possess" (5.7). With this ambivalent verdict, Augustine casts Faustus in the mold of Patricius.

Whereas Faustus is Augustine's pagan father figure, Ambrose is his surrogate Christian father.[3] Augustine makes explicit the filial dimension of his relationship with Ambrose: "This man of God received me like a father and, as bishop, told me how glad he was that I had come" (5.13). The trajectory of Augustine's attitude toward Ambrose is the obverse of that toward Faustus. At first, despite the bishop of Milan's kindness and erudition, Augustine is "uninterested" and even "contemptuous" of his sermons, which he failed to deliver in a "soothing and gratifying manner" (5.13). Only gradually does the young man begin to listen seriously to Ambrose's arguments in defense of the Catholic faith.

Ambrose's role as a paternal ideal for Augustine is confirmed by an incident involving Monica, who had journeyed to Milan to be with her son. Although it had been her custom in Africa to bring offerings of bread and wine to the shrines of the saints, she immediately ceased doing so in Milan upon learning that the practice had been prohibited by Ambrose. According to Wills, a devotion to the shrines of martyrs was characteristic of the Donatists, a puritanical sect that had taken hold in Thagaste and of which Augustine's mother was at one time likely an adherent. This ritual had permitted Monica to partake of the wine herself, though Augustine insists that she did so only out of noble motives. As Augustine surmises, Monica's "pious submission" (6.2) to Ambrose's edict would not have been forthcoming had it been issued by anyone she venerated less deeply.

In evaluating his parents' marriage, Augustine stresses that Monica never disobeyed Patricius in any way. Indeed, she would reproach other wives who complained about being beaten by their husbands, blaming them instead for the looseness of their tongues: "Her manner was light but her meaning serious when she told them that ever since they had heard the marriage

---

[3] Wills (1999) draws attention to Augustine's relationship with Rominian, a wealthy friend from his North African birthplace of Thagaste, of whom he wrote a decade earlier in *Answer to Skeptics*, "And when I was deprived of my father, you compensated for that by your patronage, encouragement, and financial help" (qtd. p. 20). Wills suggests that the pears stolen by Augustine may have come from Rominian's orchard, but there is no evidence for this in the *Confessions*.

deed read over to them, they ought to have regarded it as a contract which bound them to serve their husbands, and from that time onward they should remember their condition and not defy their masters" (9.9). Monica espouses the gender roles of late classical culture, but her subservience to Patricius exists in tension with the force of her personality and her grip on the reins of power within the family. As Fabio Troncarelli (1993) has documented, Monica continued to assert her dominance in the household of friends and disciples formed by her son after his conversion. Not only did she dictate when meals were to be taken, but she even reproved one wretch for having dared to sing a hymn while relieving himself in the privy! As Troncarelli comments, "Monica has a veritable phobia for the 'dirty' parts of the human body and regulates with implacable attention the satisfaction of the primary needs—alimentary and excretory—in children and in adults" (p. 183).

The chain of Augustine's substitutions is less easy to follow in the case of Monica than in that of Patricius because her inescapable presence made it impossible for him to replace her with any other woman. The absence of a public outlet for Monica's energies caused her to live vicariously through her prodigy. As Ian Suttie has observed in *The Origins of Love and Hate* (1935), an early classic of relational psychoanalysis, in cultures where women are accorded respect and autonomy mothers will normally be able to effectuate the "psychic weaning" of their children and to "repress infantile sexuality and incest-wishes in a permanently and completely effective manner." However, if a woman lacks status apart from her maternal role, she becomes "dependent on the child, will cling to it and cultivate its dependency on herself, with contrary effect upon the Oedipus wishes" (p. 122).[4]

It follows from Suttie's analysis that the intensity of Augustine's Oedipus complex was fueled by his mother's excessively passionate and possessive love for him. Because Patricius was not a Christian, Monica sought to make Augustine feel that God was his father, thereby creating a bond between mother and son from which her husband was excluded. Monica thereby reared Augustine in an avatar of the Holy Family, in which Jesus shares with his mother, the divinely impregnated Virgin Mary, an intimacy to which his human father Joseph cannot lay claim.

That Augustine experienced acute separation anxiety is attested by his attempt—in imitation of Aeneas, about whose wanderings he had read as a schoolboy (1.11)—to escape from his mother's influence by secretly

---

[4]   In *The Glory of Hera*, Philip Slater (1968) similarly hypothesizes that "whenever one finds a mother who, by virtue of being a woman, is deprived in some way of self-expression or forced to endure narcissistic wounds of various kinds, one may expect to find also a mother whose aspect is menacing to her male children" (p. 23).

sailing at night from Carthage to Rome.[5] Augustine interprets this journey as a means by which God used Monica's "too jealous love for her son as a scourge for her own just punishment. For as mothers do, and far more than most, she loved to have me with her" (5.8). As Stephen Greenblatt (2017) has noted, Augustine's Latin phrase for Monica's "too jealous love"—*carnale desiderium*—"would seem more appropriate for a lover than a mother," and "as Augustine looked back at his relation to his mother, he cast himself in his imagination as both her child and her husband" (pp. 90–1). Even though he deceived his mother, Augustine remarks that God "did not punish me for it" (5.8), since the sea-journey passed without incident. But this negation reveals Augustine's unconscious anticipation of punishment, and he adds without further comment: "At Rome I was at once struck down by illness" (5.9). In the absence of other explanations, this illness appears to be psychogenic, as though Augustine succumbed upon arrival to the guilt feelings he had temporarily withstood in venturing to leave Monica behind in the first place.

Unlike the vengeful Dido, however, who, upon being abandoned by Aeneas, impaled herself with a sword atop her funeral pyre, Monica refused to concede defeat and followed her son on his epic journey. Thus, Augustine never separated himself from his mother and in consequence may be said to have become a Christian rather than a classical hero. The battle of wills between mother and son is symbolized by Monica's dream in Book 3, in which she and a young man in a "halo of splendour" (3.11) stand at either end of a plank, the interpretation of which hinges on the detail that *he* shall come to where *she* is, not she to him. Although the young man in the dream is not explicitly identified, he clearly represents Augustine in a state of glory. After the dream, when the disconsolate Monica talks to a priest about her wayward son, he reassures her, "'It cannot be that the son of these tears should be lost'" (3.12). As Augustine's eventual conversion goes to show, Monica did indeed get her way, but at the cost of depriving her beloved offspring of a normal process of separation and individuation.

One consequence of Monica's possessiveness can be seen when Augustine allowed his mistress, the mother of Adeodatus, to be "torn from my side" when he contemplated marriage to another woman, "a blow which crushed my heart to bleeding, because I loved her dearly" (6.15). This plan was engineered by Monica, who hoped that Augustine would "be washed clean

---

[5] On Augustine and Aeneas, see Kligerman (1957), to whom I am indebted on the oedipal configurations in Augustine's family, and MacCormack (1998). Symptomatically, Wills (1999) twice misspells the psychoanalyst's name as "Dr. Charles Klingerman" (pp. xvii, 147), while Brown (1967) renders it still more approximately as "Klegemann" (p. 31) and "Klegeman" (p. 442).

of my sins by the saving waters of baptism" following his marriage, which would have matched him with a girl who "was nearly two years too young for marriage" (6.13), although her parents had consented to their union. Greenblatt (2017), who describes the girl as a "Catholic heiress," clarifies that she "was probably only ten or eleven years old" (p. 92), whereas Augustine was thirty at the time. Not only did Augustine abandon the woman he loved at his mother's behest, but, as he admits, because "I was a slave of lust rather than a true lover of marriage, I took another mistress, without the sanction of wedlock" (6.15). It is a measure of the shadow cast by Monica over her son's life that all three of these women—his two mistresses and his prospective bride—remain unnamed in the *Confessions*; and Monica's triumph was sealed when in the end he married no one.

Although there was no external obligation that he renounce sex since Christians were permitted to marry, Augustine consistently equates his struggle to convert with a subduing of the flesh, "Though you did not forbid me to marry, you counselled me to take a better course" (10.30). This preoccupation with celibacy as the solution to the demon of lust is epitomized by Augustine's notorious prayer, "Give me chastity and continence, but not yet" (8.7). What Augustine calls his "canker of anxiety" at the prospect of having "to adapt myself to living with a wife" (8.1) stems from an incestuous fixation. Having gone so far during his Carthage years "as to relish the thought of lust, and gratify it too, within the walls of your church during the celebration of your mysteries" (3.3)—presumably a reference to engaging in either masturbation or sexual intercourse during the divine liturgy— Augustine conforms to the pattern of the Don Juan who strives through promiscuity to replace the mother toward whom he feels unconscious hostility but on whom he remains emotionally dependent.

The theme of celibacy comes to a head at the moment of Augustine's conversion. Just prior to his breakthrough, Augustine sees before him, standing on the other side of a "barrier," "the chaste beauty of Continence in all her serene, unsullied joy" (8.11). He envisions Continence not as "barren" but as "a fruitful mother of children, of joys born of you, O Lord, her spouse" (8.11). This allegorical personification depicts the "unity of self" he had dissipated by the pursuit of a "variety of pleasures" (10.29). But in addition to its religious meaning, the fusion of chastity and fecundity in the figure of Continence constitutes a representation of the mother, who, in her son's eyes, is at once a nonsexual and sexual being. The "barrier" between himself and Continence instantiates the incest taboo, which is paradoxically at once restored (in that Augustine renounces sexuality) and violated (in that Augustine unites with the mother) when he crosses to the other side. Indeed, the first thing that Augustine does, after his conversion and that of his friend

Alypius, is to go indoors and tell his mother, who is "overjoyed" that her son no longer "desired a wife," but, in fulfillment of her dream of him standing where she is, is rather prepared to join her upon the "rule of faith" (8.12).

The death of Monica, recounted in Book 9, prompts Augustine to look back on his life. He recalls the night before her passing in which he and she together contemplated the superiority of heavenly joys to any earthly pleasures: "And while we spoke of the eternal Wisdom, longing for it and straining for it with all the strength of our hearts, for one fleeting instant we reached out and touched it. Then with a sigh … we returned to the sound of our own speech, in which each word has a beginning and an ending" (9.10). This evocation of transcendence, which Greenblatt (2017) terms a "spiritual climax" and "the most intense experience in his life" (p. 96), is suffused with sexuality. It likewise draws on the preverbal memories Augustine evokes in Book I. As Troncarelli (1993) explicates, "Augustine and his mother experience the 'vertigo' of fusion; they reenact the intensity of the symbiotic relation of earliest infancy just as in the sexual relation one reenacts together with one's partner the ineffable sweetness of being *two in one*" (p. 182).

Augustine's description of Monica on her deathbed elicits his sole reference to a sibling. As Augustine struggles to hold back his tears, his brother remarks on how unfortunate it is that she has to die abroad instead of in her own country. In response, Monica casts a reproachful glance and exclaims, "'See how he talks!'" (9.11). Like the women in Augustine's love life, his brother is never identified in the *Confessions*, though other sources establish that he was older than Augustine and named Navigus (Brown, 1967, pp. 29, 118).[6] Indeed, Augustine seems to introduce his brother at this juncture for no other reason than to annihilate him, following which the narrative reverts to his mother.

With her dying breath, Monica renounces the "vain desire" of being buried beside her husband. Whereas formerly she had "always wanted this extra happiness," Monica no longer sought such worldly consolations, and Augustine admits that he was "both surprised and pleased to find that this was so" (9.11). Despite Patricius's conversion to Christianity, he remains divided from Monica in death, and Kligerman (1957) observes that Augustine thereby fulfills "the infantile oedipal fantasy of separating his parents forever, and was even able to rationalize it as an act of piety" (p. 483). In a gesture of reparation, he prays, "Let her rest in peace with her husband. He was her first husband and she married no other after him" (9.13). But this sentiment does

---

6 Troncarelli (1993, p. 184) points out that Augustine is also known to have had at least one sister, whom he shrouds in silence in the *Confessions* and refused to admit into his presence for fear of slanders after he became a priest and she a nun.

not undo Augustine's symbolic patricide. At his mother's death, he vanquishes both his sibling and oedipal rivals. Monica's last wish ratifies for eternity her devaluation of her conjugal bond in favor of her spiritual communion with her son. Although Augustine devotes most of a book to his mother's death, he mentions his father's death only in passing (3.4).

In Book 12, Augustine offers a hymn of praise to Jerusalem, his "beloved mother," as well as to God: "And I shall remember you her Ruler, you who gave her light, you her Father, her Guardian, and her Spouse" (12.16). That Augustine should unite God and Jerusalem as partners in a mystical marriage, where the husband-father is the "Ruler" of his daughter-wife, culminates his family romance and enforces the gender norms of patriarchy. In Troncarelli's (1993) summation:

> Paradoxically, the symbolic accomplishment of the incest and the restoration of the symbiotic bond permit Augustine to assume a paternal role and have a stabilizing function. Having taken the place of his real father he can don the mask of the putative father: like Ambrose, he can become a pious Christian bishop, a defender of the faith against its enemies.
>
> (p. 182)

Through his replacement of Patricius and identification with Ambrose, Augustine is able to glorify God as the supreme father figure who reasserts authority over the feminine principle symbolized by Jerusalem.

3

Of the theft of pears recounted in Book 2 of the *Confessions*, Lionel Trilling (1963) remarks that "Augustine's puzzling sin is the paradigm of the modern spiritual enterprise" (p. 81). Like Raskolnikov's murder of the pawnbroker in Dostoevsky's *Crime and Punishment*, Augustine's transgression is haunting because of its apparent lack of motivation: "For of what I stole I already had plenty, and I had no wish to enjoy the things I coveted by stealing, but only to enjoy the theft itself and the sin. ... Perhaps we ate some of them, but our real pleasure consisted in doing something that was forbidden" (2.4).

Through his theft of the pears Augustine confronts as an existential reality the mystery of evil with which he wrestles intellectually in the *Confessions*: "Where then is evil? What is its origin? How did it steal into the world?" (7.5). Augustine's answer to these questions is that evil is not a substance, as the Manicheans claimed, but rather a privation of good arising from the choice of the perverted will to disobey God. Looking back on his deed, committed at the age of sixteen, Augustine declares, "I am quite sure that I would not have done it own my own" (2.8). Kenneth Burke (1961, pp. 93–101) has illuminated this collective aspect of the episode by proposing that Augustine and his fellows form a blasphemous counterpart to the corporate body of the Christian church, in that the *gratuitousness* of the sin that binds them together is counterpoised and redeemed by Christ's gift of *grace* to all who accept the offer of salvation through his blood.

Seen from a theological perspective, Augustine's theft of the pears signifies an ontogenetic reenactment of the Fall. Noting that Augustine refers to the pears as *poma*, the same word used in the Vulgate to mean "fruit" in the Garden of Eden, Freccero (1986, pp. 25–8) has argued that there is a typological relation between the pear tree, redolent of sexuality, and the fig tree, linked to that in John 1.48 under which Nathanael was first seen by Christ, beneath which Augustine is sitting when he experiences his conversion. This correspondence between Adam's sin and that of Augustine can only be imperfect, however, because it is the consequence of Adam's disobedience that none of his descendants can recapture his freedom of the will, which would once again make it possible to choose *not* to sin. But the parallel between their falls is unmistakable. As Augustine remarks in *The City of God*, not only was Adam's sin "committed about food," but the lure of Adam's tree, no less than his own, arose from the fact that it was "not bad nor noxious, except because it was forbidden" (14.12).

The unconscious aspect of Augustine's theft of the pears is thrown into relief when its mundane nature is seen to serve as what Freud (1899) terms a "screen memory" for other psychically charged experiences. Freud defines screen memories as "everyday and indifferent events" that are remembered in place of "serious and tragic" (p. 305) ones with which they are associatively linked. The unconscious determinants of Augustine's memory lie hidden in plain sight in his report of two events involving his parents. The first, to which I have already alluded, is his father's witnessing of "the signs of active virility coming to life" (2.3) in him in the public baths. Kligerman (1957) infers that this means Augustine "had an erection" (p. 473), a reading endorsed by Greenblatt (2017), who finds it more plausible than the alternative hypothesis that Patricius "may simply have remarked on his son's recently sprouted pubic hair" (p. 81). Incensed by Kligerman's interpretation, Wills (1999) is adamant that the Latin phrase *inquieta induta adulescentia* ("clothed in unquiet adolescence") signifies nothing more than that "Augustine in the public baths is a fallen Adam, not yet clothed in Christ's grace—as he will be when Ambrose immerses him in the *spiritual* bath of baptism" (p. xix). But, as Greenblatt (2017) counters, "erection—and above all the involuntary experience of erection—turns out … to be crucial in Augustine's interpretation of the story of Adam and Eve and his understanding of the Fall" (pp. 338–9). It is therefore compatible with a theological understanding of Augustine's depiction of himself as a "fallen Adam" that he should admit to having had an involuntary erection. Whatever it was that Augustine's father saw in the baths, it caused him to anticipate becoming a grandfather, which gives the incident a sexual cast.

The second psychologically significant event concerns Augustine's mother, who, "alarmed and apprehensive" that he might stray from the path of virtue, "most earnestly warned me not to commit fornication and above all not to seduce any man's wife" (2.3). Monica enjoins Augustine to refrain not merely from fornication but also from adultery. But since the first woman for whom a boy experiences sexual desire is typically his father's wife, Monica's warning is unconsciously an admonition not to violate the incest taboo. From all that we have seen of the intimacy between mother and son, this prohibition has the quality of a reaction formation, which intensifies the forbidden longings it is designed to suppress—Monica's as well as those of the overstimulated Augustine.

Either of these sexually arousing incidents with his parents would have been disturbing on its own, but their impact is compounded by their convergence. In Book 2, Augustine reaches "the age at which the frenzy gripped me and I surrendered myself entirely to lust" (2.2), and these memories distill the emotional impact of his arrival at puberty and initiation into genital sexuality. Crucially, Augustine reports these two memories in the section of Book 2 *immediately prior* to that in which he commences his narrative of the pear-stealing episode.

The disproportion between the triviality of Augustine's offense—his theft of the fruit for which he had no use and in which he took no pleasure—and the momentousness he imputes to it may thus be explained psychoanalytically as a displacement of the sense of guilt belonging to the "serious" incidents with his parents onto an "indifferent" occurrence. And since Monica's warning against fornication and adultery paradoxically both reinforces and invites the violation of the incest taboo, Augustine's screen memory of stealing of the forbidden fruit is at once a reenactment of the Fall and a symptom of the Oedipus complex as it is revived in adolescence.

Like the psychological dynamics in Augustine's life as a whole, his theft of the pears is open to interpretation on multiple levels. A far-reaching insight into the preoedipal determinants of Augustine's deed is provided by Winnicott (1964):

> But a child who, say, regularly goes and steals apples, and probably gives
> them away without himself enjoying them, is acting under a compulsion,

and is ill. He can be called a thief. He will not know why he has done what he has done, and if pressed for a reason he will become a liar. The thing is, what is this boy doing? … *The thief is not looking for the object that he takes. He is looking for a person. He is looking for his own mother, only he does not know this.*

(p. 163)

The compulsiveness of the behavior Winnicott describes contrasts with the apparently isolated nature of Augustine's theft, but his comments otherwise read as though they were an exegesis of this episode in the *Confessions*.[7] Augustine does not enjoy the fruit that he steals, nor can he provide a motive for his actions. If Augustine is looking for his mother without knowing it, the incestuous component of his fixation on her can be understood as a manifestation of the insecurity stemming from his parents' failure to meet his emotional needs.

Just as there are both oedipal and preoedipal layers to Augustine's theft of the pears, so, too, it can be set in an intergenerational context. In Book 10, he confronts the ineradicable presence of sin in his life even after he has embraced Christianity.[8] Augustine observes that images of his former habits—above all, fornication—that have diminished their hold during his waking hours return while he is asleep: "But when I dream, they not only give me pleasure but are very much like acquiescence in the act" (10.30). Unlike sex, however, which he is able to relegate to the realm of dreams, he cannot altogether repudiate the appetite for food and drink. What Augustine finds most insidious is that the "snare of concupiscence" lurks even in such biologically ordained activities, for "although the purpose of eating and drinking is to preserve health, in its train there follows an ominous kind of enjoyment" (10.31). Himself given to overeating, Augustine asks rhetorically, "But is there anyone, O Lord, who is never enticed a little beyond the strict limits of need?" (10.31).

Augustine illustrates this danger in narrating the life of his mother. As a child, Monica's upbringing had been entrusted to an aged female servant, who, except at mealtimes, would not permit Monica or her sisters "to drink even water, however great their thirst, for fear they might develop bad habits" (9.8). This severe discipline initially backfired, however, for Monica

---

7　My collocation of Winnicott's ideas and Augustine's theft of the pears has been anticipated by Hopkins (1981).

8　In the remaining three books, Augustine abandons autobiography in favor of an extended allegorical exegesis of the opening verses of Genesis, as the *Confessions* itself undergoes a "conversion" from personal to impersonal themes that mimics the trajectory of Augustine's life.

"developed a secret liking for wine." When she was sent by her parents to draw wine from the cask, "she would sip a few drops, barely touching it with her lips, but no more than this, because she found the taste disagreeable. She did this, not because she had any relish for the liquor or its effects, but simply from the exuberant high spirits of childhood" (9.8). Each day, Monica took increasingly larger sips until "it soon became a habit, and she would drink her wine at a draft, almost by the cupful" (9.8). Only when a quarrelsome servant-girl called her a drunkard did Monica realize the despicableness of her conduct and put a stop to it.

Although Augustine does not draw the connection, this story about Monica forms a pendant to his own youthful theft of the pears. Like Augustine, Monica at first drinks the liquor "not because she had any relish for it," but simply out of "high spirits." This symmetry between the emblematic sins of mother and son attests that Augustine's reenactment of the Fall, in addition to its oedipal and preoedipal meanings, has its roots in his mother's childhood. Freud (1933) emphasizes that "a child's super-ego is in fact constructed on the model not of its parents but of its parents' super-ego" (p. 67). This insight is borne out by the way that Augustine's conscience, instilled by Monica's warnings against engaging in sexual activity, can be traced back to the controlling behavior of *her* caretaker, a maternal figure who "was conscientious in attending to her duties, correcting the children when necessary with strictness, for the love of God, and teaching them to lead wise and sober lives" (9.8). Neither mother nor son could find a "middle way" between abstinence and overindulgence when it came to the sensual pleasures of wine and sex. Just as Monica's secret drinking yielded to Ambrose's prohibition against bringing libations to the shrines of the saints in Milan, so, too, Augustine's concupiscence surrendered as far as was humanly possible to Continence; and he emulated her vigilance in regulating the bodily functions of the members of his reformed household when he became the arbiter of Christian orthodoxy.

4

Freud is cognizant of being a pupil in St. Augustine's school. Impersonating a nonexistent interlocutor who fears having impregnated his mistress, he recalls in *The Psychopathology of Everyday Life* (1901) having read an article in an Italian newspaper with the title, "What St. Augustine Says about Women" (p. 10). What Freud learned from Augustine is clear from the Dora case (1905a), where he avers, "The Early Christian Father's '*inter urinas et faeces nascimur*' clings to sexual life and cannot be detached from it in spite of every effort at idealization" (p. 31). Freud quotes the same Latin phrase in his paper on debasement in love, where he insists that "the excremental is all too intimately and inseparably bound up with the sexual" (1912, p. 189); and he does so for the third time in a lengthy footnote to *Civilization and Its Discontents* (1930) in which he ascribes the origins of repression to humanity's adoption of erect posture as a result of disgust at the odor of the genitals. As Madelon Sprengnether (1990) points out, Freud's coupling of the sexual and the excremental reflects his preoccupation with "the responses of the male subject to the female body" (p. 116), which in the first instance means the body of the mother.

Extending his affinity with Augustine, Freud declares in *Totem and Taboo* (1913b) that in its postulation of the ubiquity of "prohibited impulses," psychoanalysis "is no more than confirming the habitual pronouncement of the pious: we are all miserable sinners" (p. 72). Indeed, Freud claims to have uncovered the meaning of the concept of original sin in his hypothesis of the murder of the primal father at the dawn of human history. Because of the law of talion, Freud argues, if "Christ redeemed mankind from the burden of original sin by sacrifice of his own life, we are driven to conclude that the sin was a murder" (p. 154). Taking this reasoning one step further, he maintains that if Christ's death "brought about atonement with God the Father, the crime to be expiated can only have been the murder of the father" (p. 154). In reiterating this overarching framework for his thought in *Moses and Monotheism* (1939), Freud credits St. Paul, "a Roman Jew from Tarsus," with the invention of Christianity when he "seized upon this sense of guilt" that had taken hold of "the whole civilized world of the time" and "traced it back correctly to its original source. He called this the 'original sin'" (p. 86). Since what is distinctive in Christianity is the "phantasy of redemption" whereby "a son of God had allowed himself to be killed without guilt and had thus taken on himself the guilt of all men," Freud underscores that the redeemer "had to be a son" since the original "crime against God" had been "the murder of the primal father who was later deified" (p. 86). "What was essential" in this synthesis, Freud adds, "seems to have been Paul's own contribution" (p. 86).

In juxtaposing Augustine and Freud, therefore, we form a chiasmus: Augustine reenacts the Fall in a narrative structured by the Oedipus complex, while Freud explains with the Oedipus complex the doctrine of original sin. Adam and Oedipus are the prototypes that allow Augustine and Freud, respectively, to distill out of their "neurotic conflicts" what Peter Brooks (1984) has termed a "sacred masterplot that organizes and explains the world" (p. 6), each of which stakes a claim to universality unrivaled in the repertoires of classical and Judeo-Christian culture. For both introspective geniuses, St. Paul is the crucial antecedent. Not only does his typological pairing of Adam and Christ in the Epistle to the Romans impute to Adam's transgression a phylogenetic significance it does not possess in the Hebrew Bible, "For as by one man's disobedience many were made sinners, so by the obedience of one shall many be made righteous" (5.19), but Paul's expostulation, "O wretched man that I am, who shall free me from the body of this death?" (7.24), also makes it plain that his "captivity to the law of sin which is in my members" (7.23) is personally felt.[9] When, prior to becoming a Christian, Augustine exclaims, "it was I who willed to take this course and again it was I who willed not to take it. ... So I was at odds with myself" (8.10), he echoes the "Pauline paradox" set forth in Romans, "For the good that I would, I do not: but the evil which I would not, that I do" (7.19); and it is again a passage from Romans (13.13–14) that Augustine—seated beneath a fig tree and hearing the voice of a child of indeterminate gender—takes up and reads from the Bible, which provides the final catalyst for his conversion.

But if their intellectual brilliance and force of will enabled Augustine and Freud to transform their personal struggles into canonical versions of the myths of Oedipus and the Fall, these same qualities should alert us to be on guard against the dangers of circular reasoning. The rub lies in the fact that if one stipulates that "in Adam's fall, we sinned all," or—in Freud's (1900) variation on the theme—"it is the fate of all of us ... to direct our first sexual impulse towards our mother and our first hatred and our first murderous wish against our father" (p. 262), then there is no place outside the belief systems generated by the theories themselves from which they may be called into question.

If the claims of universality in the theories put forward by Augustine and Freud are both a strength and a weakness, then what is required is a mode of reading that recognizes their power even as it subjects their conceptions of human nature to a thoroughgoing critique. Although it is incontestable that all human beings are mortal, it does not follow that death should be regarded as the punishment for an inherited sin of which we are inescapably guilty. Similarly, although sexuality is a precondition of human existence, this does not mean that we must agree with the passage from Diderot's *Rameau's Nephew* that Freud (1916–17) was fond of quoting

---

[9] With respect to St. Paul, Pagels (1988) cautions that Augustine's conviction that original sin was the direct result of Adam's disobedience is based on an "idiosyncratic interpretation" of Romans 5.12 to mean that by one man "death passed upon all men, *in whom* all sinned," instead of "for that all sinned," so that, for Augustine, Adam "brought upon humanity not only universal death, but also universal, and inevitable, sin" (p. 109). But though Augustine, who read the New Testament in Latin, may have exceeded the meaning of the Greek text, the notion of Adam as a "corporate personality" is already present in Paul.

as an illustration of his teachings: "If the little savage were left to himself, possessing all his foolishness and adding to the small sense of a child in the cradle the violent passions of a man of thirty, he would strangle his father and lie with his mother" (p. 338)—a judgment on human nature that echoes Augustine's contention that a child's wish to strike those who know better than he, including his own parents, "shows that, if babies are innocent, it is not for lack of will to do harm, but for lack of strength" (1.7).

Like Augustine's theft of the pears, the Oedipus complex comes to seem very different when Oedipus is no longer presumed to embody innate incestuous and patricidal impulses, but is rather viewed as an abused, abandoned, and adopted child, as well as the victim of an inherited curse stemming—to go back only one generation—from the rape of a boy perpetrated by his father Laius.[10] Seen in this light, both the Oedipus complex and the concept of original sin, far from revealing eternal verities, are ideological constructs that serve to blame children for the abuse and neglect inflicted by parents—including God the Father—who failed in their sacred duty to look after them. And since both Augustine and Freud were implacable "defenders of the faith" who sought to extirpate heresy from their respective churches, it should not be surprising that the tradition of which they are such enduring landmarks is ultimately that of patriarchy.

---

[10] On the concept of a "Laius complex," see Ross (1982), as well as my elaboration of these themes in the final chapter of *Mutual Analysis* (Rudnytsky, 2022).

Chapter 2

Incest and the Fall in Gottfried's *Tristan*

"Those who are faithful know only the trivial side of love; it is the faithless who know love's tragedies."

—Oscar Wilde, *The Picture of Dorian Gray*

1

In his Prologue to what Joan M. Ferrante (1990) has termed "the most effective expression of the most powerful love-story in the Middle Ages" (pp. 179–80), Gottfried von Strassburg avers that he has "offered the fruits of my labour to this world as a pastime, so that with my story its denizens can bring their keen sorrow half-way to alleviation and thus abate their anguish" (p. 42).[1] In his allegory of the Cave of Lovers, where Tristan and Isolde take refuge from the court to enjoy their most consummate bliss, Gottfried likewise affirms that he knows whereof he writes from personal experience: "I have known that cave since I was eleven, yet I never set foot in Cornwall" (p. 266).

Taken together, these passages suggest not only that the poem has a private meaning for its author but also that it is intended to serve a therapeutic purpose for its readers. Although the lack of external evidence renders all assertions about Gottfried's life conjectural, there is a compelling sense in which *Tristan* (*c.* 1210), like St. Augustine's *Confessions*, is both a *Bildungsroman* and a spiritual autobiography. As A. T. Hatto (1960) notes, "Gottfried's story is essentially that of Tristan, courtier, warrior, and lover, into which Isolde enters only at a later stage" (p. 7).[2] In the passage in which he offers his book as a balm to alleviate the "keen sorrows" of his intended audience, Gottfried goes on to say that to have such a diversion "frees our

---

[1] Page numbers are to A. T. Hatto's (1960) for the most part outstanding rendering into English prose of Gottfried's intricate Middle High German rhymed verse; line numbers refer to Rüdiger Krohn's (1980) edition of the original text.

[2] Hatto, who ventures an educated guess that "Gottfried is most readily imagined as a member of the urban patriciate of Strassburg," goes further to speculate that he "may be looking back to his own exacting education when he writes of Tristan's" (p. 10).

unquiet soul [*entsorget sorgehaften muot*] and eases our heart of its cares" (p. 42; l. 79), just as Augustine opens the *Confessions* by proclaiming that the human heart is unquiet until it finds peace in God (*inquietum est cor nostrum, donec requiescat in te*).

With good reason, therefore, W. T. H. Jackson (1971) remarks that Gottfried "introduces the person of the author into the poem, not, as is usually done, as an omniscient interpreter, but as an interpreter who knows because he has participated" (p. 237). The salience of this remark, which highlights how Gottfried, like a contemporary psychoanalyst, functions as a "participant observer" (Sullivan, 1953) in his narrative, renders it all the more regrettable that Jackson evinces an antipathy to psychological readings of medieval texts. Disregarding Gottfried's reiterated avowals that he has frequented the Cave of Lovers from an early age—"There was a time when I, too, led such a life, and thought it quite sufficient. ... I know this well, for I have been there" (pp. 264, 266)—Jackson (1971) asserts that "it would be ludicrous to claim that there is anything autobiographical in Gottfried's poem. ... There is no reason to assume that the poet himself was in love, though he may have been" (p. 190). It is not necessary to know anything about the particulars of Gottfried's life to be convinced that only someone who had, in Oscar Wilde's words, "known love's tragedies" could have written the masterpiece that he did.

When Gottfried states that his poem is addressed to inhabitants of "*this* world," he means his own esoteric realm, not the domain of the multitude. Indeed, the distinction between the many and the few is a core doctrine of his aesthetics. "Thus I have undertaken a labour to please the polite world and solace noble hearts," he writes in his Prologue, and continues:

> I do not mean the world of the many who (as I hear) are unable to endure sorrow and wish only to revel in bliss. ... Their way and mine diverge sharply. I have another world in mind which together in one heart bears its bitter-sweet, its dear sorrow, its heart's joy, its love's pain, its dear life, its sorrowful death, its dear death, its sorrowful life.
>
> (p. 42)

The conclusion of this passage, with its stirring antitheses, warrants quotation in the original Middle High German:

> ein ander welt die meine ich,
> diu samet in eime herzen treit
> ir süeze sûr, ir liebez leit,
> ir herzeliep, ir senede nôt,

ir liebez leben, ir leiden tôt,
ir lieben tôt, ir leidez leben.

(ll. 57–63)

The oxymoronic brilliance of the verse culminates in the chiasmus of the final two lines, where Gottfried at once inverts the order of "leben" and "tôt" and exploits the reversibility of the letters "ie" and "ei" in "lieb-" and "leid-" to depict both life and death as simultaneously "dear" and "sorrowful."[3]

As Hatto (1960) points out, "the novelty of Gottfried's secular usage" of the expression "noble hearts" (*edelen Herzen*) is that he transposes the mystical doctrine of the "noble soul," in the sense of one "raised to a divine plane," into a context in which "the word for 'noble' normally took its meaning from rank in feudal society, not from qualities of the heart" (pp. 15–16). Those whom Gottfried cordially despises are "unable to endure sorrow and wish only to revel in bliss," while those to whom his labor is addressed recognize the inescapability of tragedy in the blissful experience of love. This is why Gottfried daringly compares the story of his dead but immortal lovers to the sacrament of communion, "*This is bread to all noble hearts*" (p. 44), and why he even more boldly—from an orthodox standpoint, blasphemously— vows that he will be "damned or saved" (*verderben oder genesen*) (p. 42; l. 66) together with them and all other initiates into the mysteries of forbidden love.

2

Since, as Gottfried's language makes clear, Tristan's tragedy stems from the conjunction of conflicting emotions in the love of "noble hearts," the crucial question becomes how to account for this ambivalence. Here, invaluable guidance has been provided by Denis de Rougemont in his classic monograph, *Love in the Western World* (1940). De Rougemont's attempt to link the ethos of courtly love (so named by Gaston Paris in a study of Lancelot in 1883) to the ascetic heresy of Catharism that arose across Europe in the twelfth century has not gained wide acceptance, but his analysis of the Tristan myth

---

[3]   Compare the chiasmus in Othello's final couplet as he stabs himself to death over Desdemona's corpse: "I kiss'd thee ere I kill'd thee. No way but this, / Killing myself, to die upon a kiss" (V.ii.358–9). Like Gottfried's "ie-" and "ei-," Shakespeare's "kiss-" and "kill-" differ only by an air's breath; the verbal artistry of both poets conveys the fusion of love and death in the psyches of their protagonists.

engages the issues to which Gottfried's version gives sublime expression in with a depth and intensity that make most academic inquiries seem arid by comparison.

Focusing on the recurrent connection between erotic passion and adultery in Western culture, de Rougemont proposes to unravel the following enigma: "If the breakdown of marriage has been simply due to the attractiveness of the forbidden, it still remains to be seen why we hanker after unhappiness, and what notion of love—what secret of our existence, of the human mind, perhaps of our history—this hankering must hint at" (p. 17). Citing as examples the sword that Tristan places between his body and Isolde's in the Cave of Lovers and Tristan's marriage to Isolde of the White Hands, de Rougemont calls attention to the regularity with which the lovers, rather than trying to circumvent the obstacles to their happiness, instead seek them out: "It is not too much to say that they never miss a chance of getting parted. Where there is no obstruction, they invent one" (p. 37). He takes this observation to its logical conclusion: "If we delve into the recesses of the myth, we see that this obstruction is what passion really *wants*—its true object" (p. 42). According to de Rougemont, the hidden meaning of the myth turns out to be that what the lovers ultimately desire is "the absolute obstacle, which is death" (p. 41).

De Rougemont's insistence on the ubiquity of obstacles in the love of Tristan and Isolde is an insight of capital importance, and his acceptance of the premise that "the very *obscurity* which we find in the legend denotes its deep relation to a myth" (p. 20) dovetails with Freud's conviction that, like dreams, works of art possess both latent and manifest levels of meaning. But though de Rougemont asserts that "we now commonly take it for granted that the existence of a repressed wish is invariably manifested ... in such a way as to disguise the true nature of the wish," he pays no more than lip service to "the popularization of psycho-analysis" (p. 47); and the greatest defect of his inquiry is that he fails to consider the role of incest in the love of Tristan and Isolde or to ponder how this "secret of our existence" explains the phenomenon of "obstacle love" to which he calls such compelling attention.

Not only is King Mark—the husband of Tristan's beloved—the brother of Tristan's mother Blancheflor, and thus Tristan's maternal uncle, but after the loyal Marshal Rual li Foitenant reveals to Tristan (whom he has found after a long search at Mark's court in Cornwall) that not he but the deceased Rivalin was actually Tristan's father, Mark becomes legally Tristan's father and appoints Tristan his heir, although Rual retains the place of a father in Tristan's affections. Thus, the love affair between Tristan and Isolde is not only adulterous but also incestuous, since Isolde, as the wife of Tristan's legal and royal father, occupies both structurally and psychologically the position of his mother. This familial configuration that undergirds the Tristan myth makes manifest the "repressed wish" that motivates Monica's warning to Augustine in the *Confessions* "not to commit fornication and above all not to seduce any man's wife," and it lends credence to the psychoanalytic hypothesis that erotic triangles in later life are reenactments and transpositions of the oedipal triangle of early childhood.

Once it is grasped that the Oedipus complex is the hinge on which *Tristan* turns, every detail in Gottfried's poem falls into place. The "naked sword" (*swert bar*; l. 17413) that Tristan uses to separate himself and Isolde in the Cave of Lovers, which once again deceives Mark into believing in their innocence when he spies them through one of the *three* windows of the Cave, is said to cause them to sleep "a good way apart from each other, just as two men might lie, not like a man and a woman" (p. 270). (Gottfried's presumption that two men cannot engage in sexual relations reflects the "compulsory heterosexuality" that, as I shall elaborate in connection with *Sir Gawain and the Green Knight*, underlies the Oedipus complex.) The sword had originally been presented to Tristan by Mark prior to Tristan's battle with Morold, the champion of Gurman, the king of Ireland who had kept Mark and his court in thrall. Because Mark is Tristan's legal father, when the sword divides him from Isolde it represents what Lacan (1953) calls the "Name-of-the-Father" (*nom du père*), which contains in French a homonymic pun on the phrase "No-of-the-Father" (*non du père*), both meanings of which refer to the father's interposition of his own phallus between the son and the mother. From this standpoint, rivalry with the father is not a byproduct of the son's desire but rather what instigates it. As Malcolm Bowie (1991) has explained, "desire comes into being" for Lacan "when an already desiring Other intervenes to say *no*. The 'assumption' of castration is at once an acquiescence in this Other's law and an envious appropriation of his desire" (p. 162). Thus, the sword that Tristan places between himself and Isolde in their place of greatest seclusion is not merely emblematic of obstruction in a general sense, but specifically instantiates the incest barrier and its attendant threat of castration.

Another crucial episode involving the sword occurs earlier when Isolde the Fair, daughter of Isolde the Queen and Tristan's future beloved, is enthralled by the magnificent body of the man whom she believes to be the minstrel Tantris. On one occasion, the narrator recounts, while he was in the bath, "I have no idea how she could do such a thing, but she took up the sword in her hands" (p. 174), as though she were fondling his penis. She sees that a piece is missing—symbolic of Tristan's castration—and realizes that she is in possession of the fragment that had been left in the skull of Morold, her mother's brother, rendering his slayer her family's mortal enemy. Not yet sure of what it all means, "Isolde fetched the piece and inserted it—and the gap and the cursed splinter fitted each other and made a perfect whole as if they were one thing [*als ob ez ein dinc waere*], as indeed they had been, not two years past" (p. 174; l. 10084). The splinter and body of the sword together form a *symbolon*, which in Greek refers to an object divided between two people, each of whom keeps one of the segments as a means of recognition in the future. Tristan and Isolde themselves form a "perfect whole *as if* they were one thing," while remaining forever two sundered parts. After reassembling the sword, Isolde contemplates the name of the man in the bath, which uncannily reminds her of that of Morold's slayer:

> "Oh," she said, "these names trouble me. I cannot think what there is about them. They sound so very similar. 'Tantris,'" she said, "and 'Tristan.' They surely somehow go together?" … Forwards she read "Tris-tan," backwards "Tan-tris." With this she was certain of the name.
>
> (p. 174)

In a fortuitous analogue to the *symbolon* motif within the text, Gottfried's narrative itself breaks off about five-sixths of the way through, but the ending is supplied by the surviving fragments by Thomas of Britain, which Gottfried regarded as the "authentic version" (p. 41) of the story. Strikingly, in both Thomas and the French version of Béroul, the hero's name is given as Tris*tran* rather than Tris*tan*.[4] In his commentary on Tristan's name, Petrus Tax (1990) has suggested that the last syllable, *an*, may be "a variant of *on, homme*," from which he infers that "Gottfried wished to show in Tristan's life and death a typically 'manly' destiny" (p. 230). As Tax has further argued, Gottfried modified the received spelling both in order to make Tristan a "pure reversal" (p. 230) of Tantris and to accentuate its derivation from *triste*.

Like Oedipus, whose name means both "Swollen Foot" (*oidos* = swollen; *pous* = foot) and "know-foot" (*oida* = I know), Tristan's "typically 'manly' destiny" is inscribed in his name. In Sophocles, the Messenger who initially enters to bring Oedipus the news of the death of the king of Corinth whom he had believed was his father, only to reveal in the course of their exchange that he had been adopted by Polybus and Merope, tells Oedipus that his "ankles should be witnesses" (l. 1033) of why his life had been in danger as an infant, and that it is from the wounds to his feet when he was exposed to die on Mount Cithaeron by his birth parents that "you're called your present name" (l. 1036). In the Messenger's account, it is Oedipus's trauma that

---

⁴ The Penguin edition of Béroul's version, translated by Alan S. Fedrick (1970), not only deprives "Beroul" of his accent but "normalizes" the title to *The Romance of Tristan*.

gives rise to his name; but since the name goes back to Homer's *Odyssey*, it would be equally true to say of Sophocles' tragedy that it is the meaning of his name that explains the wounding to Oedipus's feet, rather than the other way around.

Similarly, in Gottfried, when Rual le Foitenant and his wife must settle on a name to bestow in baptism on the orphan they would have everyone believe is their own child, the narrator expounds, "Now 'triste' stands for sorrow, and because of all these happenings the child was named 'Tristan' and christened 'Tristan' at once. The name was well suited to him and in every way appropriate. Let us test it by the story" (p. 67). Once again, although it appears that the name was chosen because of the circumstances of Tristan's birth, Gottfried, like Sophocles, has contrived the story so that it becomes an unfolding of the destiny ordained by his name. When the abducted Tristan first arrives in Cornwall, the huntsmen who encounter this graceful adolescent purporting to be a merchant's son cannot fathom why he should have been thus inappropriately named: "*Juvente bele et la riant*—'Fair youth and smiling'—would have been a better name for you, believe me" (p. 83). But as the quintessential "noble heart" whose erotic history unfolds under the spell of an incestuous fixation, Tristan, like Oedipus, is fated to be a "man of sorrows," and can never be one of the legion who "wish only to revel in bliss."

In a further twist of the Möbius strip of language and experience, C. Stephen Jaeger (1977) has underscored how Gottfried creates a "connection between Tristan's fate and the internal, psychological state of his mother at the time of his birth" (p. 36). Devastated by the news of Rivalin's death yet unable to mourn the loss of her husband, Blancheflor becomes transfixed by depression and gives birth four days later: "Yet in all this grief her eyes never once grew moist. But God Almighty, how came it that there was no weeping there? Her heart had turned to stone. ... She twisted and turned and writhed ... until with much labour she bore a little son" (p. 63). Blancheflor's depression casts a longer shadow over Tristan than her physical death.[5] As Jaeger (1977) has elucidated, "during those four days of her difficult labor a fusion occurs between the emotions in her heart and the child in her womb, so that Tristan enters the world suffused with his fate" (p. 37).

The "pure reversal" of the two syllables in Tristan's name that leads to his recognition by Isolde as she fits the "cursed splinter" into the "gap" left

---

[5] The lasting effect of Blancheflor's "stone heart" on Tristan is illuminated by André Green's (1983) concept of the "dead mother," which is concerned not with a mother's physical death but with how maternal depression transforms "a living object, which was a source of vitality for the child, into a distant figure, toneless, practically inanimate," whose inner lifelessness leaves "psychical holes" (p. 142) in her emotionally abandoned offspring.

in his sword supplies an essential clue to how we should read the poem as a whole. Although its subject seems remote, the title of John T. Irwin's book, *Doubling and Incest / Repetition and Revenge: A Speculative Reading of Faulkner* (1975), signals its bearing on Gottfried's text. Irwin writes:

> In repetition, then, at the time that an act is performed for the first time it is never the first time; it only becomes the first time later, after its second occurrence, when in a third act it is imaginatively reconstituted by the memory. And that third act, which imaginatively reconstitutes the first act as first (and implicitly reconstitutes the state prior to the first act as zero), simultaneously reconstitutes the second act as repetition. But it does so, paradoxically, by treating the second act as primary and the first act as secondary—that is, by understanding the first act in light of the second act. Thus, though the first and second acts occur in one order, they are understood as first and second only by the mind's moving through them in reverse order.
>
> (p. 71)

Like Tristan's name, Gottfried's poem must be read both forwards and backwards. In particular, the episode of Tristan's parents, Rivalin and Blancheflor, while preceding Tristan's story in time, is thematically secondary to it and can only be understood retrospectively as a foreshadowing. What crucially differentiates the love of Rivalin and Blancheflor from that of Tristan and Isolde is that it is not adulterous. Consequently, everything that happens to Tristan's parents is an attenuated version of what is to come in the next generation. For example, Rivalin, fighting on behalf of King Mark, is "run through the side with a spear" and left "half dead," but he recovers when Blancheflor visits him in the guise of a "physician-woman" (pp. 56–7). Similarly, Tristan receives "an ugly blow through the thigh, plunging almost to the very life of him" (p. 133), from Morold, which can only be cured by Isolde the Queen and leads to his being recognized by Isolde the Fair. But Rivalin's wound is not poisonous, unlike that inflicted on Tristan by the weapon of Morold. Nor do Rivalin and Blancheflor die together, as Tristran and Isolt do at the end of Thomas's version. Rivalin is felled by Duke Morgan, to whom he owed allegiance for his lands and on whom his seemingly unprovoked attack had set the entire plot in motion, while Blancheflor, who had been impregnated by Rivalin prior to their marriage, dies giving birth to Tristan.

In short, although Rivalin attains the bliss of fusion with Blancheflor, "Thus he was she, and she was he" (p. 58), followed by sorrow and death, their experience, like that of Tristan and Isolde in the first phase of their love, is of "joy without mortal sorrow [*âne herzeleit*], for as yet they were free of mortal pain [*dakeine herzeleide*] and of such calamity as stares into one's heart" (p. 213; ll. 13078, 13080). Accordingly, when the poet eulogizes Rivalin after his death, "And may God in Heaven, who has never forgotten noble hearts, have him in His keeping!" (p. 63), it can be only in a qualified sense that he bestows on him the epithet "noble heart," just as Mark wonders how Rual li Foitenant could "'have reared his child so beautifully, unless from a noble heart'" (p. 97). For all his virtues, Rual has not tasted one drop of the sorrows of love, and none of Tristan's three fathers, including Mark, is a citizen of that world inhabited by those, including Gottfried himself, who have been to the Cave of Lovers.

The means by which Tristan and Isolde fall eternally and exclusively in love with each other is, of course, the love potion, which had been prepared by Isolde the Queen and "endowed with such powers, that with whom any man drank it he had to love her above all things, whether he wished it or no, and she love him alone. They would share one death and one life, one sorrow and one joy" (p. 192). The Queen had entrusted the philter to Brangane, Isolde the Fair's companion, with the strictest injunction that it was to be given only to her daughter and Mark after they had been joined in marriage. But when the younger Isolde and Tristan, who had been sent to fetch her from Ireland, are on the ship bringing her to Cornwall, they consume the potion in the absence of Brangane, who, upon realizing what has happened, "seized that cursed, fatal flask, bore it off and flung it into the wild and raging sea!" (p. 195).

The importance given to the potion has been faulted as a literary contrivance by Hatto (1960), who writes of Gottfried's version that "the chain of human motivation holds as far back as this, till we are suddenly face to face with magic" (p. 23), while Gaston Paris considered "the adulterous love of Trist[r]an and Yseult" to be less reprehensible than that of Lancelot and Guinevere "on the grounds that the love potion relieved the former pair of moral responsibility" (Fedrick, 1970, p. 20). Both these judgments are mistaken as far as Gottfried is concerned. In the earlier versions of the story by Béroul and Eilhart von Oberge, the effects of the love potion abate after three or four years, while in Thomas the potion does not wear off, but it is imbibed not only by Tristan and Isolde but also by Mark (Hatto, 1960, pp. 8–9). Gottfried is the first author to restrict the potion to Tristan and Isolde and to make the effects permanent. By virtue of his modifications of the source material, Gottfried transforms the potion from a magic trick into a means of revealing the psychological dynamics inherent in the structure of the situation. The love potion in Gottfried functions like the oracle in *Oedipus the King*, about which Freud (1940) wrote that its "coercive power … which makes or should make the hero innocent, is a recognition of the fate which has condemned every son to live through the Oedipus complex" (p. 192). Contrary to Paris's claims, Tristan and Isolde are not "relieved of moral responsibility" by the potion because it serves to bring to light their unconscious desires, about which they feel guilty.

Indeed, Gottfried throughout minimizes the importance of supernatural elements and uses them only to forge the links in "the chain of human motivation." In criticizing the "old Tale of Tristan" for expecting the reader to believe that a swallow flew from Cornwall to Ireland and then flew back to Cornwall with a lady's hair with which to build its nest, the poet exclaims, "I swear the tale grows fantastic, the story is talking nonsense here!" (p. 154). Brangane's "mistake" in letting the potion fall into the "wrong" hands ensures that it will reach the "right" destination—the one dictated by the logic of the unconscious. Like Oedipus, who flees Corinth thinking that the king and queen who adopted him are his parents but runs headlong into his fate in trying to escape it, Tristan, having been abducted by Norwegian sailors from Parmenie where he was being raised by Rivalin and Blancheflor, is on a storm-tossed boat for eight days until "the wind had beaten them to Cornwall" (p. 74). Upon landing, he encounters two pilgrims on a road where "his Uncle Mark of Cornwall's hounds ... had at that very moment chased a hart" (p. 78), and soon ends up meeting and becoming the companion of the king, although neither is consciously aware of their familial bond.

For both Sophocles and Gottfried, therefore, kinship is destiny. In the same way that Oedipus believes himself to be a stranger to Thebes, the city of which he has become the ruler, so, too, Gottfried writes, "Tristan has come home, even though he imagined he was homeless," and "Noble Mark, his unsuspected father, acted with great magnanimity, and there was truly great need that he should" (p. 87). Much later, when Tristan and Isolde have been banished from the court and found refuge in the Cave of Lovers, Mark goes hunting and, inevitably, his hounds go in pursuit of "a strange hart" that "eluded them and fled to where he had come from, over toward the Cave," where the occupants are "very much afraid—and events were to prove them right—that somehow someone might lose the hounds and come there, and so discover their secret" (pp. 269–70).

Just as Gottfried uses the potion to create the illusion of an external cause for the desire that originates in the unconscious, all the events that appear to be due to chance are effects of the incestuous love of Tristan and Isolde. In analyzing the structure of Gottfried's poem, Jackson (1971) observes that it contains "a number of rhyming quatrains so that the initial letters of the quatrains, had the work been completed, would have formed the names of the hero and heroine, intertwined thus: TIRSIOSL[TDAEN]." Jackson continues:

> The first letters of the immediately following narrative portions perform the same function but in different order: ITSROILS[DTEAN]. The quatrains so introduced never form part of the narrative. They are invariably comments, often gnomic and even inscrutable, on the fate of the lovers, on the impossibility of avoiding sorrow, on the inevitability of misery in love.
>
> (p. 194)

It eludes Jackson, as it does de Rougemont, that the theme of adultery in *Tristan* has anything to do with incest, and he is averse to psychological explanations. But what he points out about the acrostics distributed throughout the poem illuminates how the theme of "misery in love" is expressed by its aesthetic form. It is not merely the syllables in "Tantris" and "Tristan" that "go together" and can be read both forwards and backwards, but the letters in the names of Tristan and Isolde that can go in either order. Just as the "joy without mortal sorrow" of Rivalin and Blancheflor forms a prelude to the "mortal pain" of Tristan and Isolde, Gottfried once again shows the reader, in Irwin's words, that "though the first and second acts occur in one order, they are understood as first and second only by the mind's moving through them in reverse order."

Irwin's (1975) most provocative claim is that it is "the point and purpose ... perhaps of all narration" to "use the temporal medium of narration to take revenge against time, to use narration to get even with the very mode of narrative's existence in a demonic attempt to prove that through the process of substitution and repetition, time is not really irreversible" (pp. 3–4). The quatrains of acrostics "never form part of the narrative" because, in standing apart, they teach us how the narrative is to be read both synchronically and diachronically, with and against time. The motif of "revenge against time" is introduced by Gottfried when Rivalin attacks Morgan "*as if* Morgan had done him some wrong" (p. 46; italics added). This signals the eruption of a primordial feud with no discernible beginning in which it is impossible to tell who is at fault. The rest of the poem consists of incessant permutations of "substitution and repetition," where the end circles back to and is contained in the beginning.

It is the violation of the taboo against incest that accounts for the "mortal sorrow" of Tristan and Isolde and makes their consummation the nexus from which everything in the poem emanates. After they have felt the effects of the love potion without knowing what has befallen them, Gottfried comments, "What could have severed them from the ill which they shared but Union, the knot that joined their senses?" (p. 202). But because their sexual intoxication is shadowed by the knowledge that Isolde is bound to marry Mark when they reach land, the union that fleetingly severs them from their unrequited longing leads to an even more profound separation. When Brangane belatedly tells the lovers the story of the flask she has thrown overboard and why its contents will be fatal to them both, Tristan exclaims:

> "It is in God's hands! ... Whether it be life or death, it has poisoned me most sweetly! I have no idea what the other will be like, but this death suits me well! If my adorable Isolde were to go on being the death of me in this fashion I would woo death everlasting!"
>
> (p. 206)

The essence of incest is to deny the ineluctable sequence of generations and hence that time is "really irreversible." In normal development, a child who falls in love with his or her parent is learning to find a suitable partner in later life; but when a parent betrays the child's trust by committing the primal crime, the victim is robbed of a future and remains frozen in the hell of an eternal present. When Tristan commits "revenge against time" by becoming one with Isolde, he is sentenced to "woo death everlasting" because to enter her vagina is to emulate Oedipus by becoming a "fellow sower" (l. 458) in the same furrow that has been plowed by Mark, and thereby to realize the oedipal fantasy, which is, as Freud (1910) encapsulates it, *"to be his own father"* (p. 173).

When, in the interval between drinking the potion and their mutual confession of love, Tristan asks Isolde what is disturbing her, she replies ambiguously with the French word *lameir*, three of the meanings of which he is able to decipher: "He then recalled that *l'ameir* meant 'Love,' *l'ameir* 'bitter,' *la meir* the sea: it seemed to have a host of meanings. He disregarded the one, and asked about the other two" (p. 199; ll. 11993–8). Tristan does not speak the word "love" because it is already understood between them. But neither Tristan nor Gottfried seems to be conscious that *lameir* also contains a pun on "mother" (*la mere*).[6] This occluded fourth meaning of Isolde's riddle foreshadows Ferenczi's speculation in *Thalassa* (1923) that human life is motivated by the urge to return to the sea, the phylogenetic prototype of the mother's womb.

---

[6] According to the online dictionary of the Linguistics Research Center at the University of Texas at Austin, *mere* is spelled without an accent in Old French.

3

Because the plays of Sophocles were lost during the Middle Ages, *Oedipus the King* could not have served as a source for Gottfried. But the saga of what was called by Statius (*c.* 92 C.E.) "the troubled / House of Oedipus" (ll. 16–17), as it worked itself out in the fratricidal war between his sons Eteocles and Polyneices, was transmitted to posterity through the sprawling grandeur of the *Thebaid*. Statius's epic was quarried by the anonymous author of the first extant romance, the Anglo-Norman *Romance of Thebes* (*c.* 1150), and again by the twelfth-century chronicler Richard of Devizes, who lamented that the dynastic turmoil during the reign of Henry II of England was making "our Royal house troubled like that of Oedipus" (Giles, 1841, p. 3).[7] When the genre of romance arose in the twelfth century, most notably in the works of Chrétien de Troyes, its creators therefore had the entire Oedipus legend as a resource for their newly self-conscious explorations of sexual desire. This helps to explain why, beneath the adulterous love of Lancelot and Guinevere, the incest theme lies at the heart of the grandest of medieval narratives—that of King Arthur and the Round Table, in many versions of which Arthur's death is brought about by his illegitimate son Mordred, the product of Arthur's union with his half-sister Morgan le Fay. The story of Tristan, imagined to take place a generation after Arthur's reign, makes explicit this conflation of incestuous and adulterous triangles.

In addition to the classical tradition derived from Statius, the Oedipus theme reverberated throughout the Middle Ages in the twinned legends of Judas and the apocryphal Pope Gregory, "the one," according to Richard A. McCabe (2008), "concluding in despair and damnation, the other in salvation and grace" (p. 44). As McCabe summarizes "the earliest Latin version" of the life of Judas:

> Judas was exposed at birth with pierced shins because of a vision that he would kill his father. Saved by passing shepherds, the abandoned child grew to manhood and entered the service of Herod on whose behalf he stole fruit from his father's garden, killed the owner unaware of their kinship and wed the widow, his natural mother.
>
> (p. 43)

---

[7] I am indebted in this paragraph to the essay by Daniel Rubey (1988), which deserves to be better known by medievalists.

In an apparently unwitting echo of Nietzsche's exegesis in *The Birth of Tragedy* (1872) that "the horrible triad of Oedipus' destinies" means that "the same man who solves the riddle of nature—that Sphinx of two species— must also break the most sacred natural orders by murdering his father and marrying his mother" (sec. 9; p. 69), McCabe (2008) writes that the tale of Judas exemplifies how it is inevitable that "the man destined to betray the Lord of Nature violates the most sacrosanct natural law in anticipation of his future outrage" (p. 44). In the circular logic that makes him the scapegoat of the Christian narrative, "we are to understand that fate selected Judas for incest" since he was the one who would later betray Christ, "but also that the taint of incest fitted him to be such a character" (p. 44). Gregory, by contrast, is the product of an incestuous union between a sister and a brother who goes on unwittingly to marry his mother, but becomes a penitent when his enormity is discovered and eventually ascends to the papacy.[8]

Judas's theft of the fruit from his father's garden, like Augustine's theft of pears in his adolescence, is an allusion to—and reenactment of—the Fall. Thus, as Charles Méla (1992) remarks, this makes Judas into "the new Oedipus of a new Eden" for the Middle Ages, "whose fault discloses the unexpected meaning of original sin" (p. 209). As in the *Confessions*, the Oedipus complex is again shown to be the latent content of the Fall. Méla likewise establishes a connection between Gottfried's *Tristan* and medieval Oedipus lore inasmuch as the scene in which Isolde identifies the bathing Tristan as the slayer of her uncle Morold by the missing fragment from his sword draws on the episode in the *Romance of Thebes* (Ferrante and Hanning, 2018, ll. 537–42) where Jocasta recognizes Oedipus after twenty years of marriage upon seeing the scars on his feet in the bath.

In the Cave of Lovers, Tristan and Isolde console themselves by recounting the tales of unfortunate lovers of the past, including the Ovidian heroines Canacea and Biblis, both of whom committed incest with their brothers. Gottfried expressly states that Biblis, whose story is found in Book 9 of the *Metamorphoses*, "died broken-hearted for her brother's love" (p. 267), while Canacea laments in Book 11 of the *Heroides*, "Brother, why did you love me more than a brother should, / And why was I not merely what a sister should be to you? / I also burnt with it" (ll. 25–7). As John Jay Parry (1941) remarks in his introduction to Andreas Capellanus's *De amore* (c. 1185)—the title of which he renders as *The Art of Courtly Love*— "for all practical purposes we may say that the origin of courtly love is to be found in the writings of the poet Ovid," and "the men of the Middle Ages

---

[8] On the twinship of Judas and Gregory, see also Rank's encyclopedic study, *The Incest Theme in Literature and Legend* (1912, pp. 277–87).

thought that they had his approval for the dictum that the best partner in a love affair is another man's wife" (pp. 4–5).

Complementing these allusions to Ovid, Gottfried in his Literary Excursus praises "the Nightingale of the Vogelweide"—that is, Walther von dar Vogelweide, considered to be "the greatest of the Minnesinger" (Hatto, 1960, p. 368)—by saying that this melodious bird "has come down to us from Cithaeron, on whose slopes and in whose caves the Goddess of Love holds sway" (p. 107). Hatto points out that "Cithaeron" is "a confusion of the mountain with Aphrodite's island of Cythera," Cithaeron being the mountain sacred to Dionysus where Oedipus had been left to die as an infant by his parents. But while Mount Cithaeron figures prominently in Sophocles, there is no mention of a mountain in Statius, and in the *Romance of Thebes* the servants to whom King Laius gives his newborn son "pierced both his feet / and hung him from a tall oak" (ll. 121–2). In an eruption from the cultural unconscious, Gottfried conflates his own Cave of Love (*Minnegrotte*) with the "slopes" of Cithaeron. He thereby reinforces the filiation that makes Tristan—like Judas and Pope Gregory—a scion of Sophocles' hero.

4

Despite his neglect of the incest theme and the tenuousness of his argument concerning the influence of Catharism on the poets of courtly love, de Rougemont (1940) rightly points out that "antiquity has left no record of an experience akin to the love of Tristan and Iseult," which renders it necessary to explain its "belated appearance" in Western culture (p. 60). De Rougemont adds a pertinent corollary when he brands Don Juan—like Faust, another postclassical archetype of the Western imagination—"an inverted reflection of Tristan" (p. 210). Although adultery has been a source of calamity since Homer's *Iliad*, its sympathetic treatment in the courtly love tradition is without precedent. This development can be understood as the result of the tension between the feudal assumption that marriage, rather than being based on romantic love between the spouses, was a legally binding arrangement for the begetting of children, on one hand, and the culture of the twelfth-century court of Champagne, presided over by the Countess Marie—the daughter of Louis VII and Eleanor of Aquitaine and herself the wife by an arranged marriage to Henry I, Count of Champagne—which afforded men increasing prospects for social mobility and accorded women heightened dignity, on the other. The presence of the feudal attitude toward marriage in Gottfried's text can be seen in the fact that Tristan is dispatched to bring Isolde to Cornwall to allay the fears of his enemies that Mark would designate him as his heir.

As John F. Benton (1961) has summarized the thesis of Gaston Paris, Marie "encouraged Chrétien to write a work which seemingly praised Lancelot, a knight who committed adultery with his sovereign's wife," and it was at her request that Andreas Capellanus wrote *The Art of Courtly Love*, in which he quoted his patroness "as making pronouncements on love which seemed to advocate adultery and to elevate women to the rank of high priestesses of a cult of love" (p. 39).

Despite Benton's caution in using the qualifiers "seemingly" and "seemed," the soundness of Paris's argument is attested by the explicitness with which Chrétien credits Marie with having furnished him with "the material and treatment" of *Lancelot, the Knight of the Cart* (c. 1180), as well as by his avowal that he "is simply trying to carry out her concern and intention" (Comfort, 1914, p. 274) in telling Lancelot's story. In his dialogical treatise, Andreas not only has a "man of the higher nobility" express the view that "'everybody knows that love can have no place between husband and wife'" because its "'true definition'" is "'an inordinate desire to receive passionately a furtive and hidden embrace'" (Parry, 1941, p. 100), but he quotes a letter from Marie herself in which she maintains, "'We declare and we hold as firmly established that love cannot exert its powers between two people who are married to each other.'" Marie proceeds to reject the double standard of sexual morality by extending this principle to women as well as men:

> "And we say the same thing for still another reason, which is that a precept of love tells us that no woman, even if she is married, can be crowned with the reward of the King of Love unless she is seen to be enlisted in the service of Love himself outside the bounds of wedlock. But another rule of Love teaches that no one can be in love with two men. Rightly, therefore, Love cannot acknowledge any rights of his between husband and wife."
>
> (pp. 106–7)

The radical ideas expressed in these passages from Andreas constitute a gloss on Gottfried's innovation in restricting the love potion to Tristan and Isolde. Why the belief that true love can occur only "outside the bounds of wedlock" first emerged in the literature of courtly love is illuminated by Freud's (1912) observation that "the ascetic current of Christianity created psychic values for love which pagan antiquity was never able to confer on it" (p. 188). Freud's insight here builds on his pronouncement in a footnote he added in 1910 to *Three Essays on the Theory of Sexuality* (1905b):

> The most striking distinction between the erotic life of antiquity and our own no doubt lies in the fact that the ancients laid stress on the

instinct itself, whereas we emphasize its object. The ancients glorified the instinct and were prepared on its account to glorify even an inferior object; while we despise the instinctual activity in itself, and find excuses for it only in the merits of the object.

(p. 149)

De Rougemont's thesis concerning the influence of Catharism—which allowed women to serve as spiritual leaders while preaching extreme asceticism and forbidding sexual intercourse—on the proponents of courtly love gains a measure of credence from Freud's (1912) contention that the "psychical values" placed on love for the first time in Christian culture "assumed its greatest importance with the ascetic monks, whose lives were almost entirely occupied with the struggle against libidinal temptation" (p. 188).

The emotional power of Gottfried's text derives from the way he has tapped into the universal structure of the Oedipus complex in a cultural context in which adultery is countenanced and even glorified. When Tristan and Isolde have consumed the potion but not yet avowed their love, Gottfried captures his hero's conflict between longing for the wife/mother and loyalty to the husband/father, in which the former emotion at first overmasters him:

The loyal man was afflicted by a double pain: when he looked at her face and sweet Love began to wound his heart and soul with her, he bethought himself of Honour, and it retrieved him. But this in turn was the sign for Love, his liege lady, whom his father had served before him, to assail him anew, and once more he had to submit. Honour and Loyalty harassed him powerfully, but Love harassed him more. Love tormented him to an extreme, she made him suffer more than did Honour and Loyalty combined.

(p. 196)

But, as we have seen, the bliss enjoyed by Tristan and Isolde while on the ship is "haunted by fear of the future," that is, the knowledge "that fair Isolde was to be given to one to whom she did not wish to be given" (p. 204). Like the Cave of Lovers, their idyll on the ship is only a temporary refuge from law and society, and even in these interludes the awareness of the existence of an injured third party, and the unstoppable passage of time, means that the triumph of love "outside the bounds of wedlock" is never final or complete. Even before they have reached Cornwall, Tristan veers around to the opposite pole in his conflict between love and honor:

His loyalty laid regular siege to him so that he kept it well in mind and brought Mark his wife. Honour and Loyalty pressed him hard: these two, who had lost the battle to Love when Tristan had decided in her favour, this vanquished pair now vanquished Love in turn.

(p. 206)

But whether honor or love is in the ascendant, Tristan is "afflicted by a double pain." As Gottfried expounds, "*When all is said, if we pursue pleasure it cannot remain so without our having to suffer pain as well*" because "when we are unwilling to seek anything but the body's delight, it means the ruin of honour" (p. 206), an outcome no less intolerable than is the loss of love or forgoing sexual pleasure.

Because Isolde has lost her virginity to Tristan during their sea voyage, the lovers are forced to resort to deception so as not to be exposed upon reaching Cornwall. Their plan is to ask Brangane, who is "beautiful and a virgin" (p. 205), to take Isolde's place with Mark on the wedding night. As Gottfried observes, "Thus Love instructs honest minds to practice perfidy, though they ought not to know what goes to make a fraud of this sort" (p. 205). Agreeing "most reluctantly," Brangane dons Isolde's robes and allows Mark to have his way with her. Having sacrificed her virginity, Brangane slips away and Isolde, "in great distress and with secret pain in her heart," lies down beside the king, who "resumed his pleasures" (p. 208). As the narrator comments, "To him one woman was as another. ... There was nothing to choose between them—he found gold and brass in either. Moreover, they both paid him their dues, one way and another, so that he noticed nothing amiss" (p. 208).

Mark's inability to tell one woman from the other, his being satisfied with the "fine brass" of Brangane which is nonetheless a "counterfeit" that he accepts "as bed-money for a payment due in gold" (p. 207), shows that for him both she and Isolde are merely sexual objects and underscores the lack of refinement that disqualifies him from being a "noble heart." In Freud's terms, Mark, like the ancients, "glorified the instinct" and is "prepared on its account to glorify even an inferior object," but this attitude is condemned in the world that comes into being in the literature of courtly love, in which "the ascetic current of Christianity" induces its devotees to "despise the instinctual activity in itself, and find excuses for it only in the merits of the object."

In addition to the negative light in which it casts Mark, Isolde's "perfidy" in deputizing Brangane to serve as her surrogate on the wedding night exposes the potential for conflict between the two women. At first, Isolde worries to herself, "'If she plays this bed-game over-long and too intently, I fear she will take such a liking to it that she will lie there till daylight'" (p. 207), and the deception will be exposed because Brangane's sexual desire has been awakened. Even after Brangane shows her thoughts to be "true and unsullied" by leaving Mark as promised, Isolde's anxieties are not allayed.

Despite her marriage, she and Tristan continue to have "their joy morning and night, for nobody had any suspicions," but Isolde "lived in great fear and dreaded keenly lest Brangane, perhaps loving Mark, might divulge her shameful deed to him and the whole story of what had taken place" (p. 208). She goes so far as to concoct a plot to have Brangane killed, though the latter convinces the assassins to spare her life because all she had done was loan Isolde her own white shift to wear instead of Isolde's "worn" and "soiled" one, but only after "first refusing" (p. 210) Isolde's request. Upon learning that Brangane had shown her loyalty by using a harmless metaphor for the sacrifice of her virginity in this ordeal which "had smelted her in the crucible and refined her like gold," Isolde has no further doubts, and they become "so deeply devoted in mutual love and trustfulness that no difference was ever made between them in any of their affairs" (p. 211).

Despite this reconciliation, the fact that Isolde temporarily turns against Brangane illustrates the ambivalence in all the entwined relationships in the poem. Tristan reveres Mark but usurps his place with Isolde, just as there is a fusion of love and hate in Tristan's relationship with Isolde as well as in Isolde's relationship with Brangane. The central triangle is formed by Tristan, Isolde, and Mark—two men and one woman—but it is embedded in the secondary triangles of Isolde, Mark, and Brangane as well as Isolde, Tristan, and Isolde of the White Hands, both of which comprise two women and one man.

The most far-reaching implication of the lovers' plot to deceive Mark by having him deflower Brangane on his wedding night is that it requires their "honest minds" to engage in "perfidy" and "fraud." By an irreducible paradox, the lovers are both honest, because they possess "noble hearts," and dishonest because their love (as in Shakespeare's Sonnet 138) is based on a "lie" in both the sexual and moral sense. Although the poem is aligned with the perspective of Tristan and celebrates his love for Isolde, it also exposes the sordid side of their affair.

Indeed, when Mark's Steward-in-Chief, Marjodoc, who—in a tertiary triangle—himself has a "secret attachment" to Isolde, dreams that a "fearsome and dreadful" boar "broke in through the doors" of Mark's chamber and "tossed the King's appointed bed in all directions, and fouled the royal linen with his foam" (pp. 219–20), it is obvious that the boar is Tristan, who at his investiture received a shield engraved with a boar, and that the "foam" is the semen he has ejaculated in the royal bed. As both Tristan's double and a surrogate for Mark, Marjodoc is the first to experience the primal scene of a couple engaged in sexual intercourse from which he is excluded when he approaches the bed where Tristan is lying with Isolde and "overheard the two of them and all that passed between them," which causes him to be consumed with "hatred and anger, anger and hatred towards her" (p. 220). In addition to both loving and hating Isolde, Marjodoc experiences conflicting emotions toward Tristan, just as Tristan does in relation to Mark, since on the one hand he wants nothing more than "to divulge their affair and make it known then and there," but on the other is restrained by his "fear of Tristan—that he might do him some injury" (pp. 220-1). So subtle is Gottfried's artistry that, of Tristan's four father figures in the poem, Rivalin and Rual, who are his "good" fathers, both have names that begin with "R," whereas his "bad" fathers, Mark and Morgan, both have names that begin with "M." This pattern is sustained inasmuch as not only Marjodoc but Tristan's other enemies, Morold and the dwarf Melot, likewise have names beginning with "M."

The pervasive moral ambiguity in the poem culminates in "The Ordeal." In this episode, Mark devises a trap for the lovers with the aid of Melot and Marjodoc by having flour sprinkled on the floor between their beds after the three of them have been "bled"—then regarded as an enjoyable pastime—before he goes to church. In the king's absence, despite having been alerted by Brangane to the stratagem, Tristan leaps from his bed to Mark and Isolde's, then back, bleeding profusely both in their bed and in his own, though not on the floor between them. The evidence of the lovers' guilt seems overwhelming, but because he has not seen them in bed together, Mark remains in doubt about the true state of affairs. Gottfried describes the plight of the jealous husband who "had chased and all but caught up with his mortal sorrow":

> He believed one thing, he believed another. He did not know what he wanted or what he should believe. He had just found Love's guilty traces in his bed, though not before it, and was thus told the truth and denied it. With these two, truth and untruth, he was deceived. He suspected both alternatives, yet both eluded him. He neither wished the two of them guilty, nor wished them free of guilt.
>
> (p. 242)

Mark exists in a dissociated state, unsure what to believe and whether it would be worse to be betrayed by Isolde with his nephew or not. For these reasons, Gottfried both here and in an earlier episode refers to Mark as "the waverer" (*dem zwîvelaere*); (pp. 242, 226; ll. 15265, 14010), as befits a man incapable of distinguishing brass from gold.

Because of his doubts, Mark summons a council of nobles, the upshot of which is that Isolde is compelled to undergo "the ordeal of the red-hot iron" (p. 245), which will prove her guilt or innocence depending on whether it burns her or not when she holds it in her hand. Understandably anxious,

Isolde confides her fears "to Christ, the Merciful, who is helpful when one is trouble," but also resolves to take action by propounding "to her secret self a ruse which presumed very far upon her Maker's courtesy" (p. 246). Just before her moment of truth, Isolde, who has disembarked from a ship, is carried to the harbor by Tristan disguised as a pilgrim, who, upon reaching the shore, "dropped to the ground, falling as if by accident, so that his fall brought him to rest lying in the Queen's lap and arms" (p. 246). Accordingly, when Isolde, who has given away all her jewelry and other valuables "to win God's favour, so that He might overlook her very real trespasses and restore her to her honour," is about to lay hold of the iron, she swears to Mark that "'no man in the world had carnal knowledge of me or lay in my arms or beside me but you, always excepting the poor pilgrim whom, with your own eyes, you saw lying in my arms.' I can offer no purgation concerning him" (pp. 247–8). The king accepts her oath, and when Isolde grasps the iron she is not burned.

The subversive implications of this episode, in which God allows Isolde to emerge unscathed from her ordeal and thereby to convince Mark and his court of her innocence, would be evident even without any commentary on Gottfried's part. Isolde's "ruse" in this supreme test is of a piece with her "perfidy" and "fraud" in perpetrating the bed trick with Brangane in order to convince Mark that she is still a virgin; but now God, who seems to have bestowed his "favour" on Isolde in exchange for a bribe, is in on the deception. By saying that her equivocal oath "presumed very far upon her Maker's *courtesy*" (*höfscheit*) (l. 15552), Gottfried ascribes to the Christian deity an attribute that seems better suited to one of the speakers in Andreas Capellanus's dialogues. Gottfried proceeds to make explicit the theological implications of Isolde's successful act of duplicity:

> Thus it was made manifest and confirmed to all the world that Christ in His great virtue is pliant as a windblown sleeve. ... He is at the beck of every heart for honest deeds or fraud. Be it deadly earnest or game, He is just as you would have Him. This was amply revealed in the facile Queen. She was saved by her guile and the doctored oath that went flying up to God, with the result that she redeemed her honour and was again much beloved of her lord Mark, and was praised, lauded, and esteemed among the people.
>
> (p. 248)

So disconcerted is Hatto (1960) by Gottfried's comparison of Christ to a "windblown sleeve" no less ready to come to the aid of "fraud" and a "doctored oath" than of "honest deeds" that he would have us believe that "there is no compelling reason to regard this passage in its context as blasphemous, or heretical or demoniac" (p. 20). But this is to close one's eyes to Gottfried's metamorphosis of the second person of the Trinity into a patron saint of courtly love in a way that must be anathema to orthodox Christians. As A. C. Spearing (1993) has commented, "Gottfried's poem is permeated with erotic adaptations of religious motifs" (p. 63), but it is a forbidden love that he worships as sacred. That is why Gottfried affirms in the Prologue that he is prepared to be "damned or saved" together with his coterie of denizens of the "polite world," and why he equates his poem with the consecrated "bread" that will sustain and console subsequent generations of tormented lovers.

5

Despite being aligned with the perspective of the adulterous couple to the extent that he depicts Christ as prepared to condone and conceal their affair, Gottfried does not minimize the turpitude to which its illicit nature requires them to stoop. Concerning the feigned honor shown to Tristan by Marjodoc and Melot, he asks his readers:

> State your opinions, all of you, on this point: where you have only the semblance, is that honour or no? I myself say both yes and no. No and yes both have their share in it. "No" for the man who renders honour: "yes" for the one who receives it. These two are found between the pair of them—both "yes" and "no" are found there. What more is there to say? Here we have honour without honour.

> (pp. 255–6)

In this analysis, Gottfried makes it clear that while the one who "receives" only the "semblance" of honor is honorable, the one who "renders" it is a hypocrite. The crucial point is that this critique of Tristan's enemies extends to him and Isolde in relation to Mark. In the ordeal of the iron, it is Isolde who has "honour without honour," and Mark who is honorable even though he is made of a coarser fiber and lacks a "noble heart." Later, however, Gottfried reverses himself and refers to "the life so bare of honour that Mark lived with Isolde" because he "knew well enough ... that she bore him no affection, yet he cherished her in spite of it!" He did so, Gottfried continues, because "lust and appetite suffer most obstinately what it falls to their lot to suffer" (p. 275).

At every turn, this conflict between Love and Honor renders *Tristan* a tragedy in which anguish is inseparable from bliss. As long as Mark only suspects the truth on the basis of "Love's guilty traces" but lacks the "ocular proof" that will likewise be demanded by Othello, he has "chased" but not yet "caught up with his mortal sorrow." Marjodoc, who is the first to have "overheard the two of them and all that passed between them," fuels Mark's suspicions, but his allegations are hearsay. Isolde manages to escape her ordeal on a technicality, causing Mark's "doubts and suspicions" to be "set aside once more" (p. 248); and even in the Cave of Lovers, Mark finds his wife and nephew sleeping on either side of the "naked sword" that symbolizes the Name-of-the-Father and the threat of castration hanging over Tristan for his violation of the incest taboo. Mark at first oscillates helplessly, "'Guilt?' he asked. 'Most certainly, yes!' 'Guilt?' he asked. 'Most certainly, no!,'" before being taken in by Isolde's innocent appearance:

> Over the white of her face she wore the paint of golden Denial, her most excellent cosmetic "No!" The word gleamed and shone into the King's heart. The other that would have hurt him, the unpalatable word "Yes!," Mark did not see at all. This was all done with, Doubt and Suspicion were no more.
>
> (p. 272)

By his metaphor of cosmetics, Gottfried underscores the falsity of the lovers' position, yet Mark colludes in his own deception. Indeed, in his own version of the experience of "obstacle love," Mark's passion for his wife is raised to a fever pitch by the jealousy incited by the sight of her at once together with and divided from Tristan: "He gazed and gazed at his heart's desire Isolde, who never before had seemed so lovely to him as now" (p. 272).

Only in the episode "The Parting" does Mark finally "rid himself of doubt" (p. 281) about Isolde's affair with Tristan. Gottfried goes to great lengths to stress that the moment when the lovers taste their "mortal sorrow" (*tötlîche klage*) (p. 279; l. 18125) is a reenactment of the Fall. As Janet Wharton (1990) has argued, there was probably no reference to the Fall in Thomas's version, and Gottfried has "radically remodeled the incident to establish clearer parallels with the Genesis account" (p. 143). "It was noon," Gottfried writes, when Tristan received a message from Isolde to join her in "her orchard" (pp. 279–80). What follows is an old story: "Now Tristan did just as Adam did; he took the fruit which his Eve offered him and with her ate his death!" (p. 280). Since they have been intimate on numerous other occasions, it is not the fact that they have committed adultery, which their bonds of kinship make synonymous with incest, that is the cause of their undoing, but that they are caught. In a repetition of her negligence in safeguarding the love potion,

Brangane is again remiss in her vigilance; and when Mark unexpectedly appears, other ladies tell him that Isolde is probably asleep:

> "Tell me, where is the Queen sleeping?" asked the King. They motioned him towards the garden, Mark repaired there at once—and found his mortal pain there! He found his wife and his nephew tightly enlaced in each other's arms, her cheek against his cheek, his mouth on her mouth. All that the coverlet permitted him to see ... was so closely locked together that, had it been a piece cast in bronze or in gold, it could not have been joined more perfectly. Tristan and Isolde were sleeping peacefully after some exertion or other.
>
> (p. 280)

In this blinding flash when Mark sees himself excluded from the "exertion" that has just occurred between his wife and his legal son, Gottfried fuses the motifs of the Fall, the primal scene, and the Oedipus complex. The King, too, experiences an irreversible "mortal pain," so that all three members of the triangle simultaneously suffer a "living death" (p. 281). Gottfried's description of the intertwined lovers as "a piece cast in bronze or in gold" harks back to Mark's inability to tell Brangane from Isolde on the wedding night, but it remains ambiguous whether this indeterminacy is a commentary on Mark's perception or on the morally compromised nature of the lovers. The fact that Tristan and Isolde "could not have been joined more perfectly" suggests that the threat of castration symbolized by the way the gap and the splinter in the sword given to Tristan by Mark "made a perfect whole as if they were one thing" is momentarily obliterated. Just when they are about to be forcibly parted, the lovers achieve their most perfect union, though this fantasy of erasing what Lacan (1954–5) would call the "lack of being" (*manque à être*) (p. 223) of which desire is the metonymy is only made possible when they are beheld through the eyes of a third party, and is thus shown even here to be unattainable.

Although Mark has received "ocular proof" of Isolde's betrayal, so that "he no longer fancied, he *knew*," when he informs his retinue of the catastrophe he says only that "he had been told for a fact that Tristan and the Queen were together" (p. 281). An element of doubt is thereby again introduced, and when the counselors arrive on the scene they find "Isolde alone, lying on her bed and lost in her thoughts as before" (p. 282). But though the truth remains elusive as far as the world is concerned, it is not for the three principals; and the time has come when Tristan must leave Isolde and flee Mark's wrath. Placing a ring on his finger, Isolde seals with a kiss their vow of eternal love: "'You and I, Tristan and Isolde, shall for ever remain one and undivided! Let this kiss be a seal upon it that I am yours, that you are mine, steadfast till death, but one Tristan and Isolde!'" (p. 282).

In the closing sequence of the poem, however, the "one and undivided" lovers again become divided not only physically but psychically as Tristan arrives at the castle of Karke in the duchy of Arundel, where he meets the "beautiful and unmarried" (p. 287) Isolde of the White Hands. This Isolde is the daughter of the rulers of the land and the sister of Kaedin, who becomes "deeply attached to Tristan" (p. 288). After he and Kaedin rout the enemies of Arundel, Tristan is hailed as a hero but inwardly tormented by "'how far I have gone astray over this name!'" (p. 291). In the last episode from Gottfried's pen, Tristan muses on the "'strangest quandary'" brought about by his repetition compulsion: "'My eye, which regards Isolde, does not see Isolde! Isolde is far away and nonetheless beside me! I fear I have succumbed to Isolde for the second time. It is as if Cornwall had turned into Arundel, Tintagel into Karke, Isolde into Isolde'" (p. 291). Tristan's beloved, Isolde the Fair, who becomes a queen when she marries Mark, has the same name as her mother, the first Isolde the Queen; and now Tristan becomes entranced by Isolde of the White Hands. By this insistence of the signifying chain, Gottfried conveys that all three Isoldes are imagos of the same woman—namely, the mother—and every permutation of Tristan's erotic history renders visible across time a further dimension of the structure of the Oedipus complex.

Tristan's simultaneous attraction to both younger Isoldes is a mirror of his divided self. He reproaches himself with the thought, "'I am enamoured of two Isoldes and hold them both dear, yet my other self, Isolde, loves but one Tristan. That one woman desires no other Tristan but me, while I hotly woo a second Isolde'" (p. 293). By recalling the loyalty of his "other self," Tristan temporarily subdues his desire for the "second Isolde." As Gottfried paradoxically expresses it, "Things took their rightful path. Isolde [of the White Hands] robbed Isolde [the Fair] of her Tristan through desire; but now, with desire, Tristan returned to the love he was born to" (p. 293). But this noble resolution does not last long. Tristan, his heart set aflame by the girl before him, "once more began to waver because of his thoughts and desires" (p. 294), and he convinces himself that the route to happiness is to "'divide and apportion my love among more than one. If I direct my thoughts to more than one love I might easily become a carefree Tristan!'" (p. 294). Whereas before he was chastened by the thought of Isolde's the Fair's loyalty, now Tristan, like Mark, becomes a "waverer" and veers around to the idea that he himself is "'wretched'" while she is "'happy,'" not least because she can have sex with Mark at any time while he has no one: "'The pleasure I forgo for your sake—ah, how it pains me!—you pursue as often as you please! You have your partner for it'" (p. 297). The unfairness of this deprivation becomes too much to bear, and Gottfried's text breaks off with the following words from Tristan: "'I avoid all other women for her sake, yet I must forgo her too. I cannot ask that of her which would give me joy and happiness in the world ...'" (p. 297; ellipses in original).

According to de Rougemont, Don Juan is "an inverted reflection of Tristan," and in his fantasy that he might become "a carefree Tristan" if only he were able to love "more than one" woman Tristan becomes his own "inverted reflection." In so doing, he exemplifies the dynamics of the Oedipus complex analyzed by Freud in his papers on the psychology of love. In men in whom "the libido has remained attached to the mother" to an inordinate degree, Freud (1910) maintains, the "first precondition" for loving is that "the woman should not be unattached, or that there should be an injured third party" (p. 169). Since this requirement originates in childhood, "the fact of the mother belonging to the father becomes an inseparable part of the mother's essence," and the original "injured third party is none other than the father himself" (p. 169). That is why, to return to de Rougemont's concept of "obstacle love," Freud (1912) maintains that "an obstacle is required to satisfy libido; and where natural resistances to satisfaction have not been sufficient men have at all times erected conventional ones to be able to enjoy love" (p. 188).[9]

With the recognition that "the love-objects chosen by our type" are "above all mother-surrogates" as his starting point, Freud (1910) is able to show how "the formation of a series of them, which seems so flatly to contradict the condition of being faithful to one, can now be understood" (p. 169). He explains that "the notion of something irreplaceable, when it is active in the unconscious, frequently appears as broken up into an endless series: endless for the reason that every surrogate nevertheless fails to provide the desired satisfaction" (p. 169). Isolde the Fair is the ideal "mother-surrogate" for the orphaned Tristan both by virtue of her name and by virtue of "belonging to the father." But even she "fails to provide the desired satisfaction" he is ostensibly seeking, and he therefore seeks a surrogate for his surrogate by imagining what it would be like to "divide and apportion" his desire among "more than one love" with Isolde of the White Hands.

Although Thomas's version in Old French lacks the sublimity of Gottfried's Middle High German, his psychological sophistication makes it easy to see why it was hailed by his successor as the only "authentic" source. As Thomas explicates Tristran's mental state, "He desires Ysolt of the White Hands for her beauty and the name 'Ysolt,'" and he therefore resolves "to marry the

---

[9] As Tanner (1979) notes, "Rougemont's insight is so close to Freud's description of 'obstacle love' that it is surprising he does not quote it" (p. 88).

maiden so as to know what the Queen's lot is, and how, in despite of love, he may have pleasure with his wife" (p. 304). Tristran, that is, wants to marry Ysolt of the White Hands in order to know what it is like to have sex without love, and thus to experience what the absent Ysolt does with her husband. On their wedding night, Ysolt of the White Hands is brought to bed, but as Tristran is being disrobed by his retainers "they pull from his finger the ring which Ysolt had given him in the orchard on the last day he ever saw her" (p. 306). This symbolic breaking of his vow of eternal love puts Tristran "in such anguish that he does not know what to do. Now that he might easily do his will, his power to do so fails him." Out of a sense of guilt that has its roots in the unconscious, Tristran finds himself impotent with his wife. Pleading for Ysolt of the White Hands' indulgence and discretion, Tristran tells her, "'Here on my right side I have a bodily infirmity that has long been with me,'" to which she responds with commiseration, "'I will and can well forgo that other thing you speak of'" (p. 310).

Tristran's "bodily infirmity" on his "right side" is another iteration of the castration motif that has run throughout the narrative, beginning with Rivalin's wound through the "side" from which he is healed by Blancheflor. In a variation on Freud's (1912) apothegm about incestuously fixated men, "Where they love they do not desire and where they desire they cannot love" (p. 183), where Tristran loves intercourse is forbidden, and where intercourse is obligatory, he cannot perform. Tristran's inability to achieve an erection with Ysolt of the White Hands, whom he associates with Ysolt the Fair not only on account of her beauty but also her name, illustrates Freud's hypothesis that "the strange failure shown in psychical impotence makes its appearance whenever an object which has been chosen with the aim of avoiding incest recalls the prohibited object through some feature, often an inconspicuous one" (p. 183).

In the denouement of Thomas's plot, Tristran, who has been "wounded through the thigh by a lance bated with venom" (p. 341) while fighting alongside a giant ironically named Dwarf Tristran, can only be healed by his beloved Ysolt, just as Rivalin had been healed when Blancheflor visited him in the guise of a "physician-woman" and he himself had been healed in Gottfried's version from his poisoned wound by Isolde the Queen. Bestowing on Caerdin (Kaedin) the ring he had received on parting from his beloved, Tristran persuades his brother-in-law—with whom he has been reconciled despite not having consummated his marriage to Ysolt of the White Hands— to sail to England and remind his Queen Ysolt how "'she cured me of my wound long ago, and the philtre we drank together on the sea, when it caused us to fall in love'" (p. 344). As Hatto (1960) points out in a note, "Thomas here reverts to an earlier version of the story according to which the younger

Ysolt heals Tristran, not the elder" (p. 344), but this conflation of mother and daughter makes sense psychoanalytically since all three Ysolts are incarnations of the same women in Tristran's mind.

In dispatching Caerdin on his mission, Tristran tells him what he must do when he returns with Ysolt:

> "Hide it from your sister so that she may have no suspicion of our love. You will pass the Queen off as a physician-woman who has come to heal my wound. … If you can prevail upon Ysolt to come and heal my wound, use a white sail when returning. But if you do not bring Ysolt, then use the black!"
>
> (p. 345)

In another instance of what appears to be chance but is really fate—a manifestation of the logic of the unconscious—Ysolt of the White Hands overhears this conversation, which makes her "very angry in her heart," and resolves that when the opportunity arises "she will take fearful vengeance on the one she loves above all" (pp. 345–6). Accordingly, when the ship bearing Caerdin and Queen Ysolt approaches the coast of Brittany, Caerdin unfurls the white sail but Ysolt of the White Hands with "great guile" (p. 352) tells Tristran that it is black. Tristran dies apostrophizing the absent Ysolt who he believes has abandoned him; and when this Ysolt finds that she has arrived too late, she resolves "'to do as a true lover: I will die for you in return!'" (p. 353). As the poem comes to a close, Thomas describes the two lovers united in death, while all the other characters have been forgotten: "She takes him in her arms and then, lying at full length, she kisses his face and lips and clasps him tightly to her. Then straining body to body, mouth to mouth, she at once renders up her spirit and of sorrow for her lover dies thus at his side" (p. 353).

6

This ending, which circles back to the beginning, confirms that the "absolute obstacle" which the lovers ultimately desire originates in the Oedipus complex. Such a reunion in death constitutes what Freud (1926) has called a "classical instance" of "those hysterical symptoms which have been shown to be a compromise between the need for satisfaction and the need for punishment" (p. 98). Because Tristran and Ysolt are joined "body to body" as they expire, this fulfills the "need for satisfaction." But because their love is both adulterous and incestuous, they have an equally overpowering "need for punishment," which is gratified by their deaths.

Neither Thomas nor Gottfried ever mentions an afterlife. When Gottfried writes in his Prologue that he has "another world in mind" that is not accessible to "the many who … are unable to endure sorrow and wish only to revel in bliss," he means a realm of experience that is transcendent without being supernatural. Despite Thomas's declaration in his concluding lines that he has written in rhyme in order to "please lovers" and offer them "great comfort … in the face of hardship and grief" (p. 353), however, there is nothing in the extant portion of his text that is comparable to Gottfried's credo of "noble hearts." If Thomas's star glows with a less intense heat than Gottfried's, it is because he has not been to the Cave of Lovers himself. As he acknowledges in comparing the "pain and grief" borne by Mark, Tristran, and the two Ysolts: "I do not know what to say here as to which of the four was in greater torment, nor how to tell the truth about it, because I have not experienced it" (pp. 316–17).

So comprehensive is Gottfried's analysis of "love's tragedies" that he not only depicts the sordid side of Tristan's affair with Isolde but goes so far as to interrogate the ideology of obsessive desire that he otherwise dedicates himself to championing. The unexpected reversal occurs in "The Parting," when Mark comes upon Tristan and Isolde in the orchard, causing all three characters to be smitten with "mortal sorrow." This prompts Gottfried to question whether human nature has been irremediably corrupted by the Fall. At first, he seems to suggest that the guilt of original sin has been inherited, at least by women:

> Women do many things, just because they are forbidden, from which they would refrain if they were not forbidden. God knows, these same thistles and thorns are inborn in them! Women of this kind are children of mother Eve, who flouted the first prohibition.
>
> (p. 277)

Subscribing to the teachings of the priests that "it was the fig-tree" which God "forbade her on pain of death," Gottfried avouches his "firm belief" that Eve would never have broken the divine commandment "had it never been forbidden her. In the first thing she ever did, she proved true to her nature and did what was forbidden!" (p. 277).

The misogyny of these statements is clear. But in asserting that Eve "proved true to her nature" by flouting God's prohibition, Gottfried disregards the axiom of orthodox Christianity that Eve, like Adam, possessed free will before the Fall, and reads back into the state of innocence an assumption about what is "true to her nature" derived from his observations of women in the fallen world. The circularity of this reasoning becomes evident when

Gottfried claims that the desire of women for forbidden things is "inborn," since what is allegedly inherited by women from Eve is only said to belong to the first woman by a retroactive projection of the qualities of her descendants.

By this contradiction, Gottfried deconstructs the doctrine of the Fall he ostensibly espouses. So, too, when he states that "women of this kind" are daughters of Eve, he implies that there are women of a *different* kind, and hence raises the possibility that what causes women to behave wantonly has more to do with their nurture than with nature, and, specifically, with the "evil practice" of "surveillance" (p. 277) on the part of jealous husbands such as Mark. Thus, if "women do many things, just because they are forbidden, from which they would refrain if they were not forbidden," then, Gottfried concludes, "it would be wise in a man to abstain from prohibitions," and instead to treat his wife with trust and respect:

> A wise man, therefore, that is, one who grants woman her esteem, should keep no watch over her privacy in defiance of her own good will other than by counsel and instruction, and by tenderness and kindness. ... Every worthy man, and whoever aspires to be one, should trust in his wife and himself, so that for love of him she may shun all wantonness.
>
> (p. 277)

Despite the sexism in Gottfried's declaration that "when a woman grows in virtue despite her inherited instincts ... she is only a woman in name, but in spirit she is a man," he is able to envisage an ideal of "seemly moderation" in which it is possible to reconcile love and honor:

> What can ever be so perfect in a woman as when, in alliance with honour at her side, she does battle with her body for the rights of both body and honour? ... She is no worthy woman who forsakes her honour for her body, or her body for her honour, when circumstance so favours her that she may vindicate them both. Let her deny neither the one nor the other, let her sustain the two, through joy and through sorrow, however she sets about it.
>
> (p. 278)

What Gottfried here describes is the psychological foundation of companionate marriage in which the claims of sexuality are affirmed in the context of a freely chosen fidelity to one person. As Gottfried exclaims, "'She who thinks to love many, by many is unloved!'" In contrast to the "thistles and thorns" that lie in wait when "one quenches desire as soon as one feels the urge and wishes to bestow the exalted name on such meaningless behaviour," the life of a man with a woman who "shows a true concern for her womanhood" need not be plagued by the heartache that is the penalty of the Fall:

> And on whomever she takes courage to bestow her love and person, that man was born most fortunate! He was altogether destined for present bliss, he has the living paradise implanted within his heart! He need have no fear that the thorns will vex him when he reaches for the flowers, or that the prickles will pierce him when he gathers the roses.
>
> (pp. 278–9)

Notwithstanding his warning against "surveillance," Gottfried locates the source of the problem almost exclusively in the "inherent instincts" of women, rather than in the propensity of men to split desire and love. But this patriarchal assumption does not diminish the force of his insight that the life of a "noble heart" may not be preferable to that of a man who resists the temptation of forbidden fruit in favor of the ordinary blessings of "love and devotion, honour and worldly esteem" (p. 279). Just before he recounts how Tristan, like Adam, "ate his death" with "his Eve" in the orchard, Gottfried appeals to the male reader:

> If only he would take my word for it, he would not need to exchange his life for Tristan's. For truly, to whomever a virtuous woman resigns and surrenders her honour and her person, oh, with what deep love she will foster him, how tenderly she will cherish him! How she will clear all his paths of thorns and thistles and of all the vexations of love! How well she will free him of his sufferings, as no Isolde freed her Tristan better!
>
> (p. 279)

Were Tristan to have heeded Gottfried's counsel here, he might have sought to free himself from his compulsive desires by embarking on a lengthy psychoanalysis. Perhaps Gottfried, having escaped from the Cave of Lovers, is recording what he has learned from his own experience. But this is not what anyone remembers about the author who has for nearly a millennium transported his readers to "another world" of ecstatic yet agonizing love. Certainly, in an 1874 letter to his Romanian friend Eduard Silberstein, written at the age of eighteen, Freud understood the poem to be the definitive celebration of a passion that transgresses the limits of what is permitted by religious or secular laws—though these, he went on to propound, may be merely a matter of convention:

> Mind you, I do not hold, as some aesthet[ician]s [*Ästhetiker*] do, that everything immoral according to the letter of the Civil or Mosaic Code must also be unpoetic. Gottfried's Tristan and Isolde is the most brilliant refutation of this dictum. Rather, poetry, supported by the power of our passions, can go quite some way toward transfiguring what is immoral, or, better, what society does not allow.
>
> (Boehlich, 1989, p. 53)

The cogent hypothesis of Peter J. Swales (1982) that, twenty-six years later, Freud entered into a clandestine love affair with his sister-in-law Minna Bernays—which, like Tristan's, would have been at once adulterous and incestuous—is not rendered less probable by the views he set forth here.

Chapter 3

"Where th' Offense Is"

Oedipal Temptation in *Sir Gawain and the Green Knight*

"Nevertheless, it must not be forgotten that though, on the surface, a literary work relates a manifestly coherent story, intertwined with it and simultaneously, another and secret story is being told which, in fact, is the basic theme."

—Marie Bonaparte, *The Life and Works of Edgar Allan Poe*

1

Sir Gawain and the Green Knight, at once the greatest and most psychological of Middle English romances, commands admiration for the unequalled elegance and economy of its plot. As Marie Borroff (1967) has observed, the anonymous fourteenth-century author "was surely the first to combine" (p. viii) the three separate motifs from folklore that make up the action of the poem.[1] The first of its four parts turns on the "Beheading Game," in which an unknown challenger demands that one member of a group of warriors volunteer to cut off his head and agree to accept a retaliatory stroke at a future date. The hero, who undergoes this ordeal, is miraculously spared and hailed for his bravery upon returning to the court. Subsequent action interweaves the "Temptation Story," where the protagonist is obliged to resist the attempts at seduction by a beautiful woman, and the "Exchange of Winnings," in which two men make an agreement to give to the other what each has received during a given period of time.

These three stories are revealed to be intimately linked when Gawain, having represented King Arthur's court in the Beheading Game with the Green Knight, is unable at first to find the Green Chapel where he is to meet his

---

[1] Quotations from *Sir Gawain and the Green Knight* are from Borroff's alliterative verse translation, with line numbers given parenthetically, though I have retained the spelling "Bertilak," which she alters to "Bercilak," found in the Middle English text.

opponent a year later. Instead, he comes upon a magnificent castle, belonging (as he subsequently discovers) to Bertilak de Hautdesert, who induces Gawain to pledge to exchange winnings on three consecutive days, during which Bertilak goes out hunting while Gawain is visited in his bedchamber by Bertilak's alluring wife. On the first two days, Gawain dutifully returns to Bertilak the one and then two kisses bestowed on him by the Lady, but on the third day—though he does kiss his host three times—Gawain conceals from him a green and gold lace, which the Lady had told him would protect his life in his impending trial. The climax of the poem comes in the fourth part when Gawain, after receiving a nick on the neck from the third blow of the Green Knight's ax—corresponding to his transgression on the third day—learns from the Green Knight that he and Bertilak are the same person.

The fact that the literary complexity and emotional power of *Sir Gawain and the Green Knight* derive from a story that is in many respects quite simple gives this medieval romance an unexpected similarity to Greek tragedy. To begin with, there are comparatively few characters in *Sir Gawain*. In addition to the hero, only King Arthur, Guinevere, the Green Knight/Bertilak, Bertilak's wife, Morgan le Fay, and the Guide who leads Gawain to the Green Chapel play a functional role. Like *Oedipus the King*, moreover, *Sir Gawain* is a detective story in which the hero turns out to be in search of himself. But whereas the fact that Oedipus has killed his father and married his mother was common knowledge when Sophocles' play was first performed about 429 B.C.E., so that the audience possesses a godlike omniscience that allows its members to discern the ubiquitous dramatic ironies, in *Sir Gawain* the central mystery—the identity of the Green Knight and Bertilak—is concealed from the reader as well as the hero until the denouement. This state of affairs keeps first-time readers in suspense and ensures that even those who know the story will identify with Gawain and share his perspective on the action. To juxtapose *Sir Gawain* with *Oedipus* from this standpoint illustrates the contrast drawn by Freud (1908b) between "the ancient authors of epics and tragedies" and the works of modern writers in which "only one person—once again the hero—is described from within. The author sits inside his mind, as it were, and looks at the other characters from outside" (pp. 149–50).

A. C. Spearing (1970), who speaks of the plot in Aristotelian terms as the "soul" of the poem, points out that both Gawain and the reader initially believe that the Beheading Game is the main subject, whereas in fact the Temptation Story, seemingly an interlude, turns out to be crucial. The resolution of the Beheading Game thus brings, in Spearing's words, "not the expected climax, but only knowledge of what has happened, and consequent self-knowledge" (p. 191). Analogously, in *Oedipus the King* Oedipus's initial quest to find the murderer of Laius gives way to the quest for his own origins, and Oedipus gains self-knowledge through a realization of what he himself has done. Like Oedipus when he discovers his true parentage, when Gawain is confronted by the Green Knight's knowledge of his conduct he experiences the shock of what Aristotle in the *Poetics* terms *anagnorisis*, or recognition, which is accompanied by a *peripeteia*, or reversal; and in both *Oedipus the King* and *Sir Gawain and the Green Knight* a drama of interpretation underlies the drama of action.

At the outset of *Sir Gawain and the Green Knight*, King Arthur is unwilling to begin his New Year's feasting until he has heard "Of some fair feat or fray / some far-borne tale" (93), and the sudden entrance of the Green Knight more than fulfills his expectations. By the end of the poem, Gawain's own adventures have been set down in "the best book of knighthood" (2521) and transformed into the sort of "far-borne tale" destined to be recounted at subsequent feasts. Despite not being a king, Gawain shares with Oedipus the heroic quality of experiencing in actuality what for ordinary men and women must remain fantasies. The plague on Thebes that is a manifestation of Oedipus's pollution and impels him to find the murderer of Laius mirrors the resolve of Arthur's court to wear the green and gold lace in imitation of Gawain when he returns from his rendezvous with the Green Knight. Notwithstanding the contrast between Gawain's apparent triumph and reabsorption into the fellowship of the Round Table and Oedipus's self-blinding and exile from Thebes, both serve as the representatives of their societies and assume the burden of its collective guilt.

The selection of Gawain for the Beheading Game with the Green Knight appears to be fortuitous. As J. A. Burrow (1966) has observed, "one does not feel that the beheading adventure, when the Green Knight proposes it, is *for* Gawain alone in any mysterious fashion" (p. 11). Indeed, when the Green Knight challenges Arthur's court, Gawain volunteers to substitute for the king because he is its least worthy member and his defeat would not be seriously damaging to the court's reputation: "'I am the weakest, well I know, and of wit feeblest, / And the loss of my life would be least of any'" (354–5). Gawain's profession of humility contrasts, however, with the praise he is accorded by the men in Bertilak's castle, who hail him as a paragon of knighthood: "Of all knights on earth most honored is he" (914). An analogous double valuation attaches to Oedipus in *Oedipus the King*. As the wayfarer who became king when he saved the city by solving the riddle of the Sphinx, he is celebrated by the Chorus as "the first of men / in all the chances of this life" (32–3), but when the identity of his Theban parents is revealed, the Chorus deems him "equal with those who live not at all" (1188).

Both Oedipus and Gawain, therefore, oscillate between being regarded as the least and the greatest of men, and this duality is a constitutive feature of their heroism. The seeming randomness of Gawain's offer to take Arthur's place is paralleled by Oedipus's boast that he is a "child of Fortune, / ... / She is the mother from whom I spring" (1080–3). Ironically, this fictive genealogy accurately reflects his status as Everyman. The ostensible role of chance in the singling out of Oedipus and Gawain for their fates thus signifies the opposite—that their lot might have fallen to anyone because it is universal.

Once Gawain has been singled out to represent the court in the Beheading Game, the Green Knight demands—if he himself should survive being struck by Gawain—that Gawain promise to seek him out to receive a return blow in a year's time. He refuses to divulge where he lives, however, simply instructing Gawain to "'seek me yourself, wheresoever you deem / My lodgings may lie'" (395–6). After his decapitation, the Green Knight picks his head off the floor and reiterates, "'The Knight of the Green Chapel I am well known to many, / Wherefore you cannot fail to find me at last'" (454–5).

If the Green Knight assures Gawain that he will reach his destination, the reason must be that he already knows it unconsciously. In *The Interpretation of Dreams* (1900), Freud observes that the action of *Oedipus the King*, with its "cunning delays and ever-mounting excitement," is "a process that can be likened to the work of a psycho-analysis" (p. 262). Analogously, Gawain's search for the Green Knight obeys the "fundamental rule" of free association, which invites a patient in analysis to say the first thing that comes to mind in order to arrive at otherwise repressed material. From the opening stanza, which goes back to the fall of Troy and employs the motif of *translatio imperii* to recount how a series of kingdoms from Rome to Britain were founded by Aeneas and his descendants, while alluding ominously to an unnamed knight—presumably Antenor, a counselor to Priam depicted as a traitor in medieval versions of the legend—who "knotted the nets of deceit" and "Was impeached for his perfidy, proven most true" (3–4), *Sir Gawain and the Green Knight* sets Gawain's odyssey against the backdrops of the history of the Round Table and of Western civilization as a whole.

2

Because only Gawain is, in Freud's words, "described from within," and the anonymous author "sits inside his mind, as it were, and looks at the other characters from outside," the action of the poem is experienced both by the hero and by the reader as though everything that takes place in external reality were an emanation of Gawain's psyche. This circumstance gives the romance a fairy-tale quality and makes the ideas of Melanie Klein about the mental life of children especially pertinent to understanding its imaginative power. The limited number of characters, for example, is explained by Klein's (1952) contention that "there are in fact very few people in the young infant's life, but he feels them to be a multitude of objects because they appear to him in different aspects" (p. 54).

It follows from Klein's reference to the "very few people" who populate an infant's life that almost all the figures Gawain encounters on his quest are parental imagos. Gawain is Arthur's nephew—as Tristan is Mark's—and when he first appears in the poem during the Christmastide feast the poet specifies that "the good knight by Guinevere sits" (109). This anticipates the situation in which Gawain will find himself at the castle where he meets not only the affable host and the host's beautiful wife, but also an "ancient" (948) lady who accompanies the latter. During his stay at the castle, Gawain does not yet know the identity of his host and that it was he who came to Arthur's court in the guise of the Green Knight, or that the old lady is the sorceress Morgan le Fay. But the connection between what takes place at the castle and at Arthur's court is intimated when he beholds the wife and thinks to himself that she "excelled the queen herself" (945). Indeed, when the assembled company gathers on the dais for their meals, the seating arrangement replicates that at the court inasmuch as Sir Gawain is seated "beside the gay lady," while the true power structure that will only be revealed at the end of the poem is conveyed by the fact that "The old ancient lady, highest she sits," with "The lord at her left hand" (1001–3).

The key to understanding the poem is furnished by the revelation that the Green Knight and Bertilak are the same person, which can be interpreted psychoanalytically to mean that they represent to Gawain the two faces of the father—his benign and punitive aspects—initially perceived as separate but ultimately merged into one. Indeed, in the French romance *Life of Caradoc*— asserted by Larry Benson (1965, p. 16) to be the source of the Beheading Game in *Sir Gawain*—the challenger proves to be the hero's disguised father, thus presenting in undistorted form the psychological substrate of the story of *Sir Gawain*. And because Gawain's *peripeteia* resembles that of Oedipus in involving the discovery of a father figure, his *anagnorisis* fulfills on a symbolic level the Aristotelian requirement that it should be specifically one of kinship ties.

The splitting of Gawain's father figure into the characters of Bertilak and the Green Knight finds a counterpart in the pairing of Bertilak's wife with Morgan le Fay. Although not the same person, the inference that the two women—one young and alluring, the other old and repellent—are polarized aspects of his maternal imago is compelling.[2] When Gawain first encounters them together at the castle, the host's wife is adorned with "a high headdress, hung all with pearls; / Her bright throat and bosom fair to behold" (954–5), while "A wimple the other wore round her throat, / Her swart chin well swaddled, swathed all in white" (957–8).

This contrast between the "bosom fair to behold" of the Lady and the "well swaddled" body of her "swart" companion underscores that the action of the romance takes place at the primitive level of psychic reality that Klein (1946) calls the paranoid-schizoid position, with "the first object being the mother's breast which to the child becomes split into a good (gratifying) breast and bad (frustrating) breast" (p. 2). The frustration experienced by the infant seeking oral gratification leads him or her, in Klein's (1945) view, on the one hand, to idealize "the good breast and the good mother" and, on the other, to intensify "the hatred and fear of the bad mother, which becomes the prototype of all persecuting and frightening objects" (p. 379). By the compound term "paranoid-schizoid" Klein means to describe the simultaneously operating mechanisms of projection and splitting. These cause the mental representations of the breast, followed by other objects in the external world, to take "good" and "bad" forms that are believed to be intrinsic to those objects but in actuality originate in the psyche of the child—or, later, the adult—who is doing the splitting and projecting.

There are abundant indications that the poem taps into early strata of mental life. Even before the entrance of the Green Knight, Arthur's court is described as "fair folk in their first age" (54), and thus metaphorically in their infancy, while the king is "a little boyish" (86). When the Green Knight appears, "in his one hand he had a holly bob" (206), while he carried "an ax in his other, a huge and immense" (208); and this "largest of men" (141) taunts the assembled knights with being "'but beardless children'" (280). The contrast between the festive shrub, which, as the Green Knight professes to Arthur, is meant to offer an assurance that "'I pass here in peace, and would part friends'" (266), and the ominous weapon—which, like both the Green Knight himself and his horse, has "a spike of green steel" while being also "resplendent with gold" (211)—prefigures the dichotomy between the Green Knight and Bertilak and symbolizes the conflict between the forces of life and death in the tale.

The terms of what the Green Knight calls his "'contract'" (378) and "'covenant'" (393) with whoever will serve as the representative of the court

---

[2] This configuration is a variation on the "Loathly Lady" motif, best known from Chaucer's Wife of Bath's Tale, in which a knight must decide whether to marry a woman who is beautiful but unfaithful or one who is ugly bur faithful; and when he allows her to make the choice, he is rewarded with a bride who is both beautiful and faithful.

is that he himself "'shall bide the first blow'" (290) with the ax, which shall henceforth belong to the one who delivers it, provided that this same brave soul "'grant me the guerdon to give him another'" (295) in a year and a day. When the Green Knight lies on the ground with his neck exposed, Gawain brings down the ax with such force "That the shock of the sharp blow shivered the bones / And cut the flesh cleanly and clove it in twain" (424–5). But even before he has done so, the Green Knight says to Gawain, "'Now hold *your* grim tool steady'" (413; italics added); and after the Green Knight's departure Arthur reiterates that the ax now belongs to Gawain: "'Now, sir, hang up *your* ax that has hewn enough'" (477; italics added).

Each of these details makes sense when seen as a manifestation of what Klein (1935) holds to be the "phase of sadism at its zenith, through which children pass during the first year of life" (p. 262). Although directed not at the mother or her breast but at a father figure, Gawain's decapitation of the Green Knight constitutes a sadistic attack, which, as Klein (1930) elaborates, "gives rise to anxiety and sets in motion the ego's earliest modes of defence" (p. 220). The covenant with the Green Knight makes literal the scenario envisaged by Klein in which "the weapons employed to destroy the object are felt by the subject to be levelled at his own self as well. The object of the attack becomes a source of danger because the subject fears similar—retaliatory— attacks from it" (p. 220). The ax belongs to Gawain because, having done his utmost "to destroy the object," he is gripped by a dread of the "retaliatory attack" that he knows awaits him at the end of his journey; and it is thus now primarily an internal rather than an external object. What Klein in her earlier papers describes in terms of a "phase of sadism" in children she later reformulates using Freud's concept of the death instinct, but the sequence she outlines remains the same:

> I hold that anxiety arises from the operation of the death instinct within the organism, is felt as fear of annihilation (death) and takes the form of fear of persecution. The fear of the destructive impulse seems to attach itself at once to an object—or rather it is experienced as the fear of an uncontrollable overpowering object. … Even if these objects are felt to be external, they become through introjection internal persecutors and thus reinforce the fear of the destructive impulse within.
>
> (1946, pp. 4–5)

Again, all this applies to Gawain's encounter with the Green Knight and his "introjection" of the ax as an "internal persecutor" in the first of the four parts of the poem. Everything that ostensibly happens in external reality, such as the Green Knight's appearance at Arthur's court and challenge that one of its members engage with him in the Beheading Game, can be understood as a projection of the "destructive impulse" arising from Gawain's inner world. In a circular process, that impulse "seems to attach itself at once" to one or more bad objects, which in turn "reinforce the fear of the destructive impulse within." The fairy-tale quality of *Sir Gawain and the Green Knight*, in which the exaggeratedly powerful characters Gawain encounters are both real and unreal, is captured by Klein's (1935) description of how "in the very young child there exist, side by side with its relations to real objects—but on a different plane, as it were—relations to its unreal imagos, both as excessively good and excessively bad figures, and … these two kinds of object relations intermingle and colour each other to an ever-increasing degree in the course of development" (p. 286).

Because what happens in this first installment of the Beheading Game can be accounted for in psychoanalytic terms, the seemingly miraculous ability of the Green Knight to survive his decapitation by Gawain does not detract from its plausibility according to the laws that operate on what Klein calls the "different plane" of the unconscious mind. Just as in *Tristan*, where Gottfried mocks an earlier version of the tale for "talking nonsense" when it "grows fantastic" and the love potion reveals Tristan's repressed desires, so, too, the *Gawain*-poet makes minimal use of supernatural elements. When, in Part 2, he recounts the exotic dangers through which Gawain passes in his search for the Green Chapel, he signals their unimportance by devoting as few lines to them as possible: "So many were the wonders he wandered among / That to tell but the tenth part would tax my wits" (718–19). If both *Tristan* and *Sir Gawain and the Green Knight* surpass other medieval romances, this is due not only to their authors' artistic genius but also to their psychological realism.

3

Already in Part 1, Gawain's primitive anxieties are aroused by the Beheading Game, and his fears for his survival lead him to employ the "earliest modes of defence" characteristic of the paranoid-schizoid position. But his journey to the interior does not begin in earnest until Part 2. On Christmas Eve, almost one year after the Green Knight has come and gone from Arthur's court, Gawain is riding on his horse Gringolet in the bitter cold in search of the Green Chapel. Calling on Christ and Mary, he makes the sign of the cross three times, upon which there appears a "wondrous dwelling" (764) in the forest, "A castle as comely as a knight could own" (767). It seemed, the poet writes, like "A castle cut out of paper for a king's feast," and Gawain "thought it great luck" (802–3) that he might be able to celebrate Christmas there.

The appearance of this castle is for Gawain literally an answered prayer, and he is bid "'heartily welcome'" by the lord, who assures him, "'What is here is wholly yours, to have in your power / and sway'" (836–7). An answered prayer is a wish-fulfillment, and this apparition at his hour of greatest need, combined with the host's promise that he will lack for nothing, signifies that Gawain finds himself in the realm of what Freud (1913b) terms the "omnipotence of thoughts," in which fantasies cannot be distinguished from reality.

As becomes clear in retrospect, however, what Gawain believes to be his "great luck" in coming upon the castle is in fact nothing of the sort. When the host learns the identity of his guest, "Then loudly he laughed, so elated he was" (909), but this is an act. Bertilak already knows who Gawain is, while he does not divulge his own name until he resumes the form of the Green Knight at the end of the poem. Thus, whereas to both Gawain and the unsuspecting reader the welcome Gawain is accorded appears genuine and the castle a place of refuge, the denouement reveals that Gawain has been the pawn in an elaborate conspiracy aimed at wreaking revenge on King Arthur and the Round Table. The "paranoid" component of the paranoid-schizoid position turns out not to have been a delusion because Gawain does have real enemies!

When one rereads the poem with an awareness of the true state of affairs, ironies abound. Bertilak is "elated" not because he has so renowned a guest, but at the progress of his scheme to entrap Gawain. To express his "light-hearted mood," the lord "Takes his hood from his head and hangs it on a spear," offering it as a prize to whoever "should promote the most mirth at that Christmas feast" (981–5). But Bertilak will not be a bystander in this contest; instead he vows, "'I shall try for it, trust me—contend with the best, / Ere I go without my headgear by grace of my friends!'" (986–7). To Gawain, who must face the ax of the Green Knight in a week's time, the phrase "go without my headgear" cannot conjure up pleasant associations. But since Bertilak knows what lies ahead, what appears to be a lighthearted game is designed to produce a shudder of terror in Gawain.

Upon his arrival at the castle, even before he meets Bertilak, Gawain is greeted by attendants who "bore away his brand and his blazoned shield" (828). Gawain surrenders his sword, but the separation from his shield is more ominous. Prior to his departure from Arthur's court, the poet devotes two stanzas to describing Gawain's shield, which "shone all red" and is adorned with a "pentangle portrayed in purest gold" (619–20). The colors of red and gold stand in contrast to the green and gold of the Green Knight, and the pentangle is said to be an ancient "sign by Solomon sagely devised / To be a token of truth" (625–6). Indeed, the pentangle is "an endless knot," the unbroken design of which symbolizes that "ever faithful five-fold in five-fold fashion / Was Gawain in good works as gold unalloyed" (632–3). The implications of the repetition of "five-fold" are spelled out when the poet reveals that the "five fives" (651) are Gawain's faultless "five senses" (641) and "five fingers" (642), the "five wounds" (643) of Christ, Mary's "five joys" (646) in her child, and finally the virtues of beneficence, brotherly love, pure mind, manners, and compassion, which form a second set of five, "each linked in other, that end there was none" (657), embedded in the first.

The perfection of the pentangle as a "token of truth" made of "purest gold" is an emblem of Gawain's embodiment of the ideal of knighthood at the outset of his quest, before he is put to the test in Bertilak's crucible. As the poet writes, the shield "was meet for the man, and matched him well" (622). Not only do the "five joys" belong to "the high Queen of heaven" (647), but Gawain bears Mary's image on "the inner part" (649). Such congruence between appearance and reality is possible only with a clear conscience, and Gawain at first experiences no conflict in being at once the "most courteous knight" (639) and a paragon of Christian virtue under the protection of the Virgin Mary.

The separation of Gawain from his shield exposes him not only physically but also spiritually and renders him vulnerable to the temptations that follow. In addition to promising that he will lack for nothing during his stay, Bertilak assures Gawain that he need not worry about finding the Green Chapel because his retainers "'shall see you to that site by the set time'" (1069). Gawain does not have to rush off after the Christmas festivities, on what would be the morning of December 28th, but can instead "'Tarry till the fourth day / And ride on the first of the year'" (1075–6).[3] Not only that, but the host tells Gawain, "'You shall be in your own bed, in blissful ease'" (1071), following which he is invited "'to dine / When you will, with my wife, who will sit by your side / And talk with you at table'" (1097–9), while he himself goes hunting. The only condition imposed by the host on this delightful prospect is that Gawain agree to play another "'game'" (1111), which, like the Beheading Game, also involves "covenants" (1122)—namely, that "'Whatever I win in the woods I will give to you at eve, / And all you have earned you must offer to me'" (1106–7). It is not clear what Gawain can expect to "earn" while he is reposing in the castle, but Part 2 ends with this "'bargain'" struck between the two men, about which they "laughed together" (1112–13).

---

[3] The third day of the Christmas revels is specified as being on "St. John's Day" (1022), which is December 27th, and the "guests were to go in the gray morning" (1024) of the following day. Four days after that is New Year's Day, which is when Gawain must face the Green Knight.

4

Gawain agrees with his host to participate in the Exchange of Winnings, but neither he nor the reader is forewarned about the Temptation Story with which it is conjoined in Part 3. On each of the three mornings the lord is out hunting, Gawain is visited in his bedchamber by "the lady, loveliest to behold" (1187), who engages in attempts at sexual seduction. If one bears in mind that the Green Knight and Bertilak are father figures for Gawain, while the Lady and Morgan le Fay are split images of the mother, then it becomes clear that, just as in *Tristan* and the *Confessions*, what is, in Marie Bonaparte's (1934) words, "on the surface" an incipient adulterous love triangle conceals a "secret story" of oedipal temptation that "is the basic theme" (p. 116) of *Sir Gawain and the Green Knight*.

When the Lady enters Gawain's room on the first morning, she closes and locks the door and makes a beeline for his canopied bed, where Gawain pretends to have been "startled from sleep" (1200), but from which she does not permit him to rise. Praising him as the knight "'Whom all the world worships'" (1227), the Lady wants him to know that the conditions are favorable for a tryst: "'And lo! we are alone here, and left to ourselves: / My lord and his liegemen are long departed'" (1230–1); and she leaves no doubt as to her intentions: "'My body is here at hand, / Your each wish to fulfill'" (1237–8).

When Gawain attempts to deflect her advances by reiterating the profession of modesty with which he had offered to stand in for Arthur with the Green Knight, "'I am one all unworthy, and well do I know it'" (1244), the Lady is undeterred and even voices the wish that she were married to Gawain: "'And should I hunt high and low, a husband to take, / ... / No other on earth should have me for wife'" (1472–5). Gawain is thus invited to occupy the husband/father's place with the wife/mother, and he declines in the most appropriate way possible by reminding the coquette, "'You are bound to a better man'" (1275). The poet underscores his reluctance: "For were she never so winsome, / The warrior had less will to woo, for the wound that his bane / must be" (1283–5). Given the sexual nature of his temptation, and that the Lady is not only the host's wife but also metaphorically a mother to Gawain, it follows that "the wound that his bane / must be" when he meets the Green Knight is the threat of castration for his oedipal desires, and that it is this anxiety that restrains Gawain from succumbing to her blandishments.

Before she departs, the Lady coaxes Gawain into allowing her to kiss him—the phrase "lo! he is kissed" (1306) stresses Gawain's passivity—and when the host returns from his hunt and presents Gawain with the deer he has slain, Gawain, fulfilling his obligation under their "covenant" (1384), "embraces his broad neck with his broad arms, / And confers on him a kiss in the comeliest style" (1388–9). When the host inquires of Gawain where he "'won this same award,'" however, he refuses to answer: "'That was no part of the pact; press me no further, / For you have had what behooves'" (1394–6).

The same thing happens on the second day, only this time Gawain receives two kisses from the Lady, which he repays to the lord, who has hunted a wild boar. The animals are emblematic of the defensive stratagems employed by Gawain, who is being hunted by the Lady. The timorous deer is mirrored when he says on the first morning, "'I surrender myself and sue for your grace'" (1215), while the ferocity of the boar is evoked when the wife invites him to overpower her on the second, "'You are stout enough to constrain with strength, if you choose'" (1496). The violence of the hunting scenes, including the ritualized disemboweling of the animals, shows what lies beneath the decorousness of the courtly banter. Because the Lady is a mother figure for Gawain the violence of the hunts may be construed as a representation not only of the aggression being directed *at* Gawain but also of what Klein (1930) calls the infant's "oral-sadistic desire to devour the mother's breast," as well as to "possess himself of the contents of the mother's body and to destroy her by means of every weapon which sadism can command" (p. 219).

The action of the poem reaches a climax on the following day. As the lord tells Gawain, "'I have tested you twice, and true I have found you; / Now think this tomorrow: the third pays for all'" (1679–80). Before the company retires for the night, "our gallant knight" is seated "beside the gay lady," who "With sweet stolen glances … stirred his stout heart," arousing him to the point that he was "at his wits' end, and wondrous vexed," though he knew that "he could not in good conscience her courtship repay" (1657–61). Gawain, like Tristan, is torn between Love and Honor, and has been warned that what happens on the morrow will be decisive.

When the Lady returns to his chamber on the third morning, she is as scantily clad as possible above the waist: "Her face and her fair throat freely displayed: / Her bosom all but bare, and her back as well" (1740–1). She is moving in for the kill, and the anxiety preying on Gawain about his fast-approaching ordeal is evidenced by the dreams from which she awakens him:

> Deep in his dreams he darkly mutters,
> As a man may that mourns, with many grim thoughts
> Of that day when destiny shall deal him his doom
> When he meets his grim host at the Green Chapel.

(1750–3)

The Lady bestows the first of the three kisses during this last temptation on Gawain, who is in "Great peril" lest "Mary forget her knight" (1768–9). As Geraldine Heng (1991) has noted, whereas Mary is Gawain's "sacred mistress," the nameless Lady is Gawain's "aggressively secular courtly mistress" (p. 501); and the danger stemming from the loss of his shield, with its emblems of the pentangle on the outside and Mary's image on the inside, is attested by the conflict he now faces between his identity as a Christian knight and the norms of chivalrous conduct toward a member of the opposite sex: "His courtesy concerned him, lest crass he appear, / But more his soul's mischief, should he commit sin / And belie his loyal oath to the lord of that house" (1773–5).

Gawain defends himself valiantly, saying with regret to the Lady—after she has kissed him for the second time—that he is unable to give her a suitable gift because he is "'on an errand in unknown realms'" (1808), and then declining her offer of a precious ring. When that fails, the Lady, having "released a knot" (1830) in a belt "Of a gay green silk, with gold overwrought" (1832), she had been wearing, says that he must accept this much less valuable gift. Once again, however, Gawain demurs until she tells him about its magical properties: "'For the man that possesses this piece of silk, / If he bore it about his body, belted about, / There is no hand under heaven that could hew him down'" (1851–3).

This is enough to give Gawain pause because he believes he will indeed be in need of such protection at the Green Chapel. Thinking to himself that this "piece of silk" would be "a pearl for his plight" in "the peril to come" (1856), and "Could he escape unscathed, the scheme were noble" (1858), Gawain's resistance begins to crumble; and when the Lady repeats her petition he accepts the gift. Almost as an afterthought, as "she gave him the belt," the Lady "besought him for her sake to conceal it well, / Lest the noble lord should know—and the knight agrees / That not a soul save themselves shall see it henceforth" (1862–5). The third kiss follows, and the Lady takes her leave.

This is the moment Gawain's fate is sealed. Even a first-time reader who, like Gawain, does not stop to think about the fact that the Lady's belt is green and gold cannot help registering this perception subliminally. The poet's depiction of Gawain's conduct on the third day is a masterful study of an unconscious sense of guilt. For the first time in the poem, Gawain goes to confession, but he does so only after having "Tucked away the token the temptress had left" (1874). And though the poet says that "shamefaced at shrift he showed his misdeeds / From the largest to the least" (1880–1), and the priest "absolved him of his sins as safe and as clean / As if the Day of Judgment should dawn on the morrow" (1883–4), Gawain's intention to conceal the Lady's gift from her husband cannot be among the "misdeeds" to which he confesses. Gawain has not yet committed a sin, but he must have known that what he was about to do would be wrong, which renders this external absolution irrelevant to the state of his soul. The artistic liberty with which the *Gawain*-poet turns a Christian sacrament into a hollow ritual is reminiscent of the even more subversive episode of Isolde's "doctored oath" in Gottfried's *Tristan*.

When Gawain rejoins the host who has returned from his hunt, the poet notes that "He wore rich robe of blue, that reached to the earth" (1928), about which Burrow (1966) remarks that "for his one act of duplicity Gawain wears *blue*—the traditional color of faithfulness—occurring here and nowhere else in the poem" (p. 112). Like going to confession, Gawain's choice to wear the "color of faithfulness" on this day that "pays for all" constitutes an attempt to divert not only Bertilak's attention but also his own from his guilty conscience, but this masquerade of innocence betrays what it is meant to hide. In similar fashion, as W. O. Evans (1973) has pointed out, Gawain on this occasion, "in contrast with the other two evenings, hurries to his host to give him the three kisses, and … is concerned to have the business finished with as quickly as possible" (p. 727). When the host, with feigned benevolence, congratulates him on having "'had some luck'" (1938) inside the house, Gawain brings him up short, "'Since all that I owe here is openly paid'" (1941).

Gawain's statement that his entire debt to Bertilak has been "openly paid" with the three kisses fulfills his promise to the Lady concerning the girdle to "conceal it well," but it is not true. For his part, the host apologizes to Gawain for being able to offer him only meager recompense in their Exchange of Winnings, "'For I have hunted all day, and naught have I got / But this foul fox pelt, the fiend take the goods!'" (1943–4). The "foul fox pelt" corresponds to the deception in Gawain's "scheme" to hoodwink the host when he has in reality been successfully hunted by the Lady. Both he and Bertilak then grow "So gay" and make "as much merriment as any men might" as if "they had been besotted, or brainless fools" (1953–6). Although Bertilak has reason to celebrate because Gawain has fallen into his trap, Gawain's elation exemplifies Klein's (1935) concept of the manic defense, that is, the *utilization of the sense of omnipotence*" (p. 277) in order to mask and ward off anxiety and depression. Gawain's day began with his awaking from a nightmare about what would befall him "When he meets his grim host at the Green Chapel," and the poet brings Part 3 to a close with Gawain returning to his chamber; but "How soundly he slept, I presume not to say, / For there were matters of moment his thoughts might well / pursue" (1991–3).

5

Gawain's return engagement with the Green Knight in Part 4, which fulfills his "covenant" in the Beheading Game, works out with inexorable logic the consequences of his decision to conceal from Bertilak the lace given to him by the Lady in the Exchange of Winnings, when he did not realize that he was being tested in the Temptation Story. As George Engelhardt (1955) has observed concerning Gawain's incompatible promises to the husband and wife, "he could not fulfill one compact without breaking the other. This, however, was a dilemma Gawain chose not to face; he repressed it" (p. 222). And because the girdle is "something to be concealed from a rightful husband," Heng (1991) elaborates, it constitutes "a love gift; and the necessity of its concealment entails a guilty conspiracy of silence that instates two persons in an apparent transgression against a third, in effect producing a version … of the common courtly theme of triangulated, adulterous love" (p. 507). A further gloss on Gawain's dilemma is furnished by Lacan's (1956) commentary on Poe's story "The Purloined Letter," in which the Queen (as Poe clearly implies her to be) must keep secret from the King a letter she has received from a third party because it "is the symbol of a pact and … it situates her in a symbolic chain foreign to the one which constitutes her faith" (p. 42).

When Gawain sets off from the castle, he no longer hides "his love-gift, the lady's girdle" (2030) since the lord would presumably have no reason to suspect its origins. The poet again highlights its green and gold colors, which "against the gay red" of his shield "showed gorgeous bright" (2035), but with no mention of the pentangle. Gawain donned the girdle, we are told, not out of ostentation or pride, "But to keep himself safe when consent he must / To endure a deadly dint, and all defense / denied" (2240–2). Gawain's concern about his survival when he is about to "endure a deadly dint" from the Green Knight reflects the state of mind of someone at the paranoid-schizoid position. As Klein (1935) maintains, at this primitive level of mental functioning "the persecution-anxiety is mainly related to the preservation of the ego," rather than to "the preservation of good internalized objects with whom the ego is identified as a whole," which is characteristic of the depressive position, where "the anxiety and feelings of suffering are of a much more complex nature" (p. 269).

On the night prior to his departure, Gawain had asked his host if he might "'take some trusty man to teach, as you promised, / The way to the Green Chapel'" (1966–7); and on the morning of New Year's Day he is accompanied by a Guide furnished by Bertilak. Professing to have Gawain's "'good at heart'" (2095), the Guide does everything possible to heighten his anxieties. He warns Gawain that the "'villain in yon valley'" (2098) he is about to encounter is "'the most immense in his mold of mortals alive'" (2100), and that he "'cannot but be killed'" (2111) by this outsized man. Gawain is tempted for a final time when the Guide urges him to escape his doom by running away. He swears an oath that if Gawain does so, he will "'conceal this day's deed, nor say to a soul / That ever you fled for fear from any that I knew'" (2124–5).

The Guide's offer to "conceal" the dishonorable action he has proposed makes this scene a reprise of the third morning in the bedchamber, when Gawain had acceded to the Lady's plea that he not disclose to her husband her gift of the talisman. This time, however, Gawain remains firm, "'I were a caitiff coward; I could not be excused. / But I must to the Chapel to chance my luck'" (2131–2). Gawain's resolution to press on and "chance [his] luck" at the Chapel corresponds to Oedipus's determination to find the murderer of Laius, whoever he may be, and it proves Gawain to be an equally heroic "child of Fortune." Yet the contrast between his responses to the two temptations, in Engelhardt's (1955) words, "serves less to obscure than to heighten the ironic analogy between the oath proffered by the guide and an earlier promise of secrecy—that tendered by Gawain to the more persuasive chatelaine" (p. 223). By voicing the thought about which Gawain feels most guilty—that he has already done something that makes him a "caitiff coward" in order to save his life—the Guide becomes, to invoke Klein's (1946) terminology once again, a target of Gawain's projective identification and a receptacle for his "hated parts of the self" (p. 8), which can then be subjected to withering attacks.

When Gawain finally meets up with the Green Knight, the latter twice pretends to strike him with his ax before delivering a third blow that "harmed him no whit / Save a scratch on one side, that severed the skin" (2311–12), from which "a little blood lightly leapt to the earth" (2314). Gawain springs up overjoyed at having survived the confrontation that he had feared would result in his death. He warns the Green Knight that he will "'pay back'" (2325) any further attempt to hack him because "'One stroke acquits me here; / So did our covenant stand / In Arthur's court last year'" (2327–9).

When Gawain refers to "our covenant … in Arthur's court last year," he means the agreement he had entered into with the Green Knight on New Year's Day one year ago. Both for Gawain and for the reader who shares his perspective, however, the moment of *anagnorisis* comes with the Green Knight's response, when he explains that the first time he raised his ax he had "'flourished with a feint'" (2345) without harming Gawain "'By the fair terms we fixed on the first night'" (2347), and that he had done so a second time because on the second day at the castle Gawain again "'fully and faithfully'" adhered to their agreement and "'Gave over all your gains as a good man should'" (2348–9) by restoring the kisses he had received from "'my comely wife'" (2351). But, the Green Knight continues, "'You failed at the third throw,'" and for this reason Gawain had to "'take my tap'" (2354–5), which resulted in the "scratch" that cost him a few drops of blood.

In contrast to Gawain's reference to "our covenant" in speaking to the Green Knight, when the Green Knight responds by citing the "terms *we* fixed on the first night" and alluding to "*my* wife," this opens the ground under Gawain's feet because—although his appearance remains unchanged—he is no longer speaking as the Green Knight but as Bertilak, which is at first disorienting and then becomes horrifying to Gawain as all the implications of what he has just learned begin to dawn on him. The Green Knight unobtrusively uses the first-person pronouns "we" and "my" to identify himself as being also the host at the castle, and thereby imparts that the "terms" in question are no longer those of the Beheading Game, but rather of the Exchange of Winnings that forms the second of the three interlaced rings of the plot.

How Gawain reacts to the two feigned blows of the ax takes on new meaning in light of the Green Knight's revelation. The first time that the Green Knight starts to lower the ax, Gawain's shoulders "shrank a little from the sharp iron" (2267), which earns him the rebuke that "'now you flee for fear, and have felt no harm'" (2272). This flinching mirrors both the behavior of the deer on the first day of the hunt and Gawain's "surrender" to the Lady when she visits his bedchamber on the first morning. When the Green Knight repeats his trick, Gawain at first "gave no ground" (2292); and when he is reminded that he must acquiesce, Gawain is "gripped with rage" (2299) and—like the boar and himself on the second morning—aggressively taunts his adversary, "'You make such a scene, you must frighten yourself'" (2301).

But everything hinges on the meaning and consequences of Gawain's actions on the third day. Having just informed Gawain that he "'failed at the third throw,'" Bertilak not only discloses that "'the wooing of my wife—it was all my scheme!'" (2361), but also proceeds to treat Gawain's conduct not as a failure but a success. He minimizes to the point of almost excusing altogether Gawain's deception in having concealed the "'same braided girdle'" that he is now wearing and that Bertilak says had been "'my belt'" (2358) all along. He continues by praising Gawain as "'a man most faultless by far'" (2362) and extenuating his sin inasmuch as it was motivated by the instinct for self-preservation:

> "As pearls to white peas, more precious and prized,
> So is Gawain, in good faith, to other gay knights.

Yet you lacked, sir, a little in loyalty there,
But the cause was not cunning, nor courtship either,
But that you loved your own life; the less, then, to blame."

(2364–8)

So stupefied is Gawain that he "in a study stood a long while" (2369) before responding. It is Bertilak's words, not the Green Knight's ax, that have struck him with lethal force, and he first expresses his emotions by being "So gripped with grim rage that his great heart shook. / All the blood of his body burned in his face / As he shrank back in shame from the man's sharp speech" (2370–2). Apostrophizing the girdle as "'my falsehood'" (2378), Gawain "lets go the knot" (2376) and hands it to Bertilak. He berates himself for being "'faulty and false'" (2382), and pleads for forgiveness:

"I confess, knight, in this place,
Most dire is my misdeed;
Let me gain back your good grace,
And thereafter I shall take heed."

(2385–8)

This, not the ritualized encounter with the priest, which is only reported and not shown in the poem, is Gawain's true confession. It is accepted by Bertilak, who, the poet says, "laughed aloud" (2389) and pronounced Gawain "fully confessed'" (2391). He reiterates his commendation of Gawain for being "'polished as a pearl, as pure and as bright / As you had lived free of fault since first you were born'" (2393–4). He hands back to Gawain "this girdle that is gold-hemmed / And green as my garments'" in order that he may "Be mindful of this meeting when you mingle in throng / With nobles of renown,'" and also so that it may be "'known by this token / How it chanced at the Green Chapel, to chivalrous knights'" (2395–9). The girdle, that is, is to serve both as a memento to Gawain of his rendezvous with destiny and as a "token" to other "chivalrous knights" of the lessons to be learned from his adventure.

The crucial question is what to make of the divergence between Gawain's "grim rage," his overwhelming emotions of shame and guilt, and Bertilak's genial "laughter," his repeated praising of Gawain as a "pearl" who is as "free of fault" as an infant seemingly untainted by original sin. The scholarly consensus is represented by Borroff (1967), who holds that "Gawain's own violent anger at the revelation of his fault must itself be viewed with amusement, as part of human fallibility," and that we should, "with the Green Knight, forgive Gawain for single act of cowardice" because "what he did was not out of sensual lust but for love of life, 'the less, then, to blame'" (p. x).

But since only Gawain's perspective has been "described from within" throughout the poem and the narrative has been crafted so that we "sit inside his mind, as it were, and look at the other characters from outside," it is rather the truth of his subjective experience that should guide our interpretation. Just as Borroff claims that Gawain's "violent anger" at himself ought to be "viewed with amusement," she takes at face value Bertilak's verdict that Gawain is to be forgiven because his lapse was not motivated by "sensual lust" but only by his "love of life." But even after his confession has been accepted by Bertilak, Gawain laments that his downfall was caused by a woman and makes it clear that he does not believe himself to be exempt from original sin:

> "But if a dullard should dote, deem it no wonder,
> And through the wiles of a woman be wooed into sorrow,
> For so was Adam by one, when the world began,
> And Solomon by many more, and Samson the mighty—
> Delilah was his doom, and David thereafter
> Was beguiled by Bathsheba, and bore much distress.
> Now these were vexed by their devices—'twere a very joy
> Could one but learn to love, and believe them not."
>
> (2414–21)

Complementing the way that the opening of the poem rehearses the history of Western civilization since the fall of Troy, Gawain, who, like Antenor, "knotted the nets of deceit" and stands "impeached for his perfidy," here takes us back still further to the Fall of Man and sees his own fate as a repetition of that of Adam and other Old Testament patriarchs, all of whom had been "wooed into sorrow" by "the wiles of a woman." Even Solomon, who had earlier been credited with having "sagely devised" the pentangle "To be a token of truth," is reduced to one of the "dullards" undone by his sexual urges for which women are expected to take the blame.

According to Burrow (1966), Gawain's misogynistic tirade is "a departure from the true course of the poem" (p. 148), but nothing could more mistaken. A step in the right direction is taken by Mary Dove (1972), who notes that "Gawain's outburst is one of the many features of *Gawain* given a superficially rational but at a deeper level inadequate explanation within the poem" (p. 21), though Dove's situating of the passage in the context of the medieval "*blasme des femmes* tradition" takes us only a short distance. Not only are the Lady's visits to Gawain's bedchamber attempts at sexual seduction, in which she entices him with the thought that, were she not already married, "'No other on earth should have me for wife,'" but the Green Knight and Bertilak are polarized father figures for Gawain, while Bertilak's wife and Morgan le Fay are split images of the mother. It follows that by yielding to the Lady's plea that he conceal her gift from her husband, Gawain has symbolically committed not merely adultery but also incest. The motive of self-preservation proposed by Bertilak, which Borroff accepts as a sufficient explanation for Gawain's act of deception, is no more than what Bonaparte—drawing on Freud's theory of dreams—terms the "manifestly coherent story" seen "on the surface" of *Sir Gawain and the Green Knight*, whereas his oedipal temptation is the latent content that is the poem's "basic theme."

That Gawain's temptation is oedipal finds support in the poet's reliance on the liturgical calendar as a structuring principle of the action. In addition to having Gawain set forth on his quest on All Saints' Day, the poet departs from tradition in specifying New Year's Day, instead of Pentecost, as the occasion on which Arthur's court engages in its ritual of tale-telling and adventure. This innovation is significant because New Year's Day is also the Feast of the Circumcision. Consequently, as Judith S. Neaman (1976) has proposed, Gawain's "covenant" with the Green Knight is analogous to that sealed under Jewish law by circumcision; and when he sheds "a little blood" after being grazed by the Green Knight's ax, "the literal cut is Gawain's spiritual circumcision by which he becomes a new man" (p. 40).

Although the fallen Gawain does not "become a new man," Neaman's reading of his wounding as a "spiritual circumcision" is convincing. By having both of Gawain's encounters with the Green Knight take place on New Year's Day while also making the principal characters in his psychodrama parental figures, the poet anticipates Freud's thesis in *Moses and Monotheism* (1939) that circumcision is "the symbolic substitute for the castration which the primal father once inflicted on his sons," and "whoever accepted that symbol was showing that he was prepared to submit to the father's will, even if it imposed the most painful sacrifice on him" (p. 122). Because Gawain's greatest temptation is sexual, and because the lure of adultery screens a desire to violate the incest taboo, it follows that his "scratch" on the neck is a displacement not only of circumcision but ultimately also of the castration that is the condign punishment for the son's forbidden wish to usurp the father's place with the mother.

We have seen that supernatural elements play a negligible role in *Sir Gawain and the Green Knight*, and nowhere is the psychological realism of the tale more evident than in the poet's description of the setting of the Green Chapel. In parting from Gawain, the Guide tells him to "'ride the narrow road'" until it brings him "'to the bottom of the broad valley'" (2144–5). Any doubts as to the symbolic significance of this landscape are removed when the poet proceeds to refer twice to a "mound" (2171, 2178) with "high banks on either side" (2165) and a "stream" (2173). The panorama unfolds:

It had a hole on one end, and on either side,
And was covered in coarse grass in clumps all without,
And hollow all within, like some old cave,
Or a crevice of an old crag—he could not discern
aright.

(2180–4)

Wondering to himself whether this place, where he might expect to find "'The devil himself ... / Saying matins at black midnight!'" (2187–8), could be his destination, Gawain hears a terrifying sound, "As one upon a grindstone ground a great scythe!" (2202). He is soon greeted by the Green Knight wielding "A Danish ax" (2223) with a blade measuring "four feet" (2225).

A discerning commentary on the "anatomical geography" that awaits Gawain at the terminus of his journey is provided by Robert J. Edgeworth (1985):

> The features of the chapel and its setting are readily identifiable with the features of the female genitalia. The poet mentions a ravine (the vulva) with steep banks on either side (the labia) and a stream in it (the vulva is associated with moisture for many reasons: menstruation, urination, mucous secretion and natural lubrication), and the mound above (the mons Veneris) overgrown with grass (pubic hair). The mysterious three openings correspond to the meatus, the vagina, and the anus.

(p. 318)

Edgeworth leaves no doubt that the poet's equation of the site of the Green Chapel with the female genitalia must have been deliberate, and since the essence of the Oedipus complex is a conflict between father and son over who is to possess the body of the mother, it is only fitting that the final confrontation between the Green Knight and Gawain should take place at her loins.

The sexual symbolism of the setting of the Green Chapel makes it clear why the sound of the whetting of the Green Knight's ax evokes the fear of castration. Not only does the episode lend credence to Freud's assertion in *The Ego and the Id* (1923) that "it is possible to regard the fear of death, like the fear of conscience, as a development of the fear of castration" (p. 58), but Gawain's feeling of dread as he approaches the "mound" with three holes and a "hollow" interior also becomes comprehensible. It is elucidated by Freud's (1919) contention that "neurotic men" believe "there is something uncanny about the female genital organs" because "this *unheimlich* place" is "the entrance to the former *Heim* of all human beings ... where each of us lived once upon a time and in the beginning," so that when a man dreams of having been somewhere before "we may interpret the place as being his mother's genitals or her body" (p. 245).

6

In addition to disclosing that he has masqueraded as the Green Knight and that "'the wooing of my wife—it was all my scheme!,'" Bertilak has other surprises in store. He informs Gawain that he holds his barony "'Through the might of Morgan le Fay, that lodges at my house'" (2446), and it was "'Morgan the Goddess'" (2452) who "'guided me in this guise to your glorious hall, / To assay, if such it were, the surfeit of pride / That is rumored of the retinue of the Round Table'" (2456–8). He adds that her motive in doing so was "'To afflict the fair queen, and frighten her to death'" (2460). Finally, Gawain learns that this sorceress "'was with my wife at home, that old withered lady,'" and "'Your own aunt is she, Arthur's half-sister, / The Duchess' daughter of Tintagel, that dear King Uther / Got Arthur on after'" (2463–6).

According to Benson (1965), "the reader cannot help feeling that the last-minute revelation of Morgan's scheme is too weak a foundation for this poem" (p. 34). Once again, however, this objection misses the mark. What becomes clear to both Gawain and the reader in the denouement is that he was enmeshed in a conspiracy on two levels: Bertilak was behind the stratagem to have his wife attempt to seduce Gawain, but it was Morgan le Fay, in disguise at the castle as "that old withered lady," who sent Bertilak in the form of the Green Knight to test and terrorize Arthur's court. Far from being haphazard, the "last-minute revelation" of "Morgan's scheme" holds the key to understanding the structure of the plot.

To grasp the poet's conception, all that is necessary is to recall how the Green Knight and Bertilak function as father figures, and Bertilak's wife and Morgan le Fay as mother figures, for Gawain. When Bertilak reveals that the Beheading Game he staged at Arthur's court in the guise of the Green Knight was in the service of Morgan's hatred of Guinevere, this bears out Klein's claim that the "bad mother" underlies the "bad father" as "the prototype of all persecuting and frightening objects"; and, as Klein (1926) further argues in contrast to Freud, "in both sexes it is the mother who in the deepest strata of the unconscious is specially dreaded as the castrator" (p. 129*n*1).

Klein's conviction that the anxieties and psychic structures which Freud assigned to the oedipal period originate in earlier childhood likewise helps to explain the intensity of Gawain's reaction to the Green Knight's revelation that he is Bertilak in disguise. Whereas Gawain had hitherto been functioning at the paranoid-schizoid position, with its bifurcation of "excessively good" and "excessively bad" parental imagos and dread of "retaliatory attacks," the recognition that the Green Knight and Bertilak are the same person—and that it is his "good" father whom he has wronged by his duplicity in the Exchange of Winnings—propels Gawain forward into the depressive position, where anxiety is no longer "mainly related to the preservation of the ego," but rather to "the preservation of good internalized objects with whom the ego is identified as a whole." As Klein (1946) explicates this centerpiece of her theory, "with the introjection of the object as a whole the infant's object-relation alters fundamentally. The synthesis between the loved and hated aspects of the complete object gives rise to feelings of mourning and guilt which imply vital advances in the infant's emotional and intellectual life" (p. 3).

In place of his "introjection" of the ax as an "internal persecutor" after he has beheaded the Green Knight, Gawain now heeds Bertilak's admonition to "'Be mindful of this meeting when you mingle in throng'" by agreeing to wear the Lady's girdle as a visible manifestation of his "feelings of mourning and guilt" for having yielded in fantasy to her sexual temptation:

> "But a sign of excess it shall seem oftentimes
> When I ride in renown, and remember with shame
> The faults and the frailty of the flesh perverse,
> How its tenderness entices the foul taint of sin:
> And so when praise and how prowess have pleased my heart,
> A look at this love-lace will lower my pride."
>
> (2433–8)

The *Gawain*-poet has masterfully depicted the genesis of the superego as Freud describes the process in "The Dissolution of the Oedipus Complex" (1924): "The authority of the father or the parents is introjected into the ego, and there it forms the nucleus of the super-ego, which takes over the severity of the father and perpetuates the prohibition against incest, and so secures the ego from the return of the libidinal object-cathexis" (pp. 176–7). Having experienced oedipal guilt, Gawain accepts his castration and renounces the incestuous object of his desire. As Spearing (1976) has noted, Bertilak's omniscience gives him "certain similarities to the representations of God in *Patience* and *Purity*" (p. 234), two other works in all probability written by the same fourteenth-century author. In laying bare the origins of the superego, Bertilak's role as a father figure for Gawain allows us to see how an adult's conception of God, in Freud's (1927b) words, "grows out of the intimacy and intensity of a child's relation to his father" (p. 19).

When Gawain departs the Green Chapel, the poet again calls attention to the penitential display of his "sign of excess":

> The hurt was whole that he had had in his neck,
> And the bright green belt on his body he bore,
> Oblique, like a baldric, bound at his side,
> Below his left shoulder, laced in a knot,
> In betokening of the blame he had borne for his fault;
> And so to court in due course he comes safe and sound.
>
> (2484–9)

Gawain's physical wound is healed, but the "bright green belt" takes its place as the reminder of his "fault" in having violated in fantasy the incest taboo. As A. Kent Hieatt (1970) has indicated, the "geometrical imperfection" of the cincture in "needing to be knotted" (p. 121) makes it the antithesis of the pentangle with the "endless knot" that symbolizes its function as an emblem of moral perfection.

Although Gawain is blind to the clue being dropped to the central mystery of the poem—the identity of Bertilak and the Green Knight—when the Lady dangles her bait, the belt made "Of a gay green silk, with gold overwrought" proves to be the nodal point where the strands of the plot intersect. Gawain takes it from her in the Temptation Story, he conceals it from her husband in the Exchange of Winnings, and he is punished for his transgression in the Beheading Game. He "lets go the knot" "and Hands it over in haste" (2376–7) to the Green Knight, who proceeds to return to him "this girdle that is gold-hemmed / And green as my garments" (2395–6) in order to teach Gawain a moral lesson. In thus circulating from the Lady, to Gawain, to the Green Knight, and back again to Gawain, the girdle—like the handkerchief in *Othello*—illustrates Lacan's (1956) dictum about the purloined letter that "the displacement of the signifier determines the subjects in their acts, in their destiny" (p. 43).

The poem concludes with a stanza and a half recounting Gawain's return to King Arthur's court, where "The nick on his neck he naked displayed / That he got in his disgrace at the Green Knight's hand" (2498–9). Echoing the description of how Gawain was "So gripped with grim rage that ... / All the blood of his body burned in his face / As he shrank back in shame" upon being confronted by Bertilak with his duplicity in having secreted the "love-lace," Gawain's present feeling of "disgrace" is conveyed by the poet in nearly identical language: "With rage in heart he speaks, / And grieves with many a groan; / The blood burns in his cheeks / For shame at what must be shown" (2501–4).

Once again, as in the scene of reckoning at the Green Chapel where Bertilak responds to Gawain's self-condemnation with "laughter" and by praising him as a "pearl" who is "free of fault," there is an unbridgeable gulf between Gawain's conviction of his moral failure and the "gay laughter" (2514) with which he is greeted by the members of the court. Indeed, as Heng (1991) has observed, the final "signifying system" into which the green girdle passes is that of "the entire Arthurian court and its history" (p. 506) when the king and his knights agree that they will henceforth wear it as a tribute to Gawain:

> That the lords and the ladies belonging to the Table,
> Each brother of that band, a baldric should have,
> A belt borne oblique, of a bright green,
> To be worn with one accord for that worthy's sake.
> So that was taken as a token by the Table Round,
> And he honored that had it, evermore after.
>
> (2515–20)

Gawain, by contrast, in his valedictory speech, emphasizes to Arthur that the "baldric"—a belt worn across one shoulder to the opposite hip—is for him a "token" not of glory but of humiliation:

> "Behold, sir," said he, and handles the belt,
> "That is the blazon of the blemish that I bear on my neck;
> This is the sign of sore loss that I have suffered there
> For the cowardice and coveting that I came to there;
> This is the badge of false faith that I was found in there,
> And I must bear it on my body till I breathe my last.
> For one may keep a deed dark, but undo it no whit,
> For where a fault is made fast, it is fixed evermore."
>
> (2505–12)

The same critics who censure the revelation of Morgan le Fay as the prime mover of the plot as "too weak a foundation for this poem" and disparage Gawain's comparison of himself to Adam and the other patriarchs undone by "the wiles of a woman" as "a departure from the true course of the poem" go astray once again in their commentaries on the ending. According to Benson (1965), the laughter of Arthur and his courtiers "shows that they have learned even more than Gawain" (p. 205), while Burrow (1966) reads the tale as a "comedy" that concludes with "the reincorporation of the hero into his society" (p. 152). But as has been true throughout, it is Gawain's understanding of his experience that should guide our interpretation. The knights of the Round Table emulate Gawain in their placement of the "belt borne oblique," but whereas for him it serves as a reminder of "the blame he had borne for his fault," for them it has no such connotation. Far from being a "comedy" in which Gawain is "reincorporated into his society," he is left permanently alienated from the Arthurian fellowship. The "gay laughter" of the other knights does not show their superiority to Gawain, but instead reflects a tragic incomprehension of the meaning of his quest.

It is, therefore, not only Gawain and his parental imagos whose destiny is determined by "the displacement of the signifier," but that of all "the lords and the ladies belonging to the Table" as well. As the wound to Gawain's flesh from the Green Knight's ax symbolizes his castration, so, too, the belt that he calls "'the blazon of the blemish that I bear on my neck'" bears the same significance on a linguistic level. Gawain's phrase, "'the sign of sore loss,'" makes sense in light of Lacan's (1973) concept of the "central lack expressed in the phenomenon of castration" (p. 77). From this standpoint, castration anxiety is not about the penis as an anatomical organ. It is rather an expression of the ontological "lack" that deprives every gendered being of wholeness by virtue of being a speaking subject embedded in the Symbolic order of language. Ironically, therefore, when Arthur's knights adopt Gawain's "badge of false faith" in ignorance of its meaning "as a token by the Table Round," it becomes for them what the pentangle had been for Gawain before his downfall—an inveigling mirage of unattainable perfection. In Lacan's (1949) schema, it constitutes for the court a "specular image" of the mirror stage that forms the basis of the Imaginary order of human experience, out of which "the *I* is precipitated in a primordial form, before ... language restores to it, in the universal, its function as subject" (p. 2).[4]

In revealing to Gawain how he had been ensnared not only by himself but by Morgan le Fay, Bertilak, as we have seen, alludes to the bonds of kinship that conjoin the characters: "'Your own aunt is she, Arthur's half-sister, / The Duchess' daughter of Tintagel, that dear King Uther / Got Arthur on after.'" Although the legends vary, Morgan is here understood to be the legitimate daughter of Lady Igraine and her husband Gorlois, the Duke of Cornwall, while Arthur is the illegitimate son of the same Lady Igraine, with whom his father, Uther Pendragon, had slept after having been magically disguised by

---

[4] What Lacan delineates in terms of the contrast between Imaginary and Symbolic orders can be mapped onto Klein's distinction between the paranoid/schizoid and depressive positions. For both theorists, there is both a permanent oscillation between these poles of psychic life and an important respect in which the depressive position and the Symbolic order are viewed as developmental advances on their antecedents.

Merlin to look like Gorlois. This makes Arthur and Morgan half-siblings on their mother's side. For his part, Gawain is the son of King Lot and Morgause, who is Morgan's full sister and Arthur's half-sister. Thus, as Bertilak states, Morgan, although appearing to be an "'old withered lady,'" is Gawain's "'own aunt,'" while Arthur is his half-uncle, although the poet simplifies this by calling both Gawain and his brother Agravain "nephews to the king" (112).

As the illegitimate son of Uther and Igraine, King Arthur is the product of an adulterous union, while the Round Table is destined to come to grief over Queen Guinevere's love affair with Lancelot, her husband's noblest knight. The agent of Arthur's ruin, moreover, is his illegitimate son Mordred, born from his accidental incest with Morgause, whom Arthur does not realize to be his half-sister, which makes Mordred and Gawain half-brothers on their mother's side. Morgan's desire "'To afflict the fair queen, and frighten her to death'" and her enmity against the Round Table stem from Guinevere's exposure of *her* adulterous affair with a knight named Guiomar, as a result of which Morgan leaves the kingdom and becomes, as Bertilak tells Gawain, "'The mistress of Merlin'" who "'has caught many a man, / For sweet love she shared in secret sometime / With that wizard, that knows well each one of your knights / and you'" (2448–51).

Neither Lancelot nor Mordred is mentioned by the *Gawain*-poet, nor does he explain the cause of Morgan's hatred of Guinevere. But he was clearly writing with an awareness of the entire history of the Round Table. Thus, when he introduces Arthur and his court as "fair folk in their first age" who "were still / Happiest of mortal kind" (54–6), and comments about the swiftly passing year before Gawain must set forth to meet the Green Knight that "First things and final conform but seldom" (499), the qualifier "still" conveys the ephemeral nature of their happiness in this "first age" of innocence. Given the centrality of adultery and incest to the Arthurian legends, Gawain's remorse over his "dark deed" on that third day in Bertilak's castle foreshadows the fate of the Round Table, and the green and gold girdle adopted by the inhabitants of Camelot in his honor portends its destruction.

7

"If Gawain was slightly wounded for his trivial failure in withholding the lace," writes Thomas D. Hill (1980), "we can imagine how the Green Knight might have avenged adultery" (p. 284). Hill rightly discerns an analogy between Gawain's minor wound and the punishment one would expect him to receive had he committed adultery. But not only is Gawain's "failure" not "trivial" from his perspective, a more fundamental flaw in Hill's reasoning is exposed by Sheila Fisher's (1989) questions: "what if Gawain had slept with the Lady and honored the terms of his contract with Bertilak? What if he had repaid Bertilak in kind?" (p. 86).

As the reader will recall, when Gawain tells Bertilak, "'While I lie in your lodging your laws I will follow'" (1092), Bertilak proposes that they enter into the following agreement, "'Whatever I win in the woods I will give you at eve, / And all you have earned you must offer to me'" (1106–7), to which Gawain readily agrees. Then, on the evening of the first day, when Gawain greets his host who has returned from the hunt, "'He embraces his neck with both his arms, / And confers on him a kiss in the comeliest style'" (1388–9); but when Bertilak inquires where he "'won this same award,'" he declines to answer: "'That was no part of the pact; press me no further, / For you have had what behooves'" (1394–6). On the second evening, Gawain again gives the host all his "'gains, as agreed'" (1638) by kissing him twice, and thereby repays "'every claim incurred here to date, / and debt'" (1642–3). On the third day, Gawain dutifully kisses Bertilak three times, but breaches their "covenant" by withholding the lace.

Only one conclusion can be drawn from this sequence of events. Since "the terms of his contract" require that he "repay Bertilak in kind," Gawain would have escaped punishment altogether by the Green Knight if he "had slept with the Lady" in the morning provided that he not only kissed Bertilak but also had sex with him the same night! The question then becomes why this solution to Gawain's dilemma is inconceivable within the framework of the tale. As the economic language of "claim," "debt," and "contract" makes clear, both the Beheading Game and the Exchange of Winnings are based on the principle of "traffic in women" (Rubin, 1975), in which women are treated as commodities in transactions between men—of which the institution of marriage is the prototype—designed to reproduce the patriarchal social order. This bedrock of feminist analysis is augmented by Eve Kosofsky Sedgwick's (1985) insight that the "homosocial" order in which men exchange women is predicated on the "fear and hatred of homosexuality" (p. 1), so that while the strongest affective ties are those between men, the possibility that they might desire one another sexually, let alone act on that desire, is repressed to the point of being literally unthinkable, as we have seen it to be when Gottfried assumes that two men cannot engage in sexual intercourse. Thus, the kisses that the Lady bestows on Gawain are purged of any erotic connotation because he returns them to the husband to whom she belongs. But when, on the third day, Gawain enters into his agreement with the Lady to conceal her gift of the lace, he violates his contract with Bertilak and, as Fisher (1989) has explicated, has thereby "betrayed a fundamental economic principle of feudal society. Rather than trafficking *in* women, he has traffic *with* them" (p. 85; italics added).

Because it involves "traffic with women," Gawain's transgression is sexual, but his chastisement restores the male-dominated order of things it had threatened to subvert. Yet hovering on the margins and covertly pulling all the strings is Morgan le Fay, who, by engaging in extramarital sexual relations, as Ivo Kamps (1989) has remarked, "assumes power over her own body and takes herself … out of the 'traffic in women' customary" in patriarchy (p. 320). "Morgan the Goddess," the shadowy antithesis of the Virgin Mary, is a "spectral mother" (Sprengnether, 1990) who cannot be accommodated within Freud's phallocentric framework.

Whereas a Freudian reading reveals *Sir Gawain and the Green Knight* to be structured by oedipal fantasies, and a Kleinian reading reveals Gawain's "mourning and guilt" to be a function of his transition from the paranoid-schizoid to the depressive position, the lenses of feminist and queer theory allow us to see how these pillars of psychoanalytic theory themselves rest on hidden bases and biases. Above all, the concept of the Oedipus complex presupposes what Adrienne Rich (1980) has called "compulsory heterosexuality." As Judith Butler (1990) has elaborated, "Although Freud does not explicitly argue in its favor, it would appear that the taboo against homosexuality must *precede* the heterosexual incest taboo; the taboo against homosexuality in effect creates the heterosexual 'dispositions' by which the Oedipal conflict becomes possible" (p. 64). From this it follows that the depressive position can be understood as a manifestation of what Butler calls the "heterosexual melancholy" that "is culturally instituted as the price of stable gender identities" (p. 70). At once a masterpiece of the patriarchal tradition and a dismantling of its founding assumptions, *Sir Gawain and the Green Knight*, in which the hero escapes with a "nick on his neck" from a "Danish ax," can find no better gloss than Claudius's line from Shakespeare's *Hamlet*: "And where th' offense is, let the great axe fall" (4.5.219).

Chapter 4

More's *History of King Richard III* as an Uncanny Text

"The feeling of the uncanny would seem to be generated by being-reminded-of-the-repetition compulsion, not by being-reminded-of-whatever-it-is-that-is-repeated. It is the becoming aware of the process that is eerie, not the becoming aware of some particular item in the unconscious, once familiar, then repressed, now coming back into consciousness."

—Neil Hertz, "Freud and the Sandman"

1

As A. F. Pollard remarked in 1933, the problems surrounding More's *History of King Richard III* are manifold: "its authorship, its authority, its sources, the date of its composition, the circumstances of its publication, the relation of the English to the Latin versions, the absence of any original autograph, the variations in the printed texts, the motive of its conception, and the reasons for its unfinished state and abrupt termination" (p. 421). The evidence for More's authorship of *Richard III* must now be considered conclusive, and the years 1514–18 have been generally accepted as the approximate dates of composition, but all the other puzzles cited by Pollard nearly a century ago—especially the question of what led More to undertake the work in the first place, only to abandon and suppress it—continue to resist definitive solution.

The History of King Richard III has the distinction of being the first work of history to be written not only in Latin—in which language it bears the title *Historia Richardi Regis Angliae Eius Nominis Tertii*—but also in English.[1] That this text, which was first printed only in English by More's nephew William Rastell in 1557, is extant in what Richard S. Sylvester has described as "two separate but intimately related narratives, the one, in the vernacular,

---

[1] Unless otherwise indicated, quotations from *The History of King Richard III* are from Sylvester's modernized edition (More, 1976), with page numbers given parenthetically.

for a native audience, the other … in the international language of Europe" (More, 1976, p. xi), is inconceivable apart from More's participation in the movement of Renaissance humanism. And since humanist historiography, in David Norbrook's (1987) words, is "a discipline with a philosophical basis and a literary form of expression, drawing on a bare stock of factual material in order to shape a vision of political conduct and the psychology of those in authority" (p. 81), *The History of King Richard III* is ideally suited to a reading from the complementary perspectives of psychoanalysis and new historicism, which together open up the text to a range of individual and social contexts.

I shall take as my guiding thread in the ensuing discussion the concept of the uncanny. To illustrate his contention that those plots best arouse pity and fear "when the events are unexpectedly interconnected," Aristotle in the *Poetics* tells the story of the slayer of Mitys who was himself killed at a festival in Argos when a statue of his victim fell on him. Without denying the existence of genuine chance, Aristotle acknowledges the psychological effect of such seemingly motivated occurrences: "Even chance events arouse most wonder when they have the appearance of purpose" (1452 a).[2]

In his combination of scientific skepticism and respect for the vagaries of the human mind, Aristotle displays a set of attitudes that is likewise characteristic of Freud. Indeed, in "The 'Uncanny'" (1919), Freud singles out the impossibility of disentangling chance from design as one of the constitutive features of the phenomenon. Describing the way he continually found himself wandering back to the quarter of a provincial Italian town "of whose character I could not long remain in doubt," Freud notes that "it is only this factor of involuntary repetition which surrounds what would otherwise be innocent enough with an uncanny atmosphere, and forces upon us the idea of something fateful and inescapable when otherwise we should have spoken only of 'chance'" (p. 237). Although Aristotle's parable concerns murder and Freud's illicit sexuality, what makes these incidents uncanny, as Neil Hertz underscores, is not their content but the fact of their repetition. In Freud's pithy formulation, "whatever reminds us of this inner 'compulsion to repeat' is perceived as uncanny" (p. 238).

The experience of "involuntary repetition" that blurs the distinction between chance and fate confronts the reader of *The History of King Richard III* at every turn both as an overt theme and as an aspect of the work's embeddedness in history. Lily B. Campbell (1947) has drawn attention to the Renaissance practice of "expounding the present by reference to the past, using history to teach political lessons which its authors reckoned most

---

[2]   Quotations from the *Poetics* are to Grube's translation.

pertinent to the understanding of political events in their own day" (p. 109); and this reliance on parallels between past and present forms part of More's conscious design as a humanist historian. But the "political lessons" to be learned from *Richard III* extend to the "great matter" of Henry VIII's divorce from Catherine of Aragon, which lay shrouded some ten years in the future. Thus, the work takes on new meaning in light of subsequent events, which endow it in retrospect with a prophetic—and indeed uncanny—quality.

2

There is no better illustration of the uncanny in *The History of King Richard III* than More's centrally placed account of the downfall of Sir William Hastings, Richard's Lord Chamberlain.[3] Having been unjustly denounced by his trusted retainer Catesby, Hastings is arrested by Richard in the memorable council scene where his feigned courtesy turns to savage anger after calling for a mess of strawberries from the Bishop of Ely, later Cardinal Morton. More follows his report of Hastings' execution with a recapitulation of a series of events that were "either the warnings of that he should have voided or the tokens of that he could not void" (p. 50). More's refusal to commit himself as to the epistemological status of these omens exemplifies the ambiguity that pervades *Richard III*, and the problem of deciding whether Hastings' fate could have been avoided parallels that of determining whether the hand of fate is visible in the death of Mitys's slayer.

More, who has already informed the reader that Hastings' betrayal and death took place on "Friday, the thirteenth day of June" (p. 47), arranges the four events in question in a carefully crafted sequence.[4] First, Hastings is awakened at midnight by a messenger from his ally Lord Stanley, who has had a dream that the two of them were slashed by the tusks of a boar, Richard's emblem. Hastings, however, dismisses the messenger with the reply—as though he had heard of Freud's concept of "day-residue"—that it is "'plain witchcraft'" for Lord Stanley to believe in such dreams, "'which either his own fear fantasieth or do rise in the night by virtue of his day thoughts'" (p. 50). Next, More tells us, on the morning that Hastings was riding to the

---

[3] As Sylvester points out, More, among other minor factual errors, refers to him as "Richard the lord Hastings" (p. 11).

[4] In reaffirming her view that Hastings' execution took place on Friday, June 20, 1483, rather than June 13, Hanham (1975, pp. 24–9) fails to consider More's literary motives for assigning the execution to "Friday, the thirteenth," or having it coincide with the beheading of Hastings' enemies. Her sifting of the evidence, in any case, is inconclusive.

council at the Tower, his horse stumbled, "which thing, albeit each man wot well daily happeneth to them to whom no such mischance is toward, yet hath it been of an old rite and custom observed as a token oftentimes notably foregoing some great misfortune" (p. 51). In both instances, More provides a rational analysis of the workings of superstition, but creates an effect of "most wonder" by giving these "chance events" the "appearance of purpose." The third omen received by Hastings is termed by More "no warning, but an enemious scorn" (p. 51). Upon pausing on his way to the council to talk with a priest, Hastings is taunted by a companion privy to Richard's designs, "'whereto talk you so long with that priest? You have no need of a priest yet'" (p. 51). Hastings, who "was never merrier nor never so full of good hope in his life," fails to discern the sinister meaning of his interlocutor's words; and More comments that nothing is more remarkable "than the vain surety of a man's mind so near his death" (pp. 51–2).

All these incidents serve as prologues to Hastings' fourth and final portent of his doom. "Upon the very Tower wharf so near the place where his head was off so soon after," More writes, "there met he one Hastings a pursuivant of his own name" (p. 52). The existence of this pursuivant—or royal messenger—has been disputed by scholars, but the point is that Hastings is made to encounter his "follower" or double.[5] More continues: "And of their meeting in that place, he was put in remembrance of another time, in which it had happened them before to meet in like manner in the same place" (p. 52).

By "another time," More means during the reign of Edward IV, the eldest surviving son of Richard, Duke of York, and brother to Richard III. Edward IV became king in 1461 when he deposed the Lancastrian Henry VI. He ruled until 1470, when he was himself deposed by Henry VI, with the aid of the Earl of Warwick. Edward regained the throne in 1471 and remained king until his death in 1483, following which Richard III seized the throne. Despite having been Edward's strong supporter, Hastings had fallen into the late king's disfavor by incurring the enmity of Lord Rivers, brother of the queen, Elizabeth Woodville, and feared for his life. Now, however, after Edward IV's death, Lord Rivers and other allies of the queen dowager had been arrested by Richard with Hastings' connivance, but Hastings, as he thought, was secure in Richard's approbation. In reality, Hastings is deluded, and the deaths of Rivers and the others, as inaccurately reported by More, take place on the same day as his own.

---

[5] Sylvester (More, 1963, p. 224*n*51/15) is unable to identify Hastings the pursuivant, but Hanham (1975, p. 173*n*1) finds a reference to such a person in 1480 and possibly 1483.

Freud (1919) specifies as the "most prominent" causes of uncanniness "a doubling, dividing and interchanging of the self" and "the constant recurrence of the same thing" (p. 234), and the tale of Hastings' downfall combines the motifs of doubling and repetition. More emphasizes the irony whereby the apparently chance meeting with his namesake causes Hastings to exult in a false sense of security: "And foreasmuch as he now met this pursuivant in the same place—that jeopardy so well passed—it gave him great pleasure to talk with him thereof" (p. 52). The Tower wharf is the "same place" as their previous encounter and also "so near the place" where Hastings will meet his end. Following Rank, Freud (1919) explains that the idea of the double "was originally an insurance against the destruction of the ego," but underwent a reversal, and "from having been an assurance of immortality, it becomes the uncanny harbinger of death" (p. 235). Just such a reversal occurs in the case of Hastings, who at first takes the encounter with his alter ego to be a confirmation of his good fortune, not realizing that it actually foretold his doom.

That participation in politics under a tyrant induces what Freud in *Studies on Hysteria* called a "blindness of the seeing eye," or "the strange state of mind in which one knows and does not know a thing at the same time" (Breuer and Freud, 1895, p. 117), is one of the bleakest lessons of *The History of King Richard III*. Early in the work, after the Archbishop of York has buckled under pressure from Richard, then still the Duke of Gloucester, and reversed his decision to entrust the Great Seal to the queen dowager who has sought sanctuary near the palace of Westminster, Hastings smoothes over the ensuing protests with persuasions "whereof part himself believed, of part he wist the contrary" (p. 24). Hastings' dissociative state grows more acute when he is not disturbed by the fact that Richard, by now the Lord Protector, and the Duke of Buckingham have arranged to hold two separate councils— one ostensibly devoted to preparing for the coronation of Prince Edward, the elder of Edward IV's two sons with Elizabeth Woodville, the other in reality contriving to make Richard the king—because he regards the perfidious Catesby with unwarranted complacency as an extension of himself.

When Hastings is congratulated by his double on having escaped his enemies' machinations, he replies with an oblique reference to the imminent execution of Lord Rivers and his cohorts, "'Thou wouldest say so,' quoth he, 'if thou knewest as much as I know'" (p. 52). To this boast More appends the ironic postscript, "which he well wist, but nothing ware that the axe hang over his own head," and intones in choric commentary: "O good God, the blindness of our mortal nature! When he most feared, he was in good surety; when he reckoned himself surest, he lost his life, and that within two hours after" (pp. 52-3). After Richard has been crowned king in an ill-managed ceremony presided over by the Duke of Buckingham, More remarks that "there was no man so dull" that he did not perceive the collusion between the dissemblers, but many of the citizens nonetheless excused the proceedings because "men must sometime for the manner sake not be aknowen what they know" (p. 82). He compares matters of state to "kings' games, as it were, stage plays, and for the more part played upon scaffolds"—"scaffolds" meaning both theatrical platforms and places of execution—with which "lookers-on" who know what is good for them "will meddle no farther" (p. 83).

Hastings' precarious rise and abrupt fall conform to the pattern of tragedy set forth in Boccaccio's collection of exemplary biographies, largely written between 1355 and 1360, *De casibus virorum illustrium* (On the Fates of Famous Men). But, as Judith Anderson (1984) has noted, the literary subtlety and psychological sophistication with which More deploys this "fall of princes" tradition—so named after John Lydgate's sprawling poem of the early fifteenth century—owes an "undeniable" debt to Chaucer's mock heroic *Nun's Priest's Tale*, particularly in its "handling of dreams as omens" (p. 219*n*42) and pondering of the interplay between divine foreknowledge and human free will. Not only does the sexually prodigious protagonist, the rooster Chauntecleer, invert the Latin admonition about the Fall of Man, "*Mulier est hominis confusio*" (3164), which he takes to mean "'Womman is mans joye and al his blis'" (3166), but he—like Hastings—encounters and then eludes his nemesis in the shape of a fox on a Friday.[6]

The fox seizes Chauntecleer by the throat when, having flattered him into proving he can outcrow his deceased father, Chauntecleer does so with such exuberance that he closes his eyes. But Chauntecleer turns the tables on his captor by persuading the latter to open his mouth in order to taunt his human pursuers. After his escape, the rooster propounds the moral to his own story: "'For he that wynketh, whan he sholde see, / Al willfully, God lat him nevere thee [thrive]!'" (3430–1). In crowning the rivalry between son and father with the oedipal motif of blindness while depicting Chauntecleer's apparent demise as a fortunate fall, Chaucer's metaphysical comedy provides a prototype for More's somber portrayal of Hastings by bringing together both master-myths of the patriarchal tradition.

---

[6] Quotations from the *Nun's Priest's Tale* are to Robinson's (1957) edition of Chaucer. Anderson points out that both Chaucer and More specify Friday as the fateful day for their careeners on Fortune's wheel.

3

An excavation of the oedipal underpinnings of *The History of King Richard III* lays bare the pervasiveness of More's concern with sexuality. Although it is true, as Sylvester has pointed out, that "it was More who first gave real literary shape and form" (More, 1976, p. xii) to the image of Richard as "a symbol of the evils which permeate a kingdom when tyranny is allowed to take the place of wise government and good order" (p. xv), it does not follow, as Anderson (1984) supposes, that More presents a contrast between "good King Edward and wicked King Richard" (p. 81). Far from portraying Edward IV as an ideal ruler in opposition to the diabolical Richard, the lesson of More's text, as Alistair Fox (1983) has discerned, is that "the reality underlying Edward's reign … is not essentially different in kind from that which Richard will try to erect," and "Richard's reign merely manifests in extreme form circumstances that pertain in all political situations" (pp. 80–1).

In the first place, Edward is no less guilty than Richard of the murder of their brother George, Duke of Clarence, although he agonizes about it afterwards. As More puts it, Edward, "(albeit he commanded it) when he wist it was done, piteously bewailed and sorrowfully repented" (p. 8). Compounding the indictment, More accentuates the "fleshly wantonness" to which the monarch was "greatly given" (p. 5) in his youth. Richard, on the other hand, like a deranged superego, conceives of himself as "a goodly continent prince, clean and faultless of himself, sent out of heaven into this vicious world for the amendment of men's manners" (p. 55). As Richard's parading of Jane (properly Elizabeth) Shore, who had been one of Edward IV's mistresses, in public penance "out of all array save her kirtle only" (p. 55) goes to show, however, his facade of virtue is a reaction formation that conceals a repressed attraction to the forbidden object.

Together with Hastings, Jane Shore serves as a nexus for the sexual motifs of *The History of King Richard III*. In an imitation of Tacitus, More apologizes for speaking at length about so insignificant a personage: "I doubt not that some shall think this woman too slight a thing to be written of and set among the remembrances of great matters" (p. 57). But this disclaimer of Jane Shore's importance ironically signals her central role in the "great matters" under discussion. As More is at pains to stress, after Hastings' beheading Richard issued a proclamation that was so clearly premeditated that "every child might perceive that it was prepared before" justifying his condemnation on the grounds that he had been an evil counselor to Edward IV, but above all for "the vicious living and inordinate abuse of his body, both with many other, and also specially with Shore's wife, which was one also of his most secret counsel of this heinous treason, with whom he lay nightly, and namely the night last passed before his death" (p. 54). Richard's accusations are a trumped-up pretext, but once the ferocity of his revulsion against sexuality is recognized, it becomes comprehensible why Hastings should have been put to death for the "inordinate abusion of his body," and particularly for engaging in sexual intercourse with Jane Shore on the night before his arrest.

Earlier, Richard had blamed Shore's wife, together with the queen, for his "werish, withered arm" (p. 48), which, according to More, was known to have been deformed from birth. Richard's suspicion is again preposterous not only because of the congenital nature of his presumed defect but also because Jane Shore was the woman whom Elizabeth Woodville "most hated, as that concubine whom the king, her husband, had most loved" (p. 49), and hence the last person with whom she would join in a conspiracy. But such considerations count for nothing in Richard's misogynistic logic, in which each woman is branded as a "'sorceress'" and a "'witch'" because both incarnate the threat of female sexuality.

Notwithstanding the queen's suspicions, More reports that although Hastings was "sore enamored" of Shore's wife during Edward IV's lifetime, out of either respect or friendship he "forbare her" (p. 56) until after the monarch's death, when he took her as his own mistress. Richard's perception of the queen and Jane Shore as allied contains a kernel of truth given Jane's role as the tabooed object of desire whom Hastings can possess only after the death of the paternal surrogate. Hastings had originally aroused the ire of the queen not only because of "the great favor the king bare him, but also for that she thought him secretly familiar with the king in wanton company" (p. 11). From the beginning, then, Hastings is portrayed as Edward IV's double in the domain of sexual transgressions. The two periods of Hastings' disgrace are linked in that a carnal offense leads to his undoing—the first harmless, the second fatal—in both instances.

After the execution of Hastings and the queen's allies, Richard moves to take possession of the English crown. In order to advance his own claim, he must invalidate that of the young princes, Edward and Richard. Although it would seem to suffice for Richard III's purposes to assert the bastardy of Edward IV's children, he goes so far as to question his brother's legitimacy, and thereby to impugn the chastity of his own mother:

> But the chief thing and the weighty of all that invention rested in this: that they should allege bastardy, either in Edward himself, or his children, or both, so that he should seem disabled to inherit the crown by the Duke of York, and the prince by him. To lay bastardy in King Edward sounded openly to the rebuke of the protector's own mother,

which was mother to them both; for in that point could be none other color but to pretend that his own mother was one adulteress, which not withstanding to further this purpose he letted not.

(pp. 60–1)

The superfluity of Richard's aspersions concerning Edward IV's legitimacy, like his accusations against Hastings and Jane Shore, betrays the influence of unconscious fantasies, and indeed it explains these latter two vindictive outbursts. Rather than being an unfortunate byproduct of his charges, the compulsion to reveal his mother's supposed adultery constitutes Richard's underlying motive. His loathing of sexuality, and particularly the female body, is rooted in the idea of his mother as promiscuous.[7] In a sermon on the theme "'bastard slips shall never take deep root,'" delivered at St. Paul's Cross, Ralph Shaa, brother to the Lord Mayor of London, proclaimed on Richard's behalf that "neither King Edward himself, nor the Duke of Clarence, among those that were secret in the household, were reckoned very surely for the children of the noble duke, as those that by their favors more resembled other known men than him" (pp. 67–8). Richard's insistence on the bastardy of not one but both his brothers, and that only he was the legitimate son of Richard, Duke of York, exemplifies the psychology of "the exception," the rubric under which Freud (1916) analyzed Shakespeare's depiction of the effects of the spinal deformity that was a staple of Richard's demonization by Tudor historians.

Richard's second allegation, his impugning the legitimacy of Edward's children, leads More into a lengthy flashback in which he informs the reader about "some things long before done about King Edward's marriage" (p. 61). After having ousted Henry VI for the first time and consolidated his position on the English throne, Edward IV, being then in his early twenties, determined to take a wife, and for that purpose sent the Earl of Warwick to negotiate an alliance with the heiress to the king of Spain. While Warwick was on his mission, Edward chanced to receive a petition from Dame Elizabeth Grey (by birth Elizabeth Woodville), a widow of noble birth known from other sources to have been some five years his senior, with two sons from her previous marriage. Edward, More writes, "not only pitied, but also waxed enamored on her" (p. 62). When Elizabeth insisted that "as she wist herself to be too simple to be his wife, so thought she herself too good to be his

---

[7] For evidence that slander concerning the promiscuity of the Duchess of York was widespread at the time, and that "a certain archer named Blayborgne" was said to have shot her "with an arrow not tipped with steel," see Marius (1984, p. 109).

concubine," he took "counsel of his desire" and "determined in all possible haste to marry her" (p. 62).

Edward's impulsive decision had serious repercussions, not least of which was that it incurred the wrath of the Earl of Warwick and led the "kingmaker" to turn against him. Having gone over to the Lancastrian side, Warwick succeeded in restoring Henry VI to the throne and banishing Edward IV to Holland. One year later, however, Edward regrouped his forces and led an expedition back to England, where he slew Warwick in battle and resumed the throne. The other implacable antagonist to Edward's union with Elizabeth Woodville was his mother, the Duchess of York, who objected to his choice not only on the grounds "that it was not princely to marry his own subject," but above all because it would be "'a very blemish and high disparagement to sacred majesty of a prince … to be defouled with bigamy in his first marriage'" (p. 63), since Elizabeth Woodville was a widow.

But in addition to the queen's dubious past, Edward's own "fleshly wantonness" laid him open to the accusation of bigamy. As More recounts, the king boasted of having "three concubines, which in three divers properties diversely excelled: one the merriest, another the wiliest, the third the holiest harlot in his realm, as one whom no man could get out of church lightly to any place, but it were to his bed" (p. 57). "The merriest" is named by More as Shore's wife, and Sylvester tentatively identifies the two others as Eleanor Butler and Elizabeth Lucy. In her effort to block the marriage to Elizabeth Woodville, the Duchess of York promoted the claim of Dame Elizabeth Lucy, "whom the king had also not long before gotten with child," asserting that he had been betrothed to her and was "her husband before God" (p. 65). This charge was repeated by Ralph Shaa in his sermon at Paul's Cross, "for he declared then that King Edward was never lawfully married unto the queen, but was, before God, husband unto Dame Elizabeth Lucy, and so his children bastards" (p. 68). Were it proven that Edward had married Elizabeth Lucy, his hopes of marrying Elizabeth Woodville would indeed have foundered on the grounds of bigamy. But Elizabeth Lucy refused to cooperate, and "when she was solemnly sworn to tell the truth, she confessed that they were never ensured [betrothed]" (p. 65). In the end, Edward gained the hand of Elizabeth Woodville with the avowal that he "'would not be a king with that condition, to forbear mine own liberty in choice of my own marriage'" (p. 64).

But though Edward prevailed in making Elizabeth Woodville his queen, the lingering shadows cast by his relationships with the "three concubines" were posthumously exploited by Richard to accuse him of bigamy and to bar Edward V, as well as his younger brother, from succeeding to their father's throne on the grounds of illegitimacy.[8] By recording so copiously the intimate details of Edward's marriage, More makes it possible to interpret his love life as evidence of an incestuous fixation. In Elizabeth Woodville, he found reconciled the antithetical attributes of sexual experience and unimpeachable virtue that constitute a son's fantasies concerning his mother. By marrying a widow with children who was also his social inferior, Edward was unconsciously perpetuating his dependence on the mother against whom he was consciously rebelling. But—as with Tristan—even this seemingly ideal solution to his Oedipus complex was unable to satisfy him permanently.

In a speech at the Guildhall attempting to persuade "'the commons of the city'" (p. 70) to support Richard's elevation to the throne, the Duke of Buckingham castigates the former king for having made the hitherto "'honest'" Jane Shore into "'a vile and an abominable strumpet'" when, "'for his wanton lust and sinful affection,'" he "'bereft her from her husband'" (p. 73). Edward's adultery with Shore's wife, continues Buckingham, was but one example of his "'greedy appetite'" that "'was insatiable and everywhere over all the realm intolerable'":

> "For no woman was there anywhere, young or old, rich or poor, whom he set his eye upon, in whom he anything liked, either person or favor, speech, pace, or countenance, but without any fear of God or respect of his honor, murmur or grudge of the world, he would importunely pursue his appetite and have her, to the great destruction of many a good woman and great dolor to their husband."
>
> (p. 73)

As Richard's mouthpiece, Buckingham gives voice both to his misogyny and to his image of Edward as a sexual predator who specialized in stealing wives from their husbands. This allegation was designed to appeal to the householders in the audience who looked upon their wives as property not to be taken from them even by a king. Buckingham portrays Richard as a ruler who would put an end to Edward's abuses and look after "'the

---

[8] Contemporary scholars are divided on the question whether Richard's accusations against Edward IV were justified. But rather than Dame Elizabeth Lucy, it is with Dame Eleanor Butler—by birth Eleanor Talbot—that Edward was alleged in a 1484 act of Parliament, *Titulus Regius*, to have "made a precontracte of matrimonie, longe tyme bifore he made the said pretensed Mariage with the said Elizabeth Grey." For the full text and historical context, see the website of the Richard III Society, where the *Titulus Regius* is called "the single most important contemporary document establishing Richard III's title to the crown of England."

surety of your own bodies, the quiet of your wives and your daughters, the safeguard of your goods—all of which things, in times passed, ye stood evermore in doubt'" (p. 70). The popular fear that Edward's sons would fall under the influence of the Woodville faction had been exploited by Richard when he assumed the office of Lord Protector, and in becoming king he escalated his attacks by accusing Edward not only of being a serial philanderer but also, like his children with Elizabeth Woodville, of being a bastard.

In a deathbed speech intended to reconcile the warring factions in his realm, Edward IV laments the regularity with which conflict supervenes among those who ought to be bound by love: "'And nowhere find we so deadly debate as among them which by nature and law most ought to agree together. Such a pestilent serpent is ambition and desire of vainglory and sovereignty, which among states [noblemen] where he once entereth creepeth forth so far, till with division and variance he turneth all to mischief'" (p. 13). In having Edward decry ambition as "a pestilent serpent," More, who had delivered a series of lectures on St. Augustine's *City of God* around 1501, grafts a reference to Tiberius's hypocritical denunciation of the power of imperial authority in Suetonius's *Lives of the Twelve Caesars* onto an evocation of the temptation of Adam and Eve by the serpent in the Garden of Eden.[9]

Although Edward implicitly equates Richard with Satan, the "pestilent serpent," because his own vices caused his reign to be corrupted by "division and variance" More conveys that the Fall, like the Oedipus complex, rather than being a one-time catastrophe, is a paradigm that imposes itself time and again throughout human history. And in recognizing that "deadly debate" is most often found among people who should be conjoined by "nature and law," More concurs not only with Freud but also with Aristotle, who maintains in the *Poetics* that tragedies most powerfully strike the spectator with pity and fear when "suffering is inflicted upon each other by people whose relationship implies affection, as when a brother kills, or intends to kill, his brother, a son his father, a mother her son, a son his mother" (1453 b)—that is, by members of a family.

---

[9] As Sylvester notes in the bilingual Yale Edition (More, 1963, p. 174n12/21–2), the phrase "Such a pestilent serpent is ambition" reads in More's Latin version *Adeo execrabilis belua est superbia*, which echoes Suetonius's *quanta belua esset imperium*, although *belua* means "beast" or "monster" rather than "serpent." In *Utopia*, More puns on a false etymology when Hytholday reports that the Utopians "despise war [*bellum*] as an activity fit for beasts [*belua*]" (Logan, 2016, p. 89), and he recalls Augustine's *City of God* (14.13) in Hythloday's peroration condemning pride as a "monster [*belua*], the prime plague and begetter of all others" (p. 112).

4

A clue to the riddle of why More failed to complete *The History of King Richard III* is provided by *A Dialogue of Comfort against Tribulation*, written in the Tower of London during the fifteen months prior to his execution on July 6, 1535, much of the brilliance of which resides in the way that More manipulates the interplay between fiction and history.[10] More sets his imaginary dialogue, purportedly "made by a Hungarian in Latin, and translated out of Latin into French, and out French into English," neither in 1526, when Hungary lay open to the Turks after the battle of Mohács, nor in 1534–5, when it was actually composed, but in the years 1527–8, a period of calm between the coronation of Ferdinand of Austria as king of Hungary in 1527 and a second invasion by the Turkish Sultan, Suleiman the Magnificent, in 1529, which resulted in the installation of John Zápolya on the throne on the condition that he make Hungary a vassal state. The effect of this choice of dates is that More contrives to suggest that the work concerns not merely the threat of a Turkish invasion in Europe but also the danger posed by those Christians—Zápolya and Henry VIII—who ally themselves literally or figuratively with infidels and persecute those of the Catholic faith, whether in England or in Hungary. The reader's response to More's text is thus conditioned by the knowledge of subsequent events. But whereas in *A Dialogue of Comfort* More deploys these ironies to his creative advantage, in *Richard III* both he and his narrative are engulfed by them.

In its lengthier English version, the narrative of *Richard III* ends with the future Cardinal Morton inciting the Duke of Buckingham to rise in revolt against the king he had helped to install on the throne. Pollard (1933) points out that in 1514, when More was likely composing *The History of King Richard III*, Henry VIII had no heir since Mary Tudor was not born until 1516, and the third Duke of Buckingham, son of the duke portrayed by More, was next in line to the throne. Because "incitement to treason was no safer in 1514 than in 1483," and the circumstances of the present paralleled those of the recent past about which he was writing, Pollard argues that More was forced to suppress his work because its conclusion "brought him back, with a shock, from dramatic art to real politics" (p. 430). Sylvester adds that "for More himself the text was essentially a private matter," and he therefore "does not refer to it in any of his other writings, published or unpublished" (More, 1976, p. xvi). Although More is often careless with names and dates, when he mistakenly gives the name of the *third* Duke of Buckingham, Edward, to his

---

[10] This paragraph draws on Frank Manley's introduction to *A Dialogue of Comfort* (More, 1973, pp. cxx–cxxxv) in the Yale Edition of the *Complete Works*.

father, Henry, Pollard's suggestion that this lapse is unconsciously motivated gains credence from its political ramifications.

In "The 'Uncanny,'" Freud (1919) differentiates between the production of an uncanny effect in literature and in life. Because of the greater license of the imaginative writer, he contends, "in the realm of fiction many things are not uncanny which would be so if they happened in real life" (p. 250). If, however, "the writer pretends to move in the world of common reality," then "everything that would have an uncanny effect in reality has it in his story" (p. 250). Freud's distinction between the criteria for the uncanny in "fiction" and in "real life" assumes that there is a clear line of demarcation between these two domains, but just such a stable boundary is called into question by the concept of the uncanny. As Freud points out a few pages earlier, "an uncanny effect is often and easily produced when the distinction between imagination and reality is effaced, as when something that we have hitherto regarded as imaginary appears before us in reality, or when a symbol takes on the full functions of the thing it symbolizes, and so on" (p. 244). In highlighting the sexual—and indeed incestuous—origins of the motifs of doubling and repetition in *Richard III*, More corroborates Freud's definition of the uncanny as "something which is secretly familiar, but has undergone repression and then returned from it" (p. 245). But the "factor of involuntary repetition" in the work pertains not merely to such brilliant devices as More's invention (or perhaps discovery) of a second Hastings to heighten the pathos of the story of the first, but above all to the way that "the distinction between imagination and reality is effaced" by its applicability to the present as well as to the past.

Just such a collapse of the distinction between the realms of art and life is central to the experience of what Stephen Greenblatt (1980) has called More's "self-fashioning." William Roper begins his biography of his father-in-law—written nearly twenty years after More's death, when the accession of Mary Tudor had made it safe to pay tribute to a Catholic martyr—by recounting an anecdote about how More, who in his youth had been placed as a page in the household of Morton, at the time Lord Chancellor to Henry VII, would "at Christmas-tide suddenly sometimes step in among the players, and never studying for the matter, make a part of his own there presently, which made the lookers-on more sport than all the players beside" (Sylvester and Harding, 1962, p. 198). Exploring More's dazzling yet disturbing capacity for self-invention, Greenblatt (1980) observes that "a distinction between text and lived reality ... is precisely abrogated by More's mode of existence. For one consequence of life lived as a histrionic fiction is that the category of the real merges with that of the fictive; the historical More is a narrative fiction" (p. 31; see also Sylvester, 1967). As More's improvised mode of being blurs the boundary between "text and lived reality," so, too, he participates by his writing simultaneously in "dramatic art" and "real politics."

Pollard's investigations into the historical ironies of *Richard III* have been carried forward by Fox. Citing More's exposition of how Buckingham's attempt to induce the London citizens to ratify Richard's coronation is exposed as a travesty by their insistence that he address them through the person of the recorder, who "so tempered his tale that he showed everything as the duke's words and no part his own" (p. 77), Fox (1983) remarks that the episode "is strangely prophetic of More's actions as Speaker in the Parliament of 1523," when he "frustrated Wolsey's attempt to bully the Commons" (p. 91) by asserting the ancient privileges and customs of the House. Once again More found life imitating art, in that the history of his own time repeated—albeit with a saving difference—the events of 1483. More could not have known this would happen at the time of writing, but the factor of "involuntary repetition" invests "what would otherwise be innocent enough with an uncanny atmosphere" and leaves us with "the idea of something fateful and inescapable" in our minds.

Even more haunting than More's foreshadowing of his own conduct as Speaker through the indirections of the recorder is the parallel between the fates of the two Buckinghams, father and son. Not only could Morton's advice to the former be taken in 1514, no less than in 1483, as an "incitement to treason," but the third duke was in fact indicted for treason in 1521 at Wolsey's instigation and subsequently executed in a judicial murder that More himself was forced to defend before the Court of Aldermen on the King's behalf.[11] This pattern of recurrence in the Buckingham family is exploited by Shakespeare in *Henry VIII*, when the third Duke, having been arrested for treason on the grounds of possibly perjured testimony provided by his surveyor, compares his treatment at the hands of Henry VIII with that accorded his father by Richard III:

> I had my trial,
> And needs must say a noble one; which makes me
> A little happier than my wretched father.
> Yet thus far we are one in fortunes: both
> Fell by our servants, by those men we lov'd most;
> A most unnatural and faithless service.

(2.1.118–23)

---

[11] Fox (1983, p. 100) extends Sylvester's proposed *terminus ad quem* for Richard III of 1518 to 1522. Long after the birth of Mary in 1516, however, Buckingham continued to loom as a claimant to the throne because Henry did not have a legitimate male heir until Jane Seymour gave birth to Edward VI in 1537.

The analogy between father and son—and between the conduct of Richard III and Henry VIII with respect to the two Buckinghams—that Shakespeare discerned with the benefit of hindsight More experienced as a lived reality. In Fox's (1983) words, his "complicity in these events" (p. 103) must have "shocked More into recognizing that the history of King Richard III was beginning to be rewritten in his own time, and also forced him to confront the severe effects on his own moral being of having decided to enact Morus' advice in *Utopia*" (p. 101) by entering Henry's service in late 1516.

In *Utopia*, More's conflict between his impulses toward moral absolutism and political pragmatism finds expression in the clash between the attitudes of Hythloday and his own eponymous persona. In *Richard III*, the revered figure of Morton begins to implement the "'indirect approach'" to politics advocated by the character More in *Utopia*, according to which "'what you cannot turn to good, you may at least make as little bad as possible'" (Logan, 2016, p. 37), but More the author is unable to carry his narrative beyond the point where such a compromise with principle would have to be shown in action. The consequences of the threats to More's integrity after his decision to enter Henry's service, according to Fox (1983), were a breakdown and a reversion "to the dualities and *contemptus mundi* of the earlier English poems," epitomized by the "unrelieved morbidity" (p. 101) of *The Four Last Things*, an incomplete and posthumously published treatise probably written in the 1520s after Buckingham's execution.[12]

More gives every indication of having foreseen, if not the severity, at least the nature of the perils awaiting him as royal minister. In his *Life of More*, Roper tells of a time, prior to Henry VIII's decision to initiate divorce proceedings against Catherine of Aragon in 1527, when he sought to rejoice with his father-in-law at "the happy estate of this realm that had so catholic a prince that no heretic durst show his face," to which More replied:

> "And yet, son Roper, I pray God … that some of us, as high as we seem to sit upon the mountains treading heretics under our feet like ants, live not in the day that we would gladly wish to be at a league and composition with them to let them have their churches to themselves, so they would be content to let us have ours to ourselves."
>
> (Sylvester and Harding, 1962, p. 216)

---

[12] Fox's argument that *The Four Last Things* represents a response to Buckingham's execution rests on a quotation from the work in which More cites the anonymous example of "a great Duke" who is condemned for "secret treason lately detected to the king … *the matter out of question*" (p. 101; Fox's italics).

This exchange casts More in a sinister light as one whose merciless "treading heretics under our feet like ants" is chastened only by the thought that the king might one day choose to persecute Catholics. But that More harbored no illusions concerning the tyranny of Henry VIII is evident once more when Roper congratulates him on enjoying a degree of favor heretofore bestowed only on Wolsey, and More cynically answers, "'I have no cause to be proud thereof, for if my head could win him a castle in France (for then there was war between us) it should not fail to go'" (p. 208).

Similarly, Roper recalls that after More resigned the chancellorship, he warned Thomas Cromwell, then basking in royal approbation, that he would do well always to tell Henry VIII "'what he ought to do but never what he is able to do. … For if a lion knew his own strength, hard were it for any man to rule him'" (Sylvester and Harding, 1962, p. 228). The same metaphor of the king as a lion appears in *The History of King Richard III*. To kindle the fires of rebellion in Buckingham, Morton relates the pseudo-Aesopian fable (for which there is no known source) of the beast with a lump of flesh on his forehead who, when the lion proclaimed a death sentence on all those with horns, fled for his life. When the fox assured the beast that his lump was not a horn, he replied, "'No, marry, … that wot I well enough. But what and he call it a horn, where am I then?'" (p. 95). As More could not have failed to discern, Morton's parable was no less applicable to his own situation under Henry than to Buckingham's under Richard, and the need for circumspection in dealing with an absolute monarch was as great in the present as it had ever been in the past.

Because More is largely responsible for casting Richard III, as Philippa Langley and Michael Jones (2013) have written, in the role of the "grand villain" of his time—a conception of his character that, when More's text "was finally printed in the mid-sixteenth century, was quickly incorporated into the chronicles of Edward Hall and Raphael Holinshed," which in turn "became the principal sources for William Shakespeare's play" (pp. 45–6)—he is often thought to have been a proponent of the "Tudor myth."[13] In this schema of English history, stemming from Polydore Vergil and given definitive shape in Hall's *The Vnion of the Two Noble and Illustre Famelies of Lancastre and Yorke*, Richard's reign was a descent into unmitigated tyranny not overcome until the end of the Wars of the Roses, when order was providentially restored

---

[13] Langley, the independent scholar who animated the Search for Richard project, proved all the scoffers wrong when his remains were discovered beneath a car park in Leicester on September 5, 2012. The much-maligned king was reburied on March 26, 2015 "with due dignity and honour in Leicester Cathedral" (p. vii). A film directed by Stephen Frears, based on the book by Langley and Jones, originally titled *The Lost Grave: The Search for Richard III*, was released in 2022.

under Henry VII. But though More enshrines the received view of Richard, he is also capable of criticizing Edward IV and Henry VIII, both of whom resemble Richard more closely than one might have anticipated. Indeed, so far is More from offering a piece of Tudor propaganda that his ambiguous vision has finally less in common with Shakespeare's early *Richard III*, which offers a stark contrast between good and evil in the characters of Richmond (the eventual Henry VII) and Richard, than it does with Shakespeare's mature analysis of the opacities of theatricality and power in *Henry V*, or with what I have termed the "deconstruction of history" (Rudnytsky, 1991) in his valedictory *Henry VIII*.

More's clairvoyance permits the delineation of a final respect in which he contrived to make *Richard III* a script for contemporary events. Not only is Henry VIII adumbrated in the absolutism of Richard III, but he also shares the "fleshly wantonness" that flaws Edward IV. Although the increase in Henry's girth, which led to him to weigh almost 400 pounds by the time of his death in January of 1547, at the age of fifty-five, still lay in the future when More wrote his manuscript, it is again eerily prescient that he should have said of Edward that he was "of body mighty, strong and clean made, howbeit in his later days with over-liberal diet somewhat corpulent and burly, and nevertheless not uncomely" (p. 5). Parallels between Edward IV and Henry VIII were widely recognized in the sixteenth century. Polydore Vergil begins his laudatory account of Henry's reign in the *Anglica Historia* by drawing the comparison between grandfather and grandson:

> For everybody loved him; and their affections were not half-hearted, because the king on his father's side descended from Henry VI and his mother's from Edward IV. For just as Edward was the most warmly thought of by the English people among all English kings, so this successor of his, Henry, was very like him in general appearance, in greatness of mind and generosity, and for that reason was the more acclaimed and approved by all.[14]
>
> (Hay, 1950, p. 151)

---

[14] Vergil began work on the *Anglica Historia* in 1512–13, and the first printed edition, which ended its narrative in 1509, appeared in 1534. In 1555, the year of Vergil's death, a third edition was published containing an additional book that dealt with the history of Henry's reign to 1537, from which the quoted passage is taken. See Hay's introduction (pp. xiii–xvii). On More's possible familiarity with Polydore's manuscript, see Sylvester's introduction in the bilingual Yale Edition of *The History of King Richard III* (More, 1963, p. lxxvi).

More follows Vergil in acknowledging Edward's popularity, but he qualifies the tribute by commenting ironically on the king's gift of venison to the common people, "which oftentimes more esteem and take for greater kindness a little courtesy than a great benefit" (p. 6). In keeping with his revision of the Tudor myth, More uses the analogy between Edward and Henry not to glorify Edward's "greatness of mind and generosity," but to show him as a skillful manipulator of his subjects.

Henry was discreet in the prosecution of his love affairs, but as early as 1510 he gave rise to scandal by his pursuit of Anne Hastings, Buckingham's sister, during Catherine's first, abortive pregnancy. In 1519, his mistress, Elizabeth Blount, gave birth to a son, Henry Fitzroy, whom he ennobled in 1525 in an effort to secure a male heir (Ridley, 1985, pp. 49, 113, 152). Above all, when Henry initiated divorce proceedings against Catherine, he did so on the same grounds that the Duchess of York had sought to impede her son's union with Elizabeth Woodville—namely, that he had been "defouled with bigamy in his first marriage." Catherine had been previously married to Henry's elder brother, Arthur, who died at the age of fifteen in 1503 a few months after their nuptials; and Henry's marriage to Catherine in 1509 was made possible by a dispensation granted by Pope Julius II. But when, after eighteen years of marriage, Catherine had not borne him a male heir, the fear that he was being punished for violating the scriptural injunction against marrying his brother's wife (Lev. 18.16, 20.21) formed the basis of the "scruple" used by Henry as the justification for his divorce proceedings, even though Catherine insisted that her marriage to Arthur had not been consummated.

This analogy between not merely the amorous propensities of Edward IV and Henry VIII but also the circumstances of their marriages could not have escaped More's notice even at the time of his writing of *Richard III*, and it must have been with an uncanny sense of déjà vu that he watched the history he had chronicled being "rewritten in his own time" in the king's "great matter" over which he ultimately lost his own life. More's inability to complete his work and his refusal to permit its publication become comprehensible in view of both its private meanings and its political implications.

Drawing on More's account, I have argued that Edward IV's marriage to Elizabeth Woodville and ensuing pattern of adulterous behavior have their origin in an incestuous fixation. The vehemence with which Edward insisted on preserving "mine own liberty in choice of my own marriage" attests paradoxically to the extent to which he was controlled by unconscious determinants. It completes the cycle of recurrence linking Plantagenet and Tudor history to propose that the same may be said of Henry VIII. Not only did his marriage to his brother's wife entail the violation of an incest taboo, but as J. C. Flügel (1920) pointed out in a paper published in the inaugural issue of *The International Journal of Psycho-Analysis*, Henry—again like Tristan, who brought Isolde from Ireland to Cornwall so that she might marry Mark—"led his sister-in-law and future wife to the altar" (p. 27) when she married Arthur.

To add to Henry's psychological burden, Flügel continues, after the death of Arthur—who had stood in his way to the throne—Henry VII initially proposed that he himself should marry Catherine since he was a widower, thereby bringing about a situation in which young Henry "could scarcely but regard himself in some sense as a sexual rival of his father, while at the same time it was likely to reinforce the transference of the mother-regarding feelings on to Catherine" (p. 29). Thus, the dying exhortation of Henry VII that his son complete the long-delayed project of marrying his sister-in-law was carried out by the newly crowned monarch "with almost indecent haste" in less than a month because these instructions "coincided with the tendencies emanating from his own unconscious Oedipus complex; enabling him in this way to combine a conscious obedience to the behests of filial piety with a realisation of unconscious desires connected with hostility and jealousy toward his father and brother" (p. 30). Like Edward IV, Henry VIII would seem to have found in his marriage to Catherine an ideal solution to his Oedipus complex, but subsequent events were cruelly to give the lie to this hope.

It is not necessary to impute mystical powers to More to account for the accuracy with which he was able to divine what lay hidden in the hatch and brood of time. A keen insight into his own nature, and that of the tyrant whom he chose to serve, was enough. As Warwick comments in Shakespeare's *2 Henry IV*:

> There is a history in all men's lives,
> Figuring the natures of the times deceas'd,
> The which observ'd, a man may prophesy,
> With a near aim, of the main chance of things
> As yet not come to life, which in their seeds
> And weak beginnings lie entreasured.

(3.2.80–5)

But though More's prophetic gifts are susceptible of rational explanation, it is impossible to dispel the sensation of "most wonder" aroused by his obliteration of the barrier between art and life, and by the "appearance of purpose" with which he imbues the rhymes of history.

Chapter 5

The Purloined Handkerchief in *Othello*

"The letter as a signifier is thus not a thing or the absence of a thing, nor a word or the absence of a word, nor an organ or the absence of an organ, but a knot in a structure where words, things, and organs can neither be definably separated nor compatibly combined."

—Barbara Johnson, "The Frame of Reference"

1

Implicitly or explicitly, every interpretation of a literary text is a thematization of the problem of reading. Any such undertaking must situate itself within the context of previous readings of the same text as well as within the crosscurrents of diverse trends in contemporary thought. As Hans-Georg Gadamer (1960) has shown, it is not necessary for an interpreter to be aware of the "history of effects" (*Wirkungsgeschichte*) of a work to be subjected to its power, but the likelihood of a productive interpretation is enhanced by a recognition of one's embeddedness in history and on "the achievement of the right horizon of enquiry for the questions evoked by the encounter with tradition" (p. 269).

The significance of the handkerchief is one of the most time-honored cruxes in the interpretation of *Othello*, from the first major commentary on the play by Thomas Rymer to the present day. Indeed, Rymer (1692) set the terms for subsequent discussion by chastising Shakespeare for allowing the plot of his tragedy to depend upon something so trivial as a lost handkerchief:

So much ado, so much stress, so much passion and repetition about an Handkerchief! Why was not this call'd the *Tragedy of the Handkerchief?* ... Had it been *Desdemona*'s Garter, the Sagacious Moor might have smelt a Rat: but the Handkerchief is so remote a trifle, no Booby, on this side of *Mauritania*, cou'd make any consequence from it.

(p. 160)

As so often, the strictures of an intelligent neoclassical critic go directly to the central issues raised by a literary work. Rymer's sense of the incongruity between the cause and the effects of Othello's downfall is warranted and should be attended to by any reader who seeks to gain insight into Shakespeare's virtuosity in the play.

In speaking of the handkerchief as "purloined," I mean to suggest a relation between this perennial problem in Shakespeare exegesis and a cluster of writings in twentieth-century literary theory centered on Edgar Allan Poe's 1844 short story "The Purloined Letter." In his influential "Seminar on 'The Purloined Letter,'" Jacques Lacan (1956) offered a reading of Poe's story that is also a meditation on Freud's concept of the repetition compulsion and an elaboration of his own contention that "it is the symbolic order which is constitutive for the subject" (p. 29). Lacan's "Seminar" provoked a polemical reply from Jacques Derrida (1975), who reanalyzed Poe's story from the standpoint of deconstruction to argue that Lacan's version of psychoanalysis, seemingly so radical, remains tethered to metaphysical beliefs about truth and presence that have undergirded Western philosophy from Plato to phenomenology. Derrida names the system he seeks to dismantle "phallogocentric transcendentalism" and insists that it must be rejected in favor of a recognition of the priority of writing, with its endless deferrals and traces, over the illusion of fullness and a pristine moment of origin in speech. Finally, Barbara Johnson (1977), in a masterful subversion of the possibility of mastery, showed how "Derrida's own reading of Lacan's text reproduces precisely the crimes of which he accuses it" (p. 218)—simplification and distortion—to the point where it becomes impossible to know "whether Lacan and Derrida are really saying the same thing or only enacting their differences from themselves" (p. 250).

This series of responses to Poe's story bears on *Othello* because the handkerchief—like Poe's purloined letter and the green and gold girdle in *Sir Gawain and the Green Knight*—functions as what Lacan (1956) calls a "floating signifier," the circulation of which "determines the subjects in their acts, in their destiny" (p. 43). But in addition to circulating among the characters, the handkerchief has swirled in the discourses on race and sexuality that have figured so prominently in the reception history of what is, with *King Lear*, the most agonizing of Shakespeare's tragedies. On a more theoretical level, the controversy between Derrida and Lacan exemplifies a tension between deconstructionist and psychoanalytic readings of literature. In his essay on yet another purloined object, the ribbon stolen by Rousseau in Book 2 of his *Confessions,* Paul de Man (1979) writes: "Once it is removed from its legitimate owner, the ribbon, being in itself devoid of meaning and function, can circulate symbolically as a pure signifier and become the articulating hinge in a chain of exchanges and possessions. As the ribbon changes hands it traces a circuit leading to the exposure of a hidden, censored desire" (p. 283). Whereas a psychoanalyst might expect the "hidden, censored desire" revealed by the "symbolic circulation" of all three objects in their respective texts to stem from the Oedipus complex, de Man counters that Rousseau's ribbon is "devoid of meaning and function" other than "substituting for a desire which is itself a desire for substitution" (p. 284).

My "horizon of enquiry" is thus constituted by a rhizome: the "history of effects" that can be traced in recent criticism of *Othello*, the debates in literary theory arising from Poe's story, and my own repeated readings of Shakespeare's play. Perhaps the best reply to Rymer's objections is contained in Geoffrey Hartman's (1981) remarks on the use of images and metaphors in philosophical discourse:

> Something in appearance marginal, supplementary, accidental (a "case" cited by chance, an illustrative metaphor) tells us that the essence or thing itself is missing. The thing instanced becomes, as it were, a disgruntled representative of the absent (perhaps always absent) thing, and paradoxically gains more authority than the argument it was intended to supplement. And here is where literary study sees *its* chance. ... It seizes on the images and metaphors that slip, deliberately or not, into pure or scientific discourse, and reflects on whether this allowance of dream or icon may not be closer to the real subject.
>
> (p. 3)

The handkerchief may seem too "remote a trifle" to serve as the occasion for tragedy, but this "marginal, supplementary, accidental" object, which "tells us that the essence or thing itself is missing," comes as close as anything to being "the real subject" of *Othello*.

2

The paradoxes that attend the handkerchief—and the tragedy—in all its aspects are signaled by the way that Shakespeare introduces this apparently "marginal" object at the midpoint of the action, at the culmination of the "Temptation Scene" after Iago has planted the seeds of jealousy in Othello. Desdemona enters, and the following exchange occurs:

Oth. I have a pain upon my forehead, here.
Des. Faith, that's with watching, 'twill away again.

Let me but bind it hard, within this hour
It will be well.
Oth. Your napkin is too little.

(3.3.284–7)

Othello's "pain upon my forehead" alludes to the horns of cuckoldry, which he believes he wears due to Desdemona's infidelity, but also insinuates that his headache may be a psychosomatic symptom of jealousy. Subsequently, when Othello falls into a trance, Iago refers to his condition as "an epilepsy" (4.1.50), but when he asks Othello upon his recovery, "Have you not hurt your head?" (59), the latter interprets his question as a mocking allusion to cuckoldry. Iago's diagnosis is racially charged because, as Daniel Vitkus (2003) has observed, "Othello's epilepsy recalls that of the ur-Moor, Muhammed," and "Christian polemics against Islam printed in Shakespeare's time frequently allege that Muhammed was an epileptic who falsely maintained that his ecstasies were brought on by divine possession" (p. 85). Desdemona's attempt to reassure Othello that his agitation is the result of "watching," while having the literal meaning of "not sleeping," evokes the voyeurism that is a prominent feature of his character. Her offer to "bind" his head with her handkerchief, beyond being an attempt to minister to his physical needs, is an expression of Desdemona's love, which Othello rejects by branding her handkerchief "too little" to ease the anguish of his fears of betrayal.

After being brushed aside by Othello and falling to the ground, the handkerchief is picked up by Emilia, Desdemona's lady-in-waiting and wife to Iago, who surrenders it to her husband. Iago uses the handkerchief to further his schemes of revenge by planting it in the chamber of the disgraced Cassio and informing Othello that he has seen it in Cassio's possession. Cassio brings the handkerchief to his paramour, the courtesan Bianca, who accepts it, although she suspects that it had been given to him by "a newer friend" (3.4.181). Later, in Act 4, Scene 1, she angrily returns the handkerchief to Cassio, and at the worst moment possible—when Iago has hidden Othello and arranged for him to spy upon a bantering conversation between himself and Cassio, ostensibly about Desdemona but in reality about Bianca. The appearance of Bianca with the handkerchief convinces Othello that Cassio must have received it from Desdemona and causes him to resolve to murder them both. After this exchange, the handkerchief is not mentioned again until the last scene of the play. Both during and after the murder of Desdemona, Othello appeals to Cassio's possession of the handkerchief as his justification, until Emilia reveals the truth about its disappearance: "O thou dull Moor, that handkerchief thou speak'st of / I found by fortune, and did give my husband" (5.2.225–6). As Robert B. Heilman (1956) has commented, in this final twist to the "court metaphor" that pervades the drama, "the handkerchief does have evidential value—but the reverse of what Othello had supposed" (p. 161), since Emilia's words establish at one stroke the innocence of Desdemona and the guilt of Iago.

Beginning with Desdemona, the handkerchief comes into contact with all three of the female characters in the play and their male counterparts. It becomes evident how pertinent are Lacan's (1956) formulations. The handkerchief "circulates symbolically" because it is the itinerary of the signifier, and "it is not only the subject but the subjects, grasped in their intersubjectivity, who … model their very being on the moment of the signifying chain which traverses them" (p. 43). But if the characters are defined by their place in the "signifying chain," the handkerchief, in Karen Newman's (1987) words, becomes a "snowballing signifier," and "as it passes from hand to hand, both literal and critical, it accumulates myriad associations and meanings" (p. 91). Had the handkerchief returned to Desdemona, its circle completed, Iago's plot could not have succeeded. But the circuit it traces is an open one and does not save the life of Desdemona, though it does expose the machinations that are the cause of her death.

When Emilia finds the dropped "napkin," she recalls that it was Desdemona's "first remembrance from the Moor" but rejoices because "My wayward husband hath a hundred times / Woo'd me to steal it" (3.3.290–3). Why Iago wanted Emilia to steal the handkerchief is never explained, but a class motive may be at play since, as Ian Smith (2013) has pointed out, "the introduction of the handkerchief to blow and wipe one's nose, as opposed to using hands or clothing, marked a significant shift in a civilizing process that was aimed at shoring up class distinctions," and "handkerchiefs remained signifiers of wealth and status for both men and women during the early modern period" (p. 5).[1] Lacan's (1956) insistence on "the materiality of the signifier" (p. 38) gains a new meaning in light of the function of handkerchiefs as status symbols for Elizabethans. It may be for the same reason that Emilia resolves to "have the work ta'en out" (3.2.296)—that is, have the pattern copied—before she gives the handkerchief to Iago, just as Cassio requests that Bianca "Take me this work out" (3.4.180) so that he can keep a duplicate of this precious article for himself. Once the handkerchief "is removed from its legitimate owner," it gives rise to a "desire for substitution" and "can circulate

---

[1] In Toni Morrison's (2012) dramatic reimagining of Shakespeare's play, Emilia voices her resentment of Desdemona for treating her like a servant, "Someone beneath you, beneath your class which takes devotion for granted" (p. 33).

symbolically as a pure signifier and become the articulating hinge in a chain of exchanges and possessions."

3

According to Lacan (1956), the signifier is "by nature symbol only of an absence" (p. 39); Hartman concurs that the "illustrative metaphor" serves as "a disgruntled representative of the absent (perhaps always absent) thing." For Othello, the "always absent thing" takes the form of the sight of Desdemona engaged in intercourse with Cassio. "Would you, the supervisor, grossly gape on? / Behold her topp'd?" (3.3.95–6), Iago demands of his prey. But because Desdemona is not guilty of adultery, such a sight is inherently unobtainable and the handkerchief "gains more authority than the argument it was intended to supplement." Othello cries out for the "ocular proof" (3.3.360) of his wife's infidelity, but it is in his own delusions of betrayal that Iago's power lies. Upon being shown the "thing instanced"— Cassio with the handkerchief—Othello is persuaded that he has seen the nonexistent "thing itself."

Othello's futile quest to catch Desdemona in the act of being "topp'd" by Cassio duplicates the fears of her father Brabantio. In the opening scene, Iago taunts Brabantio with a pornographic description of Desdemona having sex with Othello, "Now, now, very now, an old black ram / Is tupping your white ewe" (1.1.90–1).[2] Although Othello's race lies at the heart of the play's sexual obsessions, the repugnant fascination of Iago's bestial image is heightened by the fact that Othello is an unlikely and even tabooed partner for Desdemona also because of his age. As Valerie Barnes Lipscomb (2001) has observed, "Othello and Desdemona may be separated by as much as a generation" (p. 209), and just as "the very first adjective in Iago's verbal plot to destroy Othello refers to age" (p. 210), so, too, Othello's "first words about age are linked his sexuality" (p. 215). In requesting that Desdemona be permitted to accompany him to Cyprus, he assures the Duke that he does it "not / To please the palate of my appetite, / … (the young affects / In me defunct)" (1.3.261–4). Othello's disavowal of a sexual motive for wanting his young wife's company, Lipscomb adds, "fits seamlessly with Shakespeare's subversion of racial stereotypes in the first act" since Ham, the son of Noah whose "failure to abstain from sexual intercourse during the flood" was believed to have incurred God's curse that made "his offspring dark-skinned,

---

[2] Neill (1989) points out that "'topped' … is simply a variant of 'tupped,' a verbal form deriving from the dialectical 'tup' = ram (*OED*)" (p. 400*n*43).

thereby founding the African peoples" (pp. 215–16). But Othello's seemingly praiseworthy "defunct" libido leads to his undoing "in the second half of the play" when "he becomes not only the barbaric Moor, but also the jealous, foolish old man who doubts his ability to satisfy a young wife" (p. 216). Just before he brushes aside the handkerchief, Othello himself couples his race and age as reasons why Desdemona is bound to have left him:

> Haply, for I am black,
> And have not those soft parts of conversation
> That chamberers have, or for I am declin'd
> Into the vale of years (yet that's not much),
> She's gone.
>
> (3.3.263–7)

By anxiously echoing the prejudices of which Iago is the leading spokesman, Othello reveals that he has identified with Desdemona's father. In the same way that Brabantio believes his daughter's marriage to be "Against all rules of nature" (1.3.102), Othello's self-hatred leads him to fear that Desdemona's choice of him must be a case of "nature erring from itself" (3.3.227). By inventing the character of Brabantio out of a passing reference to "the Lady's relatives" (Bullough, 1973, p. 242) in the sixteenth-century Italian novella by Giraldi Cinthio that is his principal source for the play, Shakespeare shows that Desdemona's love for Othello is rooted in a female Oedipus complex. Whereas at the outset Othello's calm and confident demeanor makes him seem utterly unlike the hotheaded Brabantio, and Desdemona's willingness to marry a black man is a repudiation of everything her father stands for, the tragedy of the play lies in the fact that her husband turns out to be an even more violent and abusive repetition of her father.

The decisive moment in the marriage between Othello and Desdemona comes when she appeals to her father before the Venetian Senate to sanction her transition from the role of daughter to that of wife. In her plea, Desdemona asks Brabantio's permission to do the same thing that her mother had done when she left her father to marry him:

> you are the lord of duty,
> I am hitherto your daughter. But here's my husband,
> And so much duty as my mother show'd
> To you, preferring you before her father,
> So much I challenge I may profess
> Due to the Moor, my lord.
>
> (1.3.184–9)

Desdemona, as Stephen Greenblatt (1980) has pointed out, "does not question the woman's obligation to obey, invoking instead only the traditional right to transfer her duty" (p. 239). Yet even this assertion of limited freedom proves intolerable to Brabantio, who immediately disowns her, "I had rather to adopt a child than get it" (1.3.191). He exits the scene with a curse against Othello: "Look to her, Moor, if thou hast eyes to see; / She has deceiv'd her father, and may thee" (292–3).

Brabantio's racially charged hatred of Othello is a psychotic manifestation of his antipathy to any suitor for his daughter's hand. Desdemona's first wooer in the play is not Othello but Roderigo, Iago's gull and another character added by Shakespeare to Cinthio. When the two schemers awaken Brabantio with their clamors, his reaction is one of annoyance with Roderigo: "In honest plainness thou hast heard me say / My daughter is not for thee" (1.1.97–8). But upon learning that Desdemona has eloped with Othello, Brabantio makes common cause with the Venetian, who at least is white, in his detestation of the Moor: "O would you had had her!" (175). Desdemona's Oedipus complex is cemented by Brabantio's incestuous fixation, which stifles his daughter's right to a sexual life. That her choice of Othello confirms Brabantio's worst fears is evinced by his response to the news of her elopement, "This accident is not unlike my dream, / Belief of it oppresses me already" (1.2.142–3).

By marrying Desdemona, Othello moves into the proprietary position formerly occupied by Brabantio and is similarly unable to tolerate any display of independence on her part. Even his summit of happiness in the play, which comes when they are reunited on Cyprus after having been separated during their voyages from Venice, is clouded by a shadow of anxiety. Othello exclaims:

> If it were now to die,
> 'Twere now to be most happy; for I fear
> My soul hath her content so absolute
> That not another comfort like to this
> Succeeds in unknown fate.
>
> (2.1.189–93)

Like Brabantio, who seeks to halt the sequence of generations, Othello longs to freeze Desdemona in the stasis of an eternal present in which the pun on "die" fuses the bliss of orgasm with a necrophilic fantasy. As she did with her father, Desdemona initially demurs and warns Othello against the danger of equating happiness with death: "The heavens forbid / But that our loves and comforts should increase / Even as our days do grow!" (193–5). But Othello, "Like to the Pontic Sea, / Whose icy current and compulsive course

/ Nev'r feels retiring ebb, but keeps due on" (3.3.453–5), is not to be deterred, and Desdemona's resistance crumbles. Indeed, as Michael Neill (1989) has commented, when "she perfects her tableau of murderous consummation" by asking Emilia to put "the sheets from the wedding night" on what will now also be her deathbed, Desdemona is acting "in unconscious collusion with Othello's fantasies" (p. 401), thereby making manifest the reciprocal incestuous fixations that caused them to be irresistibly drawn to one another in the first place.

Having ascended to the position of Brabantio, Othello centers his anxieties of betrayal on Cassio, whose race, youth, and social graces make him seem to possess everything that he himself lacks and that Desdemona, according to all the ideologically constructed "rules of nature," would want in a man. Iago, whose rage has been triggered by being passed over when Othello promoted Cassio to the rank of lieutenant, reminds Othello of what Brabantio had said about Desdemona's capacity for dissimulation: "She did deceive her father, marrying you" (3.3.204). By blocking rather than blessing Desdemona's coming of age, as Edward A. Snow (1980) has observed, Brabantio bequeaths to the newlyweds an exaggerated version of "the Oedipal curse every sexual relationship undergoes in the process of being assimilated by the patriarchal order of things" (p. 402). He secures his revenge when Iago "is able to make Othello look at himself and Desdemona in terms of Brabantio's warning" (p. 399), which means that Othello can only see in Cassio a perfected version of his former self.

Because the fear of cuckoldry is endemic to "the patriarchal order of things," the father's "Oedipal curse," in André Green's (1969) words, functions as "the equivalent in *Othello* of the oracle" (p. 102) in Greek tragedy. Even chance events such as Emilia's finding of the handkerchief and Bianca's entrance with it in her hand as Othello is spying on the conversation between Iago and Cassio become instruments of fate when Iago opportunistically turns them to his advantage. They are cogs in what the Voice calls in Jean Cocteau's (1934) self-consciously modern adaptation of *Oedipus the King* "one of the most perfect machines devised by the infernal gods for the mathematical annihilation of a mortal" (p. 6).

4

That Shakespeare's characters, although not real people, are nonetheless "imagined human beings" (Paris, 1997) to whom it is legitimate to impute both childhoods and unconscious fantasies is attested by his invention of Brabantio, which allows us to see Desdemona's marriage to Othello as a repetition of her relationship to her father. No less strikingly, Shakespeare supplies both Othello and Desdemona with childhood memories for which there is no precedent in his source. For Desdemona, these are preserved in the "Willow Song" she sings as she prepares for bed at the close of Act 4. As Ernest Brennecke (1953) points out, whereas the ballad was traditionally sung by a forsaken male lover, Shakespeare not only invents "Desdemona's mother's maid Barbara [*sic*], whose lover went mad and who died while singing this song" (p. 36). He also changes the line "Let nobody chide her, her scorns though I prove," so that Desdemona sings "Let nobody blame him, his scorn I approve" (4.3.52), which reminds the audience "how the Moor had so brutally struck her in public that very afternoon" (p. 36).[3] Othello's corresponding early memories all center on the handkerchief that he believes constitutes the "ocular proof" that Desdemona has betrayed him with Cassio.

In the history of *Othello* criticism, there has been no more radical idea than Ian Smith's hypothesis that the handkerchief is not white—as had been assumed in all previous discussions—but black. Smith amasses a great deal of evidence that makes this seem plausible. In contrast to Lynda E. Boose (1975), who places her interpretation of the "square piece of white linen spotted with strawberry-red fruit" as a "visually recognizable reduction of Othello and Desdemona's wedding-bed sheets, the visual proof of their consummated marriage" (pp. 362–3), in an exclusively European context, Smith (2013) points out that both Leo Africanus, "a converted Moor who grew up in Fez in North Africa," in his *Geographical History of Africa*— written first in Arabic and then in Italian in 1526 and translated into English in 1600—and Robert Burton, in *The Anatomy of Melancholy*, documented the practice "among Africans and Jews of displaying wedding sheets stained with blood" (p. 2). Smith quotes from Leo's account of how, "immediately after the consummation of the marriage," a designated woman "takes the bridal 'napkin stained with blood,' shows it to the guests, 'proclaiming with a loud voice that the bride was euer till that time an vnspotted and pure virgine'" (p. 2).

There could be no more precise gloss on *Othello*, in which the handkerchief is termed a "napkin" and in his last words before the murder scene Othello vows, "Thy bed, lust-stain'd, shall with lust's blood be spotted" (5.1.36), than these excerpts from Leo; and in an early study Lois Whitney (1922) concluded

---

[3] Morrison (2012) portrays Barbary as Desdemona's black African nurse and second mother, but who protests in the afterlife that she was in reality Desdemona's "slave" and that her true name was "Sa'ran" (p. 35). Desdemona counters Sa'ran's insistence on the racial gulf that divides them by pointing to their common bond of gender: "We are women. I had no more control over my life than you had. My prison was unlike yours but it was prison still" (p. 38).

that the *Geographical History* "contains so much which throws light on the character of Othello that it is hard to believe that Shakespeare was not acquainted with it" (p. 475). With reference specifically to the handkerchief, Smith (2013) documents that "black handkerchiefs were not unknown" (p. 6) in Elizabethan England. He observes further that, when Othello tells Desdemona "That handkerchief / Did an Egyptian to my mother give" (3.4.55–6), this establishes its "African provenance" (p. 15). Most saliently, Smith contends Othello's statement that it was "dy'd in mummy" (74) must "refer to the process of dying cloth so that it appears other than white" (p. 16). Indeed, because mummy is a "bituminous black dye" that became fused with "the popularly circulated idea of mummy as black flesh," this invests "Othello's description with a self-referential power to enforce a connection in the audience's mind between the handkerchief and Othello's own black skin" (p. 20). Finally, in pointing out that mummy was "credited among medieval Arab scholars as having medicinal properties" (p. 18), Smith cites a note from Neill's edition of *Othello* that it was especially "'celebrated for its anti-epileptic virtues'" (p. 16*n*75)—a fact that takes on heightened significance in view of Vitkus's argument that Othello's epilepsy is evocative of that of "ur-Moor, Muhammed."[4]

After Smith, it is no longer possible to take for granted that the handkerchief about which there is "so much ado" in *Othello* is white. His thesis, drawing on Toni Morrison's *Playing in the Dark*, that "'until very recently,'" readers of Shakespeare have almost without exception been "'positioned as white'" (p. 25), reminds us that we must be no less vigilant concerning the hazards of the white gaze than we have learned from Laura Mulvey (1975) to be concerning those of the male gaze. At the same time, when Smith (2013) writes that, "read properly," the handkerchief must be understood to be "dyed black" (p. 20), he falls into the trap into which he has been preceded by so many other critics of *Othello* of assuming something to be true that remains unresolved in the play. Had Shakespeare had wanted his audiences to realize this, it is curious that he would have made it so difficult to discern that no one before Smith had thought of it in over 400 years, especially in a play with so much racially charged language. Africans, like Europeans, had the custom of displaying "wedding sheets stained with blood" to prove to onlookers that the bride was a virgin, but nowhere does Leo Africanus say those sheets were black. And while "black handkerchiefs were not unknown" in Shakespeare's time, this is not dispositive concerning the handkerchief in Shakespeare's play.

---

[4] On the medicinal properties of mummy, see the misogynistic last lines of Donne's "Loves Alchymie," which portray sex as a transient remedy for lust, "Hope not for minde in women; at their best / Sweetnesse and wit, they'are but *Mummy*, possessed."

As is well known, whereas Cinthio describes the handkerchief as "embroidered most delicately in the Moorish fashion" (Bullough, 1973, p. 246), Shakespeare modifies this when Iago asks Othello in the Temptation Scene: "Have you not sometimes seen a handkerchief / Spotted with strawberries in your wive's hand?" (3.3.434–5). Although Smith (2013) contends that "Shakespeare takes the reference to the handkerchief's 'Moorish fashion' more seriously than has been allowed" (p. 15), the replacement of Cinthio's generic "Moorish" design with the vivid specificity of "strawberries" implies, on the contrary, that Shakespeare has "Englished" the handkerchief.[5] As Smith himself acknowledges, "the embroidered strawberry pattern suggests a home-grown tradition since the 'strawberry plant … is among the most frequently occurring of such objects represented in English domestic embroidery surviving from the period'" (p. 3).[6] And since the handkerchief is associated with wedding sheets through the word "spotted," it seems at least as justified to think of the "napkin" as white as it would be to think of it as black.

For Smith, the "African provenance" of the handkerchief underscores its "role as substitute for Othello" (p. 14) in the play. But there is an equally compelling respect in which the handkerchief, as what Newman (1987) calls "a *feminine* trifle" (p. 92), constitutes a metonymy for Desdemona. Building on Snow's (1980) interpretation that "the 'napkin' spotted with strawberries evokes the menstrual cloth as well as the wedding sheets, thereby facilitating an identification between virginal and menstrual blood" (p. 392*n*12), Newman (1987) discerns in the handkerchief a figuration of "female sexual topography," and particularly of Desdemona's "own sexual parts: the nipples—sometimes, incidentally, represented in the courtly love *blason* as strawberries—lips, and even perhaps the clitoris, the berry of sexual pleasure, nestled within its flanged leaves" (p. 92).[7] But since the handkerchief is equated with both Othello and Desdemona, at once exotic and domestic, and

---

[5] In *The Tragedy of Richard III*, Shakespeare appropriates from More's *History of Richard III* the incident in which Gloucester demands strawberries from the Bishop of Ely as a prelude to arresting Hastings for treason because he protected the "damned strumpet" (3.4.74) Jane Shore.

[6] The embedded quotation is from Lawrence Ross's (1960) article on strawberries in Shakespeare.

[7] Calling attention to Ludovico's exclamation after Othello has stabbed himself to death with a concealed dagger, "O bloody period!" (5.2.357), David Willbern (1997) explicates this phrase as an invitation to view Othello's deed not only in a rhetorical sense as "a final and fatal punctuation to an excellent discourse" but also as "a mark of female sexuality: of virginity (bridal sheets), murder (deathbed sheets), and menstruation ('napkin' also bears this significance)" (p. 5).

with the sheets of the bed in which they are united in death as they may or may not have been in life, rather than trying to decide whether it is black or white, perhaps it should be construed as oscillating between these poles—or as neither, or as both simultaneously.

5

Othello's mission to obtain the "ocular proof" of Desdemona's adultery with Cassio is replicated by the curiosity aroused in the readers or spectators of Shakespeare's play with respect to the sexual relations between Othello and Desdemona. In both instances, the handkerchief becomes the "disgruntled representative" of the "essence or thing itself" that is "always absent." Iago taunts Othello by insinuating that Desdemona's appearance of virtue may be feigned, "Her honor is an essence that's not seen; / They have it very oft that have it not. But for the handkerchief—" (4.1.16–18). But whereas Othello's voyeurism is condemned to deferral and displacement because what he is looking for has never existed, the audience's desire to pry into the secrets of the matrimonial bedchamber remains unsatisfied because there are grounds for questioning whether Othello and Desdemona were ever, in Iago's words, "fast married" (1.2.11).

This question about the marriage of Othello and Desdemona is paradigmatic of all the issues in the play of which it may be said that to be once in doubt is never to be resolved, notwithstanding the efforts of a phalanx of critics to settle the matter. Boose (1975), for example, not only assumes that the handkerchief is white but also concludes too hastily on the basis of the analogy between the handkerchief and the wedding sheets that it constitutes "the visual proof of their consummated marriage" (p. 363).[8] But the strawberry-spotted handkerchief is no more the "visual proof" of the consummation of Desdemona's marriage than it is of her adultery. It remains an "illustrative metaphor" that "gains more authority than the argument it was intended to supplement."

The best examples of what Lacan (1956) would call the "realist's imbecility" (p. 40) on this question of the marriage are the essays by T. G. A. Nelson and

---

[8] Perhaps unavoidably, Morrison (2012), too, resolves this crucial ambiguity in the play when she has her version of Desdemona tell Othello, "You broke my hymen and thought I was unfaithful the next day? Me?" (p. 41). Morrison thereby reverts to Cinthio's version of the story in which Disdemona is said to have "feared that through the abundance of lovemaking which he had with her he might have become tired of her" (Bullough, 1973, p. 248).

Charles Haines, on the one hand, and Norman Nathan, on the other. For Nelson and Haines (1983), it suffices to explain Othello's failure to perform his masculine duty to point to "the pressures placed on him during the couple's turbulent first night in Cyprus," and they assert that "the continued cleanliness of the sheets must mean that they have never been stained with virgin blood" (p. 1). To this Nathan (1988) rejoins, "if a lack of consummation is so important to this play, why isn't the audience so informed?," and "who is to say that the wedding sheets Desdemona requested were unstained!" (p. 81). Since "the existence of a hymen was considered proof of virginity," he continues, if the sheets were indeed unstained and Desdemona still a virgin, all she would have "had to do when Othello said he would kill her was to say something as obvious as, 'The proof of my virtue is even now in my body'" (pp. 81–2). The fact that she did not "offer the simplest and most obvious defense to save her life," according to Nathan, confirms that "a lack of consummation cannot be a part of Shakespeare's play" (p. 82).

As Neill (1989) has remarked, the "ironic effect" of Nathan's attempt at "a point-by-point rebuttal of Nelson and Haines … is to entrap him in the very speculation he wishes to cut short," and the reason why the audience is not "informed" about something "so important to this play" is "to make them ask the question" (p. 396). As with the color of the handkerchief, Shakespeare leaves the audience in suspense about something to which many people would like to have a definite answer. What cannot be disputed is that on every occasion when the newlyweds might be expected to consummate their marriage—at the outset, when they are both at the Sagittary, and subsequently on Cyprus—they are interrupted by alarms raised by Iago. "The purchase made, the fruits are to ensue; / That profit's yet to come 'tween me and you" (2.3.9–10), Othello says to Desdemona as they retire for the night after their reunion on the island. These lines, as Stanley Cavell (1979) has observed in an epistemological analysis, give us "reason to believe that the marriage has not been consummated," or at least "reason to believe that Othello does not know whether it has" (p. 131); and the uproar attendant on Iago's stage-managed brawl pitting the inebriated Cassio against Roderigo renders it doubtful whether they have managed to harvest their "fruits" even at this time.

Because of this pattern of what Heilman (1956) has called "imperfect consummation" (p. 189), Othello and Desdemona appear to be engaged in a perpetual act of *coitus interruptus*, which leads Cavell (1979) to assert that his "guiding hypothesis about the structure of the play is that the thing *denied our sight* throughout the opening scene … is what we are shown in the final scene, the scene of murder" (p. 132). Yet the question of Desdemona's virginity remains unresolved to the last, and the notion that it could be settled by an inspection of her vagina is the height of absurdity. The assumption that virginity is a matter of either/or, of which the presence or absence of the hymen can provide the "ocular proof," was deconstructed by Shakespeare long before Derrida (1972) instanced the membrane to illustrate his conception of a nonbinary logic: "the *hymen* is neither confusion nor distinction, neither identity nor difference, neither consummation nor virginity, neither the veil nor unveiling, neither the inside nor the outside, etc." (p. 43).

The undecidability of the color of the handkerchief comports with its function as a "supplement" for what Neill (1989) describes as "the hidden marriage-bed, an inalienably private location, shielded, until the very last scene, from every gaze" (p. 396). Despite Othello's protests that his "young appetites" are now "defunct," Greenblatt (1980) cites the ambiguity in Iago's declaration that he intends to "abuse Othello's ear / That he is too familiar with his wife" (1.3.395–6)—where "he" may refer not only to Cassio but to Othello himself—to argue that "the dark essence of Iago's whole enterprise" is "to play upon Othello's buried perception of his own sexual relations with Desdemona as adulterous" (p. 233), in keeping with the Christian teaching promulgated by rigorists from St. Jerome to Calvin that, in Calvin's words, the "man who shows no modesty or comeliness in conjugal intercourse is committing adultery with his wife" (qtd. p. 248). But, as Neill (1989) points out, Greenblatt's concern with Othello's "specifically sexual transgression" gains traction when "the ideas of adultery and disproportionate desire are specifically linked to the question of race" (p. 408). This is especially true in a culture in which adultery is understood to be "in the profoundest sense a violation of the natural order of things," and is thus viewed as "quite literally a kind of *adulteration*—the pollution or corruption of the divinely ordained bond of marriage" (p. 408).

Othello's internalization of Brabantio's view that his marriage to Desdemona is unnatural makes him susceptible to Iago's double truth that, as Neill (1989) has put it, infidelity is "the inevitable expression of Desdemona's Venetian nature, as the denizen of an unnatural city of prostituted adulterers," but also that it is "actually Desdemona's marriage that constituted the adulterous lapse, from which a liaison with one of her own kind would amount to … a penitent reversion to her proper nature" (p. 410). This line of argument has been extended by Arthur L. Little, Jr. (1993), who observes that "Cassio, like Othello, is a foreigner to the Venetian community, but while Othello represents the sinister outsider, the Florentine Cassio signifies a kind of white knight from abroad. He is the courtier *par excellence*, who is more 'gentleman' than any Venetian" (p. 314). Consequently, "Cassio and Desdemona have about them a social legitimacy that grants them cultural invisibility," and "without Desdemona's marriage to Othello, she and Cassio would be the play's most probable and conventional couple" (p. 314). Yet on the one occasion when Desdemona permits herself to imagine being with another partner, after she has asked Emilia to shroud her in her wedding sheets should she predecease her, it is not Cassio but her kinsman Lodovico whom she describes as "a proper man" (4.3.35); and Emilia concurs that she knows "a lady in Venice would have walk'd barefoot to Palestine for a touch of his nether lip" (38–9).

Shakespeare further blurs the lines between marriage and adultery in the interactions among the female characters whose destinies are determined by the handkerchief, all three of whom are white but of different social classes. Although Emilia is married, she attacks the double standard that makes it acceptable for men but not for woman to "change us for others" (4.3.97) and is comfortable with the idea of adultery on the part of a wife, calling it "a small vice" (69) for which she would "venture purgatory" (77). As a respectable lady-in-waiting, however, Emilia has only scorn for the courtesan Bianca. After the melee in which Cassio and Roderigo wound each other—and Iago then stabs Roderigo to death, though Emilia does not know this—Emilia echoes her husband's pronouncement that Cassio's injuries are "the fruits of whoring" (5.1.115) and brands Bianca a "strumpet" (121). Bianca, however, anticipates Engels when she retorts that Emilia's marriage is merely a form of legalized prostitution: "I am no strumpet, but of life as honest / As you that thus abuse me" (122–3).

If the marriage bed is "an inalienably private location," it is also a public space, not only because, as Neill (1989) observes, "it was the site of important public rituals of birth, wedding, and death" (p. 411) in the early modern period, but more radically because Shakespeare shows that the psychological (or "inside") cannot be disentangled from the social (or "outside"). With good reason, Little (1993) designates the "neither consummation nor virginity" that does and/or does not take place on the bed between Othello and Desdemona—of which the handkerchief becomes the "illustrative metaphor"—as "the 'primal scene of racism'" (p. 305) in the play. In his depiction of how racism infiltrates the most intimate areas of life, Shakespeare foreshadows Frantz Fanon (1952), whose chapter in *Black Skin/White Masks*, "The Man of Color and the White Woman," opens with an anecdote about "a black man of the darkest of hues, in full coitus with a vivacious blonde," who "exclaimed at the moment of orgasm: 'Long live Schoelcher!'" (p. 45)—Victor Schoelcher having been a politician and journalist who played a leading role in the abolition of slavery in 1848 during the French Second Republic.[9] The ecstatic ejaculation—in both senses—of Fanon's emancipated lover is at the

---

[9] Fanon incorrectly states that Schoelcher "had the Third Republic vote for the abolition of slavery" (p. 45).

opposite extreme from what Neill (1989) calls "the unnamed horror that Othello fatally glimpsed in the dark cave of Iago's imagination" (p. 412), but both furnish proof that culture is inescapable even in the "inalienably private" spaces of our minds.

In the final speech of the play, Lodovico commands Iago, but also the audience, to "Look on the tragic loading of this bed" (5.2.363), but immediately afterward ordains that what must be looked upon should not be seen: "The object poisons sight, / Let it be hid" (364–5). As Neill (1989) has commented, "the object that 'poisons sight' is nothing less than a mirror for the obscene desires and fears that *Othello* arouses in its audiences" (p. 412); and what we are being asked both to see and turn away from is "the site of racial transgression" (p. 395) as well as of "adulteration" in a more literal sense, inasmuch as Emilia's dying wish, "O lay me by my mistress' side" (5.2.237), must be a "dramatized stage direction" that means there are not two but three bodies in this terminal "alliance of corpses" (p. 407). Also buried in the rubble is Brabantio, of whom his brother Gratiano brings the news, "Poor Desdemon! I am glad thy father's dead. / Thy match was mortal to him, and pure grief / Shore his old thread in twain" (5.2.204–6). The Oracle has been destroyed by its own infernal machine.

6

In psychoanalysis, the primal scene in a literal sense refers to childhood memories or fantasies of witnessing sexual intercourse between one's parents that fuel the "obscene desires and fears" that are their derivatives in adult life. That this concept pertains not only to the audience's curiosity concerning the marriage between Othello and Desdemona but also to Othello's preoccupation with beholding Desdemona "topp'd" by Cassio is corroborated by the elaborate story he tells Desdemona about the history of the handkerchief after Iago has informed him that he saw Cassio wipe his beard with it. Demanding that she produce what Emilia has already revealed was his first gift to her, Othello admonishes his wife:

> That handkerchief
> Did an Egyptian to my mother give;
> She was a charmer, and could almost read
> The thoughts of people. She told her, while she kept it,
> 'Twould make her amiable, and subdue my father
> Entirely to her love; but if she lost it,
> Or made a gift of it, my father's eye

Should hold her loathed, and his spirits should hunt
After new fancies. She, dying, gave it me,
And told me, when my fate would have me wiv'd,
To give it her. I did so, and take heed on it,
Make it a darling like your precious eye.
To lose it or give't away were such perdition
As nothing else could match.

(3.4.55–68)

As Arthur Kirsch (1978) has noted, this passage depicts "the primitive world of a child's merger with his mother, and there is already implicit in what Othello says the seeds of his own primal betrayal" (p. 736). In the same way that his father would have "loathed" his mother were she "To lose it or give't away," Othello becomes enraged when Desdemona no longer has the handkerchief in her possession, though the effect is inverted because it is now not he but she who is accused of wanting to "hunt / After new fancies."[10] Rymer's comparison of the handkerchief to a "Garter" comes to seem inspired because it acquires the status of a fetish in the clinical definition of the term, without which Othello is incapable of experiencing desire for Desdemona.

Beneath the three-person structure of the primal scene and the Oedipus complex prominent in Othello's jealousy lies the dyadic relationship of mother and child. That Othello alleges the handkerchief had been given to his mother by an "Egyptian charmer" who "could almost read / The thoughts of people" reflects how he has been transported by its disappearance into a mental state in which fantasy is indistinguishable from reality. Othello's declaration that he felt "most happy" when he was reunited with Desdemona on Cyprus following their separation on the high seas becomes comprehensible in light of his disclosure that he received the handkerchief from his mother at her death. The thought of death brings a "content so absolute" to Othello's soul because it means being reunited with his mother, whose death is the primal betrayal that underlies his overwhelming separation anxiety and fears of abandonment. As Janet Adelman (1992) has remarked, his mother's death provides a template for the way that "the handkerchief becomes imaginatively present to Othello only in its absence, and after he believes that Desdemona has been lost to him" (p. 68).

---

[10] In *The Interpretation of Dreams* (1900), Freud illustrates the concept of "psychical displacements" with the way that "a lost handkerchief precipitates an outburst of rage" (p. 177) in Othello.

That Othello's bond with the mother has been traumatically severed is clear from his apology to the Venetian nobles for his unrefined language in recounting how he had wooed and won Desdemona:

For since these arms of mine had seven years' pith,
Till now some nine moons wasted, they have us'd
Their dearest action in the tented field.

(1.3.83–5)

Othello's revelation that he became a soldier at the age of seven means that his mother must already have died and that he kept the handkerchief through the intervening years. His bereavement was compounded by the fact that he was plucked from the world of women and thrust into the "tented field" at such a tender age. The "occupation" (3.3.357) that became the bulwark of Othello's identity—the "plumed troops and the big wars" that he believed to be the sources of his "tranquil mind" and his "content" (348–9)—was no more than a facade of masculinity that crumbled when his connection to Desdemona was broken because she lost the handkerchief that had belonged to his mother.

In the same speech in which he says he has been a soldier since his arms "had seven years' pith," Othello specifies that "some nine moons" have passed since he retired from military service, before being summoned by the Venetian Senate to lead the defense of Cyprus against the Turkish invasion. Nine months is, of course, the normal duration of a human pregnancy, while the moon is a feminine symbol. Since this interval coincides with his courtship of Desdemona, Othello's imagery signifies that he has reentered the maternal realm in which he experienced devastating losses and abandonments as a child. In his soliloquy lamenting all the reasons why Desdemona would leave him—his age, his race, his uncouth ways—Othello traces what he believes to be the inevitable fate of husbands to the moment of their conception in their mothers' wombs: "'Tis destiny unshunnable, like death. / Even then this forked plague is fated to us / When we do quicken" (3.3.275–7). No attachment to a woman can be secure for Othello because of the traumatic rupture of his bond with his mother, first through her death and then when he was sent off to the wars as a boy. Thus, when Othello exclaims, "Perdition catch my soul / But I do love thee! and when I love thee not, / Chaos is come again" (90–2), Shakespeare captures the primitive mental state in which psychic "chaos" and spiritual "perdition" supervene upon the loss of the woman who had filled the void left by a dead mother.

The preoedipal function of the handkerchief can be analyzed with the aid of Winnicott's classic paper "Transitional Objects and Transitional

Phenomena" (1953). Winnicott's thesis is that "the mother's main task (next to providing opportunity for illusion) is disillusionment" (p. 13), and when this process is traumatically disrupted because the mother has failed to place "the actual breast just there where the infant is ready to create, and at the right moment" (p. 11), the transitional object—such as a doll, blanket, or teddy bear—loses its paradoxical quality of belonging both to the inner world and to external reality and "may eventually develop into a fetish object and so persist as a characteristic of the adult sexual life" (p. 9). When this happens, Winnicott adds, the transitional object "becomes a thing in itself, something that has dangerous properties and must be mastered" (p. 19); and though the capacity for illusion "is inherent in art and religion," it "becomes the hallmark of madness when an adult puts too powerful a claim on the credulity of others, forcing them to acknowledge a sharing of illusion that is not their own" (p. 3).

Othello's process of disillusionment has been shattered first by his mother's death and by then being thrust from the world of women at the age of seven. As a result, the handkerchief "becomes a thing in itself" and acquires "dangerous properties" in his attempt to cope with the anxieties aroused by his fears of being abandoned by Desdemona. For Othello, illusion is not something that belongs, as Winnicott puts it, to "an intermediate area of *experiencing*" (p. 2), or what Winnicott will later call "potential space." Illusion has instead become *delusion* for Othello. He "puts too powerful a claim on the credulity of others," and his obsession with the handkerchief "becomes the hallmark of madness" when he murders Desdemona rather than listen to her protestations that she never gave it to Cassio.

In remarking how, in pathological cases, the transitional object may turn into a sexual fetish, Winnicott cites a paper by Mosche Wulff (1946), who offers the apropos clinical example of a four-year-old boy with enuresis who, after having been given a *handkerchief* by his mother to take with him to bed at night in order to alleviate his symptom, "demanded this handkerchief again and again, smelled of it, and refused to be parted from it," going so far as to stuff it into his pajamas and press it against his genitals, "saying that in this way it could not get lost" (p. 457). Wulff's paper is likewise cited by Martin Wangh (1950), who makes the point that "the handkerchief, on which the tragedy hinges, has long been identified as a fetish, the child's substitute for the breast," and on this basis claims that the strawberries are "easily recognized symbols of the nipples" (p. 212).[11] Since Winnicott's prototype for how the process of disillusionment can go wrong is the mother's failure to

---

[11] In Morrison's (2012) fantasia, Othello refers to Desdemona's "strawberry nipples" (p. 15) during his courtship of her.

present her breast to the infant at the moment he desires it and is thus "ready to create" the breast in his mind, Wangh's equation of the strawberries with nipples, which might otherwise seem fanciful, gains cogency when set in this interpretative context.

Whereas Winnicott invites us to see the handkerchief as a failed transitional object that becomes a fetish for Othello because of its association with the mother's breast, Freud (1927a) remains on the phallic level when he contends that fetishism in men stems from "the fright of castration at the sight of a female genital" (p. 154). Because to acknowledge that women lack a penis would mean that they themselves might suffer the same dreaded fate, the reality of this perception must be denied. The fetish provides reassurance against castration anxiety by serving as the surrogate for the hallucinated maternal penis on the woman's body, and thereby enables these psychically fragile men to perform sexually.[12] In addition to serving as a "disgruntled representative" of the "primal scene" of Desdemona having sex with Cassio, the handkerchief is the surrogate for Othello's fixation on his mother's "always absent thing." For Lacan (1973), finally, the handkerchief in *Othello*—like Poe's purloined letter and the girdle in *Sir Gawain and the Green Knight*— is what Gawain terms "the sign of sore loss" that exposes the "central lack expressed in the phenomenon of castration" (p. 77). It does so, however, not because the handkerchief represents the fantasy of the female penis as an anatomical organ, as it does for Freud, but rather because it signifies the phallus that seals the fates of the male and female characters alike when, as Lacan (1956) elaborates in his "Seminar" on Poe, "falling in possession of the letter … its meaning possesses them" (p. 44).

7

Just as Shakespeare's work lends itself to multiple psychoanalytic interpretations, it provides the ammunition that makes possible the deconstruction of psychoanalysis. For once we have located the handkerchief, in Derrida's (1975) words, "between the legs of the woman" (p. 66), have we not committed ourselves to accepting "the *transcendental* position of

---

[12] Without specifying a source, Newman (1987) writes that the handkerchief "*has been read* symptomatically as the fetishist's substitution for the mother's missing phallus" (p. 93; italics added). Since I advanced this argument in the 1985 essay that is the original version of this chapter, where I likewise proposed that the handkerchief could be viewed as a "floating signifier" and cited Wangh's interpretation of the strawberries as nipples, I cannot help wondering whether I am the elided subject in Newman's use of the passive voice.

the phallus" (p. 94), that is, to a doctrine of "castration as truth," in which something indeed "is missing from its place but the lack itself is never missing" (p. 63)?

In the final scene of the play, after Desdemona's murder, Othello seems to have forgotten his earlier story of how the handkerchief had been given to his mother by an Egyptian sorceress and offers a *second* account of its origin: "It was a handkerchief, an antique token / My father gave my mother" (5.2.216–17). One plausible explanation of this discrepancy is that the later, unembellished version, wrung from Othello by the horror of his deed— though he has not yet heard Emilia's testimony exonerating Desdemona—is the true one, and the account of its occult powers is a jealous fantasy he had fabricated to test Desdemona's love for him. But to Derrida (1975), any such attempt to assign priority to one story over another is yet another instance of trying to decide the undecidable, the point of their juxtaposition being the impossibility of arriving at any "unity of the signifier, that is, of the phallus" (p. 66).

How, then, are we to choose between these views of the handkerchief as, in de Man's words, "devoid of meaning and function" other than a "desire for substitution" and the "hidden, censored desire" of the Oedipus complex? Johnson (1977) points the way forward with her critique of Derrida's "Disseminar." "When Derrida says that a letter *can* miss its destination," she observes, "he reads 'destination' as a place which preexists the letter's movement" (p. 248). But to hypostasize the notion of "destination" in this manner is to miss Lacan's point, which is that "the letter's destination is not its literal addressee, nor even who possesses it, but whoever is possessed by it" (p. 248). Thus, Johnson continues, "the very rhetoric of Derrida's differentiation of his own point of view from Lacan's" bears out what Lacan is saying, and "Derrida's remarks against psychoanalysis ... are not objections to psychoanalysis but in fact a profound insight into its very essence" (p. 245). Even the difficulty in reconciling Othello's two narratives concerning the handkerchief is not an argument against psychoanalysis since it is the French psychoanalyst Green (1969) who insists that "the mystery of this double origin" must not be attenuated by "any simplistic explanation such as, for example, that the Moor made it all up in order to frighten Desdemona" (p. 100).

The conundrums that both invite and resist solution in *Othello* range from textual cruxes to enigmas at the heart of the play's concern with issues of race and sexuality, though to distinguish between text and theme is itself artificial. The cruxes include the choice between the First Quarto's "base Indian" and the First Folio's "base Judean" (5.2.347) in Othello's suicide speech, the choice between the Quarto's "tragic lodging of this bed" and the Folio's "tragic loading of this bed" (393) in Lodovico's closing speech, and the choice between the Quarto's "world of sighs" and the Folio's "world of kisses" (1.3.159) in Othello's account of how Desdemona responded to the story of his life. The enigmas, as we have seen, include the questions of the color of the handkerchief and whether the marriage of Othello and Desdemona was consummated.

In his authoritative study of textual problems in Shakespeare, John Jones (1995) has made the case that "Quarto and Folio *Othello* represent two acting texts of the one play" (p. 242). Although "we cannot be sure" that the 1622 First Quarto version is identical to what "King James heard" when Shakespeare's new play was performed in the Banqueting Hall at Whitehall on November 1, 1604, Jones argues, "we can be confident it was close" (p. 242). There is likewise a "high probability" that sometime after May 1606, when the Act to Restrain Abuses of Players required the removal of the fifty-two oaths found in the Quarto, Shakespeare "wrote out the whole of *Othello* afresh" (p. 242), "making a few big changes and many small ones" (p. 249), including the addition of Desdemona's Willow Song in Act 4, Scene 3, of which Emilia sings the refrain at her death, as well as the tweaks in diction of which I have given a minute sample. This, Jones maintains, is what became the 1623 First Folio version. This is all, in Jones's considered opinion, evidence that Shakespeare "was bent on improving his play" (p. 245), and—apart from the expurgations demanded by the Act of Parliament—guided by "the single thread of the worse that becomes the better" (p. 243).

It follows from Jones's reasoning that, whenever there are variants, the Folio text should be preferred to the Quarto, except when it comes to the oaths, as the expression of Shakespeare's mature artistic judgment. It is not certain that this is the right decision in every case, but there is a "high probability" of its being correct. This is equivalent to concluding that, on balance, the handkerchief is more likely to have been white than black, or that the marriage was not consummated than that it was, though these are purely interpretative and not textual questions, and one could argue them either way. Even when it comes to the textual cruxes, moreover, since Shakespeare wrote both the Quarto and the Folio versions of the play, the two together may be said to form a "hypertext" in which both variants—"base Indian" and "base Judean," for example—contribute to the semantic field and should be viewed as complementary rather than mutually exclusive. At every turn, what we have, as Derrida has said, is "neither identity nor difference," a situation in which it is both necessary and impossible to choose.

In no respect is this truer than that of the mystery of Othello's race. But I mean this less as it pertains to what Neill (1989) has described as the "sterile and seemingly endless debate about the exact degree and significance of

Othello's racial difference" (p. 392) than to what it means that Othello is called a "Moor," although—once again—these two issues cannot be completely disentangled. Iago's declaration in a soliloquy that, were Desdemona to ask him to do so, Othello would "renounce his baptism, / All seals and symbols of redeemed sin" (2.3.343–4), makes it clear that Othello was not born a Christian, but as Julia Reinhard Lupton (1997) underscores, "the play never decisively determines whether he has converted from a pagan religion or from Islam" (p. 73).[13] On the one hand, Brabantio fumes that if Desdemona is allowed to marry Othello "Bond-slaves and pagans shall our statesmen be" (1.2.99); on the other, Iago spurs Roderigo to attempt to murder Cassio in order to forestall Othello's departure from Cyprus and taking Desdemona with him "to Mauritania" (4.2.224), a homeland of Muslims in Northwest Africa. Vitkus (2019), therefore, falls into the same trap as Smith and Boose of assuming what cannot be proved when he posits that, because "Othello is known throughout the play as 'the Moor,'" this means that he is not only a "figure of blackness" but also "retains traces of Islamic identity" (p. 218) from his past life, though this is not to say that Othello did *not* have an Islamic identity either.

The crucial passage comes in Othello's suicide speech when, preparing to stab himself with a weapon concealed on his person—having already been deprived of two others he had brandished—Othello recalls the crowning moment in which he demonstrated his loyalty to the city of Venice:

> Set you down this;
> And say besides, that in Aleppo once,
> Where a malignant and a turban'd Turk
> Beat a Venetian and traduc'd the state,
> I took by th' throat the circumcised dog
> And smote him—thus.
>
> (5.2.351–6)

In inflicting on himself the violent death he had once visited on "a malignant and a turban'd Turk," Othello is at once executioner and victim, insider and outsider. But does Othello's use of the epithet "circumcised dog" to describe the slain Turk constitute a confession that he himself is circumcised? If read in this way, the passage would support the thesis of his repudiated "Islamic identity" since Muslims as well as Jews, unlike Christians, practice

---

[13] Morrison (2012) has Othello's mother say to Desdemona's mother, Madam Brabantio, "I spoke to my gods for guidance" (p. 17), after Othello committed suicide in remorse for murdering Desdemona, which makes him a polytheistic pagan rather than a Muslim.

ritual circumcision, generally at the age of seven, which we have seen to be fraught with significance in the play as associated with traumatic ruptures. It could, however, also be read as Othello's reaffirmation of his bond with the Christians of Venice because he is *not* circumcised, even as he slays himself as mercilessly as he had the enemy alien, in which case it would mean he had practiced a "pagan religion" in Africa before he converted to Christianity.

As I have noted, the first recorded performance of *Othello* was at Whitehall before King James I on November 1, 1604. The significance of this fact has been explored by Emrys Jones (1968), who proposes that, "like *Measure for Measure, Macbeth*, and possibly other plays" written in the years following James's accession to the English throne in March of 1603, *Othello* was "intended to reflect James I's opinions and tastes" (p. 47). In addition to many other attributes for which James could be lauded—including "his wisdom and learning, his piety, and his love of peace," as well as for having united the crowns of England and Scotland—"he could also be celebrated as a poet-king" (p. 47). And of all James's poems and translations, "the best known was his original heroic poem *Lepanto*" (p. 47), first published in 1591 in a collected volume of James's verse and reprinted separately in London in 1603 with the title *His Maiesties Lepanto, or, Heroicall Song.*

By linking *Othello* to James's poem, Jones throws into sharp relief the topicality of the concern with the "Cyprus wars" (1.1.50) that figures so prominently at the outset of the play. As Jones (1968) explains, the battle of Lepanto was "the culmination of a military episode which had begun in 1570 with the Turkish attack on Cyprus, at the time one of Venice's richest territorial possessions," and it was this naval conflict on October 7, 1571, "the only great Christian victory over the Turks in the sixteenth century" (p. 47), that was the monarch's theme. As Jones further points out, "Shakespeare has so arranged it that the night of Othello's elopement with Desdemona is also the night when the news arrives in Venice of the movements of the warlike Turkish fleet," and the historical context makes it possible to date the action of *Othello* "to the crucial years round about 1570, the year of the Turkish attack on Cyprus" (p. 49). Indeed, Cinthio's novella, which was published in 1565, had been "written before the Turkish attack" and "makes no mention of a Turkish threat to Cyprus" (p. 50), so this entire dimension of the play was added by Shakespeare to his source. It would therefore have seemed to "Shakespeare's first audience" that everything in Act 1 was "moving towards the naval action which culminated in Lepanto and which was fought over the same issue as that presented in the play: the possession of Cyprus" (p. 50). Surprisingly, however, "as soon as the main characters are arrived in Cyprus, the action moves into an entirely fictive realm. ... The military and naval clash which we seem led to expect never takes place. For instead of a battle between Christians and Turks Shakespeare substitutes a storm which disperses the Turkish fleet" (p. 50).

As in his other great tragedies, Shakespeare allows the "great stage" of politics to recede into the background in *Othello* in order to undertake his culturally informed psychoanalysis of the hero. But this does not mean he has forgotten the poem by the most important member of his "first audience." For in the opening lines of his "Heroicall Song," James promises to tell of the "bloody battell bolde, / … / Which fought was in Lepantoes gulfe, / Betwixt the baptiz'd race, / And circumcised Turbaned Turkes" (qtd. in Vitkus, 2003, p. 80); and it is clear that Shakespeare has recalled this passage in the "baptiz'd" Othello's memory of how he took the life of the "circumcised" and "turban'd Turk."

But though Shakespeare's borrowing from *Lepanto* underscores the centrality of the issue of Othello's religious as well as racial identity to the play, it does not settle the question of whether Othello himself had been circumcised. Indeed, it further complicates it because, after the Christian victory, a chorus of Venetian citizens in James's poem praises God for having "redeemed" them "from cruell Pagans thrall" (qtd. in Vitkus, 2003, p. 80), which establishes that Muslims could be included along with polytheists in the class of "pagans." But this should not surprise us in a play in which everything that we might like to see remains veiled. And if the "floating signifier" around which the characters' destinies pivot is not only the "disgruntled representative" of the primal scene but also simultaneously a "feminine napkin" as well as a transitional object *and* a phallic signifier in the senses of both Freud and Lacan, then it is indeed—in Barbara Johnson's words—"not a thing or the absence of a thing … nor an organ or the absence of an organ, but a *knot*" in which Desdemona's hymen and Othello's foreskin "can neither be definably separated nor compatibly combined." Rymer spoke more truly than he knew when he protested that Shakespeare ought to have called the play "the *Tragedy of the Handkerchief.*"

Chapter 6

"The Dark and Vicious Place"

The Dread of the Vagina in *King Lear*

"*At puberty a normal boy has already acquired a conscious knowledge of
the vagina, but what he fears in women is something uncanny, unfamiliar,
and mysterious. If the grown man continues to regard woman as the
great mystery, in whom is a secret he cannot divine, this feeling of his can
only relate ultimately to one thing in her: the mystery of motherhood.
Everything else is merely a residue of his dread of this.*"
—Karen Horney, "The Dread of Woman"

1

As a belated fellow traveler of what Harold Bloom has sardonically termed the
School of Resentment, I have been impressed by the collective achievements
of feminist and new historicist scholarship in transforming the received
understanding of classic works of Western literature. Thus, although "I find
[he] names my very deed of love" (1.1.71) for Shakespeare, I cannot agree with
Bloom's (1994) contention that "nothing crucial in this largeness is culture-
bound or gender-confined" (p. 52). With respect to *King Lear*—from which
I have culled Regan's words—arguably the summit of the Western canon,
Bloom insists that "the flames of invention burn away all context and grant us
the possibility of primal aesthetic value, free of history and ideology" (p. 65).
In order to challenge Bloom's idealist aesthetics, I shall draw on a tradition
of criticism whose touchstones include Coppélia Kahn's essay, "The Absent
Mother in *King Lear*" (1986), and Janet Adelman's *Suffocating Mothers* (1992)
in order to read the play through a feminist psychoanalytic lens. Its guiding
hypothesis, first systematically expounded by Kahn in *Man's Estate* (1991), is
that Shakespeare's plays are written from a male perspective and at their core
depict conflicts of masculine identity.

My point of entry into *King Lear* is furnished by Edgar's lines in the
final scene in which he recounts to Albany how, while in disguise as Poor

Tom, he encountered his eyeless father: "and in this habit / Met I my father with his bleeding rings, / Their precious stones new lost" (5.3.189–91). The phrase "precious stones," referring to the eyeballs that had been gouged out by Cornwall's sword, also carries the connotation of "testicles," while "rings," completing the metaphor of eyes as jewels and signifying the gaping sockets, has the additional meaning of "vagina."[1] Gloucester's blindness is thus a symbolic castration that leaves him with a bleeding vagina—or rather two bleeding vaginas—on his face in place of his excised testicular eyeballs.

Shakespeare's conflation of blindness with castration underpins the connection between the fates of Lear and Gloucester. It is elementary that *King Lear* is structured by a double plot that juxtaposes its two protagonists, but what has not been sufficiently recognized is that Lear and Gloucester form two halves of a single masculine psyche whose histories must be interpreted with continuous reference to one another. This contention is supported not only by the fact that both Lear and Gloucester are fathers whose wives are absent from the play and whose offspring are polarized into "good" and "evil" figures, but also by their attitudes toward sexuality.

The fleeting prelude to the tragic symphony is a scene involving Gloucester, Edmund, and Kent, in which, as Stanley Cavell (1969) has brought out in a profound exegesis, Gloucester's coarse humor deflects his shame at having sired an illegitimate son. Not by chance, his question to Kent, "Do you smell a fault?" (1.1.16), combines an obscene allusion to the vagina as a "flaw" or "crack" with the meanings of "fault" both as a moral defect and as a break in the line of scent in hunting (Astington, 1985). These associations to the olfactory apparatus prefigure not only the Fool's misogynistic barb that "Truth's a dog must to kennel, he must be whipt out, when the Lady Brach may stand by the fire and stink" (1.4.111–13), but also Lear's revulsion at the "stench" (4.6.129) of the female genitals at the height of his madness.

The counterpart to Gloucester's transgression is Lear's fantasy that he has been cuckolded by his wife, an anxiety first intimated in his repudiation of Cordelia in the opening scene: "Here I disclaim all my paternal care, / Propinquity and property of blood" (1.1.113–14). Later, when confronted by the treachery of his elder daughters, Lear brands Goneril a "Degenerate bastard" (1.4.262) when she demands that he reduce the number of his retainers, and then admonishes Regan when she professes to be pleased to see him at her doorstep, "If thou shouldst not be glad, / I would divorce me from thy mother's tomb, / Sepulchring an

---

[1] Shakespeare uses "stones" with the same bawdy connotation in Thisbe's lament to Wall for separating her from Pyramus in *A Midsummer Night's Dream*, "My cherry lips have often kiss'd thy stones" (5.1.190), as well as Shylock's protest in *The Merchant of Venice* at the loss of "two rich and precious stones, / Stol'n by my daughter" (2.8.20–1), while Gratiano refers to "keeping close Nerissa's ring" (5.1.307) at the close of the same play.

adult'ress" (2.4.131–3). These lines containing the odd trope of "divorce" from a "tomb"—meaning efface her from his memory, though "womb" might seem more appropriate—are the only allusion to Lear's wife in the play. Lear's attacks on his daughters establish a parallel between his own lawfully begotten progeny and Edmund, Gloucester's literal bastard. Although only Gloucester's adultery is actual, both protagonists blame the conception of their repudiated children on the women in question—namely, Lear's wife and the anonymous whore with whom Gloucester enjoyed "good sport" (1.1.23) when he fathered Edmund. The character of Gloucester is unique in Shakespeare's canon in portraying male adultery as having tragic consequences, although these stem not from the husband's wronging of his wife, who goes unmentioned in the play, but rather from the way that the illegitimate son returns from an unexplained absence of "nine years" (1.1.32) to exact retribution from his prodigal father.

Lear and Gloucester's psychic twinship is borne out by the inscription of the female genitals on Gloucester's face as a result of his blinding. An analogous process occurs when Lear's attempt to combat the threat of female sexuality is subverted by the welling up within himself of the femininity he has repudiated. Upon finding Kent placed in the stocks by Regan and Cornwall, he exclaims: "O how this mother swells up toward my heart! / *Hysterica passio*, down, thou climbing sorrow, / Thy element's below" (2.4.56–8). In the Renaissance medical lexicon, for which the most commonly cited source is Edward Jorden's treatise *A Brief Discourse of a Disease Called the Suffocation of the Mother*, "mother" means the womb, and Lear diagnoses his malady as a suffocation caused by its wandering. Thus, just as Gloucester's "bleeding rings" corroborate Edgar's pitiless judgment on the dying Edmund, "The dark and vicious place where thee he got / Cost him his eyes" (5.3.173–4), so, too, Lear, a male hysteric, fears that he harbors within himself the internal organs of the despised female body. The mothers who are demeaned and excluded from the play return as spirits to possess the minds and bodies of both patriarchs.

2

A study of how Shakespeare transmuted the baser metal of his sources into the gold of his masterpiece is of immense value in understanding his artistry, though these changes cannot be detected merely by reading the play. The story of the legendary King Lear was told and retold numerous times by authors from Geoffrey of Monmouth to Spenser, but Shakespeare's principal source for his main plot was the anonymous play *The True Chronicle Historie of King Leir*, probably written in the early 1590s and published in 1605 as he was about to begin work on his tragedy.[2] By contrast with the abundant sources available to him for the Lear plot, Shakespeare's sole source for the Gloucester plot is Book 2, Chapter 10 of Sir Philip Sidney's *Arcadia*, from which he appropriated the episode of the Paphlagonian king. This king has two sons, one legitimate and loyal, the other a bastard and treacherous; the latter not only deceives his father into hating and trying to kill the good son but also blinds him and seizes the crown. The parallel to Gloucester, Edgar, and Edmund is evident, and Shakespeare is indebted to Sidney for crucial details, including the blind father's attempt to persuade the loyal son who has been guiding him to assist him in committing suicide by jumping off a rock.

But Gloucester is an earl rather than a king, and when the heroes of Sidney's pastoral romance are compelled "to seeke some shrowding place within a certaine hollow rocke offering it unto them ... against the tempests furie," they encounter "an aged man, and a young ... both poorely arrayed, extreamely weather-beaten" (Bullough, 1973, pp. 402–3). In Shakespeare this becomes the scene in which Lear, accompanied by the Fool and Kent, comes upon Edgar disguised as Poor Tom in the hovel where he has taken shelter from the raging storm and shows his solidarity with the Bedlam beggar by stripping off his own clothes. Shakespeare thereby substitutes Lear for Sidney's dethroned king, who is in most respects his model for Gloucester, and we continue to be reminded of Lear when Sidney's blind father recounts that, after being undone by his "unlawfull and unnaturall sonne," he "had left my self nothing but the name of a King," and even those who pitied him "yet durst they not shewe it, scarcely with giving me almes at their doores" (p. 405). Thus, Shakespeare has conflated Lear and Gloucester in his borrowings from Sidney, which adds a latent dimension to the way that Gloucester's blinding is a symbolic castration mirroring Lear's feminization by his hysteria.

The workings of Shakespeare's imagination are further illuminated by what Bloom (1973) would call his "poetic misprision" of another of his most important sources for *King Lear*, Samuel Harsnett's *A Declaration of Egregious Popish Impostures*—a debunking by a pious Anglican chaplain of exorcism as a charade practiced above all by Catholics but also by Puritans—published, like Jorden's *Brief Discourse*, in 1603. In "Shakespeare and the Exorcists," his exemplary new historicist essay showing how much more Shakespeare took from Harsnett than "the names of the foul fiends by whom Edgar, in his disguise as the bedlam beggar Poor Tom, claims to be possessed" (p. 94), and other bits of local color, Stephen Greenblatt

---

[2] Quotations from *The True Chronicle Historie* are taken from Geoffrey Bullough's (1973) invaluable anthology of Shakespeare's sources, with line numbers given parenthetically.

(1985) quotes a passage that must have attracted Shakespeare's attention. The passage is "a sardonic explanation of why, despite the ... rule that only old women are to be exorcised," the Jesuit ringmaster "Father Edmunds and his crew have a particular fondness for tying in a chair and exorcising young women" (p. 120). Harsnett writes, "It would (I fear me) pose [i.e., foil] all the cunning Exorcists, that are this day to be found, to teach an old corky woman to writhe, tumble, curvet, and fetch her morris gambols" (pp. 120–1). As Greenblatt notes, "Shakespeare's eye was caught by the word 'corky,'" and he applies it to Gloucester in the horrific scene in which Cornwall commands his servants to tie his victim to a chair and "Bind fast his corky arms" (3.7.29), as he puts out first one eye and then the other. By transvaluing the epithet that Harsnett had used to describe an "old woman" so that it refers to Gloucester's withered arms, Shakespeare buttresses the feminine identification inherent in his blinding.

As Geoffrey Bullough (1973) points out, moreover, it is not only Edgar and Gloucester but also Lear who "shows the influence" (p. 300) of Harsnett when he attempts to suppress his "climbing sorrow" in Act 2, Scene 4. Here Shakespeare recalls the case of Robert Maynie, one of the confederates (or dupes) purported by Father Edmunds to be possessed by devils, "who had 'a spice of the *Hysterica passio*, as seems, from his youth, hee himself terms it the Moother'" (p. 300). Bullough bolsters his claim with the observation that "the word 'meiny' ('Household') is used in the same scene" (p. 300) by Kent. Jorden (1603), too, employs the expression "*Passio Hysterica* ... In English the Mother, or the Suffocation of the Mother" (p. 25); and his project closely resembles that of Harsnett in seeking to expose—albeit from a medical rather than a theological perspective—the delusions of those who "are ignorant of the strange affects that naturall causes may produce, and ... have sought above the Moone: ascribing these accidents either to diabolicall possession, to witch-craft, or to the immediate finger of the Almightie" (p. 2). Shakespeare may well have consulted Jorden as well as Harsnett to glean what it meant for Lear to be afflicted by "the Mother," but the evidence of his extensive indebtedness to the latter—as well as his use of the word "meiny" and perhaps also that he says "*Hysterica passio*" rather than "*Passio Hysterica*"—attests that *A Declaration of Egregious Popish Impostures* was the primary source for his depiction of Lear as a male hysteric.

As Lear succumbs to madness in response to his daughters' cruelties, he experiences a conflict between his desires to grow angry and to weep, which are coded, respectively, as masculine and feminine forms of protest. When Goneril demands that he halve his train of 100 knights, Lear responds:

> Life and death! I am asham'd
> That thou hast power to shake my manhood thus,
> That these hot tears, which break from me perforce,
> Should make thee worth them.

> (1.4.296–9)

He continues:

> Old fond eyes,
> Beweep this cause again, I'll pluck ye out,
> And cast you, with the waters that you loose,
> To temper clay.

> (301–4)

Later, when Regan seeks to deprive him of every last knight, he implores the gods, "touch me with noble anger, / And let not women's weapons, water-drops, / Stain my man's cheeks!" (2.4.276–8).

Each of these passages deprecates crying as effeminate, and collectively they underscore the threat to Lear's manhood posed by the tears that, like the "mother," involuntarily rise up within him when humiliated by his daughters. Lear vows that he would sooner "pluck out" his "old fond eyes" rather than permit them to give way to weeping. But if weeping means becoming feminized, then his proposed remedy—to blind himself—also entails self-castration and leads to the same result. As Thomas Clayton (1983) has observed, the same "ominous subliminal irony" (p. 125) occurs in Lear's initial resolution to divide his kingdom "that future strife / May be prevented now" (1.1.44–5), since "prevented," besides meaning "forestalled," has the etymological meaning of "anticipated," and thus signals that by his abdication Lear has brought about the very "strife" he consciously sought to avoid. When, in the climactic encounter with Gloucester in Act 4, Scene 6, Lear breaks through to genuine compassion, his empathy is expressed by accepting the tears formerly disdained as unmanly: "If thou wilt weep my fortunes, take my eyes" (4.6.176).

3

The antithesis between anger and weeping confirms that the play's dichotomizing of "good" and "evil" characters is based on a gender polarity. The character of Kent furnishes an apt example. When, after his banishment in the opening scene, he returns as Caius to offer his services to Lear, the king poses a series of questions. Concerning his age, the disguised Kent responds: "Not so young, sir, to love a woman for singing, nor so old to dote on her for any thing. I have years on my back forty-eight" (1.4.37–9). Having already declared that he "eat[s] no fish" (17)—anachronistically signaling that he is a Protestant as well as his aversion to the female genitals—Kent presents himself as immune to feminine seductions, and only after he has done so does Lear break off his interrogation and pronounce Kent worthy to be his follower.

Whereas Lear is torn between anger and tears, Kent's utter masculinity, expressed philosophically by his stoicism, obviates any such psychic fissure. "Anger hath a privilege" (2.2.70), he tells Cornwall to justify his beating of Oswald, for which he is placed in the stocks. Kent's ideology of gender fuels his contempt for Oswald, his antipode in terms of attitudes to service. The barrage of epithets with which Kent reviles Oswald culminates with calling him "the son and heir of a mungril bitch" (22–3)—an apt insult given Oswald's function as Goneril's lackey, but one that reflects Kent's misogyny. When Kent threatens to "daub the wall of a jakes" with Oswald (66–7), his regression to anality is reinforced by the fact that for him phallic heterosexuality is not even an option.

A similar imperviousness to female charms characterizes Edgar, whom many commentators have felt to function, in Bloom's (1994) words, as "Shakespeare's personal representative in the play" (p. 67)—an insight enhanced by Greenblatt's (1988) analysis of how in his feigned madness Edgar embodies "the inauthenticity of a theatrical role" (p. 117) that "elicits from us complicity rather than belief" (p. 119). Edgar's celibacy is crucial to Shakespeare's refusal so much as to hint at a love interest between him and Cordelia, who never speak to each other in the tragedy.[3] Indeed, Edgar is positively hostile to women. His verdict that Edmund's malevolence is due to the "dark and vicious place" where he was conceived is endorsed by the play. Apart from Edmund's soliloquy that opens Act 1, Scene 2, in which he rails against the "plague of custom" (3) that has discriminated against him both on account of his illegitimacy and by virtue of being a younger brother in a system of inheritance governed by the rules of primogeniture, only in Gloucester's callous banter in the opening scene is the possibility intimated that Edmund's wickedness could be due to any social stigma. As Kent alleges of Oswald, Edmund is "the son and heir of a mungril bitch," irrevocably doomed by the whore at his origins.

The motherless Edgar's function as the voice of patriarchy in the play is highlighted when, disguised as Poor Tom, he constructs an imaginary history of his past life as a courtier who "serv'd the lust of my mistress' heart,

---

[3] That Nahum Tate concludes his Restoration adaptation, which eliminates the character of the King of France, with the marriage of Edgar and Cordelia points up the calculated oddity of Shakespeare's design.

and did the act of darkness with her" (3.4.86–8). He warns his companions in the hovel to "Let not the creaking of shoes nor the rustling of silks betray thy poor heart to woman" (94–6). Lear deludedly believes that Poor Tom, like himself, has been betrayed by his daughters; but the disguised Edgar's contempt for women, like the disguised Kent's, feeds into Lear's obsessions. On another level, Edgar's feigned sexual history can be seen as an unpacking of his father's "old lecher's heart" (111), with which he has unconsciously identified himself despite his disavowals.

In addition to Edgar and Kent, the only other character left standing at the end of the play is Albany, who also earns his survival by purging himself of any feminine taint. In the first act, Goneril reviles his "milky gentleness" (1.4.341)—that is, his effeminacy—when he queries her actions, and he barely registers a protest. Once Albany learns of Gloucester's blinding and the casting of Lear out into the storm, however, he denounces his wife's demonic nature: "Proper deformity shows not in the fiend / So horrid as in woman" (4.2.60–1). This view of Goneril and Regan is also Lear's, and again it is ratified by the play. Whatever their limitations, Albany, Edgar, and Kent are portrayed as virtuous characters, and this virtue is in each case predicated on an immunity to, or escape from, the threat posed by female sexuality.

In taking a census of the virtuous characters one must not overlook the Fool, and his role, too, comes into focus when mapped onto the grid of gender. If Cordelia's relationship to Lear is defined by his identity as father, and Kent's by his identity as king, the Fool mirrors Lear in his existential capacity as a man. The Fool functions as Lear's psychotherapist, whose task is to confront him with the painful truths he would otherwise prefer to ignore. Despite—or because of—his devotion to Lear, the Fool preys on Lear's misogyny and sexual anxiety. Even before Lear voices his suspicion that Goneril is a "Degenerate bastard," the Fool insinuates: "'The hedge-sparrow fed the cuckoo so long, / That it had it head bit off by it young'" (1.4.216–17). This jingle refers to the female cuckoo's practice of depositing her eggs in the nests of other birds, which upon hatching consume the food of the "legitimate" fledglings, causing them to starve to death—or, in this instance, even devour the mother bird. The motif of cuckoldry recurs in the Fool's explanation for why a snail has a house: "to put 's head in, not to give it away to his daughters, and leave his horns without a case" (1.5.30–2). Having surrendered his crown, Lear becomes an impotent, and hence feminized, male. In a passage that conflates gender and generational reversals, the Fool tells Lear that he has grown full of songs "ere since thou mad'st thy daughters thy mothers" and "gav'st them the rod, and put'st down thine own breeches" (1.4.172–4). As Roberto Speziale-Bagliacca (1998) remarks, the Fool implies that Lear his given his elder daughters his "phallus-scepter" (p. 111), with which they can penetrate as well as beat his proffered buttocks.[4]

If Edgar is the voice of patriarchy, the Fool is the voice of Lear's unconscious. As such, he articulates the castration anxiety that is at once the cause and effect of Lear's loss of royal power. This function helps to explain such otherwise obscure jests as the Fool's parting address to the audience at the close of Act 1: "She that's a maid now, and laughs at my departure, / Shall not be a maid long, unless things be cut shorter" (1.5.51–2), where "things" has a phallic meaning and the allusion to castration is explicit in "cut shorter."

Concomitant with the Fool's obsession with castration is his view of the female genitals as a place of absence and foul odor. Again, there are sexual undertones to the Fool's answer to the riddle about why the nose is placed in the middle of the face: "Why, to keep ones eyes of either side 's nose, that what a man cannot smell out, he may spy into" (1.5.22–3). Echoing the reference to "smelling a fault" in the Gloucester plot and reinforcing the psychic indivisibility of Lear and Gloucester, the Fool's lines contrast the senses of sight and smell, which are coded respectively as masculine and feminine. The Fool's riddle emphasizes the nose's location in the middle of the face. As he earlier tells Lear, "Thou hast par'd thy wit o' both sides, and left nothing i' th' middle" (1.4.187–8), where "nothing i' th' middle" equates the nose with the vagina, now defined not in terms of its odor but its lack.

As so often, the strands of Shakespeare's sexual imagery are mutually reinforcing. Only when "nothing" is accorded its vaginal significance, as it has been by David Willbern (1980) in a scintillating essay, can the phallic resonance of "thing" be properly heard, and vice versa. Because Shakespeare, like Freud, presupposes a phallocentric model of sexual difference based on an opposition between male presence and female absence, Lear's characterization of Edgar, in the latter's disguise as Poor Tom, as "unaccommodated man" takes on a gendered meaning. When Lear describes Tom as "the thing itself"

---

4 In disowning Cordelia, Lear likens her to "The barbarous Scythian, / Or he that makes his generations messes / To gorge his appetite" (1.1.116–18), while he raves on the heath that Poor Tom has taken revenge on his flesh for having begotten "pelican daughters" (3.4.75). Yet it is Lear himself who is consumed with oral-sadistic rage, and the pelican—traditionally an emblem of maternal sacrifice because it sheds its blood to feed its young—undergoes a mutation to connote ruthless destructiveness on the part of Tom's imaginary offspring, and by extension Lear's own heartless daughters. In *The True Chronicle Historie*, Leir initially describes himself as being "as kind as is the Pellican, / That kills it selfe, to save her young ones lives" (512–13)—where, as in Shakespeare, the father in fantasy becomes the mother—whereas later in the play it is the loyal Perillus who invites Leir to "Feed on this flesh, whose veynes are not yet dry" (2125), to which the king responds, "I am no Caniball, that I should delight / To slake my hungry jawes with humane flesh" (2130–1).

(3.4.106), the genital connotation of "thing" makes Tom into an emblem of the exposed penis. The phrase "unaccommodated man" thus undergoes a mutation in which "man" comes to designate not human beings in general but males in particular, just as in his counterfeited ravings, "Pillicock sat on Pillicock-Hill" (76), Edgar employs a term of endearment for the penis, while "Pillicock-Hill" refers to the *mons Veneris*. Lear psychotically identifies with Poor Tom because he sees in the Bedlam beggar a visible manifestation not only of suffering humanity but also of himself as a "discarded father" (72) as well as of his own mutilated member.

4

Nowhere can the interdependence of character and language be seen more clearly than in Lear's tirade against female sexuality in Act 4, Scene 6, instigated by being brought face-to-face with the eyeless Gloucester:

> Down from the waist they are Centaurs,
> Though women all above:
> But to the girdle do the gods inherit,
> Beneath is all the fiends': there's hell, there's darkness,
> There is the sulphurous pit, burning, scalding,
> Stench, consumption. Fie, fie, fie! pah, pah!
> Give me an ounce of civet; good apothecary,
> Sweeten my imagination: There's money for thee.

(4.6.124–31)

In branding the female genitalia a "sulphurous pit," Lear's speech brings to a climax the olfactory imagery in the play. The anatomical references here warrant a sexual reading of Lear's apostrophe to the storm as "You sulph'rous and thought-executing fires" (3.2.4). Indeed, if the storm represents nature as an unleashed female body wreaking its destructive havoc, then it becomes plausible to construe Lear's exhortation to blow "Till you have drench'd our steeples, drown'd the cocks" (3) as a depiction of the endangered penis. Thus, the storm can be viewed as a primal scene fantasy, which exists in the mind of Lear as a character but also becomes real in the universe of the play. The storm is a hallucination of sexual intercourse as an act of violence, in which the pregnant female body is at once menacingly powerful and equated with the "thick rotundity o' th' world" that the masculine thunder threatens to "strike flat" (7).

In addition to evincing repugnance toward the "hell" of the vagina, Lear's rant bifurcates the female body, doing so not once but twice in parallel constructions ("Down from the waist," "but to the girdle"). The line of demarcation is the loins, with the human or divine region being "all above" and the bestial or demonic region yawning "beneath." The "horizontal" split in Lear's image of the female body is replicated by the "vertical" split in the structure of the tragedy between the vicious and virtuous characters—that is, Goneril and Regan and their allies, on one hand, and Cordelia and her allies, on the other.

The idealization of Cordelia is the obverse of the demonization of Goneril and Regan and should thus be viewed as a symptom of, rather than an antidote to, the play's misogyny.[5] Thus, when a Gentleman affirms to the fleeing Lear, "Thou hast one daughter / Who redeems nature from the general curse / Which twain have brought her to" (4.6.206–8), he speaks on behalf of the ideology endorsed by the play. As Adelman (1992) has argued, the "condensation of Adam and Eve with Goneril and Regan" in the word "twain" used by the Gentleman "offers a revised version of the fall, making our fallen nature entirely derivative from Eve and her daughters" (p. 119). The oppressive implications of the veneration of Cordelia are evident in Lear's eulogy over her dead body, as he strains to hear the words that will never issue from her lips: "Her voice was ever soft, / Gentle, and low, an excellent thing in woman" (5.3.273–4). That women should be chaste, silent, and obedient is a cornerstone of patriarchy, and Lear's praise of Cordelia merely gilds the shackles he has imposed on her.

As the distillation of the patriarchal ideal of femininity, Cordelia is the logical culmination of the misogyny that distinguishes the virtuous male characters in the play. But whereas Edgar, Kent, and Albany all survive and their fates vindicate a belief in poetic justice—exemplified by Albany's vow that "All friends shall taste / The wages of their virtue, and all foes / The cup of their deservings" (5.3.303–5)—Cordelia's death shatters this morality-play pattern and casts *King Lear* into the abyss of tragedy. The rivalry between good and evil siblings is found in both the Lear and the Gloucester plots, but the Lear plot, with its venerable history and multiple sources, provides the prototype, while the enmity between Edgar and Edmund refracts that between Cordelia and her sisters. The priority of the Lear plot shows that the polarization of characters in *King Lear* cannot be explained by Shakespeare's

---

[5] In *A Thousand Acres* (1991), a novel set on an Iowa farm in the 1970s, Jane Smiley implicitly critiques the idealization of Cordelia (Caroline)—and reworks Shakespeare's incest theme—by narrating the story of *King Lear* from the point of view of Goneril, here named Virginia ("Ginny"), who, along with her middle sister, Rose, has been sexually abused during childhood by their father.

concern with moral issues, but that this fairy-tale pattern is an epiphenomenon of the underlying gender dynamics.

The action of *King Lear* moves implacably toward a climax in which Edmund kills Cordelia—that is, the epitome of masculinity slays the quintessence of femininity, as these stereotypes are defined in patriarchal culture. But since Edmund's virility is tainted by his identity as a "whoreson" (1.1.24)—the same word is used by Kent to abuse Oswald (2.2.18)— his masculinity, like that of Lear and Gloucester, is haunted by a spectral femininity. Indeed, Edmund's hypersexuality, which culminates in his adulterous entanglements with both Goneril and Regan, is inherited from his father, whose licentiousness led to his blinding by Cornwall after having been betrayed by Edmund. "But have you never found my brother's way, / To the forfended place?" (5.1.10–11), the widowed Regan demands of Edmund, referring to her sister's vagina as the property of her husband Albany; and all the men who have not abjured this temptation—Lear, Gloucester, Edmund, Oswald, and Cornwall—pay with their lives for their contamination by female sexuality.

The dilemma of Lear's elder daughters, conversely, is that they cannot achieve their political aims without allying themselves with the Bastard. Emancipated women are by definition evil and dangerous, but they are barred by their gender from openly seeking power in Shakespeare's patriarchal universe. Thus, although Edmund orders the murder of Cordelia, he operates as Goneril and Regan's instrument. The formulation that, in the tragic climax of the play, masculinity slays femininity should accordingly be modified to read that the demonic half of the bifurcated image of the female body destroys its angelic counterpart.

First the Lear plot and then the Gloucester plot are set in motion when Cordelia and Edmund, respectively, utter the word "nothing." This verbal echo signals the latent antagonism between these two characters. And since an allusion to the vagina always hovers subliminally in "nothing," both plots of the play explore the dark continent of female sexuality. A comic antecedent for Shakespeare's erotic obsessions is furnished by *The True Chronicle Historie* when Cornwall and Cambria—the prospective grooms of Gonorill and Ragan, respectively—contemplate their good fortune as Leir's heirs. To Cornwall's musing, "If I have one halfe, and you have the other, / Then betweene us we must needs have the whole," the Welshman bawdily responds that they will be receiving more from his daughters than just land, "The hole! how meane you that? 'Zlood, I hope, / We shall have two holes between us" (452–5). Not to be outdone, the sisters in their own private colloquy jest that Cordella would make a fit wife for a parson because, as Ragan says, such men will often marry women "with nothing," which Gonerill pretends to believe is an impossibility, "With nothing! ... why, are there any such?," until Ragan clarifies, "I meane, no money" (490–2). Since "nothing" is a synonym for "vagina," to marry a woman "with nothing" is a paradoxical double negative meaning "no vagina," which even the most impoverished bride possesses. When the Fool calls Lear "an O without a figure" and flings the taunt, "I am a Fool, thou are nothing" (1.4.192–4), he highlights the dethroned king's identification with the femininity he repudiates.

The phrase used by the Fool to impugn Lear's wit, "nothing i' th' middle," amplifies the connections between the nose and the vagina in the imagery of the play. In his misogynistic diatribe, Lear maligns the "simp'ring dame, / Whose face between her forks presages Snow" (4.6.118–19). Although his consciously intended meaning is that an affected woman's ostensible disdain of sexuality belies her "riotous appetite" (123), the phrase "face between her forks" insinuates that the face and what lies between her legs are one and the same. In George Wilkins's *The Miseries of Enforced Marriage* (1607)—a play pervasively indebted to *King Lear* as well as to *Twelfth Night*—the Clown banters with the libertine Ilford, "Nothing comes of nothing" (46).[6] Then, as Scarborrow diffidently woos Clare, who becomes his betrothed but then commits suicide when he is forced by his guardian to marry another woman, she stands in silence as Scarborrow resolves to "walk by her, in hope she can open her teeth" (196). He continues in soliloquy: "I think if I should take up her clothes too, she would say nothing to me" (199–200). As Frank Whigham (1996) observes, "if he lifts her skirts" Scarborrow "thinks he'll find the notorious ... *vagina dentata*, the fiendish face between her forks, saying 'nothing'" (p. 137). By adding the detail of the teeth, Wilkins, who is now generally agreed to have collaborated with Shakespeare on *Pericles*, hones the equation between the mouth and the vagina posited in *King Lear*; and Whigham's commentary captures how "nothing" issues from both pairs of not only Clare's but also Cordelia's female lips.

The associations between the nose as well as the mouth and the vagina, mediated by the references to "nothing," illuminate the excruciating ending of Shakespeare's tragedy, in which Lear dies comforted by the delusion that the hanged Cordelia has come back to life: "Pray you undo this button. Thank you sir. / Do you see this? Look on her! Look her lips, / Look there, look there!" (5.3.310–12). In his final speech, Lear hears a reprise of the

---

[6] I have modernized the quotations from *The Miseries of Enforced Marriage* (Blayney, 1964) and given the line numbers parenthetically.

"nothing" uttered by Cordelia at the outset, though it now takes the form not of a spoken word but of the eternal silence of death. Lear's exhortation to "undo this button" is usually understood to pertain to his own clothes—or, by extension, to his body, seen as the garment of the soul—but the button might instead belong to Cordelia, whose breath Lear wishes to resuscitate. In that case, it would mean that Lear in dying desires to expose his daughter's body, much as Oedipus uncovers the body of his hanged wife and mother when he seizes the brooches from Jocasta's robe to put out his eyes.

5

In "The Theme of the Three Caskets" (1913a), Freud takes the test imposed by Portia's deceased father on her suitors in *The Merchant of Venice*, which requires them to choose between gold, silver, and lead caskets as the condition for gaining her hand in marriage, as the starting point for a meditation on the numerous myths and fairy tales in which a man must choose one of three women, frequently sisters, "of whom the third is the most excellent one" (p. 293). It is, of course, the lead casket that contains Portia's portrait and—after the failures of the Princes of Morocco and Arragon—is correctly chosen by her beloved Bassanio. If this were a dream, Freud says, "it would occur to us at once that caskets are also women, symbols of what is essential in woman, and therefore of a woman herself" (p. 292). Bassanio, therefore, is choosing among three women, synecdochically represented by the genitalia that are, in Freud's estimation, "what is essential" about them.

Freud then points to the "many hidden similarities" (p. 292) between the love test in *The Merchant of Venice* and the test King Lear imposes on his daughters where they must each say how much they love him as a condition for receiving their share of the kingdom he has resolved to divide among them. The key common denominator is that, just as Cordelia demurs, "I cannot heave / My heart into my mouth" (1.1.91–2)—a reticence that Lear misinterprets as rejection and causes him to disown and disinherit her—so, too, the "paleness" of the lead casket that Bassanio declares moves him "more than eloquence" (3.2.106) signifies "dumbness" or silence. Because Freud finds evidence both in dreams and in fairy tales that "dumbness is to be understood as representing death," this leads him to conclude that the third of the "sisters between whom the choice is made" signifies not merely "a dead woman," but rather "Death itself, the Goddess of Death" (p. 296). In Greek mythology, the women are incarnated in the Three Fates, of whom once again the third, Atropos, "stands for 'the ineluctable'—Death" (p. 298).[7]

Freud's analysis highlights the crossing of love and death in the human psyche that, as we have seen in *Tristan* and *Othello*, becomes tragic when it leads to a violation of the incest taboo. Whereas in all the narrative and poetic accounts with which Shakespeare was certainly familiar—Geoffrey of Monmouth, Holinshed, *The Mirror for Magistrates*, and *The Faerie Queene*— the story of King Lear is set in a context that extends backwards and forwards in time for generations, *The True Chronicle Historie* omits the prehistory and opens with Leir's resolution to abdicate and divide his kingdom among his daughters and the husbands he intends to choose for them. This is already a bold stroke of compression by the anonymous dramatist, but in contrast to Shakespeare's play, where the only mention of Lear's wife comes in his threat to Regan to "divorce" himself from her "mother's tomb" if she, like Goneril, should prove undutiful, in the old play Leir's first speech announces the completion of the funeral rites for his "deceast and dearest Queen" (2), without whom his daughters lack "their mothers good advice" (12), which he, as a father, is unable to provide; and it is for this reason that he has decided to "resigne these earthly cares" (27) and yield the crown to his heirs.

By setting the plot in motion with the death of Leir's wife, *The True Chronicle Historie* provides a readily comprehensible motive for his actions. The opposite is true of Shakespeare's play, in which what King Lear terms his "darker purpose" (1.1.36) lacks any obvious explanation. In this departure from his principal source, Shakespeare implements what Greenblatt (2004) has argued is the "crucial breakthrough" he made with the writing of *Hamlet*, which enabled him to achieve "an intense representation of inwardness" by means of "a new technique of radical excision" (p. 47). As Greenblatt elaborates, "Shakespeare found that he could immeasurably deepen the effect of his plays … if he took out a key explanatory element, thereby occluding

---

[7] The resemblances between *King Lear* and *The Merchant of Venice* are heightened by Portia's complaint to Nerissa in her opening scene about how hard it is to "have the will of a living daughter curb'd by the will of a dead father" (1.2.24–5), which makes it appear that the casket test has been designed by her father to prevent her from marrying. Yet as Nerissa assures her, her father was "ever virtuous" (27) and foresaw that Portia would "never be rightly chosen by any rightly but one who you shall rightly love" (32–3). What seems to be an insuperable obstacle thrown up by the father to his daughter's marriage turns out in the comedy to be his way of facilitating it, just as in *The Tempest* Prospero feigns to have "too austerely punish'd" (4.1.1) Ferdinand for wanting to marry Miranda, although it was all part of his plan to bestow on the future King of Naples "a third of mine own life" (3)—an enigmatic expression that equates his daughter with the "Goddess of Death," in keeping with the mythic pattern of three women elucidated by Freud.

the rationale, motive, or ethical principle that accounted for the action to be unfolded," and he names this novel technique for representing inwardness "strategic opacity" (p. 47).

Shakespeare's use of "strategic opacity" in eliminating the death of Lear's wife from the opening scene of his play goes hand in hand with another consequential innovation. Whereas in *The True Chronicle Historie* all three of Leir's daughters are unmarried at the outset and the key feature of his "sudden stratagem" (78) to test their love for him is that each must "Accept a husband, whom my selfe will woo" (87), in Shakespeare's *King Lear* both Goneril and Regan are married when the play opens, leaving only Cordelia without a consort. Discerning the subterranean link between these changes reveals that, although Shakespeare's revolutionary technique for representing inwardness hinges on "occluding" the "explanatory elements" for the actions of his characters, this does not mean that no such explanations can be found. The crucial point is that Lear decides to divide his kingdom precisely when the time has come for Cordelia to marry. Although his announcement of his intention to abdicate precedes the arrival of Cordelia's suitors, Burgundy and France, this inverts the causal connection between these events. Unconsciously, Lear desires to maintain his incestuous hold over Cordelia, and he imposes the love test as a strategy to disinherit his youngest daughter so that she will be unacceptable to either of her prospective husbands and remain in his thrall forever.

Lear knows Cordelia well enough to intuit that she will not join her elder sisters in the bidding war for his affections. His anger at her recalcitrance, although genuine on one level, masks a deeper level of satisfaction at her failure. Lear's true surprise comes when France (in words that echo Sonnet 116, "Love is not love / That alters when it alteration finds") still wants to marry Cordelia even after she has forfeited her dowry: "Love's not love / When it is mingled with regards that stands / Aloof from th' entire point" (1.1.238–40). That Cordelia has two suitors mirrors the fact that she has two married sisters, and the clash between Burgundy and France is an externalized representation of the conflict between the materialistic side of Lear's psyche that confuses love and money and the spiritual side that is capable of genuine love.

Lear's use of the phrase "darker purpose" not only conveys that his true motives for dividing the kingdom are unconscious but also highlights that they are incestuous in nature. The changes rung by Shakespeare on the word "dark" throughout the play—in Lear's revulsion at the vagina as a place of "darkness," Poor Tom's babbling that he did "the act of darkness" with his mistress, and Edgar's telling Edmund that "the dark and vicious place" where he was begotten by their father "cost him his eyes"—all confirm that Lear desires to possess Cordelia in a sexual sense. Whereas the flattering speeches of Goneril and Regan gratify Lear's narcissistic fantasy of being loved infinitely, even though they are already married, Cordelia—like Desdemona in the same situation—tells her father that she wishes to love him "According to my bond, no more nor less" (1.1.93). The "bond" that Cordelia seeks to assert in the face of Lear's exorbitant demands is the incest taboo, which requires that he be prepared to set her free to give herself body and soul to a younger man.

The True Chronicle Historie suppresses the prehistory found in the nondramatic sources, but Shakespeare—in addition to dispensing with any rational explanation for Lear's actions—writes a play that has not only no past but also no future. There is only the nightmare of the eternal present of a consummated incestuous relationship. Shakespeare's elimination of the wives of Lear and Gloucester at the outset comes full circle when the surviving cluster of purified men is bereft of women with whom to have children. An elegy for the death of time tolls in Edgar's words with which the tragedy ends, "we that are young / Shall never see so much, nor live so long" (5.3.326–7).

6

After Cordelia leaves with France in Act 1, Scene 1, she is not seen again until what modern conflated editions call Act 4, Scene 4, when she returns alone to England at the head of the French armies. *The True Chronicle Historie* follows Holinshed, according to whom the Gallian king leads the triumphant invasion that restores Leir to his throne, Strikingly, the only scene in the 1608 Quarto version of *King Lear* to be entirely cut from the First Folio is Act 4, Scene 3, in which a Gentleman explains France's absence to Kent: "Something he left imperfect in the state, which since his coming forth is thought of, which imports to the kingdom so much fear and danger that his personal return was most requir'd and necessary" (3–6). As Gary Taylor (1980) has astutely noted, this attempt "to 'motivate' the French King's absence raises an awkward question which would be better left unasked. In this case, as in others, no excuse at all is better than a poor one" (p. 30). In another illustration of "strategic opacity," Shakespeare presumably excised this scene (and other references to France) from the Folio because he realized that it would be better to allow Cordelia's unaccompanied return simply to follow from the inexorable logic of events in the play, without the fig leaf of a cover story.

Cordelia must return to England without her husband because to bring about a reunion between father and daughter is the "darker purpose" not only of Lear as a character but also of the play as a whole. The counterpart to this structural imperative is the storm, which unleashes its destructive force when Lear has been cast out by Goneril and Regan and descends into madness, thereby making external reality indistinguishable from his inner world. Shakespeare took the idea of the storm from *A True Chronicle Historie*, but his use of it vindicates the "general proposition" advanced by Greenblatt (2015) with respect to Shakespeare's borrowing of the word "corky" from Harsnett: "the closer Shakespeare seems to be to a source … the more devastating and decisive his transformation of it" (p. 120). In the earlier play, the storm happens without forewarning when Leir and his faithful counselor Perillus—the model for Kent—are about to be murdered by a messenger suborned by his two daughters. Leir warns the assassin that hell is waiting to swallow him, at which point the "almightie power" whom Perillus calls "just *Jehova*" (1649) intervenes in the form of thunder and lightning. The villain cries out in fear, "This old man is some strong Magician" (1637), before letting fall his daggers and departing.

In both plays, the storm is summoned by Leir/Lear's fantasy, but whereas *The True Chronicle Historie* is a tragicomedy governed by a providential order whose existence is revealed by his imprecation, in Shakespeare's "devastating transformation," as Greenblatt (2015) observes, "all attempts by the characters to explain or relieve their sufferings through the invocation of transcendent forces are baffled" (p. 123). The storm therefore becomes a natural phenomenon the only explanation for which is dramaturgical. Like Lear's decision to divide his kingdoms, it is a "theatrical illusion" (p. 121) of the highest order, which requires that one look beneath the surface to detect the psychological motivation that supplies the "key explanatory element" strategically effaced by Shakespeare from his plot.

Lear's longing for reunion with Cordelia reaches its apotheosis in the "birds i' th' cage" (5.3.9) speech in which he exults, notwithstanding his political defeat, because they are imprisoned together and he can now say— like Othello when he rejoins Desdemona on Cyprus—"If it were now to die, / 'Twere now to be most happy." When Lear spurns Cordelia in the opening scene, he vows never to "see / That face of hers again" (263–4), but to do so remains his heart's desire, and it is consummated in his final lines when he implores the triad of choric commentators to look not only at her face but specifically at her lips: "Look on her! Look her lips, / Look there, look there!" (5.3.311–12).

In all the versions of the story from Geoffrey of Monmouth to Holinshed, Lear rules for several years after being restored to the throne, and upon his death is succeeded by Cordelia, who, however, kills herself when her sisters' sons overthrow and imprison her. The manner of her suicide is specified only in *The Mirror for Magistrates*, where it is said to be by a knife. Spenser follows this outline in Book 2, Canto 10 of *The Faerie Queene*, but is the first to have her hang herself. As Bullough (1973) recognizes, "this probably suggested the manner of her death in *Lear*, and Edmund's intention to suggest suicide by hanging" (p. 334). Shakespeare's radical departure from this tradition, which is a concomitant of his abrogation of the future, is to cause Cordelia to be hanged while in the prison with Lear, thus allowing them to die together and giving added poignancy to his references to her lips and breath. And since Lear's entrance bearing Cordelia in his arms constitutes a reversed Pietà, as though he were the Virgin Mary and she the crucified Christ, the relationship between father and daughters is interchangeable with that between mother and son.

Whereas in the main plot of *King Lear* Shakespeare explores the incest theme through Lear's relationship with his daughters, in the subplot he explores the theme of patricide through Gloucester's relationship with his sons. As two halves of a single masculine psyche, Lear and Gloucester together delineate both facets of the Oedipus complex. Edmund obliquely avows his wish to kill his father in the forged letter he attributes to Edgar, "'If our father would sleep till I wak'd him, you should enjoy half his revenue for ever'" (1.2.52–3), and then gulls the old man into believing that Edgar had tried to "Persuade me to the murther of your lordship" (2.1.44). Edmund carries out his plan when he denounces Gloucester as a traitor, which results in his blinding by Cornwall, who rewards Edmund by naming him the Earl of Gloucester, enabling him to usurp the place not only of his father but also of his legitimate elder brother.

Although Edgar in disguise as Poor Tom says in an aside that he is pretending to aid Gloucester in his plan to commit suicide by throwing himself off a Dover cliff with the best of intentions—"Why I do trifle thus with his despair / Is done to save it" (4.6.34–5)—it is ironically he and not Edmund who in the end causes Gloucester's death. Edgar's baffling delay in unmasking himself when he had the opportunity, like the anomalies in the Lear plot, is a dramaturgical necessity to bring about this ending. As he explains to the assembled company in the final scene, he had committed a "fault" (with all the fraught overtones of that word) by not revealing himself to his father "Until some half hour past" (5.3.193–4), when he had again been unrecognizable in the suit of armor he had donned for his duel with Edmund. Overwhelmed by the discovery that the son whom he had so grievously wronged is still alive, the old man's "flaw'd heart / (Alack too weak the conflict to support!) / 'Twixt two extremes of passion, joy and grief, /

Burst smilingly" (197–200). Piety and patricide are commingled in Edgar's report of Gloucester's death, which, like the death of Lear as he gazes on Cordelia, fuses "joy and grief" and is at once a wish-fulfillment on the part of the bifurcated figure of the son and a punishment for having unconsciously desired to kill his father and marry his mother.

The incest theme that drives the Lear plot spills over into the Gloucester subplot since the sexual rivalry of Lear's older daughters over Edmund reenacts their contest for their father's favor in the opening scene. For his part, Edmund's complicity in Goneril's desire to suborn the "speedy taking off" (5.1.65) of Albany reprises the blinding of his father by seeking to kill the husband in order to be able to marry the wife, with the ultimate aim of securing the English throne by murdering Lear and Cordelia. And because the sisters are first-order blood relatives, Edmund's illicit relations with them constitute an incestuous as well as adulterous triangle. Lear's fusion in death with Cordelia is paralleled by Edmund's confession, after having been mortally wounded in his duel with the challenger whom Goneril terms his "unknown opposite" (5.3.154), upon learning that Goneril had stabbed herself in the heart after poisoning Regan to death, "I was contracted to them both; all three / Now marry in an instant" (5.3.229–30). The converse of this carnal *Liebestod* is the separation enforced by the play between Edgar and Cordelia, which, combined with Cordelia's return to England without her husband, makes possible Lear's reunion with the reincarnation of his mother in her final iteration as what Freud (1913a) beautifully calls "the silent Goddess of Death" (p. 301) that has from the outset been his "darker purpose."

Shakespeare's plays tap into the deepest human longings, but the forms these longings take reveal the ideological imprint of the age and culture in which they arose. If we have profited from the interrogations of feminism as well as psychoanalysis, it should be possible to sort out the essential from the contingent, to acknowledge our nostalgia for the oceanic feeling without stigmatizing its portal as a "dark and vicious place," and to continue to emancipate ourselves from the legacy of patriarchy even as we reread the literary masterpieces in which its misogynistic fantasies are most powerfully inscribed.

Chapter 7

Dissociation and Decapitation

"'Do you recollect the date,' said Mr. Dick, looking earnestly at me, and taking up his pen to note it down, 'when King Charles the First had his head cut off? ... Because, if it was so long ago, how could the people about him have made that mistake of putting some of the trouble out of his head, after it was taken off, into mine?'"

—Charles Dickens, *David Copperfield*

1

With the benefit of hindsight, T. S. Eliot's theory of the "dissociation of sensibility" in seventeenth-century English poetry, promulgated in his essay "The Metaphysical Poets" (1921), can be deemed to have been the most seminal contribution to English literary history of the twentieth century. As is well known, Eliot contended that whereas "the poets of the seventeenth century, the successors of the dramatists of the sixteenth century, possessed a mechanism of sensibility which could devour any kind of experience," during the seventeenth century a "dissociation of sensibility set in from which we have never recovered; and this dissociation, as is natural, was aggravated by the influence of the two most powerful poets of the century, Milton and Dryden" (p. 247).

The enduring influence of Eliot's theory can be seen in the way that it continues to be invoked and paraphrased, often without explicit acknowledgment.[1] It has, however, also been buffeted, and nowhere more soundly than by Frank Kermode in his early book *Romantic Image* (1957). Kermode proceeds by attacking the historicity of Eliot's formulation. He

---

[1] Tacit restatements of Eliot's theory include Blair Worden's (1987) reference to "the fundamental shift that, when every reservation has been made, the middle of the seventeenth century brought about" (p. 178), as well as Francis Barker's (1984) assertion concerning the same period that "in the space of a relatively few years a new set of relations between state and citizen, body and soul, language and meaning, was fashioned" (p. 10).

demonstrates that analogous attempts to pinpoint periods of unified sensibility were made by a host of Symbolist writers of the early twentieth century, but they ascribed the rupture to incompatible moments: Pound and T. E. Hulme blamed Petrarch, Yeats put it at around 1550, and so on. As Kermode observes, "It would be quite as reasonable to locate the great dissociation in the sixteenth or the thirteenth [century] as in the seventeenth; nor would it be difficult to construct arguments for other periods" (p. 157). Branding all such attempts "quite useless historically," Kermode concludes: "A once-for-all event cannot happen every few years" (p. 161).

Although Kermode shows convincingly that the concept of a dissociation of sensibility is only one example of a broader trend in modernist thought, it does not follow that Eliot's model has been discredited. As Kermode points out, Eliot presupposes "an implicit parallel with the Fall. Man's soul, since about 1650, had been divided against itself, and it would never be the same again—though correct education could achieve something" (p. 156). But, Kermode admonishes, "it is not merely a matter of wrong dates; however far back one goes one seems to find the symptoms of dissociation" (p. 156).

As in his elucidation of the representative nature of Eliot's theory, Kermode hits the mark both in comparing the dissociation of sensibility to the Fall and in dating it to "about 1650." But what appears to have gone unremarked is that the proximate cause of the dissociation must therefore be the execution of King Charles I on January 30, 1649. As I shall document, the regicide was collectively experienced by Englishmen as a trauma for which the Fall, like the crucifixion of Christ, served as a prototype. Thus, to acknowledge that Eliot's theory relies on a parallel with the paradigm of the Fall does not, as Kermode supposed, deprive it of historicity, but is paradoxically one of the strongest arguments in its favor.

But if Eliot's formulation can withstand an objection on the grounds that it is ahistorical, what about his conservative bias? In the preface to *For Lancelot Andrewes* (1928), Eliot himself defined his outlook as "classicist in literature, royalist in politics and anglo-catholic in religion" (p. ix). In the same year, Eliot published an anonymous review in the *Times Literary Supplement* in which he lauded Sir Robert Filmer, the leading seventeenth-century proponent of the divine right of kings, as a writer "whose greatest fault was that his own time, as well as all succeeding times, had little sympathy with him," and whose views have never been "refuted or replaced" (qtd. in Bradshaw, 1995, p. 376). According to Eliot, there is nothing wrong with Filmer, and his assertion that Filmer had not been "refuted" is curious given that *Patriarcha*, probably written in the 1640s but not published until 1680, elicited a vigorous rebuttal from Locke in the first of his *Two Treatises on Government*. Eliot, it might be said, is nothing more than a latter-day Filmer, and the dissociation of sensibility a Royalist reading of history that amounts to an exercise in nostalgia.

Notwithstanding the justice of this critique, Eliot's royalism, like Filmer's, contains a kernel of psychological truth that transcends its politics. Intriguingly, Norman O. Brown begins his visionary work *Love's Body* (1966) by proposing that Freud's myth of the primal horde in *Totem and Taboo* "seems to project into prehistoric times the constitutional crises of seventeenth-century England" (p. 3). Brown compares Filmer to Freud in that he "derives constitutional structure from a primal or prehistoric mythical family, from the paternal powers of our father Adam" (p. 4). "Like Freud," Brown elaborates, "Filmer attributes to the primal father unlimited power over his sons, including the power and propensity to castrate them" (p. 4). Citing Locke's definition of Filmer's idea of fatherhood as a "strange kind of domineering phantom," Brown offers a psychoanalytic interpretation of Locke's ideological struggle with Filmer: "Locke kills Filmer's fatherhood, lays that phantom. The battle of the books reenacts Freud's primal crime" (p. 4).

Freud, who wrote to his fiancée Martha Bernays in 1882 that "the reign of the Puritans and Oliver Cromwell" was for him "the most interesting period" of English history, named his second son Oliver after Cromwell and described *Paradise Lost* to the Viennese bookseller, Hugo Heller, as one of his "favourite books" (qtd. in Jones, 1953, pp. 179, 245). He thus had more than a passing interest in the revolutionary upheavals of seventeenth-century England, and Brown highlights how closely Freud's paradigm in *Totem and Taboo* fits this historical crisis. As Filmer's title underscores, divine right monarchy is the apotheosis of the ideology of patriarchy, according to which the king is the father of the state and succession is determined by primogeniture. The day prior to his execution, King Charles I met with his daughter Elizabeth and youngest son Henry. To Henry he said, "'They will cut off my head, and perhaps make thee a king. But mark what I say, you must not be a king so long as your brothers Charles and James do live.'" To this the boy replied, "'I will be torn in pieces first,'" which caused the king to "rejoice exceedingly" (Lagomarsino and Wood, 1989, pp. 133–4). As the moment at which England literally acted out the killing of the royal father in the person of the king, the execution of Charles I is not only a collective trauma but also one to which a Freudian perspective is perfectly suited.

In "The Metaphysical Poets" (1921), quoting passages from Donne and Tennyson, Eliot attributes the differences between these writers to "something which happened to the mind of England" (p. 247) in the intervening period. By hypostatizing an entity called the "mind of England," which had been afflicted by the process of "dissociation," Eliot casts his project as a kind of cultural psychoanalysis, although he would have rejected the association with Freud. But if we assimilate the theories of Freud and Eliot, the execution of Charles I becomes comprehensible as a classic instance of the pattern in which, as Freud says in *Totem and Taboo* (1913b) of the sense of guilt produced by the primal patricide, "the dead father became stronger than the living one had been" (p. 143). It is though Freud were commenting on the regicide, which took place outside the Palace of Whitehall where court masques had been performed, when he adds: "The scene of the father's vanquishing, of his greatest defeat, has become the stuff for the representation of his greatest triumph" (p. 150). If, as both Franco Moretti (1982) and David Scott Kastan (1986) have argued, the repeated representations of the "deconsecration of sovereignty" in plays from Sackville and Norton's *Gorboduc* (1561) to Shakespeare's *Richard II* (1595) and Ford's *Perkin Warbeck* (1634) contributed to a transformation in English political culture that made it possible actually to depose and execute a king in 1649, the other side of this insight into the subversive power of theater is that the killing of Charles I took on the qualities of a tragedy that made the king's vanquishing the prelude to his posthumous triumph.

The delayed revenge of Charles I came eleven years later with the collapse of the Commonwealth and the restoration of his son Charles II to the throne. But in a further historical irony, the ultimate victory of Parliament was sealed in the Glorious Revolution of 1688 when the Whig supporters of limited monarchy deposed Charles II's Catholic brother James II and installed the Protestant William of Orange, who was married to James's daughter Mary, in his place. It is fitting that the "battle of the books" between Locke and Filmer during the Glorious Revolution reenacted the one that had taken place following the regicide between Milton in *Eikonoklastes* and Charles I in *Eikon Basilike*, his purported spiritual autobiography.[2] Milton, like Locke, was trying to "lay the phantom" of divine right kingship; and Locke, like Milton, was obliged in the preface to the *First Treatise* (1690) to defend himself against the "reproach of writing against a dead adversary" (p. 172) since Filmer had been dead for nearly three decades when *Patriarcha* appeared in 1680. But Milton, unlike Locke, had to answer the king himself, who had just been slain in the flesh. Thus, it was necessary to kill the king twice—once in his natural body in the 1640s and again by bloodlessly deposing his royal body in the 1680s—before the psychic task of deconsecrating sovereignty could be brought to completion.

---

[2] For purposes of my argument, I shall set aside the controversies concerning the authorship of *Eikon Basilike* and treat it as a work written by Charles I himself.

2

The comparisons of the king to Christ, and of his murder to the Fall, were above all Royalist tropes. In *Richard II*, the Queen chastises the Gardener who foresees her husband's overthrow for making "a second fall of cursed man" (3.4.76), and the Bishop of Carlisle warns that the ensuing civil war will cause England to be called "The field of Golgotha and dead men's skulls" (4.1.144). Even the moderate Edward Hyde, 1st Earl of Clarendon, affirmed in his posthumously published *History of the Rebellion* (1702–4) that the execution of Charles I was "the most execrable murder that was ever committed since that of our blessed Saviour" (p. 315), while in his "Elegy upon King Charles the First, murdered publicly by his Subjects" the metaphysical poet John Cleveland pledged that his "faith, resting on th' original [Christ], / Supports itself in this, the copy's fall" (5–6), and lamented: "This stroke hath cut the only neck of land / That between us and this red sea did stand" (11–12).[3] There is likewise the eyewitness testimony of Philip Henry, a childhood playmate of Charles II's and James II's who became a Nonconformist divine, that he had heard "a Grone by the Thousands then present, as I never heard before & desire I may never hear again," as well as that of the anonymous author of *The Bloody Court; or the Fatall Tribunal,* who makes explicit the collective nature of the trauma caused by the beheading of the King: "This Bloody Stroke being struck upon the royal neck ... it seemed rather to fall upon the people than the King" (qtd. in Maguire, 1989, p. 3).

But these reactions on the Royalist side are less revealing as cultural barometers than those coming from partisans of the Commonwealth cause. No poet takes us deeper into the enigmas of the seventeenth century than Andrew Marvell, and no poem is more pivotal to understanding his response to the regicide than "An Horatian Ode upon Cromwell's Return from Ireland." Written in 1650, the "Ode" shows the erstwhile Royalist coming to terms with the destiny of his allegiance to the Commonwealth that he would make his choice for next decade, but its emotional center is the image of the "*Royal Actor*" (53) on the "*Tragick Scaffold*" (54), with the sense of loss attendant on the killing of the King.

Freud's thesis that "the scene of the father's vanquishing, of his greatest defeat, has become the stuff for the representation of his greatest triumph"

---

[3] The quotation from Cleveland is to the edition of Saintsbury (1968).

is borne out by Marvell's chilling lines paralleling the founding of the Commonwealth with that of Rome:

> This was that memorable Hour
> Which first assur'd the forced Pow'r.
>   So when they did design
>   The *Capitols* first Line,
> A bleeding Head where they begun,
> Did fright the Architects to run;
>   And yet in that the *State*
>   Foresaw it's happy Fate.

(65–72)

Not only does Marvell characterize the Commonwealth as a "forced Pow'r," but he accentuates the horror of the King's execution by adding the epithet "bleeding" to Livy's narrative of the buried head (*caput*) that was taken to be an omen of Rome's future greatness, and hence became the site of the Capitol. In Livy, furthermore, the head is described as "whole and sound," giving the incident a cheery tone antithetical to that in Marvell, nor is Marvell's reference to the architects' "fright" found in his Latin source.[4] Although Marvell professes to look forward to the "happy Fate" of the Commonwealth, this note of optimism itself seems "forced" when set against the reminders of the regicide by which his poem is haunted.

In his description of the "*Royal Actor*" on the scaffold, Marvell writes that he "with his keener Eye / The Axes edge did try" (59–60) and "bowed his comely Head / Down as upon a Bed" (63–4). The tribute to the King's "keener Eye" alludes to a contemporary account that Charles told a gentleman who touched the axe with which he was about to be beheaded: "'Hurt not the Ax that may hurt me,' meaning if he did blunt the edge" (Lagomarsino and Wood, 1989, p. 142). But what might come as a surprise is how Marvell's obsession with the rupture of historical continuity brought about by the regicide can also be seen not only in the "Horatian Ode" but also in his lyric poems, often using very similar language.

A prime example is "The Unfortunate Lover," whose subject is born "In a *Cesarian Section*" (16) and exhibited by "angry Heaven" (41) as "a spectacle of Blood" (42). The only light seen by "The Orphan of the *Hurricane*" (32) is "that which breaks / Through frighted Clouds in forked streaks" (21–2), which echoes how Cromwell's irresistible "force" is compared in the "Horatian

---

[4]   See the notes to these lines in Donno's (1972) edition of Marvell's poems, where the pertinent passage from Livy is cited in Holland's translation.

Ode" not only to "angry Heaven's flame" (26) but also to "the three-fork'd Lightning, first / Breaking the Clouds where it was nurst" (13–14). Similarly, whereas the infant lover cannot "to that Region climb, / To make impression upon Time" (7–8), Cromwell is hailed for how he "Could by industrious Valour climbe / To ruin the great Work of Time" (33–4). These parallels make it clear that Marvell's lyric is an elegy for the slain King, "Who, though by the Malignant Starrs, / Forced to live in Storms and Warrs, // Yet dying leaves a Perfume here" (59–61), and "in Story only rules / In a Field *Sable* a Lover *Gules*" (63–4)—that is, he lives on as a martyr steeped in blood against a background of communal mourning.[5]

"Daphnis and Chloe" is another love lyric with a political subtext. In a parody of Donne's "A Valediction: forbidding mourning," the jaded lover Daphnis, having been rebuffed by the coy Chloe, resolves to abandon her— for more willing mistresses, as the denouement reveals—but is mortified to discover that his threat of desertion has melted her resistance:

> As the soul of one scarce dead,
> With the shrieks of Friends aghast,
> Looks distracted back in hast,
> And then streight again is fled.
>
> So did wretched Daphnis look ...

(37–41)

Daphnis's indecision whether to leave or return to Chloe is compared by Marvell to the soul's parting from the body at the moment of death, a dissonant echo of the first stanza of Donne's "Valediction":

> As virtuous men passe mildly away
> And whisper to their soules, to goe,
> Whilst some of their sad friends doe say,
> The breath goes now, and some say, no:
>
> So let us melt, and make no noise ... [6]

(1–5)

Donne's solemn celebration of constancy in love has been debased by Marvell into a cynical dissection of lust, hypocrisy, and betrayal. The

---

5 See Patterson's political reading of the poem in *Marvell and the Civic Crown* (1978, pp. 20–5).
6 Marvell's indebtedness to "A Valediction" is noted by Legouis in the revised edition of Margoliouth (1988, 1:258).

imperceptibility of the moment of death in "virtuous men" to their adjacent "sad friends" becomes the "shrieks of Friends aghast" at beholding the body of "one scarce dead" abandoned by its indecisive and panic-stricken soul. Marvell's reimagining of Donne's tranquil deathbed scene as one of trauma resembles his heightening of the horror of Livy's image of the decapitated head in the "Horatian Ode"; and in "Daphnis and Chloe," too, the memory of the regicide intrudes when Daphnis calls Chloe his "Executioner" (67) and is himself compared to one who "To his Heads-man makes the Sign, / And receives the parting stroke" (99–100). Like Marvell's tribute to Charles's scrutiny of the axe, this description of Daphnis is based on contemporary reports that when the king laid his neck on the block he said to "his Heads-man," as the latter adjusted his hair, "'Stay for the sign!'" (Lagomarsino and Wood, 1989, p. 144).

Concerning Marvell's Mower poems, where imagery of the Fall is explicit, William Empson (1984) has written, "Damon keeps saying he is in despair for love of a woman," but "it is the poet who is in love with Damon" (p. 15). The same might be said of Daphnis, whose abandonment of Chloe screens a deeper level in which he himself is the object of the poet's desire. Like the other lyrics alluding to the regicide, the Mower poems must have been written after January 1649. Unless there had been not only "War" but also a "Princes Funeral" (6), there would be no point to "The Mower to the Glo-Worms," in which Marvell lauds the "Country Comets" (5) for "Shining unto no higher end / Than to presage the Grasses fall" (7–8). These poems epitomize Marvell's dissociated sensibility, since the phrase "Country Comets," spoken by the persona of the rustic Mower, in actuality emanates from the poet's sophisticated consciousness. As Jim Swan (1976) has observed, "in his role as urbane ironist, Marvell delights in the powers of his doubleness," but in the Mower poems this "delight is contained within its opposite, which is grief over a separation, a displacement that can never be overcome" (p. 195). The "displacement" that the Mower attributes to his love for Juliana is, theologically, a manifestation of the Fall; politically, it cannot be insulated from England's inundation by the "Hurricane" of civil war.

Upon Appleton House is Marvell's most sustained meditation on the upheavals of the mid-seventeenth century, and it resembles the "Horatian Ode" in its mixture of loyalty to the new regime and sense of devastation at the horrors that the Commonwealth has brought in its wake. At the heart of the poem is a eulogy for an idyllic England retrospectively equated with the Garden of Eden:

Oh Thou, that dear and happy Isle
The Garden of the World ere while,

Thou *Paradise* of four Seas,
Which *Heaven* planted us to please,
But, to exclude the World, did guard
With watry if not flaming Sword;
What luckless Apple did we tast,
To make us Mortal, and The Wast?

(321–8)

That Marvell's vision of a prelapsarian England is suffused with memories of his own childhood before the Civil War can be seen in his immediately ensuing lament that the "sweet *Militia*" (330) where "The *Gardiner* had the *Souldiers* place" (337) has been irrevocably lost: "But War all this doth overgrow / We Ord'nance Plant and Powder sow" (333–4). As Blair Worden (1987) has noted, these lines are echoed in Marvell's first surviving letter, written in 1660 to the Corporation of Hull: "I cannot but remember, though then a child, those blessed days when the youth of your own town were trained for the militia, and did methought bear their arms better than any soldiers I have seen there since" (p. 179).

If Marvell sees the Civil War as a reenactment of the Fall, it follows that General Fairfax, the addressee of *Upon Appleton House*, must be one of its principal agents. But this paradox again follows the precedent of the "Horatian Ode," where Marvell daringly invokes the motif of the Fortunate Fall by pairing the "bleeding Head" of Charles I with the "happy Fate" he forecasts for the new state led by Cromwell. Fairfax, moreover, withdrew from the trial at which the King was condemned and, in contrast to Cromwell, was openly troubled by his execution. According to Clarendon (1702–4), when her husband was summoned on the first day of the trial to serve as one of the judges, Lady Fairfax exclaimed that "'he had more wit than to be there.'" When the King's impeachment was read, Clarendon continues, and it contained the phrase "'all the good people of England,'" Lady Fairfax cried out in a still louder voice: "'No, nor the hundredth part of them'" (p. 314). And in his own poem, "On the Fatal Day," Fairfax evinces his disturbance at the King's fate:

Oh Lett that Day from time be blotted quit[e]
And Lett beleefe of't in the next Age be waved
In deepest silence th'Act concealed might
Soe that the King-doms—Credit might be saved.

(qtd. in Norbrook, 1999, p. 288)

Fairfax desires to expunge or repress the memory of the regicide, a dialectical counterpart to the guilty fascination with which Marvell obsessively returns to this trauma in his poetry.

Thus, not only is Marvell's phantasmagoric vision of the havoc wrought by the "tawny Mowers" (388) in *Upon Appleton House* an allegory of the Civil War, but the "*Rail*" slain "unknowing" (395) by one of the mowers is yet another incarnation of Charles I. The "Edge" of the scythe is drawn "all bloody" (397) from the stricken bird; and Marvell adds that, like Damon, this Mower "does his stroke detest; / Fearing the Flesh untimely mow'd / To him a Fate as black forebode" (398–400).

Despite his allegiance to the Commonwealth and employment by Fairfax, Marvell remains haunted by the regicide and evinces nostalgia for the Royalist cause. These attitudes were not shared by the Levellers, whose mutiny had been suppressed by Fairfax in May 1649 and whose radical politics Marvell satirizes in *Upon Appleton House* when he describes the newly mown fields as a "naked equal Flat, / Which *Levellers* take pattern at" (449–50). In his December 1649 manifesto, *A New-Yeers Gift Sent to the Parliament and Armie*, Gerrard Winstanley—the foremost member of the splinter group known as the True Levellers or Diggers—approved of the King's execution. In contrast to Marvell's obsession with the shedding of the King's blood, Winstanley celebrates having "cast out the Head of oppression which was Kingly power," which has delivered "this distressed bleeding dying nation out of bondage" (Erskine-Hill and Storey, 1983, p. 155).[7] Winstanley, however, recognizes the difficulty of eradicating kingship: "for Kingly power is like a great spread tree; if you lop the head or top-bow, and let the other Branches and root stand, it will grow again and recover fresh strength" (p. 156).

By his allusion to the 1642 Root and Branch petition, which called for the abolition of episcopacy, Winstanley warns lest the evils of "Kingly power" spring up again among moderate elements in the Parliament and New Model Army, which had joined forces with the Commoners to overthrow the King. Although Winstanley's horticultural metaphors appear to betray no anxiety that decapitating the sovereign might be a sacrilegious act with psychological repercussions, the undertones in the phrases "Head of oppression" and "lop the head" suggest that the memory of what had just been done to deliver the "bleeding dying nation out of bondage" could not be banished from his exhortations not to neglect to extirpate the "Branches and root" of "Kingly power."

---

[7] See Loewenstein's (1991, pp. 69–70) analysis of Winstanley's pamphlet.

3

As the foremost defender of the regicide, Milton's politics resemble Winstanley's. To be sure, as Stephen Greenblatt (2011) notes, Milton was "never sympathetic" to Winstanley's project of abolishing private property and "taking communion in the nude with a gaggle of wild-eyed would-be Adams and Eves" (p. 196) on St. George's Hill in Surrey, only twenty miles from London. But it was his purpose to strip the regicide of its aura, to make killing the King seem no more than an ineluctable, albeit solemn, consequence of his unlawful actions. Like Winstanley, Milton reserved his greatest scorn for the Presbyterians, the members of his own party who had taken up arms against the King but then shirked from imposing the death sentence. He rails in *The Tenure of Kings and Magistrates*, probably published within a month of the execution, against those backsliders who "begin to swerve, and almost shiver at the Majesty of som noble deed, as if they were newly enter'd into a great sin" (Hughes, 1962, p. 194). But even as he seeks to define the regicide as a "noble deed," a tyrannicide that itself possesses "Majesty," Milton cannot escape the realization that not only the Cavaliers but also many of his fellow Roundheads, in Marvell's phrase, did the "stroke detest" and feared that they had committed "a great sin." That Milton himself does not consciously share this sense of guilt only makes his testimony about the emotional climate following the regicide more compelling.

A key element in Milton's strategy in *The Tenure of Kings and Magistrates* is to invoke the doctrine of the king's two bodies in order to argue that the deposing of the King, which stripped him of his royal body, was the true regicide, of which the death of his natural body was merely a byproduct:

> Who knows not that the King is a name of dignity and office, not of person: Who therefore kills a King, must kill him while he is a King. Then they certainly who by deposing him have long since tak'n from him the life of a King, his office and his dignity, they in the truest sense may be said to have killd the King.
>
> (Hughes, 1962, p. 233)

Milton's attempt to sanitize the regicide by claiming that Charles was no longer a king when he went to the scaffold, and that there should therefore be no stigma attached to his death, is intellectually brilliant but psychologically naive. Even his executioner, upon being requested to wait for a signal before striking the fatal blow, responded with an acknowledgment of Charles's sovereignty: "'Yes I will, and it please Your Majesty'" (Lagomarsino and Wood, 1989, p. 144).

Not only does Milton's denial that the regicide constituted the violation of a taboo fail to carry emotional conviction, but the allusions to Shakespeare in his pamphlets unwittingly reveal that he shared the sense of guilt he reprehended in his fainthearted colleagues. In *Eikonoklastes*, Milton seeks to indict the King on the peculiar grounds that Shakespeare "was the Closet Companion of these his Solitudes" and likens him to Richard III in being "a deep dissembler, not of his affections only, but of Religion" (Hughes, 1962, pp. 361–2). Milton's desire to equate Charles I with the villain of Tudor historiography is understandable, but the King's love for Shakespeare is hardly something his subjects would have held against him; and since Shakespeare consistently presents the killing of a legitimate ruler as a sacrilegious act, the natural inference to be drawn from a reading of his works is by no means favorable to Milton's case. Seen in this light, that Milton mentions Shakespeare at all comes to seem rather odd, and his comparison of Charles I to Richard III can be understood as a defensive stratagem designed to divert attention from other parallels in Shakespeare that the theme of regicide would be likely to call to mind.

Beneath his manifest struggle with the "domineering phantom" of Charles in the regicide tracts, the future author of *Paradise Lost* finds himself in a latent conflict with the ghost of Shakespeare. In the preface to *Eikonoklastes*, Milton proposes an analogy between the malignant effect of the King's posthumous book, *Eikon Basilike*, and the "will of Caesar, being read to the people," which "wrought more in that Vulgar audience to the avenging of his death, then all the art he could ever use, to win their favor in his life-time" (Hughes, 1962, p. 342). Although one version of this story occurs in Suetonius, its best-known source was Shakespeare's *Julius Caesar*, a fact that Milton passes over in silence. That he does so, whereas he quotes a passage from *Richard III* to illustrate what he regards as the king's feigned piety, is not surprising since Shakespeare's staging of Mark Antony's rhetorical success in overwhelming Brutus's cogently reasoned but emotionally tone-deaf defense of tyrannicide bodes ill for Milton's battle of the books with *Eikon Basilike*.

Just as Milton begins *Eikonoklastes* with a self-subverting echo of *Julius Caesar*, he seems to have the play in mind again at the close. Relying on the political success of the Puritan Revolution as proof of its divine sponsorship, Milton asserts of the regicide that "god hath testifi'd by all propitious & evident signes ... that such a solemn, and for many Ages unexampl'd act of due punishment, was no *mockery of Justice*, but a most grateful and well-pleasing Sacrifice" (Hughes, 1962, p. 596). The desire for "Sacrifice" also informs Brutus's plea, "Let us be sacrificers, Caius, but not butchers" (2.1.166). He goes on to rue the conspirators' need to destroy Caesar in the flesh in order to achieve their objectives:

We all stand up against the spirit of Caesar,
And in the spirit of men there is no blood;
O that we then could come by Caesar's spirit,
And not dismember Caesar! But, alas,
Caesar must bleed for it!

(167–71)

Brutus's dilemma is psychologically identical to Milton's since his wish that it might be possible to slay "Caesar's spirit" without shedding Caesar's blood parallels Milton's fantasy that since those who deposed the King "in the truest sense may be said to have killd the King," depriving Charles of his head amounted to a technicality. And just as the violence of the assassination in Shakespeare's play undermines Brutus's distinction between sacrifice and butchery, so, too, the "bloody stroke" on Charles's neck produced a collective groan that drowned out Milton's plea that the regicide be regarded as a "well-pleasing Sacrifice" rather than a "mockery of Justice."

If *Richard III* is Milton's preferred precedent for Charles's execution, while his reminiscences of *Julius Caesar* do not have the effect he intended, there is a third Shakespeare play whose subterranean currents run through the regicide tracts. In *The Tenure of Kings and Magistrates*, as part of his attack on the Presbyterians, Milton charges that they "who now so much condemn deposing, were the men themselves that deposed the King, and cannot with their shifting and relapsing, wash off the guiltiness from their hands. For they themselves, by these their late doings have made it guiltiness, and turned their warrantable actions into rebellion" (Hughes, 1962, p. 227).

Milton's purpose is to show that the "guiltiness" produced by the regicide is due to the Presbyterians' pusillanimity concerning their "warrantable actions," not to the deed itself. But it is impossible to read this reference to handwashing without thinking, first, of Pontius Pilate and, second, of Lady Macbeth. Like his mention of Caesar's will, Milton's evocation of *Macbeth* inadvertently subverts his argument since it equates Charles I not only with Christ but also with Duncan, an anointed king whose murder was tantamount to a deicide.

That Milton's mention of handwashing carries an overtone not only of Pilate but also of Lady Macbeth is confirmed by further echoes of *Macbeth* in *The Tenure of Kings and Magistrates*. At the outset of the tract, Milton derides those fainthearted divines who, "after they have juggel'd and palter'd with the world" (Hughes, 1962, p. 227), betrayed their principles by abandoning the fight against the King. The words "juggel'd" and "palter'd" recall Macbeth's imprecation of the Witches: "And be these juggling fiends no more believ'd, / That palter with us in a double sense, / That keep the word of promise to our ear, / And break it to our hope" (5.8.19–22). And in a reference to the theme of equivocation in the Porter scene—a topical allusion on Shakespeare's part to Father Henry Garnet, the Jesuit priest who had recently been executed for his complicity in the 1605 Gunpowder Plot—Milton insists that there is "nothing that so actually makes a Subject of *England* as those two Oaths of Allegiance and Supremacy observ'd *without equivocating, or any mental reservation*" (p. 228). Drawing attention to these echoes, Martin Dzelzainis (1979) notes Milton's "reluctance to be ... explicit about his source" in the case of *Macbeth* and attributes it to "a wish not to underwrite any unfortunate parallel between the murderer of Duncan and those responsible for the execution of Charles I" (p. 58).

Although Dzelzainis explains convincingly why Milton obscured his borrowings from *Macbeth*, he does not sufficiently emphasize the strangeness of their appearance in Milton's text, since the effect of his comparison of the Presbyterian divines to the Witches and Lady Macbeth is precisely to enforce the "unfortunate parallel" between Charles and Duncan that he should at all costs have wanted to avoid. As David Norbrook (1987) has documented, Shakespeare in *Macbeth* sought "to revise the more radical views implicit in its sources" (p. 99), including the writings of the Scottish humanist George Buchanan, in order to blacken Macbeth and promote a Royalist ideology. "All Shakespeare's political plays," Norbrook adds, "are arguably as interested in emotional and unconscious motivations for political action as in rational principles" (p. 99). Shakespeare's politics are thus antithetical to Milton's. The tacit allusions to *Macbeth* in *The Tenure of Kings and Magistrates* are symptoms of an anxiety of influence in which both Shakespeare's royalism and his belief in the primacy of "emotional and unconscious motivations for political action" return to subvert the republicanism and rationalism of Milton's own texts.

Milton, that is, seeks consciously to equate Charles I with Richard III, but he unconsciously equates him with Duncan; and, in so doing, he casts himself as Macbeth. He thereby trades places with Charles I and becomes not the tyrannicide but the tyrant. The doubling of Milton and Charles I is exemplified by the following passage from *Eikonoklastes*: "That mind must needs be irrecoverably deprav'd, which either by chance or importunity tasting but once of one just deed, spatters at it and abhorrs the relish ever after" (Hughes, 1962, p. 374). Contrary to what one might expect, Milton refers here not to the regicides whose remorse has "turned their warrantable actions into rebellion," but rather to Charles himself, whom he ridicules for the contrition expressed in *Eikon Basilike* over having yielded in 1641 to demands by Parliament for the Earl of Strafford's execution. But though Milton intends "spatters" to mean "eject particles of food from the mouth," the word also conjures up the image of sprayed blood. This leads the reader to think not only of Strafford but also of the King, whose beheading Milton regards as the Presbyterians' "one just deed," but of which their "deprav'd" minds caused them to "abhor the relish ever after."

Milton thus imputes his own disavowed guilt for his role in the regicide to Charles's response to Strafford's execution. As in the case of Brutus, Milton's covert equation of himself with Charles is mediated by his repressed identification with the Presbyterians, whom he reviles for the conflicts that he cannot acknowledge in himself. These psychological dynamics are captured by Marvell's observations in *Upon Appleton House* about the Mower who "does his stroke detest" after he kills the rail, "Fearing the Flesh untimely mow'd / To him a Fate as black forebode." After the Restoration, Milton, blind and politically defeated yet spiritually triumphant in his final poetic masterpieces, ironically comes to occupy a position analogous to that of Charles I on the scaffold, over whom he had exulted in the regicide tracts.

In *Eikonoklastes*, Milton charges Charles I with both patricide and incest. Upon assuming the throne in 1625, he states, the King immediately dissolved Parliament "to protect the Duke of *Buckingham* against them who had accus'd him, besides other hainous crimes, of no less then poysoning the deceased King his Father" (Hughes, 1962, p. 352). By conflating Charles and Buckingham in the phrases "accus'd him" and "deceased King his Father," Milton implies that they conspired to assassinate James I. Later, Milton uses metaphors of gender to censure Charles's abuse of royal power. According to the King, he inveighs, "the Parliament, it seems, is but a Female," incapable of producing laws without his "procreative reason." But in that case, Milton continues:

> He ought then to have so thought of Parliament, if he count it not Male, as of his Mother, which, to civill being, created both him, and the Royalty he wore. And if it hath been anciently interpreted the presaging signe of a future Tyrant, but to dream of copulation with his Mother, what can it be less than actual Tyranny to affirme waking, that the Parliament, which is his Mother, can neither conceive or bring forth *any authoritative Act* without his Masculine coition.

> (p. 467)

Since Parliament in Milton's view "created" the King, if Charles believes it can do nothing "without his Masculine coition," he stands condemned of "copulation with his Mother," the prototypical crime of a tyrant, which compounds his alleged complicity in killing the "King his Father." Yet it is

Milton who has done precisely this in his regicide tracts. Seen in this light, his decision to write *Paradise Lost* comes into focus not only as an attempt to recoup the religious meaning of the Fall from Royalist propaganda, but also as a means of working out his own unconscious sense of guilt at having, like Satan, revolted against the King.

In August 1667, the same month in which Milton probably published his ten-book version of *Paradise Lost*, Marvell wrote *Last Instructions to a Painter*. This scathing satire of political affairs during the Dutch War, which anticipated Clarendon's forced resignation from his post as Lord Chancellor, culminates in a retrospective commentary on the trauma of the regicide. In the concluding section, Marvell portrays King Charles II—like Shakespeare's Richard III, sleepless and seeing by the light of a taper infected with "blue streaks" (916) indicative of the presence of ghosts—haunted by the specters of two ancestors, his maternal grandfather, the French King Henry IV, assassinated in 1610, and his father, Charles I:

> *Harry* sits down, and in his open side
> The grisly Wound reveals, of which he dy'd.
> And ghastly *Charles*, turning his Collar low,
> The purple thread about his Neck does show.
>
> (919–22)

Marvell's evocation of Richard III as a prototype for Charles II, unable to banish the memory not of those he has himself killed but of the predecessors whose violent ends serve as a warning of his own fate should he fail to dismiss Clarendon in time, reworks Milton's equation of Charles I with Richard III in *Eikonoklastes*. Marvell completes the pattern set forth by Milton by portraying Charles II not only as visited by the ghosts of his slain fathers but also as tempted to violate the incest taboo when he sees "a sudden Shape with Virgins face" (891), a metaphorical representation of his endangered kingdom to which he is illicitly attracted, though this bound and gagged naked female is—like Sin for Satan—a hallucinatory emanation from his own mind:

> He wonder'd first, then pity'd, then he lov'd:
> And with kind hand does the coy Vision press,
> Whose Beauty greater seem'd by her distress;
> But soon shrunk back, chill'd with her touch so cold,
> And th' airy Picture vanisht from his hold.
>
> (900–4)

If, as Milton wrote in *Eikonoklastes*, it is "the presaging signe of a future Tyrant, but to dream of copulation with his Mother," a transgression of which Charles I became guilty when he sought to impose his will on Parliament, then the lesson that Marvell draws from recent history is that the only way Charles II can avoid having the "purple thread" encircle his own neck is if he refrains from repeating his "ghastly" father's crime of committing incest with the kingdom. Fortunately, from Marvell's standpoint, the son recoiled in the nick of time and resolved instead on cashiering his insidious Lord Chancellor.

4

In the letter to the Prince of Wales with which he ended *Eikon Basilike*, Charles I predicted of those responsible for his execution that "inward horrour will be their first Tormentor" (Almack, 1907, p. 261). As though he had been reading Melanie Klein (1935), who uses the concept of reparation to refer to the desire of the child who has reached the depressive position to atone for his or her destructive impulses directed against the mother and the fantasied contents of her body, the king assured his eldest son that these malefactors would soon evince "earnest desires to make some reparations for their former defects" (Almack, 1907, p. 256). The Kleinian overtones of Charles's prophecy concerning the "inward horrour" that was bound to afflict the regicides bring out the association of their primal crime with matricide beneath its primary psychological meaning of patricide.

That the king could be the mother as well as the father of his people was acknowledged by James I when he described himself in *Basilikon Doron* as the "loving nourish-father" who gave his subjects "their very nourish-milke" (qtd. in Goldberg, 1983, p. 142). In his iconography of regicide, Shakespeare feminizes the corpses of both Julius Caesar and Duncan, whose assassinations, as Gail Kern Paster (1989) has written, "cause the fallen patriarch to reveal a womanly inability to stop bleeding" (p. 285). The antithesis between sacrifice and murder that links *Eikonoklastes* to *Julius Caesar* recurs in *Othello* when the Moor rebuffs Desdemona's protestations of her chastity before strangling her to death, "thou dost stone my heart, / And mak'st me call what I intend to do / A murther, which I thought a sacrifice" (5.2.63–5). To kill a king is for Shakespeare metaphorically to kill a woman—a woman who is a substitute for the mother—and the "inward horrour" of violating the taboo against matricide is part of the penalty visited on Milton and his fellow regicides. Charles's feminine aspect is highlighted by Marvell's encomium of the King's "comely Head" in the "Horatian Ode," and it also explains Marvell's otherwise puzzling specification of the slaughtered rail as a female through his use of the possessive adjective "her" (396) in *Upon Appleton House.*

According to Norbrook (1999), James Harrington's *The Commonwealth of Oceana*, published in 1656, is "the most important text of English republicanism" (p. 357), and one that "shows no signs of nostalgia for the old political order" (p. 359). But as with the avowed radicals Winstanley and Milton, aftershocks of the recent political earthquake can be detected in Harrington's allegorical narrative of English history. Not only does he skip over the reigns of both Charles I and James I and go back to Panurgus's (i.e., Henry VII's) weakening of the power of the nobility to find the root causes of England's metamorphosis from a monarchy into a commonwealth, but he also alleges that "the dissolution of the late monarchy was as natural as the death of a man" (Pocock, 1992, p. 62), thereby effacing the regicide and pretending that it was due to natural causes.

This denial of the traumatic violence of Charles's execution constitutes an act of dissociation on Harrington's part. He enacts the plea voiced by Fairfax, "Let that Day from time be blotted quite," and conceals "In deepest silence" the most important event in recent English history. That Harrington had a personal reason for doing so is evidenced by John Aubrey's testimony that he not only "passionately loved his Majestie" but "was on the Scaffold with the King when he was beheaded," and that Charles's death gave Harrington "so great a griefe that he contracted a disease by it; that never any thing did goe so neer to him" (Dick, 1950, p. 124).

In "The Corollary" that forms the final section of *Oceana*, Harrington compares the Cromwellian persona of Archon to the statesman and general Timoleon of Corinth (411–337 B.C.E.), who killed his brother to liberate his people from the latter's tyranny and then was summoned by the Sicilians to restore them to freedom as well. In Timoleon's old age, however, "through some natural imperfection he fell blind," whereas Archon, despite his resemblance to the Corinthian in other ways, "had his senses unto the last" (Pocock, 1992, p. 265). At the time, Cromwell was ruling England as the Lord Protector, and, as Norbrook (1999) comments, "Harrington's raising the possibility that Cromwell might go blind, and then withdrawing it, does not seem to have any political relevance unless it is meant to link Cromwell with his most prestigious defender and to offer a vague threat" (p. 374). But the absence of "political relevance" to the motif of blindness suggests that Harrington's association of Cromwell with Milton must be psychologically motivated. Since Timoleon's rise to power was due to his having committed fratricide—however justified it may have been—Harrington is implying that Cromwell, like Milton, should fear being punished with blindness for his violation of the taboo against parricide.[8] In so doing, Harrington betrays the extent to which he, too, was traumatized by having witnessed the decapitation of the king whom he "passionately loved" and whose bloody end he sought to relegate to oblivion.

5

Combined with the other texts I have examined, Marvell's poetry and Milton's prose show that the execution of Charles I was experienced as a trauma not simply by Royalists but by English society as a whole. Even Harrington, whose defense of Cromwell and the Commonwealth seems on the surface, like Winstanley's, to be devoid of "nostalgia for the old political order," gives in *Oceana* a sanitized account of the "dissolution of the late monarchy" that denies his own heartrending "griefe" at the scene on the scaffold of which he had been a spectator.

Notwithstanding Eliot's Royalist politics, therefore, his theory of the dissociation of sensibility retains its validity as an account of the collective transformation undergone by the "mind of England" during the seventeenth century. Although Kermode is right to point out that it "contains an implicit parallel with the Fall," this does not prove that the paradigm is "quite useless historically." On the contrary, the regicide was experienced as a transgressive act by a host of contemporary figures, from the ephemeral to the enduring, many of whom invoked the archetype of the Fall to make sense of the "Storms and Warrs" that had engulfed the country. Nor does Kermode's argument that "a once-for-all event cannot happen every few years" constitute a refutation. Even if there has never been an epoch of unified sensibility, it remains true that an irreversible rupture occurred in English history with the decapitation of King Charles I in 1649. Seen from this standpoint, the dissociation of sensibility constitutes a metonymy for the Renaissance, which

---

8   In the *Second Defense*, Milton likewise invokes Timoleon, "than whom there never lived in any age, a more virtuous man, or a more incorruptible statesman," in pleading that his own "loss of sight … cannot be considered as a judicial punishment" (Hughes, 1957, p. 825).

historians beginning with Burckhardt in the nineteenth century—borrowing the metaphors of rebirth, lifting a veil, and the like that had originally been employed by Petrarch and other humanists to define their sense of themselves—have characterized as an awakening of European consciousness. And if, however far back one goes, one can find symptoms of a renascence, this does not mean that the Renaissance did not take place.[9]

---

[9] For defenses of the concept of the Renaissance, see the essays by Mommsen (1942) and Weisinger (1943), and above all Greenblatt's (2011) gripping account of "the change from one way of perceiving and living in the world to another" (p. 10) precipitated by the Italian humanist Poggio Bracciolini, whose rediscovery in 1417 of the manuscript of Lucretius's *On the Nature of Things* (c. 55 B.C.E.) in a German monastery constituted a "swerve" in—to adapt Eliot's phrase—the "mind of Europe" that modernized the world.

Chapter 8

"Here Only Weak"

Sexuality and Its Vicissitudes in *Paradise Lost*

"Whether the whole relation be not Allegorical, that is, whether the temptation of the Man by the Woman, be not the seduction of the rational and higher parts by the inferiour and feminine faculties: or whether the Tree in the midst of the Garden, were not that part in the Center of the body, in which afterward was the appointment of Circumcision in Males, we leave it unto the Thalmudist."

—Sir Thomas Browne, *Pseudodoxia Epidemica*

1

In Book 8 of *Paradise Lost*, near the end of his lengthy colloquy with Raphael beginning in Book 5, Adam describes his extreme susceptibility to Eve's beauty. In contrast to the enjoyment that he feels in objects of the natural world, but which induce in his mind "no change, / Nor vehement desire," Adam acknowledges the tumult aroused in him by his fair consort:

> but here
> Far otherwise, transported I behold,
> Transported touch; here passion first I felt,
> Commotion strange, in all enjoyments else
> Superior and unmov'd, here only weak
> Against the charm of Beauty's powerful glance.
>
> (524–33)

These lines, together with the remainder of Adam's speech in praise of Eve, are greeted by the angel "with contracted brow" (560) and a reminder of the need for a healthy "self-esteem, grounded on just and right" (572). In their insistence on Adam's vulnerability in the erotic sphere—the disparity between his "Superior and unmov'd" contemplation of all other "enjoyments" and the "commotion strange" by which he is "transported" by Eve—they open the way to a psychoanalytic reading of *Paradise Lost*. Addressing in uncannily similar language the question raised by Adam's declaration, Jean Laplanche (1970) asks, "How is it, in fact, that one's sexual life constitutes the *only weak point* on which repression … comes to bear? Why is it our sexuality alone which is repressed?" (p. 30; italics modified).

Laplanche answers the riddle of why it should be that sexuality forms the "only weak point" in human development by invoking Freud's concept of *Nachträglichkeit* or "deferred action"—James Strachey's translation of what Lacan terms *après-coup* and Laplanche in his later work renders as "afterwardsness"—a psychoanalytic model for the structure of trauma that receives its most comprehensive elaboration in the posthumously published *Project for a Scientific Psychology* (1895). In the *Project,* Freud recounts how, as a girl, his patient Emma (whom we now know to have been Emma Eckstein) had twice gone into a shop in which the shopkeeper had grabbed her genitals through her clothes, but after puberty ran away in fright when she saw two shop-assistants—one of whom attracted her sexually—laughing at her appearance. Laplanche (1970) explains Emma's fear as an instance of the "deferred action" that results from the interaction of "two scenes linked by associative chains, but also clearly separated from each other by a *temporal barrier which inscribes them in different spheres of meaning: the moment of puberty*" (p. 40). The earlier assaults could not be psychically metabolized because her sexuality had not yet been awakened. But, as Laplanche notes, puberty retains its conceptual importance for Freud even after he abandoned his "seduction theory" in 1897 in favor of a belief in infantile sexuality because it remains the case that the *diphasic onset* of human sexuality—coming as it does both "too early" in infancy and "too late" with biological maturity— is what causes it to be repressed and ensures that the experience of it will necessarily be "after the event" and hence traumatic.

The shared conviction of Milton and Freud that sexuality forms the region of paramount vulnerability in the human psyche suggests the utility of the concept of deferred action to understanding *Paradise Lost*, where one of the perennial conundrums is the relation of unfallen to fallen experience. On the one hand, as Arnold Stein (1953, pp. 75–118) has elucidated, both Adam and Eve undergo a series of events in the state of innocence that seem to prefigure the Fall. For Eve, these are (1) her attraction to her reflection in the lake when she is first created (4.449–91); (2) her questioning why stars shine at night when no one is awake to see them (4.657–8); (3) her dream of eating the forbidden fruit (5.35–93); and (4) her argument to Adam in favor of gardening separately (9.205–375). Eve's incipient threats to order find their counterparts in Adam when he (1) wonders why "So many nobler Bodies" in the heavens serve merely to shed light on Earth (8.25–35); (2) experiences "amorous delight" in dreaming of Eve's creation (8.470–80), rather than the "rational delight" (391) that was his avowed reason for asking God for a human partner; (3) confesses to Raphael his "vehement desire" for Eve; and (4) accedes to Eve's request to work separately (9.367–75). The curiosity of both Adam and Eve about astronomy seems subversively to permit human consciousness to become the measure of God's design for the universe. Indeed, so pronounced are all these anticipations of the Fall in prelapsarian experience that some scholars are driven to argue, with Millicent Bell (1953), that "there is, in effect, no longer a Fall as the Bible plot presents it. … From the first we are after the Fall" (p. 867).[1]

On the other hand, this theory of the "fallacy of the fall" in *Paradise Lost* has met with strenuous objections from other scholars (Shumaker, 1955; Ogden, 1957), who point out that Eve is described by the narrator as "yet sinless" (9.659) only moments before eating the forbidden fruit. Above all, these critics insist, the connections between the Fall and its ostensible prefigurations are imposed by our perspective as fallen readers, and in no way render its occurrence inevitable. The Fall, that is, in Stanley Fish's (1967) words, must be "thrown into brilliant relief as an incomprehensible phenomenon" (p. 228), discontinuous with everything that precedes it. If only Adam and Eve—like Jesus in *Paradise Regained*—had resisted temptation at the crucial moment, their earlier trials would not seem to foreshadow the Fall but would rather have served to demonstrate the dynamic growth and possibilities of human freedom.

Criticism of *Paradise Lost* has imitated the poem itself by exhibiting a tendency to split into opposing camps, and the concept of deferred action has the virtue of taking what is of value in these seemingly incompatible "narrative" and "theological" approaches without being bound by the limitations of either. Laplanche's account gives due weight to the critics who see the Fall as an extension of earlier episodes by recognizing that a trauma can only be formed through the conjunction of two or more "scenes linked by associative chains," as Eve's downfall is preceded by her narcissistic attraction to her reflection, the dream of eating the fruit, and so on. Yet Laplanche also endorses the contention of the critics who reject this claim by positing the existence of a "temporal barrier" that divides everything coming before

---

[1] See also Waldock (1947): "It is obvious that Adam and Eve must already have contracted human weaknesses before they can start on the course of conduct that leads to their fall: to put it another way, they must already be fallen (technically) before they can begin to fall" (p. 61). Similarly, for Tillyard (1951), "the actual eating of the apple becomes no more than an emphatic stage in the process already begun" (p. 13).

and after it into "different spheres of meaning," exactly as the Fall intervenes between pre- and postlapsarian experience in *Paradise Lost*. As an event, one might say, that is itself "after the event," the Fall is a trauma that introduces repetition into human experience and is both continuous and discontinuous with what comes before it.

Although the tension between narrative and theological readings of the Fall becomes acute in *Paradise Lost*, it is already present in the Genesis story. In *The Rhetoric of Religion* (1961), Kenneth Burke coins the term "logology" to refer to his attempt to understand the language used to talk about God without taking a position on the question of God's existence. Burke's "logological" point of view is a sophisticated version of a narrative approach to *Paradise Lost*. Despite wishing to regard the theological and logological interpretations of Genesis as existing in most respects on "different planes, so that they neither corroborate nor refute one another," Burke admits that "at one point there does seem to be a necessary opposition" (p. 252). This is the vexed question of determinism versus free will, or whether the Fall was inevitable. In Burke's formulation, "theologically, Adam could have chosen *not* to sin. He could have said yes to God's thou-shalt-not. But logologically, Adam *necessarily* sinned. For if he had chosen *not* to sin, the whole design of the Bible would have been ruined" (p. 252), for there would then have been no need for a Messiah to redeem humankind.

The theological understanding of the Fall rests on the premise that it could have been avoided. In the words of Milton's God, Man was created "Sufficient to have stood, though free to fall" (3.99). Burke's contribution is to point out that the story, as Milton inherited it from the Bible, possesses a foreordained conclusion, and hence from the narrative standpoint this sense of human freedom must be dismissed as an illusion. In a comparison that is particularly apt in a psychoanalytic context, Burke (1961) contends that Adam's fall is no less inevitable than Oedipus's fulfillment of the oracle: "Logologically, to say that Adam didn't have to sin would be like saying Oedipus didn't have to kill his father and marry his mother, except that in the case of Adam it *looks* like more of a choice" (p. 252). Although the requirements of theology cannot be logically reconciled with the sense of inevitability produced by the narrative, much of the imaginative force of Milton's epic resides in the way that it demands to be read from both of these contradictory perspectives simultaneously.

Milton builds the structure of deferred action into his poem through Raphael's visit to Eden in Books 5 through 8, in the course of which he recounts the sagas of the War in Heaven and the Creation in order to reinforce God's commandment to Adam and Eve not to eat of the Tree of Knowledge. As Stein (1957) has observed, Raphael's colloquy with Adam follows Eve's report of her dream of the Fall at the outset of Book 5, and it concludes in Book 8 "with the sudden disclosure of [Adam's] passion and the enigmatic revelation of angelic sexuality which quickly return the end of the episode to a narrative mood and tempo resembling the place where the line of action broke off" (p. 109). Adam, that is, beholds Eve asleep in Book 5 "With tresses discompos'd, and glowing Cheek" (10), and this pitch of erotic excitement is not reached again until the end of Book 8, which in turn leads to the moment when Eve returns to Adam in Book 9 after having eaten the forbidden fruit, "But in her Cheek distemper flushing glow'd" (887). Raphael's sojourn on earth supplies the "temporal barrier" that makes the Fall into a repetition in a "different sphere of meaning" of Eve's dream and the other moments that in retrospect seem to have foreshadowed it.

To view the action of *Paradise Lost* in terms of the paradigm of deferred action, with the implied analogy between the Fall and the "moment of puberty," foregrounds the problem of the sexual relations between Adam and Eve. That they consummated their marriage is expressly affirmed by Milton when he writes that "Whatever Hypocrites austerely talk," they enjoyed "the Rites / Mysterious of connubial Love" (4.742–4). But though Adam and Eve engage in intercourse in the state of innocence, Stephen Greenblatt's (2017) confidence that they had "spectacularly good sex" (p. 217) lacks textual support. Although Adam acknowledges feeling "passion" and "vehement desire" for his consort, this describes his state of mind rather than their lovemaking, and Eve for her part—to employ Ferenczi's (1933) terminology in "Confusion of Tongues between Adults and the Child"—never shows more than the "tenderness" of childhood for him. She turns away from Adam when she is first led to him by the voice of God and only yields when, as she recalls, "thy gentle hand / Seiz'd mine" (4.488–9). Her behavior is like that of a child who is being "seduced" into sex by an adult—in this instance, one who is also her parent—and Adam confirms that Eve displayed "Virgin Modesty" (8.501) and was "blushing" as he led her to their "Nuptial Bow'r" (510–11). He tells Raphael that the wedding night brought him "to the sum of bliss / Which I enjoy" (522–3), but we never hear what it was like for her.

That Eve acted with "Virgin Modesty" before having sex for the first time is not surprising, but what may give the reader pause is Milton's insistence in Book 9 that she remains a virgin until the Fall. Not content with praising her "Virgin Majesty" (270), he compares her to "*Ceres* in her Prime / Yet Virgin of *Proserpina* from *Jove*" (396–7), and describes how Satan is smitten by her as a city dweller on a rural excursion would be "If chance with Nymphlike step fair Virgin pass" (452). The corollary to Eve's prelapsarian virginity is Adam's lament upon beholding her after her undoing, "Defac'd, deflow'r'd, and now to death devote" (901). Why, if they have had sex, is Eve still a virgin, not only in a spiritual but apparently also in a physical sense? The answer is provided by St. Augustine, who in *The City of God* describes how, before the Fall, "with no corrupting influence of the body, the husband would lie on the bosom of his wife" in such a way that she could be inseminated "with the integrity of the female genital organ being preserved, just as now, with that same integrity being safe, the menstrual flow of blood can be emitted from the womb of a virgin" (14.24). Laplanche (1970) terms children who have not yet crossed the threshold of puberty "sexual—presexual" (p. 40), and this oxymoron precisely captures the "Rites / Mysterious" of Adam and Eve, which are at once innocent yet sexual. Whatever our first parents did in their "inmost bower" (4.738), Eve's hymen, like Desdemona's, is "neither consummation nor virginity" (Derrida, 1972, p. 43), and their sex assuredly did not culminate—at least for her—in the "sum of bliss" that is orgasm.

2

Whereas Eve's experience of "wedded Love" with Adam is characterized by the "tenderness" of childhood, she is initiated into adult "passion" in an extramarital tryst with Satan. Upon first encountering the newlyweds in Book 4, Satan is transfixed by a "jealous leer malign" as Adam "press'd her Matron lip / With kisses pure" (501–3). To refer to Eve as a "Matron" casts her as a middle-aged married woman and places Satan in the position of a son beholding the primal scene from which he is excluded. He voices his anguish in a soliloquy, "Sight hateful, sight tormenting! thus these two / Imparadis'd in one another's arms / The happier *Eden*, shall enjoy their fill / Of bliss on bliss, while I to Hell am thrust" (505–8). Satan's presence sexualizes the landscape of Eden, which—like the *Gawain*-poet's description of the Green Chapel—is redolent of the female genitalia. Approaching the "delicious Paradise," Satan finds "her enclosure" to be crowned by "a rural mound" whose "hairy sides / With thicket overgrown, grotesque and wild, / Access denied" (134–7). As Edward Le Comte (1978) observes, "Paradise is seen as a *mons Veneris*" (p. 77).

Once the anatomical contours of Eden come into focus, it becomes clear why Satan is said to be "better pleas'd" with its "odorous sweets" than "*Asmodeus* with the fishy fume, / That drove him, though enamor'd, from the Spouse / Of *Tobit's* Son" (4.166-70). As the apocryphal story goes, Tobias, the son of Tobit, married Sara, whose seven previous husbands had all been murdered by her demon lover on their wedding night prior to consummating the union. Asmodeus, however, was repelled when Tobias burned the heart and liver of a fish in his bedchamber. The implication is that Satan, like Asmodeus, seeks to kill Adam, the husband who is his rival, in order to possess Eve, the wife whom he desires sexually, for himself, although Satan is attracted rather than put to flight by the fragrance of the Garden. What appears to have eluded commentators on this passage, however, whose exegeses are reviewed by David R. Clark (1972), is that the "fume" that apotropaically drives Asmodeus away from Sara can be nothing other than what Lear misogynistically calls the "stench" emanating from the "sulphurous pit" of the vagina, and that the allure of the same "fishy" odor is what compelled both demons to try to steal the virginal brides from their husbands in the first place.

In the story from the Book of Tobit, it is the angel Raphael who counsels Tobias on how to thwart Asmodeus, and in *Paradise Lost*, Raphael functions similarly as the "presexual" counterpart to the "sexual" Satan. When Raphael sits down to his repast with the first couple, the narrator states that Eve "Minister'd naked" (5.444) to the two males, adding that on this of all occasions angels would have had "excuse to have been / Enamour'd at that sight; but in those hearts / Love unlibidinous reign'd, nor jealousy / Was understood, the injur'd Lover's Hell" (447–50). When in Book 8 Eve takes her leave to permit Adam and Raphael to continue their conversation, the reader is told that "from about her shot Darts of desire / Into all Eyes to wish her still in sight" (62–3). Once again, the "Darts of desire" emitted by Eve remain "unlibidinous" for both her husband and their guest, so that with Raphael the specter of adultery is conjured up only to be banished, in contrast to the threat posed by Satan, who is indeed consumed by "jealousy" of Adam and inhabits "the injur'd Lover's Hell."

Although Satan makes no headway when he first encounters Adam and Eve, and is sent packing by Gabriel at the end of Book 4, he is undeterred. In Books 5 and 6, Raphael recounts Satan's revolt against God and his defeat in the War in Heaven, but Satan does not resurface in Eden until Book 9, when he inhabits the body of a serpent as a means of advancing his scheme to seek vengeance against God by bringing about the Fall of Man. By an apparent coincidence, it is just at this moment that Eve takes it into her head to propose to Adam, "Let us divide our labors" (9.214), in order to garden more efficiently. Adam responds by cautioning her that "The Wife, when danger or dishonor lurks, / Safest and seemliest by her Husband stays, / Who guards her" (267–9). Clearly, what he fears is that Eve will "dishonor" him with their "malicious Foe" (253), whose motive may be "to disturb / Conjugal Love, than which perhaps no bliss / Excites his envy more" (262–4). By evincing what Adam calls, after they have both fallen, this "strange / Desire of wand'ring" (1135–6), Eve has brought about the most conducive conditions possible for her to succumb to the temptation of adultery.

Satan, for his part, cannot believe his luck "when to his wish, / Beyond his hope, *Eve* separate he spies" (9.423–4), and he resolves to seize this uniquely auspicious "Occasion" when he beholds "alone / The Woman, opportune to all attempts, / Her husband, for I view far round, not nigh" (480–2). That Eve, "Veil'd in a Cloud of Fragrance" from the roses that "blushing round / Her glow'd" (425–7), but otherwise naked, is tending flowers, though she herself is the "fairest unsupported Flow'r, / From her best prop so far" (432–3), leaves no room for doubt that it is her own rosebud that Satan intends to gather.

Milton throws the sexual nature of Satan's seduction of Eve into increasingly sharp relief as the poem reaches its climax. Having assumed the guise of a serpent, Satan approaches her "not with indented wave, / Prone on the ground" (9.496–7), but "erect / Amidst his circling Spires" with "his Head / Crested aloft" (499–502), becoming figuratively an aroused penis in order "To lure her Eye" (518).[2] He asks Eve not to take it amiss that he approaches her "thus single" (536), meaning "unaccompanied" but also intimating his status as a bachelor. In praising the Tree of Knowledge, from which he claims to have eaten, Satan says that its "savory odor" was more pleasing to him than that of "the Teats / Of Ewe or Goat dropping with Milk" (581–2), and that he resolved not to defer gratifying "the sharp desire I had / Of tasting those fair Apples" (584–5). The lactating "Apples" that he "desires" to "taste" are Eve's comely breasts. As Satan presses on with his flattery, "Into the Heart of *Eve* his words made way" (550), and soon "Into her heart too easy entrance won" (734), a penetration that is simultaneously verbal and sexual. Indeed, Satan is said to have "impregn'd" Eve—something Adam evidently was unable to accomplish—with "his persuasive words" that reached her through "her ears" (736–7). Satan's seduction is a demonic analogue to the Annunciation, foreshadowed in Raphael's greeting of Eve, "the Angel *Hail* / Bestow'd, the salutation us'd / Long after to blest *Mary*" (5.385–7).

In the interval between her tryst with Satan and return to Adam, Eve unburdens herself in a soliloquy in which she first idolatrously vows to tend the tree "Not without Song, each Morning, and due praise" (9.800), and then muses:

> But to *Adam* in what sort
> Shall I appear? shall I to him make known
> As yet my change, and give him to partake

---

[2]   Le Comte (1978) calls attention to the possibility that the lines, "Such pleasure took the Serpent to behold / This Flow'ry Plat, the sweet recess of Eve" (9.455–6), contain an "unconscious sexual pun" on the word "plat," meaning not only "plot" but also "plait / pleat = fold, crease," a vaginal allusion reinforced by "sweet recess" (p. 79).

Full happiness with me, or rather not,
But keep the odds of Knowledge in my power
Without Copartner? So to add what wants
In Female Sex, the more to draw his Love,
And render me more equal, and perhaps,
A thing not undesirable, sometime
Superior: for inferior who is free?

(817–25)

For the only time in the poem, Eve voices a protest against her subordination, although she is less enamored by the prospect of "full happiness" in an egalitarian relationship than by the thought of reversing the gender hierarchy and becoming "superior" to Adam.[3] Her question, "for inferior who is free?," stands in contrast to the way in which, both before her fall and after her repentance, Eve not simply acquiesces but rejoices in her inferiority. In the state of innocence, she asserts that she enjoys "So far the happier lot" (4.446) by virtue of being beneath Adam, while after having been overcome by remorse in Book 10, she laments that she is "More miserable" than he because he has sinned "Against God only," whereas she bears the double burden of having sinned "against God and thee" (930–1). Eve's suppressed resentment bubbles up in her dream in which an angelic male figure promises that if she partakes of the "Fruit Divine" (5.67), she will "be henceforth among the Gods / Thyself a Goddess" (77–8); but only in the aftermath of her liaison with Satan does her nascent feminist consciousness achieve explicit articulation.

Milton extols the "wedded love" of Adam and Eve on the grounds that marriage is the "sole propriety / In Paradise of all things common else," thanks to which "adulterous lust / Was driv'n from men / Among the bestial herds to range" (4.751–5). Milton's condemnation of adultery as "bestial" (which is unfair to animals since marriage is a human institution) is the obverse of his celebration of the ideal of companionate marriage that emerges in the early modern period. Yet, as Mary Nyquist (1988) has observed, what is

---

[3] Of the many feminist critics who have elucidated the oppression of women inherent in Milton's hierarchical conception of the universe, I am most indebted to Christine Froula (1983) and Mary Nyquist (1985, 1988). Nyquist (1988) rightly takes to task the "apologetic tendency" that "is a feature of much North American academic literature on Milton" (p. 144*n*1), whose representatives include Lewalski (1974), Webber (1980), McColley (1983), and Patterson (2001). This special pleading reaches its apogee in *Feminist Milton*, where Joseph Wittreich (1987) argues that Milton's poems "do not deepen and extend, but rather decry and explode, the biblically sanctioned and culturally reinforced tradition of patriarchy and misogyny" (p. 10).

paramount in Milton's articulation of "the Protestant doctrine of marriage" is not Eve's "creation *after* Adam *per se* ... but her creation *for* him," which ratifies her "secondary status as a 'gift' from one patriarch to another" (p. 106). Although Milton regards heterosexual marriage as the bedrock of all social institutions, through which "the Charities / Of Father, Son, and Brother first were known" (756–7), the only kinship ties he mentions are those between men. As Greenblatt (2017) notes, marriage is "the only form of private property" (p. 217) in Eden, but it is Eve who belongs to Adam, and not the other way around.

Seen from this perspective, Eve's decision to eat the forbidden fruit—like the Queen's letter in Poe's short story and the Lady's gift of her girdle to Sir Gawain—is "the symbol of a pact" with Satan that "situates her in a symbolic chain foreign to the one which constitutes her faith" (Lacan, 1956, p. 42) to both her divine and human patriarchs. She desires to be an autonomous subject rather than an object of exchange between men, which is why she is initially more attracted to her own "smooth wat'ry image" (4.480) in the lake than she is to Adam, but this aspiration is condemned as sinful by the poem. She has to be instructed first by the voice of God and then by Adam to subdue her narcissism and accept that it is her fate to be ruled by her husband, "Whose image thou art" (472). When Eve concludes the recitation of her creation story by assuring Adam that she now sees "How beauty is excell'd by manly grace / And wisdom, which alone is truly fair" (490–1), what Christine Froula (1983) has termed her "indoctrination into her 'identity' is complete," and she "is so successfully colonized by patriarchal authority that she literally becomes its voice" (p. 329).

In the soliloquy after her fall, Eve contemplates turning the tables on Adam by not sharing the apple with him, which would allow her to keep the "odds of Knowledge" permanently in her favor and become not simply "more equal" but "Superior" to him by wielding the "power" she now possesses "Without Copartner." When she reflects that such a refusal would enable her to "add what wants in Female Sex," it is impossible to avoid diagnosing her as suffering from a cosmic case of penis envy. But since Eve feels this resentment because of her subaltern status in the hierarchy of creation, her complaint about what women lack is not evidence of any innate inferiority—anatomical or otherwise—but is rather a symptom of how Eve has been so thoroughly "colonized by patriarchal authority that she literally becomes its voice." As Karen Horney (1926) has put it in her critique of the Freudian shibboleth of penis envy, "women have adapted themselves to the wishes of men and felt as if their adaptation were their true nature" (pp. 56–7), and because of "the hitherto purely masculine character of our civilization," a girl is "exposed from birth onward to the suggestion—inevitable, whether conveyed brutally or delicately—of her inferiority, an experience that constantly stimulates her masculinity complex" (p. 69).

Horney's analysis allows us to trace the arc from Eve's "birth," when she is "delicately" initiated into an acceptance of her inferiority, to the full-blown manifestation of her "masculinity complex" after her fall. The most "brutal" expression of the ideology of a "purely masculine" civilization is Adam's outburst at his nadir of despair in Book 10, when Eve seeks to effect a reconciliation with him:

> O why did God,
> Creator wise, that peopl'd highest Heav'n
> With Spirits Masculine, create at last
> This novelty on Earth, this fair defect
> Of Nature, and not fill the World at once
> With Men as Angels without Feminine,
> Or find some other way to generate
> Mankind?
>
> (888–95)

Adam's diatribe echoes Eve's internalized conviction that women are constituted by an ontological "defect," and his fantasy of a "World ... without Feminine" takes to its logical conclusion the misogyny that is exemplified throughout Milton's epic.[4]

After the revolt of Satan and his legions has been crushed, God sends his Son "in Paternal Glory" (7.219) into the realm of Chaos, where the "Filial Godhead" (175) takes out "the golden Compasses" (226) with which he has been furnished and brings Creation into being through a process of long division. As Froula (1983) has discerned, Milton's cosmos is organized according to the principle of "hierarchical dualism" (p. 334), in which a binary logic goes hand in hand with the axiom of Western metaphysics that one element in every pair of opposites must be superior to the other. Thus, when God makes "two great Lights," the sun is the "greater" and the moon the "less" (7.346–8), subserviently "borrowing her Light / From him" (377–8). And what is true in the heavens, where there is "Male and Female Light" and "two great Sexes animate the world" (8.150–1), is all the more true in the relations between the sexes. For Milton, gender roles are natural, but a feminist analysis reveals that his gendered conception of nature is a cultural

---

4   For antecedents of these sentiments, see the invectives of Posthumous Leonatus in Act 2, Scene 5 of Shakespeare's *Cymbeline* and of Hippolytus in lines 616–19 of Euripides' eponymous tragedy.

construct. Whereas Adam, when he awakens for the first time, springs upward "with quick instinctive motion" toward the "ample Sky" (258–9) at which he has been gazing, Eve looks downward into the lake in which she sees the mediated reflection of "another Sky" (4.459). And when Raphael recounts to Adam how he and Eve were created by God, "Male he created thee, but thy consort / Female for race" (7.529–30), he addresses Adam directly but not Eve, whose sole defining characteristic is her procreative function.

Adam's lament at the need for women to "generate / Mankind" may be distorted by despair, but his assertion that "highest Heav'n" is inhabited exclusively by "Spirits Masculine" is factually accurate. To be sure, the narrator affirms that "Spirits when they please / Can either Sex assume, or both ... / Not ti'd or manacl'd with joint or limb" (1.423–6), but this allowance for the possibility of female—and even nonbinary—angels remains theoretical, and no such beings are shown to exist in the poem. Indeed, one wonders whether Raphael's blushing "Celestial rosy red" (8.619) when Adam asks him how angels "thir / Love express," whether "by looks only" (615–16) or also by some form of touch, may not be due to the absence of "Spirits Feminine" in Heaven. Similarly, although Raphael goes on to disclose that "if Spirits embrace, / Total they mix" (626–7), this celestial commingling is left to the reader's imagination. One has to look to Hell, where Satan sleeps beside Beëlzebub, his "Nearest Mate" (1.192) and "Companion dear" (5.672), to find not only the female body but also the overt expression of same-sex desire for which there is no room in the Father's homosocial house.

3

Satan's role as Eve's seducer in the marriage plot of *Paradise Lost* is a reprise of his failed uprising against God. As Beëlzebub says in the Council in Hell, it "would surpass / Common revenge" were one of the Devils able to lure the "puny inhabitants" of Earth "to our Party, that thir God / May prove thir foe" (2.367–71). What Satan could not accomplish in a frontal assault against God he hopes to achieve via an attack on Adam by committing adultery with his wife. In both phases of his campaign, Satan is in the position of the son in an oedipal configuration, but in the second—the repetition—he takes aim at the Father indirectly in the person of the Husband.

In a creative act without literary or theological precedent (Gilbert, 1942), Milton makes the occasion of Satan's rebellion the Father's proclamation that he has "begot" his "only Son" and "anointed" him the "Head" to whom "shall bow / All knees in Heav'n" (5.603–9). As Nyquist (1985) has expounded, "the deity emerges as, specifically, the Father" in *Paradise Lost* by virtue of this decree that calls into being the Son as the visible manifestation of a "a self-presence that is both patriarchal and divine" (p. 188). Yet the paradoxical effect of this assertion of identity is the generation of "an order split by an adversary who habitually appropriates the Father's Word only as a negative and alienating *(non) du père*" (p. 188). The alienation of patriarchal self-presence manifests itself as otherness in the forms of femininity, sexuality, homosexuality, and a universe governed by the principle of "hierarchical dualism."

To all appearances, the Father's decision to "anoint" the Son—chronologically the first thing that happens in the poem, from which everything else follows—is without any precipitating cause. As Bernard Paris (2010) has shown, however, it is possible to look beneath the surface and find a psychological explanation for this ostensibly unmotivated deed. When Gabriel captures Satan in Paradise, he responds to Satan's taunt that he and the other obedient angels "cringe" (4.945) before the throne of God with the following retort:

> And thou, sly hypocrite, who now wouldst seem
> Patron of liberty, who more than thou
> Once fawn'd, and cring'd, and servilely ador'd
> Heav'n's awful Monarch? wherefore but in hope
> To dispossess him, and thyself to reign?
>
> (957–61)

Despite being an "exchange of insults," Paris contends, "Gabriel's charge of hypocrisy rings true, for Lucifer's adoration was clearly insincere" (p. 14). What is more, Lucifer's discontent must have been perceived by God because, as the narrator affirms, hypocrisy is "the only evil that walks / Invisible, except to God alone" (3.683–4).

In this analysis, which goes beyond a logological reading by using evidence from the poem to demonstrate how what Milton actually does directly contravenes his avowed theological intention—how, in Blake's famous phrase, he "was of the Devil's party without knowing it" (Noyes, 1956, p. 211)—God emerges as anything but a serene and supremely just sovereign of the universe. Rather, he is a touchy tyrant who, as Shelley wrote in *A Defence of Poetry*, "in the cold security of undoubted triumph inflicts the most horrible revenge upon his enemy" (p. 1107). As Paris (2010) spells out God's devious strategy, having been narcissistically injured by Satan's recalcitrance, he elevates the Son as a means of "penalizing the ungrateful angels with what they feel to be demotion on the pretext of making them happy, while preparing to cast them out should they disobey an edict that is calculated to make them rebel" (p. 16). This pattern repeats itself in human history when God allows the sacrificial offering of Abel to catch fire but rejects that of Cain, "for his was not sincere; / Whereat hee inly rag'd" (11.443-4), just as Satan rages when God withdraws his love and showers favor on the rival brother—now officially recognized as the "only Son"—who gives him the unqualified adoration and obedience he demands from all his progeny.

What is tragic in this situation, though no less obscured by the ideology of the poem than God's responsibility for Satan's rebellion, is how God imposes a double bind on his creations that requires them to choose between obedience and disobedience, leaving them no room to follow a path of genuine independence without regard to his wishes and expectations. This is why, the instant Satan begins to have a thought of his own—to want to escape from God's authoritarian straitjacket—femininity bursts into the poem, shattering the tranquility of the heretofore exclusively masculine preserve of Heaven, and is given the name of Sin.

Yet it is not in Heaven but at the Gates of Hell, through which he needs to pass to accomplish his mission on Earth, that Satan first encounters the character of Sin, as well as of Death; and when he does he fails to recognize them. The narrator describes the scene:

> Before the Gates there sat
> On either side a formidable shape:
> The one seem'd Woman to the waist, and fair,
> But ended foul in many a scaly fold
> Voluminous and vast, a Serpent arm'd
> With mortal sting.
>
> (2.648–53)

This hideous depiction of the female body, which amalgamates Spenser's allegory of Error in Book 1 of *The Faerie Queene* with Ovid's portrayal of Scylla in Book 14 of the *Metamorphoses*, literalizes King Lear's rant, "But to the girdle do the gods inherit, / Beneath is all the fiends." Nor does Milton's phantasmagoria of the female genitalia end here. Around Sin's loins "A cry of Hell Hounds never ceasing bark'd," only to "creep" periodically "into her womb," where they would "kennel" and "howl'd / Within unseen" (655-9). The other menacing figure, a shapeless shape, shakes "a dreadful Dart" at Satan, and "what seem'd his head / The likeness of a Kingly Crown had on" (672-3).

What ensues is a classic father/son confrontation between Satan and Death in which the antagonists, like Laius and Oedipus, do not realize their familial bond. Only when Sin melodramatically throws herself between them is lethal combat averted:

> O Father, what intends thy hand, she cried,
> Against thy only Son? What fury, O Son,
> Possesses thee to bend that mortal Dart
> Against thy Father's head?
>
> (727–30)

Bewildered by her words and not believing he has ever seen "A sight more detestable than him and thee" (745), Satan denies knowing them, which leads Sin to remind him how, while still in Heaven and in the presence of all the rebel angels, she had sprung from the "left side" (755) of his head, "a Goddess arm'd" (757), following which he fell in love with her and they engaged in sexual intercourse:

> Thyself in me thy perfect image viewing
> Becam'st enamor'd, and such joy thou took'st
> With me in secret, that my womb conceiv'd
> A growing burden.
>
> (764–7)

Sin becomes pregnant in Heaven before the outbreak of the war with God, but when Satan's forces are defeated and cast into Hell, she is ejected along with them; and it is in Hell that she gives birth to her "odious offspring," Satan's "own begotten," whose violent passage through her "entrails" causes her "nether shape" to become "Distorted" (781–4) in monstrous fashion.

Sin's narrative combines an allusion to Hesiod's account of the birth of Athena from the head of Zeus in the *Theogony* with the exposition of how "every man is tempted" in the Epistle of James: "Then when lust hath conceived, it bringeth forth sin: and sin when it is finished bringeth forth death" (1.14,16). Satan is tempted, in Milton's ideology, when he harbors resentment against God and "conceives" of Sin in his mind; but this thought leads to "lust," which in turn leads to Sin literally "conceiving" and "bringing forth" Death. That Sin springs from the "left side" of Satan's head betokens her inferior position in Milton's hierarchical dualism, just as Eve is taken from the "left side" of Adam (8.465), whereas the Son sits at the "right hand" (5.606) of the Father. As a female, Sin's extrusion from Heaven is inevitable. The classical and the feminine are equated with the demonic in Milton's Christian universe, and Sin, who masqueraded in Heaven as the Goddess of Wisdom, is unmasked in Hell as Error and Scylla.

Satan's love for Sin, his "perfect image," is quintessentially narcissistic, but because he takes "secret joy" with her, it is also a case of incest between a father and his adult daughter.[5] Indeed, incest is the *sexualized form of loving one's image*, and Satan's sexual relations with Sin complete the oedipal dynamics in his averted showdown with Death. Unlike Satan's intercourse with Sin, however, which is consensual, Death rapes his fleeing and terrorized mother, causing her to bear the Hell Hounds Satan has already seen—and heard—crawling in and out of her body:

> And in embraces forcible and foul
> Ingend'ring with me, of that rape begot
> These yelling Monsters that with ceaseless cry
> Surround me, as thou saw'st, hourly conceiv'd
> And hourly born, with sorrow infinite
> To me, for when they list, into the womb
> That bred them they return, and howl and gnaw
> My Bowels, thir repast.
>
> (793–800)

This, too, is an act of incest, but one that is infinitely more horrific and with the roles reversed, so that Sin is now the mother rather than the daughter. By his act of violence, Death has not only imitated but surpassed his father, begetting his own "yelling Monsters," which makes Sin's womb the site not of one or two, but of three generations of incest.[6]

Just as Death outdoes his father in the sexual sphere, so, too, he has the upper hand in their initial encounter. Satan, who at the beginning of Book 2 sits in splendor "High on a Throne of Royal State" (1), at first expresses disdain for the specter that seeks to prevent him from passing through the

[5]	For real-life examples of consensual father/daughter incest, see Kathryn Harrison's memoir, *The Kiss* (1997), where she remarks on "the fascination of our likeness, that we resemble each other in ways that transcend physical similarities" (p. 57) but is too smitten to be able to see that "my father himself is selfish, a narcissist, dangerous" (p. 80), and the unexpurgated volume of Anaïs Nin's diary, *Incest* (1992), as well as Nin's fictional rendering of her experience in "Winter of Artifice" (1948).

[6]	In a footnote added in 1920 to the *Three Essays on the Theory of Sexuality*, Freud (1905b) writes that "the genital apparatus remains the neighbour of the cloaca, and actually ... 'in the case of women is only taken from it on lease'" (p. 187). The embedded quotation, taken from Lou Andreas-Salomé's paper "'Anal' and 'Sexual'" (1916), reprises Freud's Augustinian theme that *inter urinas et faeces nascimur*, a view of the female anatomy made literal in Sin's conflation of her "womb" and her "Bowels."

gates, "Retire, or taste thy folly, and learn by proof, / Hell-born, not to contend with Spirits of Heav'n" (2.686–7). But he is met with a defiant rejoinder:

> And reck'n'st thyself with Spirits of Heaven,
> Hell-doom'd, and breath'st defiance here and scorn,
> Where I reign King, and to enrage thee more,
> Thy King and Lord?
>
> (696–69)

There are two would-be rulers in Hell, and as Roland M. Frye (1978) notes, although "Milton provides Satan with the most stunningly ornate throne in literature," it is only Death who is given "the dignity of a crown" (p. 117); and he would surely have been victorious in their combat had Sin not warned Satan not to count on his armor to save him, "for that mortal dint, / Save he who reigns above, none can resist" (813–14). Once Sin has made it clear that they are all on the same team, however, the conflict is averted. Satan assures his "Dear Daughter" and his "fair Son," the "dear pledge / Of dalliance" (817–19) with her in Heaven, that he comes "no enemy, but to set free / From this dismal house of pain, / Both him and thee" (822–4).

Because Satan attempted to "dispossess" God in order to "reign" in his place, he has undermined the principle of paternal authority and cannot prevent his own son from rebelling against him. This oedipal logic makes it impossible for him to rest securely on his throne. The same process plays itself out in the human realm when Adam, at his nadir of despair after the Fall, checks his lament that he did not ask to be created by God with the thought that his own son could one day level the same reproach against him:

> and though God
> Made thee without thy leave, what if thy Son
> Prove disobedient, and reprov'd, retort,
> Wherefore didst thou beget me?
>
> (10.759–62)

Again, in Book 11, when Michael informs Adam that he is to be banished from his "Capital Seat" in Eden, to which future generations would have come "to celebrate / And reverence thee thir great Progenitor," he underscores that Adam has forfeited not only his moral and political but also his geographical authority: "But this preëminence thou hast lost, brought down / To dwell on even ground now with thy Sons" (343–8).

The oedipal dynamics of *Paradise Lost* culminate in Book 10 when Satan, having successfully tempted Adam and Eve, once more encounters his spawn on his return journey to Hell. Upon seeing her father emerge intact "From out of *Chaos*" (317), Sin rhapsodizes how "My Heart, which by a secret harmony / Still moves with thine, join'd in connexion sweet" (358–9), to which Satan responds by acknowledging his bond not only with his "Fair Daughter" but also with his "Son and Grandchild both" (384). As in *Oedipus the King*, where Oedipus's incest with Jocasta makes him, in Teiresias's words, her "son and husband" as well as the "father and brother" to his children (456–8), Satan's incest with Sin creates a doubling of kinship ties. And now that the Fall has taken place, Death has with his mace constructed a massive bridge allowing for easy passage between Hell and Earth:

> and now in little space
> The confines met of Empyrean Heav'n
> And of this World, and on the left side Hell
> With long reach interpos'd; three several ways
> In sight, to each of these three places led.
>
> (320–4)

Satan's family reunion takes place near the foot of this highway, and the junction of "three several ways" uncannily replicates the "place where three roads meet" (716) that is the site of Oedipus's fatal collision with Laius in *Oedipus the King*. In the creative imaginations of both Milton and Sophocles, the crossroads symbolize the womb of the daughter/mother where three generations commingle. Since "Empyrean Heav'n" is the realm of God, while Hell on the "left side" belongs to Satan and "this World" is the implicitly feminine prize over which they are contending, Milton restores the infernal triad of Satan, Sin, and Death to the larger context in which Satan is not the father in danger of being slain by his son, but the son who seeks in vain to challenge the sovereignty of his omnipotent Father.

4

In their first recorded conversation, Adam tells Eve that God has enjoined upon them "no other service than to keep / This one, this easy charge" (4.421–2) not to eat of the Tree of Knowledge. It is, he continues, "The only sign of our obedience left / Among so many signs of power and rule" (428–9). In *The Christian Doctrine*—the Latin treatise Milton probably completed by the early 1660s, but the manuscript of which was not discovered until 1823— he elaborates on the significance of the prohibition: "It was necessary that something should be forbidden or commanded as a test of fidelity, and that an act in its own nature indifferent, in order that man's obedience might thereby be manifested" (Hughes, 1957, p. 993). St. Augustine writes in exactly the same way in *The City of God* of "that one tree, which was interdicted not because it was in itself bad, but for the sake of commanding a pure and simple obedience" (13.20).

For both Milton and Augustine, there is nothing intrinsic to the tree that makes its fruit forbidden. Rather, it becomes forbidden *because* God has prohibited it, and he could as easily have chosen any other tree. The prohibition, in other words, is *arbitrary*—or, as Milton puts it, "in its own nature indifferent"—since the point of the interdiction is to serve as a "test of fidelity" of unfallen Adam and Eve, or what Adam calls "the sole sign of our obedience" to the Creator who has laid down the conditions of their existence to which they must adhere. Adam and Eve's succumbing to temptation in the Garden of Eden furnishes the prototype of the pear-stealing episode in Augustine's *Confessions,* and in both instances there is a puzzling lack of motivation, at least on a conscious level, for their actions. Augustine reiterates in *The City of God* that the Fall was "committed about food," the lure of which arose from the fact that it was "not bad nor noxious, except because it was forbidden" (14.12).

That the "indifferent" prohibition on the Tree of Knowledge imposed as a "test of fidelity" and "sign of obedience" on Adam and Eve is, like Augustine's theft of the pears, a screen for the Oedipus complex is illuminated by the observation of Claude Lévi-Strauss (1949) that *the fact of being a rule, independent of modalities, is indeed the very essence of the incest prohibition*" (p. 32). The insight of structuralist anthropology that the central point of the incest taboo, like that of the prohibition on the Tree of Knowledge, is simply "*the fact of being a rule*" can be reformulated in psychoanalytic terms to mean that the eating of the forbidden fruit by Adam and Eve constitutes the "manifest content" of the Fall, the "latent content" of which is a violation of the incest taboo.

When Sin recounts her origin story to Satan at the Gates of Hell, she says that after she burst forth from his head, all the angels "recoil'd afraid / At first, and call'd me *Sin,* and for a Sign / Portentous held me," until her "attractive graces won / The most averse, thee chiefly" (2.759–63). Beyond the consonance of "Sin" and "Sign," Milton has the angels shrink from Sin as a "Sign Portentous" because she is the "sign of disobedience," a counterpart to the "sign of obedience" in the Tree of Knowledge and a personification of the consequences of defying God. The Fall of Man brings sin and death into the world, and in the allegory of Satan, Sin, and Death Milton renders visible what it means to eat from the Tree of Knowledge.

In addition to being born from the "left side" of their male progenitors, Eve is the "image" (4.472) of Adam, who addresses her the "Best Image of myself and dearer half" (5.95) after she tells him her frightening dream, just as Sin is the "perfect image" of Satan. And as Sin is both Satan's daughter and his lover, so, too, Adam is both the husband and father of Eve, whom he twice calls "Daughter of God and Man" (4.660, 9.291). Yet Milton mutes the incestuous aspect of the "wedded love" of the human characters and highlights their narcissism. Whereas Sin metamorphoses from Athena into Scylla, Eve is Narcissus in being drawn to her own "smooth wat'ry image" in the lake. Only in the fall of Satan do we see enacted the violation of the incest taboo that is screened by the "indifference" of the prohibition against eating from the Tree of Knowledge. Indeed, since incest is the sexually explicit form of loving one's own image, the conclusion follows that *the fall of Satan is to the fall of man as incest is to narcissism.*

It is integral to the patriarchal logic of *Paradise Lost* that Sin should be the first female in the history of the universe. To be sure, Milton in his opening invocation appeals to his "Heav'nly Muse" (1.6), who is identified with Urania and the Celestial Patroness in the invocations to Books 7 and 9. Yet, as Froula (1983) points out, this female figure, who is said also to have inspired Moses—understood to be the author of Genesis and the following four books of the Pentateuch—is "transformed from *witness* of Creation to *Creator*" (p. 337) when Milton proclaims:

> Thou from the first
> Wast present, and with mighty wings outspread
> Dove-like satst brooding on the vast Abyss
> And mad'st it pregnant.
>
> (19–22)

By the end of the invocation, Froula continues, the Muse "is 'transsexualized' … precisely at the point at which Milton has most at stake in establishing his epic authority," and thereby turns "not just into a Creator-figure but into that powerful self-sufficient *male* Creator so crucial to Adam in his relations with Eve" (p. 338). The Muse, now renamed the "Spirit" (17) and identified with the Holy Spirit, which in *The Christian Doctrine* is said to have appeared "in the likeness of a dove" (Hughes, 1957, p. 966), impregnates the "Abyss" and hatches the life he has produced. Thus, just as there are no female figures in Heaven, while both Sin and Eve have fathers but no mothers, the metamorphosis of the Muse reveals that "the repression of the mother is the genesis of Genesis" (Froula, 1983, p. 337).

Not only do Sin and Eve have fathers but no mothers, but the same is true of Satan and Adam. Everything in Creation goes back to God the Father. And if what Eve sees reflected in the lake may be interpreted as a reflection of her lost mother, it is from the illusion of having a feminine creator that she must be delivered in order to be socialized into the patriarchal order. By drawing out the implications of the Genesis narrative in which woman is created from the body of the first man, rather than males being born from the body of women, as Froula (1983) argues, Milton underscores that "it is not that Adam is an imperfect image of his God, rather, his God is a *perfected* image of Adam: an all-powerful *male* Creator who soothes Adam's fears of female power by Himself claiming credit for the original creation of the world" (p. 332).[7]

The relation between the two male creators is displayed in Book 8 when Adam petitions God to bestow on him a human partner:

Thou in thyself are perfet, and in thee
Is no deficience found; not so is Man,
But in degree, the cause of his desire
By conversation with his like to help,
Or solace his defects.

(415–19)

The difference between God and Adam is between God's perfection, which is absolute, and Adam's perfection, which is only relative or "in degree," and the reason he seeks a companion. Before God accedes to Adam's request, he permits himself to banter with his lieutenant because the "nice and subtle happiness" (399) Adam envisions for himself shows that he will "Taste no pleasure, though in pleasure, solitary" (402). The phrase "in pleasure" alludes to the Hebrew meaning of Eden as a "place of pleasure," but God's joke insinuates that even in Paradise Adam will not remain contented with the "solitary pleasure" of masturbation. Thus, Eve originates in Adam's masturbation fantasy, which God gratifies when he creates Eve just as she appears to Adam in his ensuing dream. In so doing, he makes her literally, in Nyquist's words, "a 'gift' from one patriarch to another."

---

[7] Milton combines an allusion to the Witches' riddle of Macduff's Caesarean section, which makes him the incarnation of pure masculinity, and to the character of Macbeth in Shakespeare's tragedy when—in the course of the prophetic vision of human history revealed to him by Michael—Adam beholds the innumerable "Diseases dire" (11.474) with which his descendants will be afflicted as a consequence of the Fall: "Though not of Woman born; compassion quell'd / His best of Man" (496–7).

The "repression of the mother" that is ubiquitous in *Paradise Lost* is a symptom of the "fears of female power" that haunt patriarchy. Indeed, as Froula (1983) elaborates, the cultural fantasy that Eve is created from Adam's rib "dramatizes an archetypal womb envy as constitutive of male identity" (p. 332). Ironically, therefore, the penis envy confessed by Eve as the colonized "voice of patriarchy," even when she is most in rebellion against it, constitutes a defensive projection onto women of the "mystery of motherhood" analyzed by Horney (1932) as a bedrock of masculine pathology since "That Shepherd, who first taught the chosen Seed" (1.8) the story of Genesis.

From this standpoint, the grotesque nether regions of Sin become explicable as a graphic representation of the "womb envy" and "dread of woman" that are the underside of patriarchy. By its iron law, independence is equated with disobedience—that is, Sin—and Sin in turn is equated with the female body, the "attractive graces" of which shatter the tranquility of the heavenly monastery of "Spirits Masculine." The punishment for Eve's fall, relayed on behalf of the Father by the Son, likewise centers on her reproductive organs, "Thy sorrow I will greatly multiply / By thy Conception; Children shalt thou bring / In sorrow forth," while ratifying her subaltern status, "to thy Husband's will / Thine shall submit, hee over thee shall rule" (10.193–6). To counteract this disruption of the patriarchal order, as Adam comes to understand, it must be a "Virgin Mother" (12.379) from whose "Womb the Son / Of God most High" (381–2) is miraculously born. But though it is granted to Mary to bring forth Christ, she herself is not divine.

5

The mirror image of the oedipal logic that governs Satan's rebellion plays itself out with respect to the "anointed" Son. Just as any desire for independence from God is treated as an act of disobedience and punished accordingly, so, too, obedience to Him is a product of coercion, although this painful truth is masked by the ideology of the poem. What Milton would have us believe is summed up in Raphael's statement to Adam, "freely we serve / Because we freely love" (5.538–9). But this admirable sentiment, which would hold true if God were a genuinely loving and not an authoritarian father, is belied by Raphael's immediately preceding declaration, "Myself and all th' Angelic Host that stand / In sight of God enthroned, our happy state / Hold, as you yours, *while our obedience holds*" (5.535–7; italics added). This shows that the love and service of the "Angelic Host" are *not* free since they would be met with the same fate as Satan and his followers should they cease to pay homage to God.

A few lines earlier Raphael asserts, "Our voluntary service he requires, / Not our necessitated" (529–30). This statement again unwittingly lays bare the bad faith on which God's sovereignty depends since to "require" something "voluntary" is a contradiction in terms. In Paris's (2010) words, God "seems to need to feel that their love is free so it can give him pleasure and at the same time to behave coercively so as to be sure of receiving the adoration he requires" (p. 12). Like his elevation of the Son because he perceives Lucifer's discontent and wishes to provoke him into open war in order to be able to exact retribution, this is the behavior of a narcissistic parent. What Abdiel calls the "Golden Sceptre" with which God presides over the souls in Heaven is simply the "Iron Rod" that he uses "to bruise and break" (5.885) anyone who steps out of line in a velvet glove.

By the Son of God—the one perfect created being—love and service are indeed freely given, but instead of facing the threat of damnation he must forfeit his life. Unlike the angels, all of whom "stood mute" (3.217) when the Father asked which of them would "be mortal to redeem / Man's mortal crime" (214–15), the Son implores, "On mee let thine anger fall" (237), and volunteers to undergo the Crucifixion, "on me let Death wreck all his rage" (241). Although the Father frames the issue in impersonal terms as one of justice, which demands that the human race be irrevocably damned unless someone offers to "pay / The rigid satisfaction" (210–11) for Adam's "Treason" (206), "the whole design of the Bible"—as Burke called it—which makes the Fall inevitable from a narrative standpoint, can be viewed as an elaborate scheme to gratify what William Empson (1961) has described as the Father's "craving to torture his Son" (p. 246), while washing his hands of responsibility for this sadomasochistic scenario.

It might at first appear that the Son is an equal partner in what Paris (2010) has termed the "glory system" (p. 11) that governs his relationship with the Father, as it does Heaven as a whole. Resplendent with "Filial obedience: as a sacrifice / Glad to be offer'd, he attends the will / Of his great Father" (3.269–71), who promises him, "Therefore thy Humiliation shall exalt / With thee thy Manhood also to this Throne" (313–14). Having been "Anointed universal King," the Son is told he will wield "all Power" and "reign for ever" (317–18). For his part, prior to ascending "The Chariot of Paternal Deity" (6.750) in which he will vanquish Satan and his legions on the third day of the War in Heaven, the "filial Godhead" assures his only begetter, "thou always seek'st / To glorify thy Son, I always thee, / As is most just" (6.724–6).

But the appearance of reciprocity in this two-person mutual adoration society is an illusion because the Son's reign turns out to have an expiration date. As the Father explains in the presence of "the Heav'nly Choir" (3.217), after the Son has presided over "the general Doom" (328) in which "The

World shall burn, and from her ashes spring / New Heav'n and Earth" (334–5), there will be no further need for his services, "Then thou thy regal Sceptre shalt lay by, / For regal Sceptre then no more shall need, / God shall be All in All" (339–41). By the same token, at his moment of greatest triumph, the Son looks forward to abdicating his throne at the end of time:

> Sceptre and Power, thy giving, I assume,
> And gladlier shall resign, when in the end
> Thou shalt be All in All, and I in thee
> For ever, and in mee all whom thou lov'st.

> (6.730–3)

To readers who do not share Milton's Christian fundamentalism—as it may justly be called despite some heterodox wrinkles—the prospect of the world being burned to a crisp is unlikely to seem as appealing as it did to him. But the underlying problem is that God places all his subordinates in a double bind. In a universe ruled by the law of the excluded middle, obedience is coerced, dissent is not tolerated, and the Son's "happiness entire" (6.741) consists in abject submission to the Father, first by volunteering for a suicide mission, and finally by obliterating himself when he—and the rest of Creation—become absorbed into the "All in All" that is synonymous for Milton with the paternal principle.[8] Satan's attempt to overthrow "Heav'n's awful Monarch" is punished with castration when he loses his authority as a father and encounters his son Death wearing a "Kingly Crown," but the same is true of the Son's display of "Filial obedience," which illustrates Otto Fenichel's (1945) explanation of the unconscious logic at work in the boy's feminine castration complex: "if I act as if I had no penis any more they will not cut it off. … If castration cannot be avoided anyhow I prefer it actively in anticipation of what is to come, and I shall at least have the advantage of ingratiating myself with the threatening person" (p. 79).

Of Milton's three heresies—material monism, mortalism, and Arianism— the most psychologically significant is the third, named after Arius, a Cyrenaic theologian of the late third and early fourth centuries who denied the doctrine of the Trinity and held the Son to be subordinate to the Father. As Milton writes in *The Christian Doctrine*, "it is so self-evident as to require

---

[8] In the *Art of Logic*, the Latin treatise expounding the method of the Huguenot Petrus Ramus, probably sketched out during Milton's years at Cambridge but not published until 1672 (Hartig, 1972, pp. 14–16), he defines the law of the excluded middle by quoting the statement of Boethius that "between affirmation and negation there is no middle ground" (Patterson, 1935, p. 139).

no explanation ... that the Father alone is a self-existent God, and that a being that is not self-existent cannot be God" (Hughes, 1957, p. 937), from which it follows that "the Father is greater than the Son in all things" (p. 939), while the Holy Spirit "must evidently be considered as inferior to both Father and Son" (p. 968). And because "the Son derives his essence from the Father, he is posterior to the Father not merely in rank ... but also in essence," and since he "did not beget, but was begotten," the Son "is not the first cause, but the effect, and therefore is not the supreme God" (p. 956).

To employ the categories of Burke (1961), it is axiomatic for Milton that God the Father is at once "first in time," "first in importance," and "first in the sense of a logical grounding" for all other beings, a "'causal ancestor'" from whom all others are "deduced or derived as lineal descendants" (p. 180). But there is a fault in this bedrock principle because, notwithstanding Milton's claim in *The Christian Doctrine* that "it was in God's power consistently with the perfection of his own essence not to have begotten the Son" (Hughes, 1957, p. 934), it is impossible to be a father without having a child. As Milton himself writes in *The Tenure of Kings and Magistrates*, "We know that king and subject are relatives, and relatives have no longer being than in the relation" (p. 767). Indeed, inasmuch as the concept of fatherhood only has meaning "in the relation," Milton's assertion in *The Christian Doctrine* is self-contradictory and his unprecedented decision to make the Father's "begetting" of the Son the primal event in the history of the universe is the ultimate self-deconstructive act. What Nyquist (1985) terms the "originary utterance" that establishes the Son as "the Word" is also the means by which God emerges as the Father, but what is supposed to ground a patriarchal and divine order of self-presence turns out to be "traversed as if endlessly by the enmity of Satan" (p. 188), in whose wake trail the traces of what Derrida (1972) calls "différance" or "the generative movement in the play of differences" (p. 27), of which the most disruptive is that of gender.

6

If there is one truth that is universally acknowledged about *Paradise Lost*, it is that God and Satan are engaged in a cosmic war. The narrator echoes not only the Father and the Son but also Adam in terming Satan "the Adversary of God and Man" (2.630), while in his opening dialogue with Beëlzebub Satan proclaims his intent to thwart the will of God:

> If then his Providence
> Out of our evil seek to bring forth good,

Our labor must be to pervert that end,
And out of good still to find means of evil.

(1.162–5)

The three days of the War in Heaven in Book 6 typologically foreshadow Christ's victory over Satan through his death and resurrection, when "Death his death's wound shall then receive" (3.252)—an interim victory that will be sealed with "the general Doom" (328), when "Hell, her numbers full, / Thenceforth shall be for ever shut," and from the ashes of the incinerated world shall "spring / New Heav'n and Earth, wherein the just shall dwell" (332–5) for all eternity.

But though this conflict between God and Satan takes center stage in *Paradise Lost*, its prominence makes it easy to overlook, as Augustine Habeck (2024) has astutely pointed out, that "even when warring with God, the fallen angels adhere to and value the system of order he has created."[9] Habeck notes that in the Council in Hell Mammon "proposes that they use Heaven as a model" in making the best of their plight: "as he our darkness, cannot we his Light, / Imitate when we please?" (2.269–70); and "later in his speech Mammon says they should organize their efforts into a 'settled state / Of order'" (279–80). Thus, even though Satan is the antagonist in the poem, he and his legions are fighting the battle on God's terms, in which good and evil are objectively existing coordinates of the universe and their doomed mission can only be to attempt to "pervert" God's providential design. Because all created beings, including the Son, owe their existence to God the Father, they are caught in a double bind in which they must either obey his "Golden Sceptre" or be smitten with the "Iron Rod" of death or damnation if they go their own way.

Habeck's insight that "though the good of Heaven and the evil of Hell might seem like the ultimate dichotomy, Heaven, Hell, and Earth are all made from God's will, and all are part of the same patriarchal system," is, however, only the first step in a more far-reaching argument. And that is that the only domain in *Paradise Lost* "that exists apart from God is the realm of Chaos, a realm that, since before the beginning of time, God has been slowly crushing between his creations." It is this—and not the war between God and Satan— that is "the true war" in *Paradise Lost*, one in which, paradoxically enough, God and Satan are on the *same* side, since they are both aligned with "the

---

⁹ It is a pleasure to acknowledge my indebtedness to Augustine Habeck, one of my undergraduate students at the University of Florida, whose paper inspired the ideas developed in this section.

created universe" that values "the masculine, stratified, and the orderly," as opposed to the "feminine, egalitarian, and disorderly," which Milton equates with the realm "where eldest *Night* / And *Chaos*, Ancestors of Nature, hold / Eternal Anarchy" (2.894–6). But the third and final step that needs to be taken to bring out the full force of Habeck's thesis is to recognize that Milton is indebted for his conception of Chaos to Lucretius's philosophical epic *On the Nature of Things*, and that the "battle against Chaos" in *Paradise Lost* is thus simultaneously Milton's battle against Lucretius. Only when one steps outside the oedipal and patriarchal framework that fills almost the entirety of the vast canvas of *Paradise Lost* does it, as David Quint (2004) has written, "become apparent how the epic poet who would justify the ways of God to men and explain the Fall that brought death into the world engages, beneath the surface of his text, the godless Roman poet and his doctrine of sheer contingency and purely natural mortality" (p. 848).

When Satan enters the "nethermost Abyss" where "*Chaos* and *ancient Night*" sit jointly enthroned, he assures them that he comes "no Spy" (2.969–70), and indeed that it will bring them "no mean recompense" if he "that Region lost / All usurpation thence expell'd, reduce / To her original darkness and your sway" (981–3). He claims, in other words, to be acting for their benefit in seeking to destroy the universe newly created by God, "Yours be th' advantage all, mine the revenge" (986). Chaos, described by the narrator as "a brok'n foe" (1040), replies:

> I upon my Frontiers here
> Keep residence; if all I can will serve
> That little which is left so to defend,
> Encroacht on still through [y]our intestine broils
> Weak'ning the Sceptre of old *Night*: first Hell
> Your dungeon stretching far and wide beneath;
> Now lately Heaven and Earth, another World
> Hung o'er my Realm, link'd in a golden Chain
> To that side Heav'n from whence your Legions fell.[10]
>
> (998–1006)

Persuaded that they have a common interest, Chaos concludes by wishing Satan success in his mission: "go and speed; / Havoc and spoil and ruin are my gain" (1008–9).

---

[10] I follow Leonard's (1998) edition of Milton's poems in accepting the emendation, first proposed in 1733, of "our intestine broils" to "your intestine broils." Leonard notes that "Heaven" in line 1004 refers to "the universe surrounding our earth," which belongs to Creation, "as distinct from *Heaven* (1006), the abode of God" (p. 743).

In describing the war between God and Satan as "*your* intestine broils," Chaos makes it clear that, from his perspective, their conflict is indeed a civil one in which he has no stake, but which has resulted in the increasing loss of his territory. "First Hell" and "lately Heaven and Earth" have been carved out of his domain, leaving him with "little … to defend." As Habeck observes, the fact that Night, who "is given female pronouns," wields the "Sceptre" in Chaos—as God and Satan do in their respective kingdoms—makes this realm of "Eternal Anarchy" at once "patriarchal and matriarchal," as well as one in which all the other entities—Orcus, Ades, Demogorgon, and the rest—are not "said to be below them," but rather "all share the same space in Chaos's palace." This leaves only God's Heaven as never having belonged to Chaos, from which, as John Leonard (2000) has commented, "the natural inference is that Heaven and Night are coeternal" (p. 213). And since—as Leonard likewise underscores—it is Night, and not Chaos, to which a womb is repeatedly ascribed in the poem, whereas Milton "speaks of Chaos as 'embryon atoms' (2.900) within Night's womb," which "is an 'abortive gulf' (441) that conceives, but cannot deliver, embryonic matter" (p. 207), the relation of Chaos to Night comes into focus as that of atoms to the void in Lucretius's awe-inspiring conception of the universe in which human life happens to have evolved.

In the event, however, Chaos, like Eve, is deceived by Satan's promises. When Satan returns to Hell from what he believes to have been his triumphant voyage to Earth, he recounts how he was "forc't to ride / Th' untractable Abyss, plung'd in the womb / Of unoriginal *Night* and *Chaos* wild," but proceeds to lie to his followers when he adds that, "jealous of thir secrets," Chaos and Night "fiercely oppos'd / My journey strange, with clamorous uproar / Protesting Fate supreme" (10.475–80). In fact, they would have been better advised to put up a fiercer resistance, since, as we know, after the Fall of Man has brought Sin and Death into the world, Death, with his "Mace petrific" (294), smites the "raging Sea" (286) of Chaos to construct a "stupendous Bridge" (351) between Earth and Hell, which further encroaches on the already-diminished dominion of "the Anarch old" (2.988). As Satan descends "The Causey to Hell Gate," the narrator relates, "on either side / Disparted *Chaos* over-built exclaim'd, / And with resounding surge the bars assail'd," but they "scorn'd his indignation" (10.415–18), and his protests are to no avail. Death and Sin prove unwittingly to be God's agents—he calls them "My Hell-hounds" (630)—and Chaos and Night are losers rather than winners in their negotiations with Satan.

Whereas what is at stake in God's war with Satan is the choice between salvation and damnation, in God and Satan's joint war against Chaos— and Milton's battle with Lucretius—it is the choice between existence and extinction. As Belial puts it in responding to Moloch's appeal to the fallen angels to renew their war with God, even if it means his "utmost ire" might "reduce / To nothing" their hitherto "eternal being" (2.95–8), this is a counsel of despair:

> To be no more; sad cure; for who would lose,
> Though full of pain, this intellectual being,
> Those thoughts that wander through Eternity,
> To perish rather, swallow'd up and lost
> In the wide womb of uncreated night,
> Devoid of sense and motion?

(146–51)

In these beautiful lines, which advocate eternal torment as preferable to annihilation, Night is "uncreated," just as Satan terms her (or it) "unoriginal," as Hughes explicates in a note to the later passage, "because nothing existed before it to originate it"; and in both instances Milton employs the image of a womb to convey the idea of being "swallow'd up and lost" (whether with or without motion) like an atom in the void of infinite space.

In the most famous example of this image cluster, the "wild Abyss" into which Satan gazes prior to commencing his epic ascent from Hell to Earth is described by the poet as "The Womb of Nature and perhaps her Grave" (2.910–11). As scholars have long recognized, Milton here alludes to Book 5, line 259 of *On the Nature of Things*, where Lucretius calls the earth *omniparens eadem rerum commune sepulchrum*, or, in Philip Hardie's (1995) literal translation, "both universal parent and common grave of things" (p. 20*n*2). But what appears to have been overlooked is that Milton replaces "earth" with "womb," thereby linking this passage to all the other references to Night's womb in *Paradise Lost*; and, even more consequentially, it is now Chaos and Night that are not only the "womb of Nature" but also "perhaps her Grave." The implications of this from a Christian perspective are indeed alarming. As Quint (2004) explains, "Lucretius would have it that Chaos is the condition of the whole universe and that worlds created by chance within it are due in time to fall back through entropy into its disorder" (p. 859). Although it is axiomatic for Milton that God, and not chance, has created the world, he nonetheless acknowledges the possibility that Lucretius might be right, which to a Christian "would ultimately render the universe and human life absurd" (p. 860).

This is the supreme anxiety that Milton must try to stare down in *Paradise Lost*, and it is voiced yet again by Satan in his speech seeking to deter any of the other devils from undertaking his heroic mission. Not only are they imprisoned behind the Gates of Hell, but a still greater danger awaits anyone who succeeds in escaping:

> These past, if any pass, the void profound
> Of unessential Night receives him next
> Wide gaping, and with utter loss of being
> Threatens him, plung'd in that abortive gulf.
>
> (2.438–41)

Like Belial, Satan recognizes that he risks the "utter loss of being" by casting himself into "the void profound / Of unessential Night," another echo of what Lucretius terms in Book 1, line 1104 "the vast void" or *inanum profundum*. Strikingly, as Quint (2004) has shown, in his flight through Night "Satan is himself reduced to a Lucretian atom in freefall" and "is saved from drowning in deep oceanic space only by a chance explosion of the nitrous particles of Chaos" (p. 859). As Milton describes it:

> Flutt'ring his pennons vain down he drops
> Ten thousand fadom deep, and to this hour
> Down had been falling, had not by ill chance
> The strong rebuff of some tumultuous cloud
> Instinct with Fire and Nitre hurried him
> As many miles aloft.
>
> (933–8)

Since Chaos is outside God's sphere of influence, it is not due to divine providence but simply to "our ill luck," in Quint's words, that Satan is rescued from his endless fall and "hurtled back on track to earth and to the seduction of humanity" (p. 859)—though Burke might well counter that "the whole design" of *Paradise Lost* "would have been ruined" had Chance not intervened as it did.

And what is true of Satan is true of both the earth and the universe as a whole. When Eve asks Adam why the stars shine at night, her question may reflect her limited human understanding, but Adam supplies the proper theological answer:

> they set and rise;
> Lest total darkness should by Night regain
> Her old possession, and extinguish life
> In Nature and all things.
>
> (4.664–7)

When the Son rides "in Paternal Glory" into Chaos to "circumscribe / This Universe" (7.226–7), his first act is to divide "light from darkness" and to name "Light the Day, and Darkness Night" (250–1); but the ever-present danger is that "total darkness" will "regain / Her old possession, and extinguish life" and light entirely. This would mean the victory of entropy over order, and by extension of Lucretius over Milton; and hence the stars perform the essential function of keeping Chaos at bay. Similarly, as James Grantham Turner (2024) has noted, "when Adam calls 'this Earth a spot, a graine, / An atom with the Firmament compar'd' (8.17–18), little does he know that, as we learn from Satan's epic journey through Chaos, this entire universe is but 'a starr of smallest magnitude' (2.1052–3) and this planet but a quark within that 'Atom'" (p. 12). What if—Milton dares to contemplate—there were no Eternal Providence, but only "sheer contingency and purely natural mortality," and "*Chaos* and *ancient Night*" were to resume their thrones?[11]

As Satan approaches the "dark Pavilion" (2.960) of these Lucretian powers, his ears are assaulted by "a universal hubbub wild / Of stunning sounds and voices all confus'd" (951–2). Whereas the "Filial Godhead" (7.175) is the "Omnific Word" (217) by which the Father brings order out of anarchy, Chaos is a prelinguistic realm devoid of intelligibility or meaning, just as it is before rather than beyond good and evil. Unlike the Adversary who, as Nyquist has put it, "appropriates the Father's Word only as a negative and alienating *(non) du père*," Chaos and Night exist outside the "hierarchical dualism" that is the cornerstone of patriarchy. They seize us with the "delight and horror" of the antioedipal.[12]

---

[11] Like Quint, Turner (2024) highlights the "astonishing" quality of "the Lucretian echoes in Milton's oeuvre" given that "asserting Eternal Providence is precisely the superstition that *De Rerum Natura* aims to demolish" (p. 2). What has not been sufficiently appreciated, however, is that whereas Milton's Arianism has to do with the specifically Christian doctrine of the Trinity, his other two heretical beliefs—mortalism (that the soul dies with the body) and material monism (that all forms of life, even the most ethereal, are transmutations of what Raphael calls "one first matter" [4.472])—while also being departures from Christian orthodoxy, are consistent with Lucretius's views, and may indeed have been influenced by them, though Lucretius would, of course, dismiss as nonsense the Christian promise that both body and soul will be resurrected at the Last Judgment. Milton's confrontation with Lucretius goes back to his Latin verse exercise at Cambridge, "That Nature Is Not Subject to Old Age," and Edward Phillips mentions Lucretius (with Manilius) as one of the "two egregious poets" (Hughes, 1957, p. 1029) that his uncle drilled into his pupils.

[12] In his seminal article, Hardie (1995) was the first to remark that in his 1674 tribute, "On *Paradise Lost*," Marvell "expresses his reaction to the Miltonic sublime" by translating Lucretius's homage to "the divine mind" of Epicurus in Book 3, lines 28–30 of *On the Nature of Things*, "At all this a kind of godlike delight and horror seizes us" (p. 20).

Chapter 9

Milton, Marriage, and Blindness

"The spiritual disillusionment and bodily deprivation to which most marriages are thus doomed puts both partners back in the state they were in before their marriage, except for being the poorer by the loss of an illusion, and they must once more have recourse to their fortitude in mastering and deflecting their sexual instinct."
—Freud, "'Civilized' Sexual Morality and Modern Nervous Illness"

1

According to Stephen Greenblatt (2017), "the decisive event of Milton's life—the experience to which his imagination ever afterward obsessively returned—was not his meeting with Galileo in Florence, not the outbreak of the English Civil War, not the beheading of the anointed king, not even his own descent into blindness. Rather it was the scant month or five weeks that he spent as a newlywed in the summer of 1642 with his young bride, Mary Powell" (p. 162). Although I concur that Milton's marriage at the age of thirty-three to this sixteen-year-old daughter of Royalist parents, which he realized had been "a catastrophic mistake" (p. 176) when Mary left him and returned to her family and friends in Oxfordshire, was his greatest trauma, I must take issue with Greenblatt's further contention that "Milton had not, he fervently believed, compromised the chastity on which, for so many years, he had founded his sense of himself, his moral authority, and his poetic vocation" (p. 174) when he took this disastrous step.

In my interpretation of Milton's life and career, I am guided by Ernest Sirluck's article, "Milton's Idle Right Hand" (1961), the linchpin of which is the thesis that, about 1637, Milton had made a "covenant and pledge" of "sacrificial celibacy" as the basis of his "renewal yet again of his self-dedication as God's poet" (p. 767). As early as 1629, at the age of twenty-one, Sirluck notes, Milton had written in Elegy 6, a Latin poem to his closest friend from St. Paul's School, Charles Diodati, that "he who sings now of the sacred counsels of the gods on high, and now of the infernal realms," should "drink sober drafts from the pure spring"; and, above all, "his youth must be innocent of crime and chaste, his conduct irreproachable and his hands stainless," for "truly the bard is sacred to the gods and is their priest" (Hughes, 1957, p. 52). At about the same time, Milton wrote in his second Prolusion, "On the Music of the Spheres," a prose oration also in Latin, that Prometheus's theft of fire from Zeus "deprived us of that felicity which we shall never be permitted to enjoy as long as we wallow in sin and are brutalized by our animal desires." Only if "our hearts were as pure, as chaste, as snowy as Pythagoras' was" would our ears "resound and be filled with that supremely lovely music of the wheeling stars" (p. 604).

It is because Milton had already set forth his credo in 1629 that Sirluck terms his later texts a "*renewal ... of his self-dedication as God's poet*," and he adduces three passages from Milton's poetry in support of his argument. The first was added by Milton in 1637 to *A Mask Presented at Ludlow Castle*—since 1738 popularly known as *Comus*—which he had written for a performance three years earlier before the Earl of Bridgewater at this splendid edifice on the border between England and Wales. In Milton's interpolation, the Lady expatiates on "the Sun-clad power of Chastity" (762) and proclaims her adherence to "the sage / And serious doctrine of Virginity" (785–6).[1] The second passage is from "Lycidas," Milton's celebrated elegy to Edward King, also written in 1637, where the poet affirms that his drowned friend from Christ's College, Cambridge—where, as Milton acknowledges in his sixth Prolusion, he himself had mockingly been given "the title of Lady" (Hughes, 1957, p. 620)—"hears the unexpressive nuptial Song" (176) reserved in the Book of Revelation for the 144,000 followers of the Lamb who "were not defiled with women; for they are virgins" (14.4). Sirluck's third exhibit is *Epitaphium Damonis*, a 1639 Latin eulogy of the recently deceased Diodati, to whom Milton had confided his lofty dreams in Elegy 6 and whom he now assures that "because you did not taste the delights of the marriage bed, lo! the rewards of virginity are reserved for you" (p. 139).

But if, as these passages establish, Milton had rededicated himself to "sacrificial celibacy" as he approached his thirtieth birthday, he must have changed his mind by the time, as his nephew and pupil Edward Phillips wrote in his *Life*, he "took a journey into the country; no man about him knowing the reason," and, "after a month's stay, home he returns a married

---

[1] Since Milton was celibate at the time, Comus's attempt to persuade the Lady that the advantage of beauty "Consists in mutual and partak'n bliss, / Unsavory in th'enjoyment of itself" (741–2), not only constitutes, as Le Comte (1978) discerns, "a criticism of the practice of masturbation" (p. 2), but must also reflect the poet's own struggle to subdue his sexual urges.

man, that went out a bachelor" (Hughes, 1957, p. 1031). As explanations for this change of heart, Sirluck (1961) adduces, first, that "perhaps the glamour of the sacrifice had begun to wear off" four years after Diodati's death; second, that "Milton was now living in the busy world of London, not in the virtual cloister of Horton," the village where he had spent the two years prior to his Italian journey of 1638–9; but third and "most influential of all … was the fact of his participation in the fight against Episcopacy" (p. 769). This plunge into "meaningful action," which had the justification of being "in the service of God's church," Sirluck adds, was "just the kind of thing needed before Milton would release himself from the pledge which was both symbol and counterpart of the service yet to be performed in God's church" (p. 769) as a poet.

The title of Sirluck's article alludes to Milton's 1642 pamphlet, *The Reason of Church Government*, in which he imparts to "the elegant and learned reader" that only the extraordinary circumstances of the present time had caused him to resort to "this manner of writing, wherein knowing myself inferior to myself, led by the genial power of nature to another task, I have the use, as I may account it, but of my left hand" (Hughes, 1957, p. 667). Milton's foray into the political arena on the side of Parliament, which coincided with the outbreak of the English Civil War, was his justification for redirecting his "genial power" away from poetry to the "inferior" medium of prose; and, Sirluck (1961) argues, by taking up his pen in the service of the Puritan cause, Milton could try to convince himself that "the left hand had earned the commutation of the sacrifice pledged in the name of the right" (p. 769).

The internal conflict caused by Milton's sacrifice of his yearning for the celestial "rewards of virginity" for the all-too-human desire to "taste the delights of the marriage bed" can be observed in *Apology for Smectymnuus*, a pamphlet probably printed in the late spring of 1642, shortly before the excursion "into the country" that astonished his friends and family. There, after extolling "what a noble virtue chastity sure must be," and remarking on how, if unchastity "be such a scandal and dishonor" in a woman, it is far more so in a man, who is "both the image and glory of God" as well as "the perfecter sex," Milton builds to a peroration in which he invokes the same passage from Chapter 14 of Revelation to which he had appealed in his encomium of Diodati: "Nor did I slumber over that place expressing such high rewards of ever accompanying the Lamb with those celestial songs to others inapprehensible, but not to those not defiled with women, which doubtless means fornication; for marriage must not be called a defilement" (Hughes, 1957, pp. 694–5).

Here, in what Sirluck (1961) characterizes as an "incongruous afterthought" (p. 769) that indeed constitutes a head-spinning reversal,

Milton goes back on his earlier insistence that the "rewards of virginity" in the afterlife were *not* granted to married men and preemptively excuses his own rash conduct by claiming that to be "defiled with women" means only engaging in "fornication" but not sexual intercourse in marriage. It is because Milton here patently attempts to rationalize the intention to abandon his vow of "sacrificial celibacy" that Greenblatt's claim that he "had not, he fervently believed, compromised the chastity on which, for so many years, he had founded his sense of himself, his moral authority, and his poetic vocation" is untenable. On the contrary, as Caitlin Weatherly (2020) has wryly put it, Milton attempted to carve out for himself a "marriage loophole" that would allow him "to have his apple and eat it too" because he could revise his heretofore unqualified espousal of "the sage / And serious doctrine of Virginity" without having to acknowledge even to himself that he had done so.[2]

The humiliation—at once private and public—that Milton experienced when he was deserted by Mary led him almost immediately to publish, anonymously, *The Doctrine and Discipline of Divorce* (1643). This was followed by an augmented edition under his name the following year, as well as by three more pamphlets devoted to rebutting the attacks to which he had been subjected: *Judgement of Martin Bucer Concerning Divorce* (1644), *Tetrachordon* (1645), and *Colasterion* (1645). In seeking to circumvent Christ's prohibition on divorce except on the grounds of fornication—which, Milton is at pains to insist in *The Christian Doctrine*, "signifies not adultery only, but either what is called *any unclean thing*, or a defect in some particular which might be justly required in a wife" (Hughes, 1957, p. 1003)—Milton claims in *Doctrine and Discipline* that it must be contrary to the purpose of a Christian marriage to be forced "to grind in the mill of an undelighted and servile copulation" when one is joined "with such a yoke-fellow, from whom both love and peace, both nature and religion, mourns to be separated" (p. 712). He bemoans how easy it is for "the soberest and best governed men," who have "spent their youth chastely" and "are in some things not so quick-sighted," to be taken in by "the bashful muteness of a virgin," as a consequence of which "they haste too eagerly to light the nuptial torch" (p. 708). That Milton's tract was an attempt to salve both his conscience and his wounded ego was not lost on his detractors, especially those in the clergy, who met his apologia, as Greenblatt (2017) notes, with "a rush of ridicule and outrage" (p. 183).

---

[2]   It is again a pleasure to express my indebtedness to one of my undergraduate students at the University of Florida who has allowed me to continue my own education in the process of teaching her.

When Milton announced his intention to write with his "left hand" in *The Reason of Church Government*, he believed that this was only a temporary expedient and he would soon find his way back to his true path as a poet. Indeed, although he recognized that he was being "foolish in saying more to this purpose," this did not deter Milton from proceeding "to venture and divulge unusual things of myself," namely, that what he aspired to do was to "leave something so written to aftertimes, as they should not willingly let it die" (Hughes, 1957, pp. 667–8). Despite not having yet settled "what king or knight before the conquest might be chosen in whom to lay the pattern of a Christian hero," or whether a tragedy modeled on those by Sophocles or Euripides might not be "found more doctrinal and exemplary to a nation" than an epic poem, Milton knew what he wanted to accomplish: "That what the greatest and choicest wits of Athens, Rome, or modern Italy, and those Hebrews of old did for their countries, I, in my proportion, with this over and above of being a Christian, might do for mine" (pp. 668–9). His ambition was nothing less than to write an immortal work that would eclipse Homer, Vergil, Ariosto, and Tasso, not to mention the authors of the Old Testament and the Greek tragedians.

But because England had not yet "enfranchised herself from this impertinent yoke of prelaty, under whose inquisitorious and tyrannical duncery no free and splendid wit can flourish," Milton was persuaded that the time was not yet ripe for him to spread his wings. He therefore "did not think it shame" to enter into a "covenant" with the "learned reader" that "for some few years yet I may go on trust with him toward the payment of what I am now indebted, as being a work not to be raised from the heat of youth, or the vapors of wine, ... but by devout prayer to that eternal Spirit who can enrich all utterance and knowledge, and sends out his seraphim with the hallowed fire of his altar, to touch and purify the lips of whom he pleases" (p. 671).

Milton displayed only minimal signs of anxiety when he made this pledge to God and his readers in 1642. But things did not go as planned, and what he had originally expected would be a hiatus of "some few years" became his life. Milton turned away from poetry—writing only a handful of sonnets, paraphrases of Hebrew Psalms, and occasional pieces—and threw himself into the political maelstrom. His prose writings made him the preeminent polemicist on behalf of the Commonwealth and led to his appointment as Secretary of Foreign Tongues to the Council of State in 1649. As early as *Areopagitica* (1644), Milton declared that "by the concurrence of signs, and by the general instinct of holy and devout men," it was evident that God was "decreeing to begin some new and great period in his Church, even to the reforming of reformation itself," and that he had for this purpose revealed himself "to his servants, and, as his manner is, first to his Englishmen" (Hughes, 1957, p. 743). If the English were God's chosen people, Milton could feel justified in abandoning the idea that his only route to immortality was through poetry in favor of the hope that he could fulfill his sacred mission by leading the fight to plant God's kingdom on earth.

In the decades following his marriage and entrance onto the political stage, Milton was buffeted by two other calamities. The first was his blindness, which became nearly total in 1652. As Edward Phillips remarked, Milton's "adversaries gladly [took] occasion of imputing his blindness as a judgment upon him for his answering the King's book" (Hughes, 1957, p. 1034) when he published *Eikonoklastes* in response to *Eikon Basilike*. Milton, however, turned this interpretation of his blindness on its head in his Latin tract, *The Second Defense of the People of England* (1654), where he demanded, "Is there anything reprehensible in my manners or my conduct? Indeed nothing" (Hughes, 1957, p. 823). Far from being "depressed by any sense of the divine displeasure," he insisted, he enjoyed the "full experience of the divine favor and protection" by which he was "enabled to do the will of God" (p. 826). Indeed, he went on, "I am unwilling to exchange my consciousness of rectitude with that of any other person," and the "divine law not only shields me from injury, but almost renders me too sacred to attack." Milton believed that he owed this protection to "the overshadowing of those heavenly wings which seem to have occasioned this obscurity; and which, when occasioned," God "is wont to illumine with an interior light, more precious and more pure" (pp. 826–7).

But though Milton repudiated the aspersion that his blindness was a sign of "divine displeasure," it was now 1654, and he was growing increasingly anxious that his prose labors had become an evasion, not a fulfillment, of the "covenant" he had made before God and man twelve years earlier. The key text for understanding Milton's state of mind during this period is the sonnet on his blindness, "When I consider how my light is spent," probably written in 1652. In this moving piece of self-analysis, Milton refers to his "one Talent which is death to hide," which is "Lodg'd with me useless, though my Soul more bent / To serve therewith my Maker, and present / My true account, lest he returning chide" (3–6).

Previously, in *The Reason of Church Government*, Milton had invoked the parable of the talents from the Gospel of Matthew (25.14-30) to reckon with his conscience. As he took up his political cudgels, he reminded himself that "God even to a strictness requires the improvement of these his entrusted gifts," and anyone with this awareness "cannot but sustain a sorer burden of mind, and more pressing, than any supportable toil or weight which the body can labor under, how and in what manner he shall dispose and employ those sums of knowledge and illumination which God had sent him into the world to trade with" (Hughes, 1957, p. 665). What "aggravates the burden more," Milton added, is that someone who has "received amongst his allotted parcels certain precious truths as no diamond can equal"—that is, a pearl of great price (Matt. 13.46)—is under the heaviest obligation of all. Were he not to do his utmost on behalf of the reformed church in her hour of need with "those few talents which God at present had lent me," Milton concluded, he could "foresee what stories I should hear within myself, all my life after, of discourage and reproach" (p. 666).

Throughout the 1650s, Milton remained dedicated to his duties on behalf of the Puritan cause, yet his sonnet gives voice to an acute sense of "discourage and reproach." It is clear that he feels guilty about the "hiding" of his poetic "talent"—a "talent" being both an ancient unit of currency and his divine gift—as a consequence of which Milton, like the "wicked and slothful servant" in the parable who has buried in the ground the single talent given to him by his lord, fears being "cast into outer darkness" where "there shall be weeping and gnashing of teeth" (Matt. 25.26, 30). Echoing his reference to the "burden of mind" that is greater than any physical "toil or weight," Milton describes how his soul is "more bent," in the sense of "inclined," than ever to do what he knows he is supposed to do. But it is also "bent" under the weight of his guilt at not being able to present a "true account" to God, whom he called in "How soon hath time"—a sonnet probably written after his twenty-third birthday on December 9, 1631—his "great task-Master" (14). He offers his blindness as an excuse, "'Doth God exact day-labor, light denied,' / I fondly ask" (6–7), but knows that he does so "fondly," that is, foolishly and in vain. All Milton can do to subdue his "murmur" of discontent at the unfairness of his lot as a blind man asked to work during the day—that is, as a blind poet overwhelmed by his labors on behalf of the Council of State—is to appeal to "patience" (8–9) to console himself with the thought that God is best served by those "who best / Bear his mild yoke" (10–11), and "They also serve who only stand and wait" (14).

Although "When I consider" reveals Milton's anguish at having failed to redeem the promissory notes he had issued concerning his "one Talent," he asserts in the sonnet to his friend and pupil Cyriack Skinner—grandson of the jurist Sir Edward Coke—commemorating the third year of his blindness that he will not argue "Against heav'n's hand or will" (7) because he is supported by the knowledge that he sacrificed his eyesight "In liberty's defense, my noble task, / Of which all Europe talks from side to side" (11–12). Notwithstanding his doubts, he reiterates in 1655 his commitment to the "noble task" on which he had embarked in 1642, averring that "This thought" was enough to lead him "through the world's vain mask / Content though blind," although he hints that he continues to harbor a higher ambition when he ends the sonnet with the words "had I no better guide" (13–14).

In order for Milton's psychic realignment to become complete, he had to undergo a second calamity that proved to be a blessing in disguise. As Blair Worden (1998) has observed, Milton mentions Oliver Cromwell by name in only two places in his writings: a sonnet addressed to him in 1652 and a passage in the *Second Defense*, published in May 1654. In both of these Milton offers praise that is "heartfelt" but "accompanied … by doubt and by warning," and the ensuing "silence is loud" (pp. 243–4). Worden argues that very few of Milton's hopes for Cromwell "are likely to have survived September 1654," when Cromwell—who had assumed the office of Lord Protector for life in December 1653—had "forcibly expelled the commonwealthmen from parliament, declared his resolve to suppress heresies and blasphemies, and publicly scorned critics of the established ministry" (pp. 260–1). Thus, even before Cromwell died in September 1658 and was succeeded as Lord Protector by his son Richard, Milton was disillusioned, if not embittered; and everything on which he had placed his hopes for the past eighteen years came crashing down in May 1660, when, after General George Monck had thrown his support to the moderates in Parliament who wanted to restore the monarchy, Charles II triumphantly entered London and regained the throne.

In the aftermath of this disaster, Milton had to face the fact that he had made no less grievous a miscalculation in politics than he had in his private life when he married Mary Powell. He had thought that he could decipher the "concurrence of signs" and that God had a special plan in mind for "his Englishmen," but he had been mistaken and it was all for nothing. In the language of typology, the Christian method of interpreting the Scriptures according to which, as Edward W. Tayler (1979) has put it, "the people and events of the Old Testament 'prefigure' their 'fulfillments' in the New Testament" (p. 25), Milton had confused the "type" or prefiguration with the "antitype" or fulfillment. Whereas he had formerly believed that good would triumph over evil in what Adam described to the archangel Michael in his final speech of *Paradise Lost* as "this transient World, the race of Time" (12.554), Milton now understood that this would not happen until the Second Coming of Christ and time was swallowed up in "Eternity, whose end no eye can reach" (556).

It is Sirluck's (1961) thesis that "the failure of his marriage" constituted "a direct blow to [Milton's] poetic inspiration (or, what amounts to the same thing, to his faith in it)" (p. 754), and it was only with his blindness that he found a "new symbol" (p. 771) to replace the "covenant and pledge" he had originally sealed with "the Sun-clad power of Chastity." Although he insisted in the *Second Defense* that he not only enjoyed the "full experience of the divine favor and protection," but was now "too sacred to attack," his blindness acquired its full meaning only after 1660. While writing with his "left hand," he could assert in good conscience that his blindness was not a punishment for his defense of the regicide, but he continued to harbor guilt about his marriage, the impetuousness of which his Anonymous Biographer—probably either his younger nephew, John Phillips, or Cyriack Skinner—ascribed to "his practice of not wasting that precious talent" (Hughes, 1957, p. 1040), where Milton's anxiety-ridden identification with the reprobate servant in the parable is appropriated to allude wittily to his sperm, which he wished to put to better use than he could as a bachelor.

As long as he was caught up in politics, Milton could try to quiet his "murmur" not only about having broken his vow of "sacrificial celibacy" when he married but also about having abandoned poetry for prose, which had resulted in the seemingly endless deferral of his ambition to "leave something so written to aftertimes, as they should not willingly let it die." But once his political hopes had collapsed, his qualms both about his marriage and about the burial of his "one Talent" converged in his mind. He understood that his blindness was indeed a punishment, but not for the reasons alleged by his opponents. It was rather a requital for the sophistry of his argument that "marriage must not be called a defilement," yet it was also the sign of a renewed covenant with God that would allow Milton to resume his poetic vocation.

2

Upon the Restoration of Charles II, a warrant was issued for Milton's arrest. He had to go into hiding until late August of 1660, when the Indemnity and Oblivion Act seemed to make it safe for him to reemerge, but even then he was arrested and briefly imprisoned until influential friends, including Marvell, secured his release. Yet though Milton had, as he wrote in the invocation to Book 7 of *Paradise Lost*, "fall'n on evil days, / ... and evil tongues; / In darkness, and with dangers compast round" (26–8), this disaster turned out to be a fortunate fall. By abjuring the political arena as, in Michael's words, "To good malignant, to bad men benign" (12.538), such that "Tyranny must be, / Though to the Tyrant thereby no excuse" (95–6), Milton was free to assume once again the mantle of the poet-prophet, "The only righteous in a World perverse, / And therefore hated" (11.701–2). He could identify himself with Enoch and Noah in the Hebrew Bible, and most of all with Abdiel, that undaunted Puritan angel among the Satanic throngs of whom the narrator says, "His Loyalty he kept, his Love, his Zeal" (5.900). From his alienated vantage point, Milton could take it upon himself to "admonish" not only his dissolute contemporaries but all of humankind for "thir wicked ways," and "before them set / The paths of righteousness" (11.813–14).

After his disenchantment with politics, Milton realized that only by abandoning history in favor of eschatology could he hope to "assert Eternal Providence, / And justify the ways of God to men" (1.25–6). This reorientation enabled him to rectify his earlier miscalculations and transmute his boast in the *Second Defense* that God had compensated him for his blindness by illuminating him "with an interior light, more precious and more pure" into his appeal to the "Celestial Light" in the invocation to Book 3 of *Paradise Lost* to "Shine inward, and the mind through all her powers / Irradiate, there plant eyes, all mist from thence / Purge and disperse, that I may see and tell / Of things invisible to mortal sight" (51–5). It was no longer Cromwell to whom he ascribed the lion's share of responsibility for, in Worden's (1998) words, "the failure … of the momentous destiny which the poet had expected" (p. 262) for the Puritan Revolution, but rather Satan who invoked "necessity, / The Tyrant's plea" (4.393–4), in an attempt to justify his actions, just as it was Satan who tried to rally his defeated comrades by recalling how they had shaken the throne of Heaven in "the Glorious Enterprise" (1.89). Milton could continue to reject monarchy as an earthly institution by locating its origins in Nimrod, the "mighty Hunter" who sought to exercise "Empire tyrannous" (12.33–4) over his brethren, causing Adam to protest that God "gave us only over Beast, Fish, Fowl / Dominion absolute," but "Man over men / He made not Lord" (67–70), while simultaneously proclaiming God to be the "Eternal King" (3.374) with "Dominion absolute" over the universe.

As part of his stock-taking after the Restoration, Milton revisited his folly in marrying Mary Powell after having known her for barely a month. Beholding the dismal panorama of human history revealed to him by Michael, Adam is struck by a group of "just men," who "all thir study bent / To worship God aright" (11.577–8). There then arrive "A Bevy of fair Women" (582) who cause the eyes of the men "To rove without rein, till in the amorous Net / Fast caught," they "each his liking chose" (586–7). And what should these men do but "all in heat / They light the nuptial torch, and bid invoke / *Hymen*, then first to marriage rites invok't" (589–91)? This is exactly what Milton rued having done in *The Doctrine and Discipline of Divorce* when he bemoaned how easily men who have "spent their youth chastely" and "are in some things not so quick-sighted" can be taken in by "the bashful muteness of a virgin," as a consequence of which "they haste too eagerly to light the nuptial torch."

Milton's tale of entrapment is an ominous beginning to the institution of marriage in the postlapsarian world. But when Adam punningly attempts to cast the blame on women, "But still I see the tenor of Man's woe / Holds on the same, from Woman to begin," Michael harshly rebukes him: "From man's effeminate slackness it begins, / Said th' Angel, who should better hold his place / By wisdom, and superior gifts receiv'd" (11.634–7). Here, Milton implicitly accepts responsibility for having fallen into Mary's "amorous net," and the phrase "effeminate slackness" conveys by inversion how it was actually his masculine hardness—his erection—that was the cause of his undoing by inducing him to throw away his "wisdom, and superior gifts" in his haste to "light the nuptial torch."

Milton undertakes a complex series of maneuvers whereby he contrives "to have his apple and eat it too" with respect to sexuality in *Paradise Lost*. On the surface, he celebrates "wedded love," including "the Rites / Mysterious of connubial love," in a way that suggests there is nothing problematic about having sex within marriage, and by extension about getting married in order to have sex. This gets Milton off the hook for having broken his "covenant and pledge" of "sacrificial celibacy" and the ensuing debacle with Mary Powell. On a deeper level, however, since Adam and Eve are not inflamed with "Carnal desire" (9.1013) before the Fall and they experience "Lust" (1015) only after they have eaten the forbidden fruit, Milton cancels out the sexual motive for his marriage altogether. How could he have wanted to marry for sex when Eve is repeatedly said to be a "virgin" prior to her encounter with Satan, from which she returns "deflow'r'd"? In his paean to marriage Milton couples the words "adulterous" and "lust" to form the phrase "adulterous lust" (4.754), as though lust were unimaginable in a married couple.

Yet on the third and most deeply buried level, since Adam confesses to Raphael that he feels "passion" for Eve even before the Fall, and is "only weak / Against the charm of Beauty's powerful glance," his motive for asking God to make him a "human consort" (8.392) is already contaminated by sexual urges. The "single imperfection" (423) that causes him to seek a companion with whom he can engage in "Social communication" (429) turns out to be not simply his need for an attachment figure—his "incompleteness when alone"—but above all the sexual desire that is his "only flaw." This conclusion is corroborated by God's joke about Adam's discontent with the "solitary pleasure" of masturbation—a discontent that was undoubtedly shared by Milton. Adam's "vehement desire" for Eve contradicts both of Milton's two self-exculpations, which are themselves inconsistent—sex "must not be called a defilement" in marriage, but he did not take his wife's virginity—and puts Milton back on the hook for having married a teenager in order to be able to have sex with her.

Satan's role as the child in the primal scene tormented by his exclusion from the bliss of the parental couple "Imparadis'd" in each other's arms goes back to

God's ruthless suppression of what the ideology of the poem frames as Satan's heinous act of rebellion. Having failed in his attempt to supplant the Father, the son banished from Heaven repeats his behavior on Earth by undertaking to seduce the wife away from her husband. Satan temporarily turns his oedipal defeat into a victory by becoming the successful lover in a romantic triangle. By providing this cosmic backdrop to the "marriage plot" of *Paradise Lost*, Milton shows how adultery has its roots in incest inasmuch as Satan's metaphorical "impregnation" of Eve forms a reprise of the "secret joy" he took with Sin that left the "growing burden" of Death in his daughter's womb.

3

Milton remained estranged from his wife for three years. As Edward Phillips recounts, Milton wrote several letters in which he tried to persuade Mary to return, and when these went unanswered he sent a messenger who "reported that he was dismissed with some sort of contempt" (Hughes, 1957, p. 1031). Phillips surmises that the reason for this rebuff is that the King was "then in some prospect of success" in the initial phase of the civil war, and Mary's parents "began to repent them of having matched the eldest daughter of the family to a person so contrary to them in opinion; and thought it would be a blot in their escutcheon, whenever that court should come to flourish again" (p. 1031).

Understandably, Milton was "so incensed" by this behavior on the part of Mary's family "that he thought it would be dishonorable ever to receive her again, after such a repulse" (Hughes, 1957, p. 1031). In high dudgeon, he not only wrote his four divorce pamphlets but also, being "now as it were a single man again," undertook to remarry, even though he and Mary were not divorced in the eyes of the law. As the Anonymous Biographer puts it, Milton, who "had entered into that state [of matrimony] for the end designed by God and Nature"—that is, procreation—"and was then in the full vigor of his manhood"—that is, eager to have sex—"could ill bear the disappointment he met with by her obstinate absenting; and therefore, thought upon a divorce, that he might be free to marry another; concerning which he also was in treaty" (p. 1040). The object of his affections, Edward Phillips reports, was "one of Dr. Davis's daughters, a very handsome and witty gentlewoman, but averse, as it is said, to this motion" (p. 1032).

Milton had been accused of favoring polygamy in the controversies over the divorce tracts, and he defended the practice at length in Book 1, Chapter 10 of *The Christian Doctrine*. In a 1644 sermon delivered to Parliament, the Puritan clergyman Herbert Palmer demanded:

If any plead Conscience for the Lawfulness of *Polygamy*; (or for divorce for other causes than Christ and His apostles mention: Of which a *wicked book* is abroad and *uncensured*, though *deserving to be burnt*, whose *Author* hath been so *impudent* as to set *his Name* to it, and *dedicate it to your selves*), or for Liberty to *marry incestuously*, will you grant a *Toleration* for all *this*?

(qtd. in Miller, 1974, p. 122)

As Leo Miller (1974) has suggested, Palmer's "dig about polygamy" may have been prompted by an "intimation of the proposal to Miss Davis" that Milton had made at this time, and "the needle about incest" (p. 122) reflects Milton's imaginative preoccupation with this theme. In his panegyric to "wedded love" in *Paradise Lost*, Milton includes the "Saints and Patriarchs" (4.762) of the Hebrew Bible among those whose marriage beds were "undefil'd and chaste" (761), even though they had plural wives.

As to the Powells, they continued to have their eyes out for the main chance. The prospect that they might permanently lose their son-in-law, combined with "the declining state of the King's cause, and consequently of the circumstances of Justice Powell's family," caused them, in Phillips's words, "to set all engines on work to restore the late married woman to the station wherein they had late planted her" (Hughes, 1957, p. 1032). As Greenblatt (2017) elaborates, in June 1645, following "what proved to be the decisive battle of the Civil War," when "the Parliament's New Model Army, under the command of Thomas Fairfax and Oliver Cromwell, crushed the king's forces" at the Battle of Naseby, the elder Powells, "facing ruin, knew they had to act quickly" (p. 186). Enlisting the cooperation of Milton's cousins, William and Hester Blackborough, they ambushed their son-in-law and "brilliantly stage-managed" (p. 186) a scene of reconciliation, for which Phillips's *Life* of his uncle is again the contemporary source:

One time above the rest, he making his usual visit, the wife was ready in another room, and on a sudden he was surprised to see one whom he thought to have never seen more, making submission and begging pardon on her knees before him. He might probably at first make some show of aversion and rejection; but partly his own generous nature, more inclinable to reconciliation than to perseverance in anger and revenge, and partly the strong intercession of friends on both sides, soon brought him to an act of oblivion and a firm league of peace for the future.

(Hughes, 1957, p. 1032)

Phillips's use of the phrase "act of oblivion" is a fine touch since it alludes to the Act of Parliament that had led Milton to believe it was safe for him to come out of hiding after the Restoration. Not only did Milton agree to a "league of peace" after his civil war with the Powells, but he took Mary, her mother (her father having recently died), and several other members of her family to live with him and his father in London. That Milton was not happy with this arrangement is attested by a letter he wrote in Latin around Easter of 1647 to Carlo Dati, whom he had befriended in Florence during his Italian journey. Acknowledging that he was troubled by "very frequent grieving over my own lot," Milton complained that, while he was deprived of the company of those with whom he would wish to converse, including his own recently deceased father, he was forced to "live well-nigh in a perpetual solitude" with others "whom the mere necessity of neighbourhood ... has closely conjoined with me, whether by accident or tie of law, *they* are the persons, though in no other respect commendable, who daily sit in my company, weary me, nay, by heaven, all but plague me to death whenever they are jointly in the humour for it" (qtd. in Le Comte, 1978, p. 35). Despite this portrait of misery, which seems to include his wife among his tormentors, the Miltons remained yokefellows until May of 1652, when Mary died at the age of twenty-seven, after having given birth to their third daughter and fourth child. Milton's only son—who, like his father and grandfather, was named John—died shortly after his mother at just over one year of age.

Although the letter to Dati calls into question Greenblatt's (2017) contention that Milton had let go of "his most toxic feelings in the wake of the breakdown of his marriage" (p. 226), Milton undoubtedly drew upon his memory of this "stage-managed" scene in *Paradise Lost* when Eve—who may, in an inversion of the typological pattern, be called Milton's "second Mary"—begins the process of mending her relationship with her husband. Just as in Phillips's narrative, Adam's initial "show of aversion and rejection" yields to more compassionate feelings, and the description of Mary "making submission and begging pardon on her knees before him" is likewise paralleled in the poem.[3] Undeterred by Adam's vituperative greeting, "Out of my sight, thou Serpent" (10.867), and ensuing onslaught, following which he turns his back on her, Eve, "with Tears that ceas'd not flowing, / And tresses all disorder'd, at his feet / Fell humble, and imbracing them / Besought his peace" (910–13).

---

[3] Phillips, who was fifteen at the time, acknowledges that he is reporting what "might probably" have happened, not what he himself observed. It seems likely that he was influenced in his memoir, which was not published until 1694, by Milton's rendering of the scene in *Paradise Lost*.

But if this scene of reconciliation in *Paradise Lost* is autobiographical, the same holds true for the disagreement between Adam and Eve that led to the Fall. Edward Le Comte (1978) points out that their argument over how to tend their garden, in which Eve, "in a burst of unquelled perversity," falls "by separating herself from her husband and his admonitions," bears more than a passing resemblance to how "Mary Powell asserted a shattering independence many months before her husband uttered a word about divorce" (p. 67). Only Adam's uxoriousness explains why, instead of asserting his authority, he gives Eve permission to go off by herself on the ostensibly magnanimous grounds that "thy stay, not free, absents thee more" (9.372). What is puzzling in the poem becomes comprehensible when one realizes that Milton is following the script of his own life, where, according to Phillips, he allowed Mary to spend the summer with her family "on condition of her return at the time appointed, Michaelmas, or thereabout" (Hughes, 1957, p. 1031)—that is, on September 29, four months after his journey into the country "about Whitsuntide," which fell on May 29, 1642—but she broke her promise and kept him waiting for years.

In *Paradise Lost*, phylogeny recapitulates ontogeny. Milton's account of the origin of the institution of marriage in the pious men who "all in heat ... light the nuptial torch" reprises the apologia for his own marital disaster in *The Doctrine and Discipline of Divorce*, just as the argument between Adam and Eve over separate gardening and their reconciliation after the Fall represent the corresponding moments of rupture and repair in "the decisive event of Milton's life." But there is yet another passage that tantalizes the reader with unusually specific details of unhappiness in love, which has been masterfully decoded by Le Comte. Immediately after his tirade denouncing women and lamenting that there is no "other way to generate / Mankind" than heterosexual intercourse, Adam proceeds to foresee the "innumerable / Disturbances on Earth through Female snares, / And strait conjunction with this Sex" (10.896–8). He continues:

> for either
> He shall never find out fit Mate, but such
> As some misfortune bring him, or mistake,
> Or whom he wishes most shall seldom gain
> Through her perverseness, but shall see her gain'd
> By a far worse, or if she love, withheld
> By Parents, or his happiest choice too late
> Shall meet already linkt and Wedlock-bound
> To a fell Adversary, his hate or shame:

> Which infinite calamity shall cause
> To Human life, and household peace confound.
>
> (898–908)

As Le Comte (1978) observes, "the first man is being remarkably prescient," and he possesses the "gift of foreseeing the future" because Milton is "enumerating three instances that fit three women in his own life" (p. 37). The first is Mary Powell, marriage to whom was due not only to a "mistake" but also to "misfortune," with the latter word being a "punning reference" to the fact that the reason for Milton's excursion into the country when he met Mary was to collect a "bad debt" (p. 37) owed by her father to his father. The second, "whom he wishes most," is an otherwise unidentified dark-eyed Italian signorina living in England named Emilia, to whom Milton wrote five sonnets in her native language at the age of twenty-one, who either in "her perverseness" refused him or else was "withheld / By parents" because Milton was not a Catholic; and, Le Comte surmises, "very likely ended up with 'a far worse'" (p. 37).

The third woman, Milton's "happiest choice" but whom he met "too late," is the "very handsome and witty" daughter of Dr. Davis, whom Milton undertook to marry when he became "as it were a single man again" after he had been deserted by Mary. Although the syntax of the passage is ambiguous, Le Comte is surely right to construe "already linkt and Wedlock-bound" as referring to Milton himself, not to Miss Davis, both because he is the one who was married and because he had just given an example of a woman "gain'd / By a far worse." It follows that the "fell Adversary, his hate or shame," must be a posthumous indictment of Mary Powell, whose family, as his complaint to Dati makes clear, did indeed his "household peace confound." Even in *Paradise Lost*, in short, it was the recollection of his unhappiness with his first wife that led Milton to denounce marriage as the cause of "Infinite calamity … / To human life."

Like the misogynistic outburst that precedes it, Adam's vision of what lies in store for future husbands reflects his anger and despair at his lowest point in the epic, before Eve tearfully "fell humble" at his feet and begged his forgiveness. In both its tone and its diction Adam's prophecy looks ahead to *Samson Agonistes*, where Dalila is repeatedly described as a "snare," and what Le Comte (1978) calls the "Freudian image of female genitals as a trap," reinforced by "the sexual overtones of *strait* (narrow) *conjunction*" (p. 113), becomes a dominant motif.[4] But, unlike Samson, Adam succeeds in

---

4   Le Comte notes that the New Testament notion of the "narrow road" (*stricta via*) to salvation was "used as a *double entendre*" to refer to the vagina by Theodore Beza, Calvin's successor in Geneva, and rendered in English by Nicholas Grimald in *Tottel's Miscellany* of 1557 as follows: "Oh straight is vertues path, if sooth men say / And likewise, that I seek, straight is the way" (p. 140*n*37).

moving past "his most toxic feelings in the wake of the breakdown of his marriage," which, as Greenblatt (2017) observes, "suggests at least that Milton passionately longed to imagine a full reconciliation between the estranged husband and his wife" (p. 226). Perhaps the most fitting commentary on Milton's portrayal of his first marriage in *Paradise Lost* may be found in closing lines of the epic, in which Adam and Eve are once more "hand in hand" as they make "thir solitary way" (12.648–9) through the world—simultaneously back together but still "in a perpetual solitude," and never again as they once were.

Chapter 10

"What Once I Was, and What Am Now"

Paradise Regained and *Samson Agonistes*

"In such strange passion, if I may once more
Review the past, I warred against myself—"

—Wordsworth, The Prelude

1

According to Edward Phillips, "It cannot certainly be concluded when [Milton] wrote his excellent tragedy entitled *Samson Agonistes*, but sure enough it is that it came forth after *Paradise Lost*, together with his other poem called *Paradise Regained*, which doubtless was begun and finished and printed after the other was published" (Hughes, 1957, p. 1036). Somewhat more definitively, the Anonymous Biographer states that *Samson Agonistes* was one of the works that Milton "finished after the Restoration" (p. 1042). That the writing of *Paradise Regained* can be dated to the period between the publication of the ten-book edition of *Paradise Lost* in 1667 and the publication of the volume in which the brief epic appeared alongside *Samson Agonistes* in 1671 is not a matter of controversy. Matters stand otherwise with *Samson*, where a vocal minority of scholars has deemed the testimony of the Anonymous Biographer to be insufficient and seized on Phillips's uncertainty to argue that the tragedy was written decades earlier in Milton's life.

The fountainhead of the traditional view is the sixth and last volume of David Masson's (1880) monumental biography of Milton. Convinced that *Samson Agonistes* is the "latest production of Milton's muse," Masson stipulates that "we have no information as to the date of composition, except what is conveyed in the poem itself," but asserts that this "certifies it beyond all doubt as a post-Restoration poem; and the most probable date is between 1666 and 1670" (p. 662). Noting that Milton had contemplated writing a play about Samson as early as 1641, Masson comments that he did so "little knowing how much of his future life was to correspond with the fate of that particular hero of the Hebrews" (p. 664). Still, "the experience had come, coincidence after coincidence, shock after shock, till there was not one of all the Hebrew heroes so constantly in his imagination as the blind Samson among the Philistines" (p. 664). Accordingly, "a tragedy on Samson would be in effect a metaphor for the tragedy of his life," so that it was "by destiny as much as by choice" that Samson become "Milton's dramatic subject after the Restoration" (p. 664).

Notwithstanding his conviction that "the Hebrew Samson among the Philistines and the English Milton among the Londoners of the reign of Charles the Second were, to all poetic intents, one and the same person," and that this identity is established "not only by the similarity of their final circumstances, but also by the reminiscences of their previous lives," Masson asserts that "it is impossible to point out a single particular in which, having chosen for his subject the Biblical story of Samson's dying revenge, he has overstrained it for a personal purpose" (p. 670). Thus, even though Masson invites his readers to imagine how Samson's dejection about his blindness expresses Milton's own state of mind, how the Dalila episode "sums up his incredibly perverted opinion of women" (p. 674), and how "Samson's challenge to the giant Harapha" shows Milton's "unabated pugnacity, his longing for another Salmasius to grapple with" (p. 675)—Salmasius being the Latin name of the classical scholar Claude Saumaise, described by Phillips as "the great French Goliath, to whom our little English David … gave such a hit in the forehead" in the controversies over the regicide "that he presently staggered, and soon after fell" (Hughes, 1957, p. 1033)—Masson's reading of *Samson Agonistes* as a "metaphor" for Milton's life remains suggestive rather than conclusive.

Combined with the perceived lacunae in the early biographies, Masson's broad-brush approach spurred William Riley Parker (1949) to challenge conventional wisdom by advocating on the basis of resemblances to Milton's paraphrases of a series of Psalms that *Samson Agonistes* was composed in two installments from 1646 and 1653, while John T. Shawcross (1961) relied on metrical analyses to seek to narrow the window further to between 1646 and 1648. Parker's argument is coupled with an assault on "the autobiographical fallacy." He regards it as inconceivable that Milton would have wanted to lend credence to the idea, "published and talked by royalist sympathizers, that his blindness had been God's punishment on him for his misdeeds" (p. 150). It is strange that Milton chose to publish *Samson* at all if he was so sensitive to these accusations, but Parker has no explanation for this. Nonetheless, he continues, not only is Samson's blindness portrayed by Milton as "God's punishment for disobedience and loss of virtue," but he "had shown great weakness, he was possessed of more strength than wisdom, he had been uxorious, he had brought dishonor to God," and "proponents of the autobiographical interpretation ignore, of course, these central aspects of Samson's character" (pp. 150–1).

As A. S. P. Woodhouse (1949) has pointed out, however, despite his censure of Masson, Parker "is constrained by the direction of his own argument to admit a relation to Milton's life and experience" (p. 158). He quotes from Parker's article to demonstrate that he places great weight on the fact that Milton's vision deteriorated from 1646 to 1648, which is also when "'the clergy were still damning his views on marriage and divorce'" and "'he felt lonely and miserable in his life's work,'" all of which leads Parker to conclude that "'we can believe Milton felt little personal interest in Samson's attitudes until he, too, was a rejected champion facing the grim fact of blindness'" (p. 158; see Parker, 1949, p. 163). It is ironic that a castigator of "the autobiographical fallacy" himself relies on autobiography to bolster his eccentric views.[1] Still, Woodhouse joins Parker in rejecting Masson's conviction that *Samson Agonistes* was "Milton's last poem," above all because "the placing of *Samson* with or immediately after *Paradise Regained* presents very serious difficulty, so divergent are the two pieces in doctrine, temper and tone" (pp. 157–8). Woodhouse takes it for granted that "in attempting to date the tragedy, we are thrown back wholly on internal evidence" (p. 157), but he argues against Parker that "Milton's grounds for disillusion were far more complete, and his stubborn faith put to its severest test," not in the 1640s or early 1650s, but "in the year following the Restoration, between May, 1660 and May, 1661" (pp. 158–9).

Despite the apparent consensus even among those who cannot agree on the date of *Samson Agonistes* that there is no external evidence to settle the issue, this turns out not to be true. In his reading of the tragedy as a record of "the struggle of the blind poet to come to terms with the defeat of the Puritan cause" (p. 111), Blair Worden (1995) has demonstrated the extent to which *Samson Agonistes* is steeped in the discourse by and about the regicides following the Restoration of Charles II. In particular, Worden shows how the repeated attempts of Samson's father to ransom his son from his Philistine captors resemble the efforts not only by Milton's supporters but also by those of other advocates of regicide, including Edmund Ludlow and Colonel John Hutchinson, to secure clemency on their behalf from Parliament.

---

[1] In an appendix to "Milton's Idle Right Hand," Sirluck (1961) has critiqued the grounds on which scholars beginning with Parker have promoted an early date for *Samson* as amounting to nothing more than "admitted conjecture, impressionistic speculation, or demonstrable fallacy" (p. 781).

At his first appearance in the tragedy, Manoa tells Samson that he has "already made way / To some *Philistian* Lords, with whom to treat / About thy ransom" (482–4). Later, in attempting to comfort Samson in his despair, he assures him that he will not "omit a Father's timely care / To prosecute the means of thy deliverance / By ransom or how else" (602–4), while at the end of the work, after Samson has been taken to the Temple of Dagon, Manoa informs the Chorus that he has "attempted one by one the Lords" (1457) to "accept of ransom for my Son thir pris'ner" (1460). "Some," he says, "much averse I found and wondrous harsh, / Contemptuous, proud, set on revenge and spite" (1461–2). "Others," however, were "more moderate seeming, but thir aim / Private reward, for which both God and State / They easily would set to sale" (1464–6), while the third group, "more generous far and civil, who confess'd / They had enough reveng'd," were ready "to remit" any further punishment of Samson provided that "some convenient ransom were propos'd" (1470–1).

Citing contemporary testimonies, Worden (1995) documents how members of Parliament reacted to the bids for mercy by intermediaries for the imprisoned Puritans: "In Ludlow's and Lucy Hutchinson's accounts, some MPs, high-flying Anglicans among them, responded to pleas for leniency with bitter vindictiveness, others with personal opportunism, others still with heart-warming magnanimity" (p. 120). The resemblance between the three types of responses to Manoa's "attempt of ransom" for Samson in the play and those reported by Milton's contemporaries as having been undertaken in reality cannot be a coincidence. But though this suffices to refute the claims by Parker and Shawcross that the work could have been written before the Restoration, it leaves open whether *Samson* might be better imagined as stemming from the first rather than the final years of the 1660s.

In his master's thesis at the University of Richmond, Edward P. Crockett (1966) impressively investigates the autobiographical substrate of *Samson Agonistes*. Endorsing the traditional view that *Samson Agonistes* "should be regarded as the sequel to the two longer poems" (p. 34), Crockett observes that Masson is unduly cautious in asserting that Milton never allowed a "personal purpose" to break through his aesthetic frame. Early in the play, Samson complains of his mistreatment at the hands of the Philistines: "I dark in light expos'd / To daily fraud, contempt, abuse, and wrong" (75–6). Crockett highlights the anomalousness of the word "fraud" in this context since Samson is "unlikely to have had any money in his pockets when he was taken captive in Gaza" or been exploited in "any form of investments or real estate," whereas Milton not only "is reputed to have told a witness before bis death that his daughters and a maid-servant cheated him in his household expenditures and disposed of some of his books in a fraudulent manner" in 1662, but also "suffered great financial losses due to the change of the government in 1660" (pp. 46-7; see Masson, 1880, p. 448).

Also extremely telling is Crockett's citation of the passage in which the Chorus describes how God can throw down those whom he has formerly exalted. If they are not left to "the hostile sword" or "to th'unjust tribunals, under change of times, / And condemnation of th'ingrateful multitude," then "perhaps in poverty / With sickness and disease thou bow'st them down, / Painful diseases and deform'd, / In crude old age" (692-700). As Crockett notes, although Milton escaped execution and other serious reprisals following the Restoration, "he did suffer poverty, sickness, and painful disease" (p. 66). Having discussed Milton's poverty, Crockett quotes Masson's description of how his health, which had never been "particularly robust," worsened in the 1660s: "The blindness, now total for ten years, was a settled matter; but Milton's ailments besides were serious enough, and had taken the form at length of a confirmed and serious gout" (pp. 66-7; see Masson, 1880, p. 455). Given that gout is "a disease both painful and deforming when the visitation is severe," Crockett argues that "it stands to reason that the source of this 'abstract' illustration of the exemplary fallen man was Milton's personal condition in the early or middle 1660's" (p. 67).

In addition to confirming the view that *Samson Agonistes* must have been written after the Restoration, Crockett goes beyond Masson by proving that Milton's rendering of Samson's story contains elements that cannot be accounted for without situating them in the context of his life. Of utmost interest is the passage in which the Chorus states that Samson, "this heroic *Nazarite*," was prompted to break "his vow of strictest purity" when he "sought in marriage that fallacious Bride, / Unclean, unchaste" (318-21). As Crockett underscores, this indictment of Samson's marriage to Dalila "appears to be an instance of pure autobiography" on Milton's part because "there is nothing in the biblical account to indicate that Samson had made a vow of chastity" and "nothing in the Nazarite law as delivered to Moses (Numbers 6.1-21) that requires this kind of purity of one who is under the vow" (pp. 56-7). Once again, as with his health and finances, since Samson's "vow of chastity" lacks biblical authority, it can only be understood as coming from Milton, who, beginning in Elegy 6, had "claimed chastity as a necessity in the life of a young poet who proposes to sing the highest measures," and for the next thirteen years had "extolled and lived the life of chastity" (p. 57) until he married Mary Powell in 1642.

By uncovering the autobiographical roots of Milton's depiction of Samson's marriage to Dalila as a violation of "his vow of strictest purity," Crockett opens up the possibility of reinterpreting *Samson Agonistes* as Milton's most profound meditation on what it had meant to break what Ernest Sirluck

(1961) has established was the "covenant and pledge" of "sacrificial celibacy" (p. 767) in his own life. Crucially, Milton departs from the Book of Judges not only in making Samson's identity as a Nazarite—that is, as Samson says in his opening soliloquy, "a person separate to God, / Design'd for great exploits" (31–2)—conditional on preserving his vow of chastity, but also in having him marry Dalila. In Judges, the unnamed woman of Timnath is called Samson's "wife" (14.16), while Delilah is simply a woman whom he "loved" (16.4). (Between these two primary relationships, Samson in Judges also consorts with a harlot from Gaza, an episode Milton omits as alien to both his literary and personal purposes.) By this transformation of his biblical source, Milton is able to treat Samson's marriage to Dalila as a repetition of his marriage to the woman of Timna, and thereby to paint a composite portrait of the disastrous error that he believed had caused him to forfeit his own God-given Talent.

In rereading *Samson Agonistes* with the benefit of these insights, it becomes clear that the arguments advanced by Parker and Woodhouse support conclusions antithetical to the positions they espouse. Parker, as we have seen, cannot imagine that Milton would have wanted to lend credence to the idea "that his blindness had been God's punishment on him for his misdeeds," which he believes corroborates his view that *Samson* must have been written before the Restoration, but he cannot explain why Milton would have chosen to publish a work in 1671 that had been written much earlier if people were bound to read it this way. What is more, Parker believes that such "central aspects of Samson's character" as that "he had been uxorious" and "brought dishonor to God" must discomfit "proponents of the autobiographical interpretation." While taking Parker to task for his inconsistencies, Woodhouse maintains that *Samson Agonistes* should be dated to the first year following the Restoration because it is "so divergent ... in doctrine, temper and tone" from *Paradise Regained* that the two works cannot possibly have been written either simultaneously or in succession, and hence Masson must be mistaken in regarding it as "Milton's last poem."

As I shall demonstrate, however, it was precisely *because* he continued to be tormented by the realization that he had been a fool, had been uxorious, and had brought dishonor upon himself that Milton felt compelled to revisit the traumas of his marriage and blindness for the final time in *Samson Agonistes*. The fact that *Samson* is in many respects the antipode to *Paradise Regained*, moreover, far from being a reason to think it must have been written earlier, can be vastly better comprehended if Milton is envisioned as having proceeded contrapuntally, by telling the story of his life first as a Song of Innocence and then as a Song of Experience. In both works, Milton travels back in time, creating a persona through whom he can, in Samson's words, contrast "what once I was, and what am now" (22). The multiple continuities between these dialectically conceived masterpieces come into focus when *Samson* is read as a sequel to *Paradise Regained*, and both are understood to have been written by the poet who, after long travail, had fulfilled his reason for being on this earth by writing *Paradise Lost*.

2

In the Gospel of Luke, Milton's principal source for *Paradise Regained*, Jesus is said to have been "about thirty years of age" (3.23) when he was baptized, the event with which the epyllion opens. Read as autobiography, this would put Milton in 1637–9, just when he had made his vow of "sacrificial celibacy" as the basis of his renewed "self-dedication as God's poet." If we imagine the poem as set in this period of Milton's life, it becomes evident why neither sexuality nor blindness plays a role in *Paradise Regained*. Even Satan knows the folly of Belial's advice that he should seek to tempt Jesus by setting "women in his eye and in his walk" (2.153), Sirens whose "Virgin majesty" belies their "amorous Arts" and "enchanting tongues / Persuasive" (157–9) that cause the hearts of men to become "tangl'd in Amorous Nets" (162). Like the Lady in *A Mask*, who has the "hidden strength" of chastity, "Which, if Heav'n gave it, may be term'd her own" (418–19), Jesus is impervious to such temptations.

Whereas Adam had confessed to Raphael in *Paradise Lost* that he was "only weak / Against the charm of of Beauty's powerful glance," Satan tells Belial that "Beauty stands / In th'admiration only of weak minds / Led captive" (2.220–2). Belial's phrase "Amorous Nets" harks back to Adam's vision of the "Bevy of fair Women" who cause the eyes of heretofore "Just men" to rove until they are caught "in the amorous Net," and "all in heat / They light the nuptial torch" (11.577–90). Since, as we know from *The Doctrine and Disciple of Divorce*, both Adam's susceptibility to Eve and his account of the origin of the institution of marriage are grounded in Milton's own experience of having been fooled by "the bashful muteness of a virgin" and consequently having hastened "too eagerly to light the nuptial torch," Jesus in *Paradise Regained* is not only a later version of the Lady in *Mask* but also an antidote to Milton's own weakness when it came to Mary's "powerful glance" and "enchanting tongue," which led him to fall into her "amorous Net" and break his "covenant and pledge" to God by his impetuous marriage.

Both the Lady and Jesus are autobiographical masks of chastity for Milton, the former reflecting his confidence when he was practicing what he preached about "the sage / And serious doctrine of Virginity" (786–7), and the latter retroactively undoing his marriage as though it had never happened. And just as *Paradise Regained* allows Milton to imagine that he had always been proof against the lure of women, by returning him to the 1630s it also restores his eyesight. This explains why blindness is mentioned only once in passing, in connection with "Blind *Melesigenes*, thence Homer call'd" (4.259)—Meles being a river near to which Homer was supposedly born—as part of the panorama of Athens Satan sets before Jesus near the end of the second of his three temptations taken from Luke (4.1–12): to make bread out of a stone, to accept the gift of the kingdoms of the world, and to cast himself down from a pinnacle of the temple in Jerusalem.

Since Milton not only identifies with Jesus at the age of thirty but also looks back on his life from the vantage point of a man in his sixties, there are multiple temporal layers to *Paradise Regained*. Much as Samson does in *Samson Agonistes*, Jesus begins by comparing his present state of mind as an adult to his memories of childhood, "Ere yet my age / Had measured twice six years" (1.209–10), when he went to the Temple both to hear and teach the rabbis:

> O what a multitude of thoughts at once
> Awak'n'd in me swarm, while I consider
> What from within I feel myself, and hear
> What from without comes often to my ears,
> Ill sorting with my present state compar'd.
> When I was yet a child, no childish play
> To me was pleasing, all my mind was set
> Serious to learn and know, and thence to do
> What might be public good; myself I thought
> Born to that end, born to promote all truth,
> All righteous things: therefore above my years,
> The Law of God I read.

> (196–207)

Milton portrait of the Savior as a young boy "Serious to learn and know" is again reminiscent of the "Just men" in *Paradise Lost* who, until they were waylaid, "all thir study bent / To worship God aright." Further evidence for the autobiographical nature of these recollections comes from the *Second Defense*, where Milton writes: "My father destined me from a child to the pursuits of literature; and my appetite for knowledge was so voracious that, from twelve years of age, I hardly ever left my studies, or went to bed before midnight" (Hughes, 1957, p. 828). Like Jesus, Milton is "destined from a child" by his father for great things, and the fact that the age of twelve is a turning point in both their lives provides a magnet for Milton's identification with the Son of God.

At first Jesus's meditation leaves open how he will fulfill his ambition to do the "public good" and "promote all truth," but then his thoughts veer in a political direction:

> yet this not all
> To which my Spirit aspir'd; victorious deeds
> Flam'd in my heart, heroic acts; one while
> To rescue *Israel* from the *Roman* yoke,
> Then to subdue and quell o'er all the earth
> Brute violence and proud Tyrannic pow'r,
> Till truth were freed, and equity restor'd.
>
> (1.214–20)

Here Milton vicariously recounts his own exploits as a warrior-hero performing "victorious deeds" first by rescuing England from the Royalist "yoke" and then by spreading the fight against "proud Tyrannic pow'r" across "all the earth." As he had written in the Preface to the *First Defense of the English People*, "Even as successfully and piously as those our glorious guides to freedom crushed in battle the royal insolence and tyranny uncontrolled … even as easily as I, singlehandedly, lately refuted and set aside the king himself when he, as it were, rose from the grave" (qtd. in Crockett, 1966, p. 48).

Noble as these aspirations are, however, Jesus then speaks to his mother, who for the first time reveals the truth of his origins and encourages him to set his sights even higher:

> By matchless Deeds express thy matchless Sire,
> For know, thou art no Son of Mortal man;
> Though men esteem thee low of Parentage,
> Thy Father is th'Eternal King, who rules
> All Heaven and Earth, Angels and Sons of men.
> A messenger from God foretold thy birth
> Conceiv'd in me a Virgin; he foretold
> Thou should'st be great and sit on *David's* Throne,
> And of thy Kingdom there should be no end.
>
> (1.233–41)

Having been informed of the identity of his Father and that he was born to fulfill the most heroic of all destines, Jesus searches the Scriptures for "what was writ / Concerning the Messiah" and comes to the realization that "of whom they spake / I am," so that his true calling is to "work Redemption for mankind" (260–6). But all this had taken place in his youth, when he was not yet ready to begin his mission. Consequently, Jesus recalls, "The time prefixt I waited" (269), until he came to be baptized by John and heard his "Father's voice / Audibly … from Heav'n" pronounce him to be "his beloved Son, in whom alone / He was well pleas'd" (283–6). This proclamation is a terrestrial repetition of God's exaltation of the Son as king of the angelic hosts in *Paradise Lost*: "This day I have begot whom I declare / My only Son, and on this holy Hill / Him have anointed" (5.603–5). By this sign, Jesus knows "the time" is "Now full" (286–7); and led "by some strong Motion," he ventures forth "Into this Wilderness" (290–1) to find out what more God has in store for him.

Just as Milton departs from all literary and theological precedents in *Paradise Lost* by making the Father's "begetting" of Christ as his "only Son" the occasion for Satan's rebellion and the War in Heaven, so, too, *Paradise Regained* opens with the narrator's report of how "From *Nazareth* the Son of *Joseph* deem'd / To the flood *Jordan*, came as then obscure, / Unmarkt, unknown" (1.23–5). It is once again when "the Father's voice / From Heaven pronounc'd him his beloved Son" (31–2) that Satan, "with envy fraught and rage" (38), summons "his mighty Peers" (40) to a Council to investigate the situation. The question faced by Satan concerns the relation between these two "beloved Sons" of the heavenly Father:

> His first-begot we know, and sore have felt,
> When his fierce thunder drove us to the deep;
> Who this is we must learn, for man he seems
> In all his lineaments, though in his face
> The glimpses of his Father's glory shine.
>
> (89–93)

Milton's originality in making God's "anointing" of the Son the mainspring of the cosmic drama in *Paradise Lost* is matched by his choice of the story of Jesus's triple temptation in the wilderness as his blueprint for the plot of *Paradise Regained*. Even though this renewed victory over Satan is from the standpoint of orthodox theology only preparatory to the work on which the Redeemer is about to "enter, and begin to save mankind" (4.635) at the conclusion of the brief epic, Milton effectively supplants the Crucifixion—and the Resurrection—with what C. A. Patrides (1966) has termed "the one event in the life of Jesus which appealed to him" (p. 145) as the means by which the "happy Garden" of which he had formerly sung, "By one man's disobedience lost," is compensated for by "Recover'd Paradise to all mankind, / By one man's obedience fully tried" (1.1–4).

The effect of Milton's deemphasis of the traditional linchpins in the Christian narrative of the fall and redemption of humankind is to keep the theme of temptation at the center of his work by making the contest between Jesus and Satan turn on what it means to be the Son of God. Although Jesus already knows that he is "no Son of Mortal man" and his "Father is th'Eternal King," the lesson that Satan "must learn" is precisely that the "first-begot" who has already vanquished him in Heaven and this baffling successor, who would appear to be a "man … / In all his lineaments," are one and the same. In *Paradise Lost* the contest between Christ and Satan likewise turns on the interpretation of a prophecy that is also a riddle. There, it centers on the "mysterious terms" in which the Son pronounces "doom" (10.172–3) on Satan in the form of the Serpent, "Her Seed shall bruise thy Head, thou bruise his heel" (175). Satan, who was forced "This essence to incarnate and imbrute" (9.166) in order to carry out his temptation of Eve, himself unknowingly comprises two natures that are really one. When he returns to Hell in apparent triumph, Satan boasts that it is not he who has been judged, "but the brute Serpent in whose shape / Man I deceiv'd" (10.495–6); but he, along with all the other devils, is forthwith transformed into "A monstrous serpent" (514) and "punisht in the shape he sinn'd" (516). Adam, meanwhile, is progressively enlightened about the meaning of the prophecy, until in Book 12 Michael reveals that it refers to the "temporal death" (433) that Christ, the "seed of woman" (379), must undergo in the Crucifixion in order to "bruise the head of *Satan*" and "crush his strength / Defeating Sin and Death, his two main arms" (431–2).

The action of *Paradise Regained* is devoid of suspense. Indeed, it consists in Jesus repeatedly *not* acting by refusing to succumb to Satan's temptations. As the Son of God, Jesus is incapable of sin, so there is no chance he will use his free will for any purpose other than to affirm his perfect obedience to the Father. But inasmuch as Jesus is also an autobiographical mask for Milton, both as he was as a thirty-year-old with unblemished chastity and as the sixty-year-old who had written *Paradise Lost*, Milton could look back on the anxieties that had once pierced him as no more than distant memories that now glanced off him like so many harmless arrows from—in the words of the Elder Brother in *A Mask*—his armor of "complete steel" (421).

Even when he first proclaimed "his self-dedication as God's poet" in Elegy 6 and the second Prolusion, Milton was worried that time was passing him by. As he wrote in "How soon hath time":

How soon hath Time, the subtle thief of youth,
Stol'n on his wing my three-and-twentieth year!

My hasting days fly on with full career,
But my late spring no bud or blossom showeth.

(1–4)

To make matters worse, Milton's "inward ripeness" had not manifested itself in the manner of "more timely-happy spirits" (7–8), so he felt belated by comparison with other poets—especially Spenser, who despite having published *The Shepheardes Calendar* in 1579, when he was twenty-six or twenty-seven, wrote the following year in a Latin verse-letter to Gabriel Harvey: "it is not meet / A youth with genius not unblest, should spend / In duties mean, repeated to no end, / The precious morning of his fairest years, / Nor see the hoped-for fruit crown the green ears."[2] If, as seems likely, Milton was imitating Spenser's complaint in his sonnet, he was avowing his ambition by emulating his preeminent Protestant precursor (and fellow Cambridge graduate) even as he chafed at his own barrenness. Milton sought to allay his fears by voicing with apparent equanimity his acceptance of whatever "lot, however mean or high, / Toward which Time leads me, and the will of Heav'n" (11–12). If he could only be patient, he concluded, then what he experienced as time in the human realm he would be able to view as though it were eternity in God's sight: "All is, if I have grace to use it so, / As ever in my great task-Master's eye" (13–14).

Similarly, in "Lycidas," the drowning of Edward King "ere his prime" (8) causes Milton to fear that Atropos, the third of the three Fates whom he calls "the blind *Fury* with th'abhorred shears," will cut the thread of his own "thin-spun life" before he has had a chance to reap the "fair Guerdon" of his abstemious and celibate existence and "burst out into sudden blaze" (73–6). He acknowledges harboring the desire for fame that is the "last infirmity of Noble mind" and leads the "clear spirit" to "scorn delights, and live laborious days" (70–1).[3] But Milton seeks to check his ambition—and his anxieties—by having Phoebus, the god of poetry, remind him that "'*Fame* is no plant that grows on mortal soil'" (78); rather, it "lives and spreads aloft by those pure

---

[2] I quote the English translation of Spenser's poem from the article by R. N. Smith (1945, p. 395).

[3] The cost of the renunciation exacted by Milton's vow of celibacy is evident when he wonders, "Were it not better done as others use, / To sport with *Amaryllis* in the shade, / Or with the tangles of *Neaera*'s hair?" (68–70). As Le Comte (1978) comments, "Amaryllis and Neaera (names derived respectively from Virgil and Horace) stand for the natural pleasures. They are symbolic, but they are also girls" (p. 19). He quotes a correspondent to the *Times Literary Supplement*, "The hair is pubic, is it not? At least it must be so on a second level of interpretation" (p. 20).

eyes / And perfect witness of all-judging *Jove*; / As he pronounces on each deed, / Of so much fame in Heav'n expect thy meed'" (81–4). By the end of the elegy the language of otherworldly consolation is no longer classical but Christian. "Through the dear might of him that walk'd the waves" (173), Milton affirms, his drowned friend "hears the unexpressive nuptial Song / In the blest kingdoms meek of joy and love" (176–7), which is promised in Revelation to the followers of the Lamb "which were not defiled with women; for they are virgins" (14.4). And since Milton, too, is in this exalted company he need not dread his own death because he is assured of receiving "fame in Heav'n" even if he does not live long enough to achieve immortality through his poetry.

Milton's anxiety about his procrastination reaches its apogee in the sonnet on his blindness, where, as Sirluck (1961) comments, "the best he can manage is resignation" (p. 771). But by the time he came to write *Paradise Regained*, he no longer needed to fear that he had buried his "One Talent which is death to hide," so Milton could display his mastery of these old insecurities by echoing both "How soon hath time" and "Lycidas." Thus, in Book 3, when Satan seeks first to undermine the confidence of the Son by warning him, "Thy years are ripe, and over-ripe" (31), then to awaken his "thirst for glory" (38) by comparing the obscurity in which he labors to the fame achieved at the same age by Alexander the Great, Scipio Africanus, Pompey, and Julius Caesar, and finally to goad him into action with the promise "but thou yet art not too late" (42), it is to no avail. The Savior responds with the rebuke that earthly glory is nothing but the "blaze of fame" (47) sparked by "A miscellaneous rabble, who extol / Things vulgar, and well-weigh'd, scarce worth the praise" (50–1). Unperturbed, he explains to Satan that "true glory" consists in the "approbation" with which God views "The just man" (60–2); and since "All things are best fulfill'd in their due time" (182), he need not be in any hurry to act.

Paradise Regained culminates in the temptation on the pinnacle of the temple in Jerusalem, which turns on the question of what it means to be the Son of God. "Swoln with rage" by his previous rebuffs, Satan lays his final trap by disclosing to Jesus that he had monitored his development from infancy to the day of his baptism, which caused him to want to study this "Son of *David*, Virgin-born" (4.499–500) still more closely:

> Thenceforth I thought thee worth my nearer view
> And narrower Scrutiny, that I might learn
> In what degree or meaning thou art call'd
> The Son of God, which bears no single sense;
> The Son of God I also am, or was,

And if I was, I am; relation stands;
All men are Sons of God, yet thee I thought
In some respect far higher so declar'd.

(514–21)

Satan's reference to Jesus as "Virgin-born" is flattery, as it would appear to concede his divinity, but Satan claims he still does not understand "what more thou art than man, / Worth naming Son of God by voice from Heav'n" (538–9). Accordingly, he transports Jesus "through the Air sublime" (542) and places him atop the highest spire in the Holy City. He challenges Jesus to prove that he is the "Son of God" (555) by casting himself down since it was promised that he would be rescued by angels, "lest at any time / Thou chance to dash thy foot against a stone" (558–9).

Because Jesus knows that to attempt to prove his identity would be to forfeit it, he administers the death blow to Satan when he responds: "Also it is written, / Tempt not the Lord thy God; he said and stood" (560–1). Unlike Milton's sonnet on his blindness, where he can only pray that "They also serve who only stand and wait" (14), the passivity of Jesus's reply to Satan, like his earlier awaiting of the "time prefixt," is the supreme expression of his assurance that he is indeed the "beloved Son" and the checkmate of his opponent in a game that had already been won.

Following Jesus's refusal to take Satan's bait, Milton celebrates his triumph by comparing Satan to the thwarted nemeses of two classical heroes:

But Satan smitten with amazement fell
As when Earth's son *Antaeus* (to compare
Small things with greatest) in *Irassa* strove
With *Jove's Alcides*, and oft foil'd still rose,
Receiving from his mother Earth new strength,
Fresh from his fall, and fiercer grapple join'd,
Throttl'd at length in th'Air, expir'd and fell;
So after many a foil the Tempter proud,
Renewing fresh assaults, amidst his pride
Fell whence he stood to see his Victor fall.
And as that *Theban* Monster that propos'd
Her riddle, and him who solv'd it not, devour'd,
That once found out and solv'd, for grief and spite
Cast herself headlong from the *Ismenian* steep,
So struck with dread and anguish fell the Fiend.

(4.562–76)

In these extended similes, Milton amalgamates Hercules and Oedipus, paragons respectively of strength and wisdom, into a composite type of Jesus Christ whose exploits are "small things" compared with his vanquishing of "the Tempter," which is the "greatest." Like Jesus, Hercules, whom Milton calls "*Jove's Alcides*," is the son of a divine father—the king of the Greek and Roman gods—and a human mother. Antaeus, by contrast, although the son of Poseidon, is described solely in terms of his maternal origin, as "Earth's son." Like the "*Theban* monster," the Sphinx who "devour'd" all those who could solve her riddle, Antaeus challenged passers-by to a life-and-death contest in the form of a wrestling match and could not be defeated as long as he received "from his mother Earth new strength." Hercules, however, triumphed by raising him up "in th'Air," where he was then able to "throttle" him.

The invincibility enjoyed by Antaeus provided he maintains contact with "his mother Earth"—Gaia being literally his mother—is the incestuous tie that is both his source of strength and his fatal weakness. When he is lifted off the ground by "*Jove's Alcides*," the connection is severed and he becomes helpless. In the ensuing comparison, in which the plummeting "Fiend" is equated with the Sphinx who "casts herself headlong" off a mountain, Oedipus, who remains unnamed, is evoked purely as an intellectual hero, devoid of any taint of incest or patricide. In the same way that he effaces his marriage to Mary Powell, as well as the blindness that he experienced as first his punishment for and then his redemption from having partaken of her forbidden fruit, Milton conjures up the hologram of Oedipus without an Oedipus complex. By redeeming Oedipus from his primal crimes, Jesus becomes Christ and regains paradise for fallen humanity. He proves himself to be the son of "th'Eternal King" by extinguishing even the *desire* to compete with his heavenly Father, while in the final lines of the poem, "Sung Victor" by the angelic hosts, "hee unobserv'd / Home to Mother's house private return'd" (637–9), as devoid of sexual impulses as his conception was miraculous in the first place.

As William Kerrigan (1983) has pointed out, however, there is "a latent chiasmus in each of the two similes" (p. 90) with which Milton concludes *Paradise Regained*. Although Hercules defeats Antaeus by lifting him "in th'Air," it is Satan who had just set Jesus "on the highest Pinnacle" (4.549), thereby reversing their roles. Similarly, although in the Greek myth it is the Sphinx who "propos'd / Her riddle" and Oedipus who solved it, in Milton's poem it is Jesus whose identity as the Son of God "bears no single sense" and Satan who is unable to solve the riddle of his dual nature. This makes Jesus not only the second Oedipus but also a hybrid Sphinx, and Satan not only the

"*Theban* Monster" but also a defeated Oedipus. As Jesus had warned Satan in Book 1, "henceforth Oracles are ceast, / And thou no more with Pomp and Sacrifice / Shalt be inquir'd at *Delphos* or elsewhere" (456–8)—Delphi being the site of the oracle consulted by Oedipus, among many others—for he himself has been sent into the world as the "living Oracle" (460) of God. Jesus's victory in *Paradise Regained* is adumbrated in *Paradise Lost*, where the Son is again likened to "this Oracle," whose prophecy of Satan's "doom" is fulfilled—in an allusion to Luke 10.18—"When *Jesus* son of *Mary* second *Eve*, / Saw Satan fall like Lightning down from Heav'n" (10.182–4).

How deeply embedded these symmetries are in Milton's poetry can be seen in the continuation of the climactic passage in *Paradise Regained* that describes Satan's fall from the spire:

> So Satan fell; and straight a fiery Globe
> Of Angels on full sail of wing flew nigh,
> Who on their plumy Vans receiv'd *him* soft
> From his uneasy station, and upbore
> As on a floating couch through the blithe Air,
> Then on a flow'ry valley set *him* down
> On a green bank, and set before *him* spread
> A table of Celestial Food, Divine.[4]

(4.582–9; italics added)

In the earliest annotated edition of *Paradise Regained*, published in 1795, Charles Dunster expressed his disapproval of Milton's solecism. It is Satan who falls, but Jesus who is rescued by the "fiery Globe / Of Angels" and served the "Celestial" banquet:

> But the grammatical inaccuracy here, I am afraid, cannot be palliated. *Him*, according to the common construction of language, certainly must refer to Satan, the person last mentioned. The intended sense of the passage cannot indeed be misunderstood; but we grieve to find any inaccuracy in a part of the poem so eminently beautiful.

(qtd. in Kerrigan, 1983, p. 90)

What the neoclassical critic fails to understand is that this "grammatical inaccuracy" is Milton's poetic expression of the psychic twinship of Satan and Christ. If, as Kerrigan maintains, the "splitting of the imago of the father

---

[4] I have deleted the period after "spread" in Hughes's edition, which appears to be a typographical vagary.

constitutes the major psychological strategy of Milton's life and work" (p. 114), this proposition has as its corollary Milton's splitting of the imago of the son into enemy brothers, who form mirror images of a single divided psyche.

3

Like *Paradise Regained*, *Samson Agonistes* transports Milton back to the past while simultaneously allowing him to view his life as a completed arc. That this memory play must have been written after the Restoration of Charles II has been rendered indisputable by Crockett and Worden, but the fact that the three types of responses to Manoa's "attempts of ransom" on behalf of his son and Samson's having been the victim of "daily fraud" reflect Milton's situation in the first year or two of the 1660s does not mean that it dates from that initial post-Restoration period. Despite the despair from which Samson suffers at the outset, *Samson Agonistes* affirms the existence of a divine providence that renders its outcome no less inevitable than that of *Paradise Regained*, even though Samson remains unaware of this for most of the work. As the Chorus intones in the final speech of the play:

> All is best, though we oft doubt,
> What th' unsearchable dispose
> Of highest wisdom brings about,
> And ever best found in the close.
> Oft he seems to hide his face,
> But unexpectedly returns
> And to his faithful Champion hath in place
> Bore witness gloriously.
>
> (1745–52)

Since Milton could not have believed that his own life had been "best found in the close" or dared to call himself God's "faithful Champion" until after he had completed *Paradise Lost*, it is inconceivable that this passage could have been written before he had redeemed himself in the eyes of his "great task-Master." And while it is less important to sort out the order of *Paradise Regained* and *Samson Agonistes*, the evidence that *Samson* extends and deepens motifs in the brief epic corroborates Masson's view that the tragedy is indeed "Milton's last poem."

Whereas Jesus takes Milton back to the late 1630s, Samson has been married not once but twice, which would put Milton in the late 1650s. In 1656, four years after the death of Mary Powell, Milton married Katherine

Woodcock, who died in 1658 of complications following the birth of a daughter who also did not survive; and it was not until 1663, at the age of fifty-five, that he married the twenty-four-year-old Elizabeth Minshull, who died in 1737 at the age of ninety-nine. Even if we do not place undue weight on the date of his marriage to Katherine Woodcock, it is clear that *Samson Agonistes* must be imagined to take place after Milton's blindness had become complete and when his "sense of Heav'n's desertion" (632) was at its height, for which we have "When I consider" as a benchmark and still leaves us in the 1650s. Whereas Woodhouse assumes that the differences in "doctrine, temper and tone" between *Samson* and *Paradise Regained* must mean that they cannot have been written in sequence, I maintain that they are doctrinally compatible and that their dissonances in "temper and tone" are the consequence of Milton's technique of contrapuntal composition. Having adopted a regressive solution to the calamities of his life in *Paradise Regained* by wiping the slate clean as though they had never happened, Milton in *Samson* heals from his traumas by confronting and symbolically repeating them. *Samson Agonistes* was the perfect vehicle for his final and most profound self-analysis because it allowed Milton to depict his blindness not merely as a condign punishment for the violation of his "vow of strictest purity" but also as the direct result of his supreme act of stupidity and disloyalty to God.

The continuities between *Paradise Regained* and *Samson Agonistes* are evident from Samson's opening soliloquy, in which he laments that while he may find respite for his body, he cannot for his mind:

> Ease to the body some, none to the mind
> From restless thoughts, that like a deadly swarm
> Of Hornets arm'd, no sooner found alone,
> But rush upon me thronging, and present
> Times past, what once I was, and what am now.

> (18–22)

This closely parallels Jesus's lines from Book 1 of *Paradise Regained*:

> O what a multitude of thoughts at once
>   Awak'n'd in me swarm, while I consider
>   What from within I feel myself, and hear
>   What from without comes often to my ears,
>   Ill sorting with my present state compar'd.

> (196–200)

Although Jesus has none of Samson's anguish about having been abandoned by God, he, too, compares his past and present states as well as what he hears "from without" to what he feels "from within." Milton's artistic evolution can be seen in the transmutation of Jesus's "multitude of *thoughts*" that "Awakened … *swarm*" in his mind into Samson's more fully developed metaphor of his "restless *thoughts*" that "like a deadly *swarm* / Of Hornets arm'd" come "thronging" on him in his solitude.

Both of Samson's betrayals result from secrets he reveals about himself to his wives. As he tells his father, "Nothing of all these evils hath befall'n me / But justly; I myself have brought them on, / Sole Author, I, sole cause" (374–6). Despite having been "warn'd by oft experience" after the woman of Timna shared with his enemies a secret she had wrested from him "in her height / Of Nuptial Love profest" (382–5), Samson allowed the same thing to happen with Dalila, "who also in her prime of love, / Spousal embraces" (388–9), won from him something even more precious, "My capital secret, in what part my strength / Lay stor'd" (394–5). With both wives, Samson betrays a secret about himself during their "spousal embraces" and, indeed, at "the height of Nuptial Love"—that is, the moment of orgasm.

Unlike the "capital secret" concerning the source of his strength he discloses to Dalila, the secret Samson confides to his first wife is never spelled out in the play. But like the riddle of the Sphinx, to which Sophocles only alludes in *Oedipus the King* but everyone at the Festival of Dionysus where the tragedy was first performed would have been expected to recognize, Milton could take it for granted that his readers would be familiar with Samson's story in the Book of Judges. There, when Samson brings his parents to meet the woman of Timnath, he is attacked by a lion that he slays with his bare hands. Then, when he resolves to marry her, "he turned aside to see the carcase of the lion; and, behold, there was a swarm of bees and honey in the carcase" (14.8), which Samson eats. At the wedding feast, Samson makes a wager with his wife's companions that they cannot solve the following riddle, "Out of the eater came forth meat [i.e., food], and out of the strong came forth sweetness" (14). When they threaten to burn her and her father's house if she cannot get him to tell her the answer, she importunes him until he yields, upon which the companions say to Samson, "What is sweeter than honey? and what is stronger than a lion?" (18).

Just as the riddle of the Sphinx, which defines man in terms of the number of his feet, holds the key to the identity of Oedipus, so, too, the riddle of the bees holds the key to Samson's identity. Being the lion in whose carcass the bees make honey, he is the strong man who brings forth sweetness and the destroyer who nourishes his people. The reader who knows the answer to Samson's riddle can then see the providential meaning in the "multitude of thoughts" by which he is plagued at the outset. The "swarm of bees" to which the "swarm / Of hornets" alludes signifies that Samson—notwithstanding his despair—had never forfeited his identity as "a person separate to God, / Design'd for great exploits." Milton elaborates this image cluster when Samson tells the Chorus that most friends "in prosperous days / They swarm, but in adverse withdraw their head" (191–2). Similarly, when he describes to Manoa how "Thoughts my Tormentors arm'd with deadly stings / Mangle my apprehensive tenderest parts" (624–5), these "deadly stings" again contain the promise of Samson's redemption, although he has no inkling of it at the time.

The belief in divine providence that suffuses *Samson Agonistes* no less than it does *Paradise Regained* is manifested in Samson's opening lines: "A little onward lend thy guiding hand / To these dark steps, a little further on" (1–2). In the sonnet to Cyriack Skinner, Milton had affirmed that he was led "through the world's vain mask" by a "better guide" than the thought that he had lost his eyesight "In liberty's defense," and by the late 1660s his faith in a higher power had been vindicated. Milton never specifies who is leading the blind Samson, but when an "aged man in Rural weeds" (1.314)—an avatar of Spenser's Archimago—asks Jesus with feigned courtesy, "Sir, what ill chance hath brought thee to this place / So far from path or road of men?" (321–2), the Son of God, for whom there is no such thing as chance, upbraids his questioner, "Who brought me hither / Will bring me hence, no other Guide I seek" (335–6). What is clear from the outset to Jesus in *Paradise Regained* is only understood by Samson at the end of his play. Having initially refused to accompany the Messenger to the "Idolatrous Rites" (1378) at the pagan temple, he tells the Chorus that he begins to "feel / Some rousing motions" that "dispose / To something extraordinary my thoughts," and these assure him that he will do nothing "that may dishonor / Our Law, or stain my vow of *Nazarite*" (1382–6) if he obeys the command of the Philistine lords. The Danites respond, "Go, and the Holy One / Of *Israel* be thy guide / To what may serve his glory best" (1427–9).

These passages confirm that the mysterious "guiding hand" at the outset of the tragedy belongs to "the Holy One / Of *Israel*," who has never ceased to pilot Samson through the voyage of his life. Samson's "rousing motions" are identical to the "strong motion" by which Jesus is "led / Into this Wilderness" where he meets Satan. And just as Jesus learns from his mother that his birth was "foretold" by a "messenger from God," Samson's birth was "from Heaven foretold / Twice by an Angel" (23–4). Even though Samson and Jesus represent Milton's spiritual condition before and after his marriage to Mary Powell, for the poet who has written *Paradise Lost* Samson's regeneration is no more in doubt than is Jesus's victory over the Tempter on the pinnacle.

4

When Manoa first beholds Samson in his blindness, he questions why his prayer to have a child was granted by God only to end in ignominious fashion, "For this did th'Angel twice descend? for this / Ordain'd thy nurture holy, as of a Plant?" (360–1). Samson, however, checks Manoa's complaints, "Appoint not heavenly disposition, Father" (373), and tells him, as we have seen, that "Nothing of all these evils hath befall'n me / But justly, I myself have brought them on." As Worden (1995) has shown, in insisting that he is the "sole Author" and "sole cause" of his miseries, Samson speaks for all the defeated Puritans condemned to imprisonment or execution—including Edmund Ludlow, Algernon Sidney, and Sir Henry Vane—who needed to "confront the calamity of the Restoration and to explain it, as [they] sought to explain everything, in terms of God's providence" (p. 113). The only way they could do this was by acknowledging that "the defeat of God's cause owes nothing to its enemies … and everything to the sinfulness which God punishes in His servants" (p. 113). Samson, therefore, is a paradigm of the imperative felt not simply by Milton but by all his comrades who had "to learn to keep faith with—in Ludlow's words—God's 'seemingly dead and buried cause'" (p. 113).

But in addition to being a collective hero, what makes Samson representative of Milton is *why* he has, in Worden's words "to absorb the lesson of divine humiliation" (p. 113). He becomes a prisoner not because of a political defeat but because of his failure in the religious and domestic spheres. When Manoa seeks to ransom him from the Philistines, Samson entreats him to "spare the trouble / Of that solicitation," and instead to "let me here, / As I deserve, pay on my punishment; / And expiate, if possible, my crime, / Shameful garrulity" (487–91). He adds that while it would have been "heinous" enough "To have reveal'd / Secrets of men, the secrets of a friend," which would have warranted his being "avoided as a blab" and having "the mark of fool" set on his forehead, what he has done is far worse: "I / God's counsel have not kept, his holy secret / Presumptuously have publish'd, impiously, / Weakly at least, and shamefully" (491–9).

Samson's insistence that he deserves to be punished for the "crime" of "shameful garrulity" and because he has "presumptuously … publish'd" God's "holy secret" takes on added meaning when it is construed as Milton's autobiographical confession. In *The Reason of Church Government*, even as he excused himself to the "elegant and learned reader" for using his "left hand" despite being "led by the genial power of nature to another task," Milton acknowledged that he would "be foolish in saying more to this purpose" and "to venture and divulge unusual things of myself." Yet he could not refrain from proclaiming that he knew both from an "inward prompting" and from the plaudits he received on his Italian journey that he had been called "to leave something so written to aftertimes, as they should not willingly let it die." He also, as we know, vowed to do for England "what the greatest and choicest wits of Athens, Rome, or modern Italy, and those Hebrews of old did for their countries … with this over and above of being a Christian."

Milton "publish'd" these statements, which are indeed "presumptuous," early in 1642, shortly before he made the "journey into the country" from which he returned to London yoked to Mary Powell. Because it was his marriage that caused him to believe he had broken his "vow of strictest purity," and for decades thereby made it impossible for him to keep his promise to the reader, it would be natural for Milton to have concluded that he had been guilty of "shameful garrulity" by virtue of the fact that he had gotten married. Just as the Samson story allowed Milton to interpret his blindness not merely as a punishment for his sexual sin but as its direct consequence, so, too, it allowed him to conflate his marriage with his revelation of "God's counsel." In both instances, what had been a contiguity in Milton's life became a simultaneity in the imaginative work through which he revealed the inner truth of his experience.

Although Samson is inveigled by both his wives into divulging a secret about himself in "the height / Of nuptial love profest," there is a radical difference between these lapses. The solution to the riddle of how "out of the strong came forth sweetness," while it has a providential meaning, concerns Samson in his personal capacity, and what he lets slip with the woman of Timna causes no lasting harm. What Samson betrays to Dalila, by contrast, concerns the "Heav'n-gifted strength" (36) that was the seal of the "Promise" that he "Should *Israel* from *Philistian* yoke deliver" (38–9), which has to do with his identity as a Nazarite, the revelation of which has catastrophic consequences. But since Samson's "holy secret" is that his "strength / Lay stor'd" (394–5) in his hair, it is also his "capital secret" not only in the sense of being his most important secret, but also because it contains a play on the Latin word *caput* and refers to his head. The same etymological pun holds the key to the riddling judgment pronounced by the Son on Satan in the form of the Serpent in *Paradise Lost*, who receives his "capital bruise" (12.383) of eternal damnation when the Savior is bruised in the heel by his "temporal death" (433) on the cross. Samson's is thus literally a "head case," or what he calls one of "impotence of mind" (52), although his psychological problems manifest themselves above all in the sexual sphere.

The contrast between Samson's two marriages begins with the fact that, with the woman of Timna, Samson knows "That what I motion'd was of God," and this "intimate impulse" assures him, despite his parents' opposition, that his choice of "The daughter of an Infidel" is the "occasion" by which he "might begin *Israel's* Deliverance, / The work to which I was divinely call'd" (221–6). The same "intimate impulse" is the source of the "rousing motions" that, at the end of the tragedy, prompt him to change his mind and follow the Messenger to the festival at the Temple of Dagon. When he marries Dalila, however, Samson assumes that he can rely on reason to discern God's ways, much as Adam and Eve do when they wonder about the seeming inefficiency of the universe, and as Milton himself had done when he expected that the Puritan Revolution would establish God's kingdom on earth. As Samson says in hindsight, "I thought it lawful from my former act, / And the same end" (231–2).

By modifying his biblical source so that Samson marries not only the woman of Timna but also Dalila, Milton again creates a structure of repetition in which Samson's first marriage stands in relation to his second as unfallen experience does to the Fall in *Paradise Lost*. Like the prelapsarian sex of Adam and Eve, Samson's first marriage is, in Laplanche's terms, "sexual—presexual" and does not result in the loss of his spiritual virginity. But the seeds of his undoing are there, just as they are when Adam's "single imperfection" prompts him to ask God to create a companion for him and he confesses his "vehement desire" for Eve to Raphael before the Fall.

Milton's recurrent references to circumcision in *Samson Agonistes* as the sign of the difference between Israelites and their enemies keep the spotlight where it belongs in the story of a man whose downfall was caused by sex. Samson cannot forget how treacherous Hebrews had yielded him "To the uncircumcis'd a welcome prey" (260), but also how he had fought "Above the nerve of mortal arm / Against the uncircumcis'd" (640). Dalila, conversely, admits that her "name perhaps among the Circumcis'd / … / To all posterity may stand defam'd" (975–7)—where "Circumcis'd" is used as an epithet of contempt—but takes comfort in the thought that she will be "among the famousest / Of Women" (982–3) in her own country. Harapha likewise rues that he had not been given the opportunity to fight Samson when he was at full strength because then the "glory of Prowess" would have been "won by a *Philistine* / From the unforeskinn'd race" (1098–100).

Whereas for Samson it is the Philistines who are defined by a privative as "uncircumcis'd," for Harapha it is the Hebrews who are "unforeskinn'd." Similarly, when the Chorus advises Samson to go with the Officer to the feast at the Temple of Dagon because he is already in bondage to the "uncircumcis'd, unclean" (1364) Philistines, the negative prefixes reflect the Hebrew perspective that to be circumcised is not to have lost a piece of one's anatomy, but rather to have gained a superior penis and religion. Finally, in recalling how Samson decimated "the flower of *Palestine*" with "The Jaw of a dead Ass," the Chorus celebrates that "a thousand foreskins fell" to "his sword of bone" (143–4). While describing a slaughter, this image conjures up a fantasy of Samson performing a mass circumcision of the Palestinians whose foreskins he removes.

Milton's obsession with the penis in *Samson Agonistes* has its counterpart in his use of the word "snare" with reference to Dalila, though he never does so in connection with the woman of Timna because Samson's decision to marry her is divinely inspired. The first time Samson mentions Dalila, he calls her "That specious Monster, my accomplisht snare" (230), while later, during their confrontation, he vows that he will never "bring my feet again into the snare / Where once I have been caught" (931–2). In response to his father's plea that he should cease to punish himself so harshly for his misdeeds, Samson begins the story of his downfall by recollecting how, "Fearless of danger, like a petty God, / I walk'd about admir'd of all and dreaded" (529–30), until he was taken unawares:

> Then swoll'n with pride into the snare I fell
> Of fair fallacious looks, venereal trains,
> Soft'n'd with pleasure and voluptuous life;
> At length to lay my head and hallow'd pledge
> Of all my strength in the lascivious lap
> Of a deceitful Concubine who shore me
> Like a tame Wether, all my precious fleece,
> Then turn'd me out ridiculous, despoil'd,
> Shav'n, and disarm'd among my enemies.
>
> (532–40)

Samson's acknowledgment that he had been "swoll'n with pride" pertains at once to the hubris that had deluded him into thinking he was "a petty God" and to his erect penis, just as Oedipus's name, "Swollen Foot," alludes to *his* erect penis as well as to the hubris that inflated his ego after defeating the Sphinx. The continuity between Milton's last two works is exemplified by the fact that he ends *Paradise Regained* by comparing Jesus to Oedipus as the triumphant solver of the Sphinx's riddle in *Oedipus the King*, while *Samson Agonistes* begins, as Merritt Hughes (1957) points out, with the captive Samson being guided in a way that imitates "the opening scene of Sophocles' *Oedipus at Colonus*, where Antigone leads her blind father forward" (p. 551). Like Hamlet, whose question to Ophelia, "Lady, shall I lie in your lap?" (3.2.112), she rightly takes to be a sexual innuendo but he pretends to have been innocuous, "I mean, my head upon your lap?" (114), Samson describes how he was induced to "lay my head" in Dalila's "lascivious lap." For both Milton and Shakespeare, "lap" is a euphemism for what Hamlet obscenely terms "country matters" (116), and Samson's "head" is a metonymy for the penis he had heedlessly slipped into Dalila's "snare."

In succumbing to Dalila, Samson is simultaneously "swoll'n with pride" and "Soft'n'd with pleasure." This paradoxical conjunction of tumescence and detumescence replicates how Adam's "vehement desire" for Eve leads to the "effeminate slackness" that brings about his fall. Michael's rebuke of Adam is internalized by Samson when he rues how "a grain of manhood" might have enabled him to avoid "all her snares: / But foul effeminacy held me yok't / Her Bondslave" (408–11). When Dalila "shore" Samson of his "precious fleece," she not only caused him to his lose his erection when he ejaculated into her "lap" in "the height of Nuptial Love" but also castrated him "like a tame Wether." Both he and Adam lacked what Gabriel in *Paradise Lost* calls a properly virile "self-esteem, grounded on just and right" (8.572), which would have saved them from their destruction at the hands of their wives.

Just as Samson never refers to the woman of Timna as a "snare," it is only of Dalila that he says that his "Vessel" was "shipwreck't" because he "divulg'd the secret gift of God / To a deceitful Woman" (198–202). Milton's metaphor of the body as a ship derives from St. Paul, who enjoins the faithful Christian "to possess his vessel in sanctification and honour," not "in the lust of concupiscence," which means that he must "abstain from fornication" (1 Thess. 4.3-5). Notwithstanding the "loophole" he had tried to carve out for himself in *Apology for Smectymnuus* by claiming that "marriage must not be called a defilement," Milton could not escape the realization that he had given way to the "lust of concupiscence" and broken his vow to "abstain from fornication" that had been the bedrock of "his self-dedication as God's poet" when he fell for Mary Powell. He compounded his offense by doing so just when he had been so "foolish" as to "venture and divulge" the full extent of his ambition in *The Reason of Church Government*.

For Milton, therefore, his marriage to Mary *was* fornication, which is why, even though he departs from Judges by making Dalila Samson's wife, Samson refers to her as a "deceitful Concubine." The castration visited upon Samson as a punishment for his transgression is symbolized not only by his "shav'n" head but also by his blindness. When Samson laments in his opening soliloquy, "why was the sight / To such a tender ball as th' eye confin'd?" (93–4), the phrase "tender ball" evokes the testicles and resonates with Edgar's reference in *King Lear* to the "bleeding rings" of Gloucester's sockets that have lost their "precious stones" or eyes.

In response to Samson's lament that he has been undone by pride and betrayed the promise of his birth, the Chorus praises him for having been able to repress "Desire of wine and all delicious drinks, / Which many a famous warrior overturns," and not having allowed "the dancing Ruby" to allure him "from the cool Crystálline spring" (541–6). This passage harks back to Milton's avowal in *The Reason of Church Government* that the immortal work he was destined to write was one "not to be raised from the heat of youth, or the vapors of wine" (Hughes, 1957, p. 671), which in turn is echoed both by his insistence in Elegy 6 that the divinely ordained poet should "drink sober drafts from the pure spring" (p. 52) and by the Lady's encomium in *Comus* of Nature's "sober laws / And holy dictate of spare Temperance" (767–8).

While agreeing that he drank only "the clear milky juice" and did not envy "them the grape / Whose heads that turbulent liquor fills with fumes" (550–2), Samson meets the Chorus's praise with a crushing self-reproach:

> But what avail'd this temperance, not complete
> Against another object more enticing?
> What boots it at one gate to make defense,
> And at another to let in the foe,
> Effeminately vanquish't?

> (558–62)

Unlike Jesus in *Paradise Regained*, Samson's temperance did not afford him immunity against the "more enticing" temptations of women whose "amorous Arts" and "enchanting tongues" cause the hearts of men to become "tangl'd in Amorous Nets."

That Milton is revisiting the trauma of his marriage to Mary Powell in Samson's memories of Dalila comes into sharpest focus when she rises up from his past to appear in the play. Just as Milton modeled his description of Eve's reconciliation with Adam in *Paradise Lost* on the ambush arranged by Mary's parents with the aid of his cousins to salvage her marriage to Milton, he revisited the same scene from 1645 in the encounter between Samson and Dalila. But Milton now casts Mary's plea that they put an end to their estrangement in the harshest possible light. Like Eve, who "with Tears that ceas'd not flowing, / And tresses all disorder'd, at [Adam's] feet / Fell humble, and imbracing them / Besought his peace" (10.910–13), Dalila is tearful and apparently contrite:

> With doubtful feet and wavering resolution
> I came, still dreading thy displeasure, *Samson*,
> Which to have merited, without excuse,
> I cannot but acknowledge; yet if tears
> May expiate …

> (732–6)

Again like Eve, Dalila pleads that "conjugal affection" has overcome her "fear and timorous doubt" (739–40) to make her want to see Samson again in order to learn if she can do anything to ease his suffering and "in some part to recompense / My rash but more unfortunate misdeed" (746–7).

What is different is the reaction of Milton's personas, although this is not clear at first. As we have seen, when Eve approaches Adam, whose despair has led him to wish he were dead, he lashes out before she has had a chance to say a word, "Out of my sight, thou Serpent" (10.868), and proceeds to ask why God did not "find some other way to generate / Mankind" (894–5), without the need to engage in sexual intercourse with women. At the conclusion of his speech, Adam turns his back; but when Eve implores his forgiveness, not least because she is "More miserable" in having sinned not "Against God only" but "against God and thee" (930–1), Adam relents and, "As one disarm'd, his anger all he lost" (945).

Like Adam's, Samson's diatribe comes before Dalila has spoken, but then he brushes aside all her excuses and attempts to placate him with unappeased anger. Just as Milton's grievance was not simply that Mary had deserted him but also that she had returned to her Royalist parents, Samson indicts Dalila for siding with heathens and traitors:

> I before all the daughters of my Tribe
> And of my Nation chose thee from among
> My enemies, lov'd thee, as too well thou knew'st,
> Too well. …
> Being once a wife, for me thou wast to leave
> Parents and country …
> No more thy country, but an impious crew
> Of men conspiring to uphold thir state
> By worse than hostile deeds, violating the ends
> For which our country is a name so dear.
>
> (877–95)

Everything Samson says here about Dalila applies to Mary, whose family Milton would have regarded as an "impious crew" of opportunists who had violated "the ends / For which our country is a name so dear." In contrast to Adam, who permits Eve to embrace his feet, when Dalila asks Samson if she may "Approach thee at least, and touch thy hand," his anger reaches the boiling point: "Not for thy life, lest fierce remembrance wake / My sudden rage to tear thee joint from joint" (951–3).

In *Samson Agonistes* Milton rewrites the story he had told in *Paradise Lost* to reflect the far bleaker version of his experience with Mary as he had uncovered it in his ever-deepening self-analysis. When Samson repudiates Dalila, "thou and I long since are twain" (929), he alludes to Jesus's words about the joining of husband and wife in marriage that seem to forbid divorce except on grounds of fornication, "Wherefore they are no more twain, but are one flesh" (Matt. 19.6), but which, as Mary Nyquist (1988) has shown, were "susceptible to Milton's polemical appropriation" (p. 112) in *Tetrachordon* to defend his wish to dissolve his marriage for what he considered to be more compelling reasons.[5] It is though he had gotten his way after all and he and Mary Powell had never reconciled. Instead of the elegiac ending of *Paradise Lost*, where Adam and Eve make their "solitary" way through the fallen world "hand in hand," Dalila has no part in the providence that guides Samson, although he remains unaware of it at this point in the drama. After she reveals her true colors by proclaiming that she will always be remembered with honor by her own people because she chose "Above the faith of Wedlock bands" to save "Her country from a fierce destroyer" (985–6), the Chorus comments upon her departure, "She's gone, a manifest Serpent by her sting / Discover'd in the end" (997–8), a verdict seconded by Samson, who calls her "a viper" (1001).

Dalila proves in reality to be the "Serpent" that Adam at his most vitriolic had accused Eve of being, and since "in the end" may mean not only "at last" but also refer to the lower part of her body, she becomes the human incarnation of Sin in *Paradise Lost*, who is likewise described as "a *Serpent* arm'd / With mortal *sting*" with a body that "*ended* foul in many a scaly fold" (2.651–3; italics added). In view of this degradation of Dalila's body, compounded by Milton's allusions to her not only being but also having a "snare," the "Amber scent of odorous perfume" (729) that the Chorus detects wafting from Dalila when she first approaches Samson at once distills and disguises the "fishy fume" emanating from her vagina, just as Lear begs for "an ounce of civet" to blot out the "stench" he imagines coming from the "sulphurous pit" of the female genitalia when he encounters the blinded Gloucester.

5

Just as Samson's hornets are the "type" of which Milton's allusion to the riddle of the bees in Judges is the "antitype," Dalila's shearing of Samson's "precious fleece" contains the promise of his redemption inasmuch as it is in the nature

---

5   In his sketch of Milton's life, John Aubrey allows that Mary did "not wrong his bed" during the years she was separated from Milton, but points out the possibility must have occurred to him, for "what man (especially contemplative) would like to have a young wife environed [and stormed] by the sons of Mars, and those of the enemy party" (Hughes, 1957, p. 1022; brackets in original).

of hair to regrow. Having been not only "soft'n'd" by his ejaculation in the sexual act but made "a tame Wether," Samson laments his existence as a "burdenous drone"—a male bee that lacks a stinger—with his "redundant locks / Robustious to no purpose hanging down" (567–9). Manoa, however, urges that God could easily "Cause light again within thy eyes to spring," because "why else this strength / Miraculous yet remaining in these locks? / His might continues in thee not for naught" (584–8). Manoa is mistaken in thinking that Samson's eyesight will be restored any more than was Milton's. But he is right in his belief that God still has a plan for Samson, for Samson's "redundant" locks, far from being "robustious to no purpose," are the sign of his returning physical and spiritual potency.

Although Samson's regeneration is already in progress while he is in a state of despair due to his "sense of Heav'n's desertion" (632), he does not show an awareness of his changed condition until his confrontation with Harapha. When the Philistine giant taunts him with having gotten his strength from "spells / And black enchantments" (1132–3), Samson rejects the aspersion, "My trust is in the living God who gave me / At my nativity this strength" (1140–1), although he acknowledges that God did so only "while I preserv'd these locks unshorn, / The pledge of my unviolated vow" (1143–4). Harapha then redoubles his mockery, sneering that Samson has been abandoned by his supposed God "to grind / Among the Slaves and Asses" (1161–2), notwithstanding his "boist'rous locks" (1164) that are "by the Barber's razor best subdu'd" (1167).

Samson does not attempt to defend himself against Harapha's insults, but for the first time voices the hope that his father had formerly pleaded for in vain:

> these evils I deserve and more,
> Acknowledge them from God inflicted on me
> Justly, yet despair not of his final pardon
> Whose ear is ever open.
>
> (1169–72)

Like Samson's words "redundant" and "robustious," which mean, respectively, "flowing" and "strong" or "healthy," Harapha's "boist'rous" connotes "thick-growing," and thus attests that Samson once again has a full head of hair. But both "robustious" and "boist'rous" also mean "noisy," just as "redundant" means "superfluous," so all these words describing Samson's newly abundant hair hark back to the "garrulity" that twice led him to surrender his "fort of silence to a Woman" (236) and to be "shorn" by Dalila. With the regrowing of his hair Samson regains his "strength / Miraculous" and begins to express hope for a "final pardon" from God. Whereas Samson stains his "vow of *Nazarite*" when he repeats his disclosure of a secret during intercourse, the "robustious" sprouting of his hair, which signifies his restoration to God's favor, represents the miracle of a second virginity, as though he had never been "defiled with women" and is therefore once again eligible for the "high rewards of ever accompanying the Lamb with those celestial songs to others inapprehensible."

Like Harapha's ridicule of Samson's belief in the sacredness of his hair, "Where strength can least abide" (1136), his scorn that Samson has been forced "to grind / Among the Slaves and Asses" shows that Samson's punishment is simultaneously a repetition of his sin and God's way of effecting his salvation. In his opening soliloquy, Samson bemoans that he must "grind in Brazen Fetters" (35) as the prisoner of his enemies, "Eyeless in *Gaza* at the Mill with slaves" (41). Samson appears to have read *The Doctrine and Discipline of Divorce*, where Milton had argued that it was contrary to the purpose of a Christian marriage to be forced "to grind in the mill of an undelighted and servile copulation" (Hughes, 1957, p. 712). As Edward Le Comte (1978) notes, this phrase was added to the second edition of the work, "as if another half year of abstinence had served to increase Milton's disgust or scorn," and there was in fact "a rabbinical tradition" that Samson was "commanded to copulate" by Philistine husbands who "brought their wives to him to have a child by him" (p. 30). Through Samson, Milton relived the nightmare of that initial month of cohabitation with Mary Powell, while within the diegesis of the tragedy Samson reenacts his "servile copulation" with Dalila. Indeed, in his dialogue with Manoa Samson declares that his present "grinding is not yet so base" as was his "former servitude," which was far more "unmanly" (415–17); and because he has at least extricated himself from Dalila's "snare," Samson's abasement by the Philistines is the first step on his journey to redemption.

Although Samson begins to "despair not" in his confrontation with Harapha, his regeneration is far from complete. When the Chorus warns him of the consequences of his refusal to go with the Officer to participate in the festival at the Temple of Dagon, Samson demands, "Shall I abuse this Consecrated gift / Of strength, again returning with my hair / After my great transgression?" (1354–6). He has recovered his strength, but still believes it would be an "abuse" of his "Consecrated gift" were he to add "a greater sin / By prostituting holy things to idols" (1357–8). Only after his initial refusal does Samson recognize that God can "dispense" (1377) with his own laws and allow a chosen person to do what would ordinarily be forbidden, as he himself had done when he heeded his "intimate impulse" to marry "The daughter of an Infidel." As his downfall was caused not by his first marriage but by his second, which was not divinely inspired, so, now, he undoes the blunder of that earlier repetition by changing his mind and allowing himself to be guided by the "rousing motions" that elevate his thoughts to "something extraordinary" and are posited by the ideology of the poem to be not delusions, but truly the voice of God.

Throughout *Samson Agonistes* Samson's head has been simultaneously a phallic symbol and a barometer of his spiritual condition. At the beginning of the work, the Chorus comes upon him "With languish't head unprop't, / As one past hope, abandon'd" (119–20). The image cluster of hornets and bees is fused with the motif of Samson's "capital secret" when he tells the Chorus how most friends "in prosperous days / They swarm, but in adverse withdraw their head" (191–2). Shortly thereafter, he wonders aloud, "How could I once look up, or heave the head" (197), since he has "shipwreck't" his "Vessel" when he laid his "head" in Dalila's "lap" and blabbed about the source of his strength. Finally, according to the Messenger's report, Samson stood with his arms on "two massy Pillars" (1633) and his "head a while inclin'd" (1636) until, "with head erect" (1639), he proclaimed in his final words that he would perform a feat of strength that "'with amaze shall strike all who behold'" (1645), and brought down the roof of the pagan temple "Upon the heads of all who stood beneath" (1652). When Samson's "inclin'd" head becomes "erect," his physical *erection* is proof of his spiritual *election*, and he dies by perpetrating a mass murder that is simultaneously a suicide, though the glory of this cataclysm properly belongs not to Samson but to "the Holy One / Of *Israel*."

6

In laying the groundwork for an autobiographical reading of *Samson Agonistes*, Masson identified Harapha as "another Salmasius" and noted how the Dalila episode "sums up [Milton's] incredibly perverted view of women," but he did not attempt to connect her with Mary Powell. The breakthrough that made this possible was Crockett's insight that the premise of the tragedy that Samson had broken "his vow of strictest purity" as "a person separate to God" when he married Dalila lacked biblical support, and must therefore be "an instance of pure autobiography" on Milton's part.

Although Samson's "agon" with Dalila, which prompts him to erupt in "sudden rage" and want to tear her "joint from joint" when she asks to touch his hand, is the emotional apex of the work, she is vanquished by the close of their encounter. Harapha, Samson's political opponent, is dispatched with vastly greater ease. His most complex relationship is with his "reverend Sire" (326) Manoa, who, apart from the Chorus, is both the first to speak with

Samson and the only one to eulogize him after his death. Neither Masson nor Crockett attempts to show how Milton might be reflecting on his own relationship to his father; indeed, Crockett (1966) takes James Holly Hanford to task for being "overly bold" in claiming that Samson's conversation with Manoa can be read as "'an imaginary one between Milton and his parent.'" "Where," Crockett demands, "is there to be found any account that the elder Mr. Milton had such attitudes toward his son's marriage or career that would have made this kind of dialogue between them likely?" (p. 21; see Hanford, 1949, p. 217).

There are, however, biographical facts that serve as a skeleton on which it is possible to hang some flesh.[6] The poet was the first son and the second of six children of John Milton (1562–1647), and Sara *née* Jeffrey (*c.* 1572–1637). The senior John Milton was by profession a scrivener who earned his livelihood as a financial broker, notary, and moneylender—it was to collect an unpaid debt that his son was dispatched to the Powells—and by avocation a composer of sacred music. Of Milton's five siblings, two survived to adulthood. These were his older sister Anne, who married Edward Phillips and was the mother of Edward and John; and his younger brother Christopher, a lawyer and Royalist sympathizer who became a Catholic and was knighted and made a judge by King James II in 1686. The father's prosperity meant that he could hire tutors for both sons in classical languages and that the elder never had to work for a living, but after leaving Cambridge could instead enjoy an extended period of intense study at his family's residence in the village of Horton, travel to the Continent in 1638, and fulfill his ambition of becoming a writer. In 1643, during the period of Milton's separation from his wife, his father ceased to live with Christopher and his family in Reading and moved in with John, then living on Aldersgate Street in London. After Milton's reconciliation with Mary in 1645, Milton's father moved with him and Mary's mother and other relatives into a larger house nearby in the Barbican, where he remained until his death two years later.

Although we have no way of knowing what may have been said in the conversations between father and son, "the elder Mr. Milton" was eighty by the time of his son's marriage, so he may well have had "Locks white as down" (327), as the Chorus says of Manoa. And since he lived with his son both during his separation from Mary and after their reconciliation, he had ample opportunity to witness the tensions in their household and to convey his opinions about his prodigy's choice of a spouse. It is therefore by no means difficult to imagine that *Samson Agonistes* reflects the emotional reality of

---

[6] In what follows, I rely on Gordon Campbell's (2009) entry on Milton's father in the *Oxford Dictionary of National Biography*.

Milton's experience not only of his marriage but also of his relationship to his "reverend Sire."

With respect to the attitude of Milton's father to his career, moreover, Crockett overlooks a key source of evidence. As Kerrigan (1983) remarks, Milton's Latin poem *Ad Patrem* contains "our sole record of a disagreement between them" (p. 113). Although the date of *Ad Patrem* is uncertain, it probably stems from 1637 or 1638, when Milton had renewed his vow of "sacrificial celibacy" and was living in Horton, prior to setting off on his Italian journey. In a complex dialectic, he begins by announcing his intention to "rise on bold wings to do honor to my revered father" (Hughes, 1957, p. 82), but soon modulates into a defense of his decision to become a poet over his father's objections:

> You should not despise the poet's task, divine song, which preserves some spark of the Promethean fire and is the unrivaled glory of the heaven-born human mind and an evidence of our ethereal origins and celestial descent.
>
> (p. 83)

"Do not persist, I beg of you, in your contempt for the sacred Muses," Milton continues, "You may pretend to hate the delicate Muses, but I do not believe your hatred" (p. 84). The poet who sings a "divine song" belongs to a sacred fellowship and will receive his reward in heaven:

> When we return to our native Olympus and the everlasting ages of immutable eternity are established, we shall walk, crowned with gold, through the temples of the skies and with the harp's soft accompaniment we shall sing sweet songs to which the stars shall echo and the vault of heaven from pole to pole. Even now the fiery spirit who flies through the swift spheres is singing his immortal melody and unutterable song in harmony with the starry choruses.
>
> (p. 83)

Here Milton again alludes to Revelation, where the blessed wear "crowns of gold" (4.4) and "the voice of the harpers" who sing "a new song before the throne" can be heard only by the 144,000 who are "not defiled with women; for they are virgins" (14.2–4). These verses are the touchstones of Milton's "covenant and pledge" to remain celibate as the condition for being consecrated as "God's poet," which he first articulated in 1629 and to which he rededicated himself from 1637 to 1639. Indeed, when Milton writes of the "fiery spirit" who "even now … flies through the swift spheres … singing his immortal melody and unutterable song in harmony with the starry choruses," he could well be referring to Edward King, whom he eulogized in "Lycidas" as one who "hears the unexpressive nuptial Song / In the blest Kingdoms meek of joy and love," although by 1639 he would also say of Diodati that "because you did not taste the delights of the marriage bed, lo! the rewards of virginity are reserved for you."

All of this comports with assigning *Ad Patrem* to the late 1630s, and the tranquility of Horton is suggested by the appreciation Milton expresses to his father for permitting him to dwell "far away from the uproar of cities" in "these high retreats of delightful leisure beside the Aonian stream," where he is at liberty to walk "by Phoebus' side, his blessed companion" (p. 84). Because Milton reaffirms his "vow of strictest purity" to be the prerequisite for his poetic vocation in a poem addressed to his father, who had tried to discourage his son's devotion to the "sacred Muses," "the elder Mr. Milton" must have been aware that his son had not kept his end of the bargain. This buttresses the thesis that Milton is continuing a dialogue with his late father about his marital history in his portrayal of Samson's relationship to Manoa.

In addition to voicing gratitude to his father for having afforded him the "delightful leisure" to consort with the god of poetry, Milton is fulsome in his thanks for his education in foreign languages:

> It was at your expense, dear father, after I had got the mastery of the language of Romulus and the graces of Latin, and acquired the lofty speech of the magniloquent Greeks, which is fit for the lips of Jove himself, that you persuaded me to add the flowers which France boasts and the eloquence which the modern Italian pours from his degenerate mouth—testifying by his accent to the barbarian wars—and the mysteries uttered by the Palestinian prophet.
>
> (pp. 84–5)

Having mastered Latin and Greek at St. Paul's and Cambridge, Milton credits his father for his acquisition of Italian, French, and Hebrew. Apart from his mention of France, the "flowers" of which do not include an epic poem, this passage adumbrates Milton's "presumptuous publication" of his "holy secret" in *The Reason of Church Government*, where he resolves to surpass "the greatest and choicest wits of Athens, Rome, or modern Italy, and those Hebrews of old." Milton is spreading his wings in *Ad Patrem*, and "the Aonian stream"—a reference to the fountain on Mt. Helicon, sacred to the Muses— recurs in the invocation to Book 1 of *Paradise Lost*, where he proclaims that his "advent'rous Song" will "soar / Above th' Aonian Mount, while it pursues

/ Things unattempted yet in Prose or Rhyme" (13–16)—the last line being an appropriation of Ariosto's boast at the opening of *Orlando Furioso*.

In arguing against his father's opposition to the poetic career he had nonetheless done so much to make possible, Milton highlights their common dedication to the "sister arts" under the patronage of Apollo:

> Now, since it is my lot to have been born a poet, why does it seem strange to you that we, who are so closely united by blood, should pursue sister arts and kindred interests? Phoebus himself, wishing to part himself between us two, gave some gifts to me and others to my father; and, father and son, we share the possession of the divided god.
>
> (p. 84)

Milton adroitly appeals to his father's avocation as a composer, but in noting how they "share the possession of the divided god," he erases the generational distinction between them and effectively transforms "father and son" into siblings.

By the end of *Ad Patrem*, Milton is confident not only of being "crowned with gold" in heaven, but also of achieving earthly fame by his poetry: "Therefore, however humble my present place in the company of learned men, I shall sit with the ivy and laurel of a victor" (p. 85). Consequently, even though he reiterates that "no requital equal to your desert and no deeds equal to your gifts are within my power," the final lines of the poem shift the burden of indebtedness from his own shoulders onto those of his father: "And you, my juvenile verses and amusements, if only you dare hope for immortality and a glimpse of the light beyond your master's funeral pyre ... perhaps you will preserve this eulogy and the name of the father whom my song honors as an example to remote ages" (pp. 85–6). If these "juvenile verses" survive his own "funeral pyre," Milton asserts, "the name of the father" to whom he is so grateful will likewise be preserved "as an example to remote ages." It will then be he who has given life to his father, not the other way around.

In his master's thesis at the University of Massachusetts, Boston, on *Ad Patrem* as a "prologue" to *Paradise Lost*, C. Macauley Ward, Jr., (2011) observes that the Latin poem is "explicitly written as an expression of thanks to a generous father. Yet, within the space of seventeen lines, it becomes a challenge to the father's authority ... the poet contradicts his stated purpose, arguing that even though he is grateful for his father's generosity, it would be wrong for him not to pursue his own ends" (p. 3). Ward connects this reversal in *Ad Patrem* to Milton's espousal of the doctrine of the Fortunate Fall in *Paradise Lost*, where, at the conclusion of the poem, after Adam states that he has learned the lesson that "to obey is best, / And love with fear the only God"

(12.561–2), Michael holds out the promise that Adam will "not be loath / To leave this Paradise, but shalt possess / A paradise within thee, happier far" (585–7). As Ward sums up the paradox at the heart of *Paradise Lost*, even as Milton inculcates the precept of obedience, he "implicitly justifies man's first disobedience against God by arguing that mankind would never have known anything better than Eden if Adam and Eve had been content simply to obey God" (pp. iii–iv).

Writing in the first person in *Ad Patrem*, Milton lets it be known that he was "born a poet" and that the poet's song is evidence of "celestial descent." This claim, which reveals the sense of a heroic destiny that Milton will transmute into the miraculously "foretold" births of Jesus and Samson, underpins Kerrigan's hypothesis that the "splitting of the imago of the father constitutes the major psychological strategy of Milton's life and work." In *Paradise Regained* the only time Jesus's human father is named is when Jesus comes from Nazareth to be baptized in the "flood *Jordan*" and is described as "the Son of *Joseph* deem'd," which makes it clear that Joseph is not Jesus's true father, whereupon "the Father's voice / From Heaven pronounc'd him his beloved Son."

The same motif plays itself out in more complex fashion in *Samson Agonistes*, where Manoa is again Samson's earthly father and well-intentioned, but has at best an imperfect comprehension of his son. Lamenting how the child for whom he had prayed has been "Into a dungeon thrust, to work with Slaves" (368), Manoa asks, "Who would be now a Father in my stead?" (355). The answer, of course, is Samson's Father in Heaven, whose "guiding hand" has been steering him even in the depths of despair. Failing to grasp that Samson's marriage to the Woman of Timna was prompted by a "Divine impulsion" (422), Manoa chastises him in the unintentionally hilarious line, "I cannot praise thy marriage choices, Son" (420). Similarly, in counseling Samson that he should "repent the sin, but if the punishment / Thou canst avoid, self-preservation bids" (504–5), Manoa does not realize that Samson's punishment is integral to his redemption. Even at the end of the poem he voices the hope that "since his strength with eyesight was not lost, / God will restore him eyesight to his strength" (1502–3), but Samson's blindness cannot be reversed any more than could Milton's; and Manoa again misses the mark in attempting to perform his paternal function.

Manoa's attempts to ransom Samson from the Philistines further illustrate his inadequacy as a father. When he receives the news of Samson's death from the Messenger, he grieves that Samson has "paid his ransom now," and that his hopes for Samson's "Delivery" had proven to be "Abortive as the first-born bloom of spring / Nipt with the lagging rear of winter's frost" (1573–7). This is another misunderstanding, as Manoa himself comes to realize upon hearing the Chorus's apostrophe to Samson's "dearly bought revenge, yet glorious!," which has "fulfill'd / The work for which thou wast foretold / To *Israel*" (1660–3). He is then able to appreciate that his son's death was not a failure but a triumph:

> Come, come, no time for lamentation now,
> Nor much more cause: *Samson* hath quit himself
> Like *Samson*, and heroicly hath finish'd
> A life Heroic.
>
> (1708–11)

What Manoa believes to be "best and happiest" is that Samson has left "To himself and to his Father's house eternal fame," and "all this / With God not parted from him, as was fear'd, / But favoring and assisting to the end" (1717–20).

Manoa is correct that God has "not parted" from Samson, but has been "favoring and assisting" him "to the end." But just as in *Paradise Regained*, where what it means for Jesus to be the Son of God "bears no single sense," Manoa is unable to grasp the full extent of what it means for his "Heroic" son to bring "eternal fame" to his "Father's house." Reiterating the crucial phrase, he announces his plan to bring Samson's cleansed and purified body "Home to his Father's house":

> there will I build him
> A Monument, and plant it round with shade
> Of Laurel ever green, and branching Palm,
> With all his Trophies hung, and Acts enroll'd
> In copious Legend, or sweet Lyric song.
>
> (1733–7)

Despite the disdain evinced by Jesus in *Paradise Regained* for Satan's temptations of earthly fame and glory, they exerted a powerful hold on Milton. Whether in *Ad Patrem*, where he looks forward to sitting "with the ivy and laurel of a victor," or in "Lycidas," where he confesses that he is afflicted by the "last infirmity of Noble mind," or in *The Reason of Church Government*, where he proclaims his intention to write the greatest epic poem of all time, there can be no doubt that Milton was—as Peter J. Swales (1982) has stated of Freud—"a man of *boundless* ambition!" (p. 5).

There is, therefore, a limited truth to Manoa's desire to honor his son with all the regalia of classical culture. But in all the texts I have cited Milton qualifies his worldly aspirations with reminders that he longs to be "crowned with gold" through "the everlasting ages of immutable eternity," that "*Fame* is no plant that grows on mortal soil," and that he can go "over and above" his precursors in the epic tradition only by virtue "of being a Christian." This is what Manoa cannot comprehend about what it means for Samson to achieve "eternal fame" and return "Home to his Father's house." After he builds the "Monument" for his son, Manoa states that "all the valiant youth" will be inflamed to "matchless valor" by Samson's memory, and "The Virgins also shall on feastful days / Visit his Tomb with flowers, only bewailing / His lot unfortunate in nuptial choice, / From whence captivity and loss of eyes" (1738–4). To the end, Manoa cannot fathom that Samson's marriage to Dalila—like Milton's to Mary Powell— although a calamity that entailed the punishment of blindness, was part of God's design, without which Samson could not have fulfilled the promise of his birth.

7

In both *Paradise Regained* and *Samson Agonistes*, Milton exhibits the "splitting of the imago of the father" that goes back to *Ad Patrem* and expresses the fantasy of "ethereal origins and celestial descent" that was integral to his poetic vocation. Not only does Jesus have two fathers in *Paradise Regained*, but he and Satan are both sons of God who embody the antithetical poles of obedience and disobedience. Yet since each is both Oedipus and the Sphinx, these seeming opposites are doubles that embody two sides of the son's ambivalent relationship to his father.

In *Samson Agonistes*, there is only one son who encompasses both obedience and disobedience. As Milton honored his father in *Ad Patrem* while incurring his disapproval by becoming a poet—and again, in all likelihood, by his marriage—so, too, Samson honors Manoa but disregarded him in his "marriage choices." At the same time, although the outcome was providential, both Samson's marriage to Dalila and Milton's marriage to Mary violated their covenants with God and were therefore acts of disobedience also of the heavenly Father. The ending of the tragedy, in which Samson destroys himself along with the Philistines, confirms that he has been restored to God's grace but is likewise a self-imposed death sentence for his transgressions both carnal and spiritual.

In *Paradise Lost*, Milton combines the "enemy brothers" plot with ambivalent father-son relationships. As in *Paradise Regained*, he splits the figure of the divine Son into Christ and Satan, but these sibling rivals are mirror images in being equally, although antithetically, subordinated to God the Father. As the first man, Adam does not have a human father, but, like Samson's, his relationship to God fuses obedience and disobedience. Like Samson, Adam breaks his covenant with God by transgressing with a woman, for which he, too, receives a death sentence, but is ultimately made "happier far" with a "paradise within."

The nodal point of these motifs in *Paradise Lost* is Abdiel, whom Worden (1995) compares to Samson as Milton's "transparently autobiographical creation" (p. 115) in the epic poem. Abdiel experiences at once a "splitting of the imago of the father" between Satan and God and the choice between obedience and disobedience. Satan, however, unlike Manoa or Joseph, is not a fallible human but a fallen angel who has defied the authority of God. Consequently, Abdiel must not merely supersede but actively rebel against him. Abdiel's defiance of the negative father imago is praiseworthy because it is in the service of his obedience to the heavenly Father, who is for Milton the only true King. Because Abdiel is never tempted to disobey God, he experiences no inner conflict. In this respect, he differs from Samson, Adam, and Satan, but resembles the Son, who in *Paradise Lost*, "full of wrath bent on his Enemies" (6.826), drives Satan and his legions into Hell, while in *Paradise Regained* he employs a strategy of passive aggressiveness to win an equally crushing victory over his sibling rival. It is only against the split-off representations of the "bad" father and "bad" brother that Abdiel and Christ display their anger, and their submission to the Father's will makes them the only purely "good" son figures in Milton's major poems.

Building on Harold Bloom's (1973) theory of the anxiety of influence, Thomas Weiskel (1976) has argued that we can see in the Satan of *Paradise Lost* "the essential predicament of the modern poet" because, "as a state of mind, modernism is an incurable ambivalence about authority," and Satan is locked into "a genuine ambivalence in which authority must be at once ascribed to the Father and won from him" (pp. 8–9). To his neoclassical and Romantic successors, Milton stood in the position of the self-sufficient God the Father, while they both owed their identity to him and sought in vain to equal—let alone surpass—his achievement. Milton's most astonishing feat in *Paradise Lost* was to include a credible representation of the character and perspective of God. Because later poets were unable to replicate this masterstroke, the representative forms of the eighteenth and nineteenth centuries became the mock epic and the lyric, both of which lack the scope and majesty of genuine epic and relegated even their greatest practitioners to the status of Satan unable to match wits with God.

Milton could not have written *Paradise Lost* had he not shared, in Stephen Greenblatt's (2017) words, "Augustine's conviction that the literal truth of

Jesus Christ was bound up with the literal truth of Adam and Eve" (p. 205). Although Copernicus, Kepler, and Galileo had upended the Ptolemaic system that placed the earth at the center of the universe, Milton managed to finesse this issue. When Adam questions Raphael about astronomy, the angel cautions, "This to attain, whether Heav'n move, or Earth, / Imports not" (8.70–1), adding that God deliberately concealed such secrets from men and angels alike, "perhaps to move / His laughter at thir quaint opinions wide / Hereafter" (78–9). Despite the palpable defensiveness in Milton's disparagement of science, nothing in the upheavals precipitated by the Copernican Revolution cast serious doubt on the acceptance of the Bible as the revealed Word of God, and it would be another two hundred years before Darwin stuck a dagger in the heart of the belief in the "literal truth" of the Genesis narrative with the theory of evolution. It was therefore possible for Milton to have, as it were, the best of both world systems, and take it for granted that nothing in his Christian faith was incompatible with the scientific knowledge of his time, even though he sought to minimize its importance.

Milton's Christianity in turn furnished him with a perfect strategy for dealing with his own "anxiety of influence" with respect to his precursors in the epic tradition. Because the biblical account of Creation was sacrosanct, he could regard the monuments of Homer, Vergil, and the rest as fictional and derivative versions of the one true story that he by divine inspiration was retelling in his poem. This allowed Milton to transform his belatedness into priority, so that his predecessors became the ones who were imitating *him*. A prototypical example of how Milton at once absorbs and supersedes the classical tradition can be observed when he says of the ancient Greeks and Romans who "fabl'd" about the fall of Mulciber, "thus they relate, / Erring; for he with this rebellious rout / Fell long before"—fell, that is, when the unnamed angel who had been the architect of Pandemonium in Hell was thrown, not by "angry *Jove*" but by God, "Sheer o'er the Crystal Battlements" (1.741–8).

In synergy with this propitious moment in intellectual history, Milton reaped the reward of his blindness combined with the defeat of the Puritan Revolution. Thanks to these two blessings in disguise, he finally freed himself from the sense of guilt caused by his marriage to Mary Powell that had paralyzed his "right hand" for twenty years. Because he had once again "gotten right with God," he was no longer the son who had to prove himself in the eyes of his earthly and heavenly fathers, but could speak with the voice of—and become—the "great task-Master" himself. After *Paradise Lost*, no poet could rival what Milton had done any more than there could be a second God in the Judeo-Christian tradition.

In *Samson Agonistes*, where Milton reenacts the greatest trauma of his life, he simultaneously captures his experience of "double darkness" in the 1650s, when he had not only gone blind but felt his "genial spirits droop" and "hopes all flat" (594–6), and his certainty by the late 1660s that his tragedy had ended with a glorious rebirth. Unlike Jesus in *Paradise Regained*, who goes from triumph to triumph, Samson's fall "from the top of wondrous glory" (167) to the "lowest pitch of abject fortune" (169) leads the Chorus to ponder the vicissitudes of human existence:

> God of our Fathers, what is man!
> That thou towards him with hand so various,
> Or might I say contrarious,
> Temper'st thy providence through his short course,
> Not evenly, as thou rul'st
> Th'Angelic orders and inferior creatures mute,
> Irrational and brute.
>
> (667–73)

If God treats man with a "contrarious" hand, how can he be said to be just? This passage harks back to *The Doctrine and Discipline of Divorce*, where Milton, in the throes of his misery following the debacle of his marriage and subsequent desertion by Mary Powell, writes that a man who "sees withal that his bondage is now inevitable, though he be almost the strongest Christian, he will be ready to despair in virtue, and mutiny against divine providence" (Hughes, 1957, p. 710).

Yet, in a reprise of the invocation to Book 1 of *Paradise Lost*, where Milton proclaims his intention to "assert Eternal Providence, / And justify the ways of God to men," but with symptoms of considerably greater anxiety, the Chorus intones:

> Just are the ways of God,
> And justifiable to Men;
> Unless there be who think not God at all:
> If any be, they walk obscure
> For of such Doctrine never was there School,
> But the heart of the Fool,
> And no man therein Doctor but himself.
>
> (293–9)

The ridicule Milton heaps on those "who think not God at all" suggests that he must have been tempted not only to "mutiny against divine providence" but also by atheism when he felt he had broken his covenant with God.[7] But even his darkest days, when he feared he had buried his talent, Milton quelled his "murmur" of protest by heeding the voice of "patience" that admonished him to "stand and wait," and Masson (1880) beautifully interprets Samson's apotheosis as Milton's rendering of "his own extraordinary self-transmutation, before the eyes of the astonished Restoration world, out of his former character of horrible prose iconoclast into that of supreme and towering poet" (p. 677). The Semichorus chants:

> But he though blind of sight,
> Despis'd and thought extinguish't quite,
> With inward eyes illuminated
> His fiery virtue rous'd
> From under ashes into sudden flame. ...
> So virtue giv'n for lost,
> Deprest, and overthrown, as seem'd,
> Like that self-begotten bird
> In the *Arabian* woods embost,
> That no second knows nor third,
> And lay erewhile a Holocaust,
> From out her ashy womb now teem'd,
> Revives, reflourishes, then vigorous most
> When most unactive deem'd,
> And though her body die, her fame survives,
> A secular bird ages of lives.

(1687–707)

Whereas Satan (who acknowledges having been created by God in his soliloquy on Mount Niphates in Book 4) is in the grip of a delusion when he boasts to Abdiel in *Paradise Lost* that he and the other angels are all "self-begot, self-rais'd / By our own quick'ning power" (5.861–2), when the Chorus

---

[7] Although not an expression of outright atheism—an abyss into which Milton peers in his battle against Lucretius in *Paradise Lost*—he broods in *The Christian Doctrine* that the evidence of order and purpose in nature has "compelled all nations to believe, either that *God, or some evil power* whose name was unknown, presided over the affairs of the world" (Hughes, 1957, p. 905; italics added). He goes on to argue that those who maintain that God's foreknowledge of the Fall must mean Adam did not possess free will "do not hesitate even to assert that God is himself the cause and origin of sin," which confirms such men to be "the most abandoned of all blasphemers," while "an attempt to refute them would be nothing more than argument to prove that *God was not the evil spirit*" (p. 916; italics added).

eulogizes Samson as "that self-begotten bird / ... / That no second knows nor third," he has indeed become not only his own father but also his mother from whose "ashy womb" he perpetually "revives." As the Phoenix, Samson—who, like Jesus in *Paradise Regained*, is an Oedipus without an Oedipus complex—is also a type of Christ, through whose death and resurrection the poet himself will be "crowned with gold" through "the everlasting ages of immutable eternity," while simultaneously being "A secular bird" whose "fame survives" in human memory for "ages of lives."

On Milton's stone in St. Giles' Cripplegate, there is written: "Near this spot was buried / JOHN MILTON / Author of '*Paradise Lost*' / Born 1608—Died 1674." But Milton's true epitaph is found in the final speech of the Chorus in *Samson Agonistes*:

> All is best, though oft we doubt,
> What th' unsearchable dispose
> Of highest wisdom brings about,
> And ever best found in the close.
> Oft he seems to hide his face,
> But unexpectedly returns
> And to his faithful Champion hath in place
> Bore witness gloriously; whence *Gaza* mourns
> And all that band them to resist
> His uncontrollable intent;
> His servants he with new acquist
> Of true experience from this great event
> With peace and consolation hath dismist,
> And calm of mind, all passion spent.
>
> (1745–58)

Since 1945, the word "Holocaust," rather than meaning a completely burnt sacrificial offering of an animal, as it did for Milton, has come to signify a genocidal catastrophe that makes it impossible for many people to believe that "All is best" in this violent, fragile, and increasingly uninhabitable world. But even readers "who think not God at all," and who may mourn *with* Gaza, can bear witness to the "true experience" of Milton's "faithful Champion." As denizens of the imagination, we long for the "peace and consolation" of a genuine catharsis, and we put down *Samson Agonistes* with "calm of mind, all passion spent."

References

Adelman, Janet. 1992. *Suffocating Mothers: Fantasies of Maternal Origins in Shakespeare's Plays*, Hamlet *to* The Tempest. New York: Routledge.

Almack, Edward, ed. 1907. *Eikon Basilike; or The King's Book*. London: Chatto and Windus.

Anderson, Judith H. 1984. *Biographical Truth: The Representation of Historical Truth in Tudor-Stuart Writing*. New Haven, CT: Yale University Press.

Andreas-Salomé, Lou. 1916. "Anal" and "Sexual." Trans. Nina Hausmann et al. *Psychoanalysis and History*, 24 (2022):19–40.

Aristotle. 1958. *On Poetry and Style*. Trans. G. M. A. Grube. Indianapolis, IN: Bobbs-Merrill, 1977.

Astington, John H. 1985. "Fault" in Shakespeare. *Shakespeare Quarterly*, 36:330–4.

Augustine, St. 1950. *The City of God*. Trans. Marcus Dods. New York: Modern Library.

Augustine, St. 1961. *Confessions*. Trans. R. S. Pine-Coffin. Harmondsworth, Eng.: Penguin Books.

Augustine, St. 2005. *Letters 211–270, 1*–29**. *The Works of St. Augustine: A Translation for the 21st Century*. Ed. Boniface Ramsey. Trans. Roland Teske. Hyde Park, NY: New City Press.

Barker, Francis. 1984. *The Tremulous Private Body*. London: Methuen.

Bell, Millicent. 1953. The Fallacy of the Fall in *Paradise Lost*. *PMLA*, 68:863–83.

Benson, Larry. 1965. *Art and Tradition in* Sir Gawain and the Green Knight. New Brunswick, NJ: Rutgers University Press.

Benton, John F. 1961. The Court of Champagne as a Literary Center. In *Culture, Power and Personality in Medieval France*. Ed. Thomas N. Bisson. London: Hambledon Press, 1991, pp. 3–43.

Blayney, Glenn H., ed. 1964. *The Miseries of Enforced Marriage*, by George Wilkins. Oxford: Oxford University Press.

Bloom, Harold. 1973. *The Anxiety of Influence: A Theory of Poetry*. New York: Oxford University Press, 1975.

Bloom, Harold. 1994. *The Western Canon: The Books and School of the Ages*. New York: Harcourt Brace.

Boehlich, Walter, ed. 1989. *The Letters of Sigmund Freud to Eduard Silberstein, 1871–1881*. Trans. Arnold J. Pomerans. Cambridge, MA: Harvard University Press, 1990.

Bonaparte, Marie. 1934. *The Life and Works of Edgar Allan Poe: A Psychoanalytic Interpretation*. Trans. John Rodker. Abr. in Muller and Richardson, 1988, pp. 101–32.

Boose, Lynda E. 1975. Othello's Handkerchief: "The Recognizance and Pledge of Love." *English Literary Renaissance*, 5:360–74.

Borroff, Marie, ed. and trans. 1967. *Sir Gawain and the Green Knight*. New York: Norton.

Bowie, Malcolm. 1991. *Lacan*. London: Fontana.

Bradshaw, David. 1995. Lonely Royalists: T. S. Eliot and Sir Robert Filmer. *Review of English Studies*, 46:375–9.

Brennecke, Ernest. 1953. "Nay, That's Not Next!": The Significance of Desdemona's "Willow Song." *Shakespeare Quarterly*, 4:35–8.

Breuer, Josef, and Sigmund Freud. 1895. *Studies on Hysteria. The Standard Edition of the Complete Psychological Works of Sigmund Freud*. Ed. and trans. James Strachey et al. 24 vols. London: Hogarth Press, 1953–74. Vol. 2.

Brooks, Peter. 1984. *Reading for the Plot: Design and Intention in Narrative*. New York: Knopf.

Brown, Norman O. 1966. *Love's Body*. New York: Vintage.

Brown, Peter. 1967. *Augustine of Hippo*. Berkeley, CA: University of California Press, 1969.

Browne, Sir Thomas. 1646. *Pseudodoxia Epidemica*. Abr. in *Selected Writings*. Ed. Sir Geoffrey Keynes. London: Faber and Faber, 1968, 227–373.

Bullough, Geoffrey, ed. 1973. *Narrative and Dramatic Sources of Shakespeare. Vol. 7. Major Tragedies*: Hamlet, Othello, King Lear, Macbeth. New York: Columbia University Press.

Burke, Kenneth. 1961. *The Rhetoric of Religion: Studies in Logology*. Boston, MA: Beacon, 1970.

Burrow, J. A. 1966. *A Reading of* Sir Gawain and the Green Knight. New York: Barnes and Noble.

Butler, Judith. 1990. *Gender Trouble: Feminism and the Subversion of Identity*. New York: Routledge.

Campbell, Gordon. 2009. John Milton (1562–1647). *Oxford Dictionary of National Biography*. Online edition. https://doi-org.lp.hscl.ufl.edu/10.1093/ref:odnb/18799.

Campbell, Lily B. 1947. *Shakespeare's "Histories": Mirrors of Elizabethan Policy*. San Marino, CA: Huntington Library, 1968.

Cavell, Stanley. 1969. The Avoidance of Love: A Reading of *King Lear*. In *Must We Mean What We Say? A Book of Essays*. Cambridge: Cambridge University Press, 1976, pp. 267–353.

Cavell, Stanley. 1979. Othello and the Stake of the Other. In *Disowning Knowledge in Six Plays by Shakespeare*. Cambridge: Cambridge University Press, 1991, pp. 125–42.

Clark, David R. 1972. Asmodeus and the Fishy Fume: *Paradise Lost*, IV, 153–71. *Studies in English Literature*, 12:121–8.

Clayton, Thomas. 1983. "Is This the Promis'd End?": Revision in the Role of the King. In *The Division of the Kingdoms: Shakespeare's Two Versions of* King Lear. Ed. Gary Taylor and Michael Warren. Oxford: Oxford University Press, 1986, pp. 121–42.

Cocteau, Jean. 1934. *The Infernal Machine*. Trans. Albert Bermel. In The Infernal Machine *and Other Plays*. Norwalk, CT: New Directions, 1963, pp. 5–96.

Comfort, W. W., ed. and trans. 1914. *Arthurian Romances*, by Chrétien de Troyes. London: Everyman's Library, 1970.

Crockett, Edward P. 1966. *An Evaluation of the Autobiographical Interpretation of* Samson Agonistes. Master's thesis, University of Richmond. 91 pp.

de Man, Paul. 1979. *Allegories of Reading: Figural Language in Rousseau, Nietzsche, Rilke, and Proust*. New Haven, CT: Yale University Press.

de Rougemont, Denis. 1940. *Love in the Western World*. Rev. ed. Trans. Montgomery Belgion. New York: Harper Torchbooks, 1974.

Derrida, Jacques. 1972. *Positions*. Trans. Alan Bass. Chicago, IL: University of Chicago Press, 1981.

Derrida, Jacques. 1975. The Purveyor of Truth. Trans. Willis Domingo et al. *Yale French Studies, No. 52. Graphesis: Perspectives in Literature and Philosophy*. Ed. Marie-Rose Logan, 1975, pp. 31–113.

Dick, Oliver Lawson, ed. 1950. *Aubrey's Brief Lives*. London: Secker and Warburg.

Dickens, Charles. 1850. *David Copperfield*. Ed. Jeremy Tambling. Rev. ed. Harmondsworth, Eng.: Penguin Books, 2004.

Dodds, E. R. 1928. Augustine's *Confessions*: A Study of Spiritual Maladjustment. *The Hibbert Journal*, 26:459–73.

Donno, Elizabeth Story, ed. 1972. The *Complete Poems*, by Andrew Marvell. Harmondsworth, Eng.: Penguin Books, 1978.

Dove, Mary. 1972. Gawain and the *Blasme des Femmes* Tradition. *Medium Aevum*, 41:20–6.

Dzelzainis, Martin. 1979. Milton, Macbeth, and Buchanan. *The Seventeenth Century*, 4:55–66.

Edgeworth, Robert J. 1985. Anatomical Geography in *Sir Gawain and the Green Knight. Neophilologus*, 69:318–19.

Eliot, T. S. 1919. Hamlet and His Problems. In Eliot 1964, pp. 121–6.

Eliot, T. S. 1921. The Metaphysical Poets. In Eliot 1964, pp. 241–50.

Eliot, T. S. 1928. *For Lancelot Andrewes: Essays on Style and Order*. London: Faber and Faber.

Eliot, T. S. 1964. *Selected Essays*. New Edition. New York: Harcourt, Brace & World.

Empson, William. 1961. *Milton's God*. Cambridge: Cambridge University Press, 1981.

Empson, William. 1984. *Using Biography*. Cambridge, MA: Harvard University Press.

Engelhardt, George J. 1955. The Predicament of Gawain. *Modern Language Quarterly*, 16:218–25.

Erskine-Hill, Howard, and Graham Storey, eds. 1983. *Revolutionary Prose of the English Civil War*. Cambridge: Cambridge University Press.

Evans, G. Blakemore, et al., eds. 1974. *The Riverside Shakespeare*. Boston, MA: Houghton Mifflin.

Evans, W. O. 1973. The Case for Gawain Re-Opened. *Modern Language Review*, 68:721–33.

Fanon, Frantz. 1952. *Black Skin/White Masks*. Trans. Richard Philcox. New York: Grove Press, 2012.

Fedrick, Alan S., ed. and trans. 1970. *The Romance of Tristan*. Harmondsworth, Eng.: Penguin Books, 1978.

Fenichel, Otto. 1945. *The Psychoanalytic Theory of Neurosis*. New York: Norton.

Ferenczi, Sándor. 1923. *Thalassa: A Theory of Genitality*. Trans. H. A. Bunker. New York: Norton, 1968.

Ferenczi, Sándor. 1933. Confusion of Tongues between Adults and the Child: The Language of Tenderness and of Passion. In *Final Contributions to the Methods and Problems of Psycho-Analysis*. Ed. Michael Balint. Trans. Eric Mosbacher et al. New York: Brunner/Mazel, 1980, pp. 156–67.

Ferguson, Margaret W., Maureen Quilligan, and Nancy J. Vickers, eds. 1986. *Rewriting the Renaissance: The Discourses of Sexual Difference in Early Modern Europe*. Chicago, IL: University of Chicago Press, 1987.

Ferrante, Joan M. 1990. "Es ist eine zunge, dunket mich": Fiction, Deception and Self-Deception in Gottfried's *Tristan*. In Stevens and Wisbey, 1990, pp. 171–80.

Ferrante, Joan M., and Robert W. Hanning, ed. and trans. 2018. *The Romance of Thebes (Roman de Thèbes)*. Tempe, AZ: Arizona Center for Medieval and Renaissance Studies.

Fish, Stanley E. 1967. *Surprised by Sin: The Reader in* Paradise Lost. Berkeley, CA: University of California Press.

Fisher, Sheila. 1989. Taken Men and Token Women in *Sir Gawain and the Green Knight*. In *Seeking the Woman in Late Medieval and Renaissance Writings: Essays in Feminist Contextual Criticism*. Ed. Sheila Fisher and Janet E. Halley. Knoxville, TN: University of Tennessee Press, 1989, pp. 71–105.

Flügel, J. C. 1920. On the Character and Married Life of Henry VIII. *International Journal of Psycho-Analysis*, 1:24–55.

Fox, Alistair. 1983. *Thomas More: History and Providence*. New Haven, CT: Yale University Press.

Freccero, John. 1986. Autobiography and Narrative. In *Reconstructing Individualism: Autonomy, Individuality, and the Self in Western Thought*. Ed. Thomas C. Heller, Morton Sosna, and David E. Wellbery. Stanford, CA: Stanford University Press, 1986, pp. 16–29.

Freud, Sigmund. 1895. *Project for a Scientific Psychology*. In *The Standard Edition of the Complete Psychological Works*. Ed. and trans. James Strachey et al. 24 vols. London: Hogarth Press, 1953–74 (hereafter *S.E.*), 1:295–397.

Freud, Sigmund. 1899. Screen Memories. *S.E.*, 3:303–22.

Freud, Sigmund. 1900. *The Interpretation of Dreams*. *S.E.*, 4 and 5.

Freud, Sigmund. 1901. *The Psychopathology of Everyday Life*. *S.E.*, 6.

Freud, Sigmund. 1905a. *Fragment of an Analysis of a Case of Hysteria*. *S.E.*, 7:7–122.

Freud, Sigmund. 1905b. *Three Essays on the Theory of Sexuality*. *S.E.*, 7:126–246.

Freud, Sigmund. 1907. Contribution to a Questionnaire on Reading. *S.E.*, 9:245–7.

Freud, Sigmund. 1908a. "Civilized" Sexual Morality and Modern Nervous Illness. *S.E.*, 9:181–204.

Freud, Sigmund. 1908b. Creative Writers and Day-Dreaming. *S.E.*, 9:143–53.

Freud, Sigmund. 1909. Family Romances. *S.E.*, 9:237–41.

Freud, Sigmund. 1910. A Special Type of Choice of Object Made by Men. *S.E.*, 11:163–76.

Freud, Sigmund. 1911. Formulations on the Two Principles of Mental Functioning. *S.E.*, 12:218–26.

Freud, Sigmund. 1912. On the Universal Tendency to Debasement in the Sphere of Love. *S.E.*, 11:179–90.

Freud, Sigmund. 1913a. The Theme of the Three Caskets. *S.E.*, 12:291–301.

Freud, Sigmund. 1913b. *Totem and Taboo. S.E.*, 13:1–161.

Freud, Sigmund. 1914. On Narcissism: An Introduction. *S.E.*, 14:73–102.

Freud, Sigmund. 1916. Some Character-Types Met with in Psycho-Analytic Work. *S.E.*, 14:309–33.

Freud, Sigmund. 1916–17. *Introductory Lectures on Psycho-Analysis. S.E.*, 15 and 16.

Freud, Sigmund. 1919. The "Uncanny." *S.E.*, 17:217–56.

Freud, Sigmund. 1923. *The Ego and the Id. S.E.*, 19:12–66.

Freud, Sigmund. 1924. The Dissolution of the Oedipus Complex. *S.E.*, 19:173–9.

Freud, Sigmund. 1926. *Inhibitions, Symptoms and Anxiety. S.E.*, 20:87–176.

Freud, Sigmund. 1927a. Fetishism. *S.E.*, 21:152–7.

Freud, Sigmund. 1927b. *The Future of an Illusion. S.E.*, 21:5–56.

Freud, Sigmund. 1930. *Civilization and Its Discontents. S.E.*, 21:57–145.

Freud, Sigmund. 1933. *New Introductory Lectures on Psycho-Analysis. S.E.*, 22:5–182.

Freud, Sigmund. 1939. *Moses and Monotheism. S.E.*, 23:7–137.

Freud, Sigmund. 1940. *An Outline of Psycho-Analysis. S.E.*, 23:144–208.

Froula, Christine. 1983. When Eve Reads Milton: Undoing the Canonical Economy. *Critical Inquiry*, 10:321–47.

Frye, Roland M. 1978. *Milton's Imagery and the Visual Arts: Iconographic Tradition in the Epic Poems*. Princeton, NJ: Princeton University Press.

Gadamer, Hans-Georg. 1960. *Truth and Method*. Trans. Garrett Borden and John Cumming. New York: Crossroad, 1982.

Gilbert, Allan H. 1942. The Theological Basis of Satan's Rebellion and the Function of Abdiel in *Paradise Lost. Modern Philology*, 40:19–42.

Giles, John Allen, trans. 1841. *The Chronicle of Richard of Devizes: Concerning the Deeds of Richard the First, King of England*. Cambridge, Ontario: In parentheses Publications, 2000.

Goldberg, Jonathan. 1983. *James I and the Politics of Literature: Jonson, Shakespeare, Donne, and Their Contemporaries*. Baltimore, MD: Johns Hopkins University Press.

Green, André. 1969. *The Tragic Effect: The Oedipus Complex in Tragedy*. Trans. Alan Sheridan. Cambridge: Cambridge University Press.

Green, André. 1983. The Dead Mother. In *On Private Madness*. Trans. Katherine Aubertin. London: Hogarth Press, 1986, pp. 142–73.

Greenblatt, Stephen. 1980. *Renaissance Self-Fashioning: From More to Shakespeare*. Chicago, IL: University of Chicago Press.

Greenblatt, Stephen. 1985. Shakespeare and the Exorcists. In *Shakespearean Negotiations: The Circulation of Social Energy in Renaissance England*. Berkeley, CA: University of California Press, 1988, pp. 94–128.

Greenblatt, Stephen. 2004. The Death of Hamnet and the Making of Hamlet. *The New York Review of Books*, October 21, pp. 42–7.

Greenblatt, Stephen. 2011. *The Swerve: How the World Became Modern*. New York: Norton.

Greenblatt, Stephen. 2017. *The Rise and Fall of Adam and Eve*. New York: Norton.

Grene, David, trans. 1954. *Oedipus the King*. In *Sophocles I*. Ed. David Grene and Richmond Lattimore. Chicago, IL: University of Chicago Press, 1970, pp. 11–76.

Grene, David, trans. 1955. *Hippolytus*. In *Euripides I*. Ed. David Grene and Richmond Lattimore. Chicago, IL: University of Chicago Press, 1972, pp. 163–221.

Grierson, Herbert J. C., ed. 1912. *The Poems of John Donne*. 2 vols. Oxford: Oxford University Press, 1968.

Habeck, Augustine. 2024. "The Womb of Nature and Perhaps Her Grave": The Battle against Chaos in *Paradise Lost*. Unpublished manuscript, ENL 4221, University of Florida.

Hanford, James Holly. 1949. *John Milton, Englishman*. New York: Crown Publishers.

Hanham, Alison. 1975. *Richard III and His Early Historians, 1483–1535*. Oxford: Clarendon Press.

Hardie, Philip. 1995. The Presence of Lucretius in *Paradise Lost*. *Milton Quarterly*, 29:13–24.

Harrison, Kathryn. 1997. *The Kiss: A Memoir*. New York: Random House, 2011.

Hartig, John Joseph. 1972. *The "Art of Logic" and "Paradise Lost": Milton's Own Theory of Logic Put into Actual Practice in His Epic Poem*. Master of Arts Thesis, McMaster University, v + 138 pp.

Hartman, Geoffrey H. 1981. *Saving the Text: Literature/Derrida/Philosophy*. Baltimore, MD: Johns Hopkins University Press.

Hatto, A. T., ed. and trans. 1960. *Tristan*, by Gottfried von Strassburg, with the surviving fragments of the *Tristran* of Thomas. Harmondsworth, Eng.: Penguin Books, 1978.

Hay, Denys, ed. and trans. 1950. *Anglica Historia*, by Polydore Vergil. London: Royal Historical Society.

Heilman, Robert B. 1956. *Magic in the Web: Action and Language in* Othello. Lexington, KY: University of Kentucky Press.

Heng, Geraldine. 1991. Feminine Knots and the Other: *Sir Gawain and the Green Knight*. *PMLA*, 106:500–14.

Hertz, Neil. 1979. Freud and the Sandman. In *Textual Strategies: Perspectives in Post-Structuralist Criticism*. Ed. Josué V. Harari. Ithaca, NY: Cornell University Press, pp. 296–321.

Hieatt, A. Kent. 1970. *Sir Gawain*: Pentangle, Luf-Lace, Numerical Structure. In *Silent Poetry: Essays in Numerological Analysis*. Ed. Alastair Fowler. London: Routledge and Kegan Paul, 1970, pp. 116–40.

Hill, Thomas D. 1980. Gawain's Jesting Lie: Towards an Interpretation of the Confessional Scene in *Sir Gawain and the Green Knight*. *Studia Neophilologica*, 52:279–86.

Hopkins, Brooke. 1981. St. Augustine's *Confessions*: The Pear-Stealing Episode. *American Imago*, 38:97–104.

Horney, Karen. 1926. The Flight from Womanhood: The Masculinity-Complex in Women as Viewed by Men and by Women. In Horney 1967, pp. 54–70.

Horney, Karen. 1932. The Dread of Woman: Observations on a Specific Difference in the Dread Felt by Men and by Women Respectively for the Opposite Sex. In Horney 1967, pp. 133–46.

Horney, Karen. 1967. *Feminine Psychology*. Ed. Harold Kellman. New York: Norton, 1973.

Hughes, Merritt Y., ed. 1957. *John Milton: The Complete Poems and the Major Prose*. New York: Odyssey.

Hughes, Merritt Y., ed. 1962. *The Complete Prose Works of John Milton. Vol. 3, 1648–1649*. New Haven, CT: Yale University Press, 1970.

Hyde, Edward, Earl Of Clarendon. 1702–4. *The History of the Rebellion and the Civil War*. In *Selections*. Ed. G. Huehns. London: Oxford University Press, 1968.

Irigaray, Luce. 1974. *Speculum of the Other Woman*. Trans. Gillian C. Gill. Ithaca, NY: Cornell University Press, 1985.

Irwin, John T. 1975. *Doubling and Incest / Repetition and Revenge: A Speculative Reading of Faulkner*. Baltimore, MD: Johns Hopkins University Press.

Jackson, W. T. H. 1971. *The Anatomy of Love: The* Tristan *of Gottfried von Strassburg*. New York: Columbia University Press.

Jaeger, C. Stephen. 1977. *Medieval Humanism in Gottfried von Strassburg's* Tristan und Isolde. Heidelberg: Carl Winter Universitätsverlag.

Johnson, Barbara. 1977. The Frame of Reference: Poe, Lacan, Derrida. In Muller and Richardson, 1988, pp. 213–51.

Jones, Emrys. 1968. *Othello, Lepanto*, and the Cyprus Wars. *Shakespeare Survey*, 21:47–52.

Jones, Ernest. 1953. *The Life and Work of Sigmund Freud. Vol. 1. The Formative Years and the Great Discoveries, 1856–1900*. New York: Basic Books.

Jones, John. 1995. *Shakespeare at Work*. Oxford: Clarendon Press.

Jorden, Edward. 1603. *A Briefe Discourse of a Disease Called the Suffocation of the Mother*. London: John Windet.

Kahn, Coppélia. 1986. The Absent Mother in *King Lear*. In Ferguson, Quilligan, and Vickers, 1986, pp. 33–49.

Kahn, Coppélia. 1991. *Man's Estate: Masculine Identity in Shakespeare*. Berkeley, CA: University of California Press.

Kamps, Ivo. 1989. Magic, Women, and Incest: The Real Challenges of *Sir Gawain and the Green Knight*. *Exemplaria*, 1:313–36.

Kastan, David Scott. 1986. Proud Majesty Made a Subject: Shakespeare and the Spectacle of Rule. *Shakespeare Quarterly*, 37:459–75.

Kermode, Frank. 1957. "Dissociation of Sensibility." In *Romantic Image*. London: Fontana, 1971, pp. 153–77.

Kermode, Frank. 1975. *The Classic: Literary Images of Permanence and Change*. New York: Viking.

Kerrigan, William W. 1983. *The Sacred Complex: On the Psychogenesis of* Paradise Lost. Cambridge, MA: Harvard University Press.

Kirsch, Arthur. 1978. The Polarization of Erotic Love in *Othello*. *Modern Language Review*, 73:721–40.

Klein, Melanie. 1926. The Psychological Principles of Early Analysis. In *The Writings of Melanie Klein*. Ed. Roger Money-Kyrle et al. 4 vols. New York: Free Press, 1980 (hereafter *Writings*), 1:262–80.

Klein, Melanie. 1930. The Importance of Symbol-Formation in the Development of the Ego. *Writings*, 1:219–32.

Klein, Melanie. 1935. A Contribution to the Psychogenesis of Manic-Depressive States. *Writings*, 1:262–89.

Klein, Melanie. 1940. Mourning and Its Relation to Manic-Depressive States. *Writings*, 1:344–69.

Klein, Melanie. 1945. The Oedipus Complex in Light of Early Anxieties. *Writings*, 1:370–419.

Klein, Melanie. 1946. Notes on Some Schizoid Mechanisms. *Writings*, 3:1–24.

Klein, Melanie. 1952. The Origins of Transference. *Writings*, 3:48–60.

Kligerman, Charles. 1957. A Psychoanalytic Study of the *Confessions* of St. Augustine. *Journal of the American Psychoanalytic Association*, 5:469–84.

Krohn, Rüdiger, ed. 1980. *Tristan*, by Gottfried von Strassburg. 3 vols. Stuttgart: Phillip Reclam, 1990.

Lacan, Jacques. 1949. The Mirror Stage as Formative of the Function of the I as Revealed in Psychoanalytic Experience. In Lacan 1977, pp. 1–7.

Lacan, Jacques. 1953. The Function and Field of Speech and Language in Psychoanalysis. In Lacan 1977, pp. 30–115.

Lacan, Jacques. 1954–5. *The Seminar. Book II. The Ego in Freud's Theory and in the Technique of Psychoanalysis*. Trans. Sylvana Tomaselli. New York: Norton, 1988.

Lacan, Jacques. 1956. Seminar on "The Purloined Letter." Trans. Jeffrey Mehlman. In Muller and Richardson, 1988, pp. 28–54.

Lacan, Jacques. 1958. The Signification of the Phallus. In Lacan 1977, pp. 281–91.

Lacan, Jacques. 1973. *The Four Fundamental Concepts of Psycho-Analysis*. Ed. Jacques Alain-Miller. Trans. Alan Sheridan. New York: Norton, 1981.

Lacan, Jacques. 1977. *Écrits: A Selection*. Trans. Alan Sheridan. New York: Norton.

Lagomarsino, David, and Charles J. Wood, eds. 1989. *The Trial of Charles I: A Documentary History*. Hanover, NH: University Press of New England.

Langley, Philippa, and Michael Jones. 2013. *The Lost King: The Search for Richard III*. New York: St. Martin's Griffin, 2023.

Laplanche, Jean. 1970. *Life and Death in Psychoanalysis*. Trans. Jeffrey Mehlman. Baltimore, MD: Johns Hopkins University Press, 1976.

Le Comte, Edward. 1978. *Milton and Sex*. New York: Columbia University Press.

Leonard, John, ed. 1998. *John Milton: The Complete Poems*. London: Penguin Classics.

Leonard, John. 2000. Milton, Lucretius, and "the Void Profound of Unessential Night." In *Living Texts: Interpreting Milton*. Ed. Kristin A. Pruitt and Charles W. Durham. Susquehanna, PA: Susquehanna University Press, pp. 198–217.

Lévi-Strauss, Claude. 1949. *The Elementary Structures of Kinship*. Trans. James Harle Bell and John Richard von Sturmer. Boston, MA: Beacon.

Lewalski, Barbara K. 1974. Milton on Women: Yet Once More. *Milton Studies*, 6:3–20.

Lipscomb, Valerie Barnes. 2001. "Yet That's Not Much": Age Differences in *Othello. Journal of Aging and Identity*, 6:209–21.

Little, Arthur L. 1993. "An Essence That's Not Seen": The Primal Scene of Racism in *Othello. Shakespeare Quarterly*, 44:304–24.

Locke, John. 1690. *Two Treatises on Government*. Ed. Peter Laslett. New York: Mentor Books, 1963.

Logan, George M., ed. 2016. *Utopia*, by Thomas More. Trans. Robert M. Adams. 3rd ed. Cambridge: Cambridge University Press, 2022.

Loewenstein, David. 1991. *Representing Revolution in Milton and His Contemporaries: Religion, Politics, and Polemics in Radical Puritanism*. Cambridge: Cambridge University Press.

Lucretius. c. 55 B.C.E. *On the Nature of Things*. Rev. ed. Trans. and ed. Martin Ferguson Smith. Indianapolis, IN: Hackett, 2001.

Lupton, Julia Reinhard. 1997. *Othello* Circumcised: Shakespeare and the Pauline Doctrine of Nations. *Representations*, 57(4):73–89.

MacCormack, Sabine. 1998. *The Shadows of Poetry: Vergil in the Mind of Augustine*. Berkeley, CA: University of California Press.

Maguire, Nancy Klein. 1989. The Theatrical Mask/Masque of Politics: The Case of Charles I. *Journal of British Studies*, 28:1–22.

Margoliouth, H. M., ed. 1988. *The Poems and Letters of Andrew Marvell*. 3rd ed. Rev. Pierre Legouis with E. E. Duncan Jones. 2 vols. Oxford: Clarendon Press.

Marius, Richard. 1984. *Thomas More*. New York: Knopf.

Masson, David. 1880. *The Life of John Milton: Narrated in Connexion with the Political, Ecclesiastical, and Literary History of His Time*. 6 vols. 1858–80. Vol. 6. 1660–74. Gloucester, MA: Peter Smith, 1965.

McCabe, Richard A. 2008. *Incest, Drama and Nature's Law, 1550–1700*. Cambridge: Cambridge University Press.

McColley, Diane K. 1983. *Milton's Eve*. Urbana, IL: University of Illinois Press.

Méla, Charles. 1992. Oedipe, Judas, Osiris. In *Histoire et société: mélanges offerts à Georges Duby*, 4:201–20.

Miller, Leo. 1974. *John Milton among the Polygamophiles*. New York: Loewenthal Press.

Mommsen, Theodor E. 1942. Petrarch's Conception of the "Dark Ages." *Speculum*, 17:226–42.

More, Thomas. 1963. *The History of King Richard III*. Ed. Richard S. Sylvester. *The Yale Edition of the Complete Works of St. Thomas More* (hereafter *Yale Ed.*). 15 vols. New Haven: Yale University Press, 1963–97. Vol. 2.

More, Thomas. 1973. *A Dialogue of Comfort against Tribulation*. Ed. Louis L. Martz and Frank Manley. *Yale Ed.*, Vol. 12.

More, Thomas. 1976. *The History of King Richard III and Selections from the English and Latin Poems*. Ed. Richard S. Sylvester. New Haven, CT: Yale University Press.

Moretti, Franco. 1982. "A Huge Eclipse": Tragic Forms and the Deconsecration of Sovereignty. In *The Power of Forms in the English Renaissance*. Ed. Stephen Greenblatt. Norman, OK: University of Oklahoma Press, 1982, pp. 7–40.

Morrison, Toni. 2012. *Desdemona*. London: Methuen, 2024.

Muller, John, and William Richardson, eds. 1988. *The Purloined Poe: Lacan, Derrida, and Psychoanalytic Reading*. Baltimore, MD: Johns Hopkins University Press.

Mulvey, Laura. 1975. Visual Pleasure and Narrative Cinema. *Screen*, 16(3):6–18.

Nathan, Norman. 1988. Othello's Marriage is Consummated. *Cahiers Élisabéthains*, 34(October):79–82.

Neaman, Judith S. 1976. Sir Gawain's Covenant: Troth and *Timor Mortis*. *Philological Quarterly*, 55:30–42.

Neill, Michael. 1989. Unproper Beds: Race, Adultery, and the Hideous in *Othello*. *Shakespeare Quarterly*, 40:383–412.

Nelson, T. G. A., and Charles Haines. 1983. Othello's Unconsummated Marriage. *Essays in Criticism*, 33:1–18.

Newman, Karen. 1987. "And Wash the Ethiope White": Femininity and the Monstrous in *Othello*. In *Fashioning Femininity and English Renaissance Drama*. Chicago, IL: University of Chicago Press, 1991, pp. 71–93.

Nietzsche, Friedrich. 1872. *The Birth of Tragedy*. In *The Birth of Tragedy and The Case of Wagner*. Ed. and trans. Walter Kaufmann. New York: Vintage, 1967, pp. 17–151.

Nin, Anaïs. 1948. Winter of Artifice. In *Winter of Artifice: Three Novelettes*. Athens, OH: Swallow Press, 1999, pp. 37–86.

Nin, Anaïs. 1992. *Incest: The Unexpurgated Diary of Anaïs Nin, 1932–1934*. Ed. Gunther Stuhlmann. San Diego, CA: Harcourt Brace, 1993.

Norbrook, David. 1987. *Macbeth* and the Politics of Historiography. In *Politics of Discourse: The Literature and History of Seventeenth-Century England*. Ed. Kevin Sharpe and Steven N. Zwicker. Berkeley, CA: University of California Press, 1987, pp. 78–116.

Norbrook, David. 1999. *Writing the English Republic: Poetry, Rhetoric and Politics 1627–1660*. Cambridge: Cambridge University Press.

Noyes, Russell B., ed. 1956. *English Romantic Poetry and Prose*. New York: Oxford University Press.

Nyquist, Mary. 1985. The Father's Word/Satan's Wrath. *PMLA*, 100:187–202.

Nyquist, Mary. 1988. The Genesis of Gendered Subjectivity in the Divorce Tracts and in *Paradise Lost*. In *Re-membering Milton: Essays on the Texts and Traditions*. Ed. Mary Nyquist and Margaret W. Ferguson. New York: Methuen, 1988, pp. 99–127.

O'Donnell, James J. 1985. *Augustine*. Boston, MA: Twayne.

Ogden, H. V. S. 1957. The Crisis of *Paradise Lost* Reconsidered. *Philological Quarterly*, 36:1–19.

Ovid. c. 25–16 B.C.E. *The Heroides*. Trans. A. S. Kline. https://www.scribd.com/document/158719850/Heroides-PDF, 2001.

Pagels, Elaine. 1988. *Adam, Eve, and the Serpent*. New York: Random House.

Paris, Bernard. 1997. *Imagined Human Beings: A Psychological Approach to Character and Conflict in Literature*. New York: New York University Press.

Paris, Bernard. 2010. *Heaven and Its Discontents: Milton's Characters in* Paradise Lost. New Brunswick, NJ: Transaction.

Parker, William R. 1949. The Date of *Samson Agonistes*. *Philological Quarterly*, 28:145–66.

Parry, John Jay, ed. and trans. 1941. *The Art of Courtly Love*, by Andreas Capellanus. New York: Norton, 1969.

Paster, Gail Kern. 1989. "In the Spirit of Men There Is No Blood": Blood as Trope of Gender in *Julius Caesar*. *Shakespeare Quarterly*, 40:284–98.

Patrides, C. A. 1966. *Milton and the Christian Tradition*. Hamden, CT: Archon Books, 1979.

Patterson, Annabel. 1978. *Marvell and the Civic Crown*. Princeton, NJ: Princeton University Press.

Patterson, Annabel. 2001. Milton, Marriage and Divorce. In *A Companion to Milton*. Ed. Thomas N. Corns. Oxford: Blackwell, 2001, pp. 279–93.

Patterson, Frank Allen et al., eds. 1935. *A Fuller Institution of the Art of Logic*. Ed. and trans. Allan H. Gilbert. *The Works of John Milton*. 18 vols. New York: Columbia University Press, 1931–8. Vol. 11.

Pocock, J. G. A., ed. 1992. *The Commonwealth of Oceana*, by James Harrington. Cambridge: Cambridge University Press.

Pollard, A. F. 1933. The Making of Sir Thomas More's *Richard III*. In *Essential Articles for the Study of Thomas More*. Ed. Richard S. Sylvester and Germain Marc'hadour. Hamden, CT: Archon Books, 1977, pp. 421–31.

Quint, David. 2004. Fear of Falling: Icarus, Phaethon, and Lucretius in *Paradise Lost*. *Renaissance Quarterly*, 57:847–81.

Rank, Otto. 1912. *The Incest Theme in Literature and Legend*. Trans. Gregory C. Richter. Baltimore, MD: Johns Hopkins University Press, 1992.

Rich, Adrienne. 1980. Compulsory Heterosexuality and Lesbian Existence. In *Feminism and Sexuality*. Ed. Stevi Jackson and Sue Scott. New York: Columbia University Press, 1996, pp. 130–43.

Ridley, Jasper. 1985. *Henry VIII: The Politics of Tyranny*. New York: Viking.

Robinson, F. N., ed. 1957. *The Works of Geoffrey Chaucer*. 2nd ed. Boston, MA: Houghton Mifflin.

Ross, John Munder. 1982. Oedipus Revisited—Laius and the "Laius Complex." *Psychoanalytic Study of the Child*, 37:169–200.

Ross, Lawrence A. 1960. The Meaning of Strawberries in Shakespeare. *Studies in the Renaissance*, 7:225–40.

Rubey, Daniel. 1988. The Troubled House of Oedipus and Chrétien's Neo-Tristan: Re-writing the Mythologies of Desire. In *The Persistence of Myth: Psychoanalytic and Structuralist Perspectives*. Ed. Peter L. Rudnytsky. New York: Guilford, 1988, pp. 67–94.

Rubin, Gayle. 1975. The Traffic in Women: Notes on the "Political Economy" of Sex. In *Toward an Anthropology of Women*. Ed. Rayna R. Reiter. New York: Monthly Review Press, 1985, pp. 157–210.

Rubin, Gayle. 1984. Thinking Sex: Notes for a Radical Theory of the Politics of Sexuality. In *The Lesbian and Gay Studies Reader*. Ed. Henry Abelove, Michèle Aina Barale, and David M. Halperin. New York: Routledge, 1993, pp. 3–44.

Rudnytsky, Peter L. 1991. *Henry VIII* and the Deconstruction of History. *Shakespeare Survey*, 43:43–57.

Rudnytsky, Peter L. 2022. *Mutual Analysis: Ferenczi, Severn, and the Origins of Trauma Theory*. New York: Routledge.

Rymer, Thomas. 1692. *A Short View of Tragedy; It's Original, Excellency, and Corruption. With some Reflections on Shakespear, and Other Practitioners for the Stage*. In *Critical Works of Thomas Rymer*. Ed. Curt A. Zimansky. New Haven, CT: Yale University Press, 1956, pp. 82–175.

Saintsbury, George, ed. 1968. *Minor Poets of the Caroline Period*. 3 vols. Oxford: Clarendon Press.

Schorske, Carl E. 1973. Politics and Patricide in Freud's *Interpretation of Dreams*. *American Historical Review*, 78:328–47.

Sedgwick, Eve Kosofsky. 1985. *Between Men: English Literature and Male Homosocial Desire*. New York: Columbia University Press.

Sharpe, Kevin, and Steven N. Zwicker, eds. 1987. *Politics of Discourse: The Literature and History of Seventeenth-Century England*. Berkeley, CA: University of California Press.

Shawcross, John T. 1961. The Chronology of Milton's Major Poems. *PMLA*, 76:345–78.

Shumaker, Wayne. 1955. The Fallacy of the Fall in *Paradise Lost*. *PMLA*, 70:1185–7.

Sirluck, Ernest. 1961. Milton's Idle Right Hand. *Journal of English and Germanic Philology*, 60:749–85.

Slater, Philip E. 1968. *The Glory of Hera: Greek Mythology and the Greek Family*. Boston, MA: Beacon Press.

Smiley, Jane. 1991. *A Thousand Acres*. New York: Knopf.

Smith, Ian. 2013. Othello's Black Handkerchief. *Shakespeare Quarterly*, 64:1–25.

Smith, Robert M. 1945. Spenser and Milton: An Early Analogue. *Modern Language Notes*, 60:394–8.

Snow, Edward A. 1980. Sexual Anxiety and the Male Order of Things in *Othello*. *English Literary Renaissance*, 10:384–412.

Spearing, A. C. 1970. *The Gawain-Poet: A Critical Study*. Cambridge: Cambridge University Press.

Spearing, A. C. 1993. *The Medieval Poet as Voyeur: Looking and Listening in Medieval Love-Narratives*. Cambridge: Cambridge University Press.

Speziale-Bagliacca, Roberto. 1998. *The King and the Adulteress: A Psychoanalytic and Literary Reinterpretation of* Madame Bovary *and* King Lear. Durham, NC: Duke University Press.

Sprengnether, Madelon. 1990. *The Spectral Mother: Freud, Feminism, and Psychoanalysis*. Ithaca, NY: Cornell University Press.

Statius. c. 92 C.E. *Silvae. Thebaid, Books 1–4*. Trans. J. H. Mozley. Loeb Classical Library. Cambridge, MA: Harvard University Press, 1928.

Stein, Arnold. 1953. *Answerable Style: Essays on* Paradise Lost. Seattle, WA: University of Washington Press.

Stein, Arnold. 1957. *The Art of Presence: The Poet in* Paradise Lost. Berkeley, CA: University of California Press.

Stevens, Adrian, and Roy Wisbey, eds. 1990. *Gottfried von Strassburg and the Medieval Tristan Legend: Papers from an Anglo-American Symposium*. Suffolk, Eng.: Brewer.

Sullivan, Harry Stack. 1953. *The Interpersonal Theory of Psychiatry*. Ed. Helen Swick Perry and Mary Ladd Gawel. New York: Norton.

Suttie, Ian. 1935. *The Origins of Love and Hate*. London: Free Association Books, 1988.

Swales, Peter J. 1982. Freud, Minna Bernays, and the Conquest of Rome: New Light on the Origins of Psychoanalysis. *New American Review*, 1 (Spring/Summer):1–23.

Swan, Jim. 1976. History, Pastoral and Desire: Andrew Marvell's Mower Poems. *International Review of Psychoanalysis*, 3:193–202.

Sylvester, Richard S. 1967. A Part of His Own: Thomas More's Literary Personality in His Early Works. *Moreana*, 15:29–42.

Sylvester, Richard S., and Davis P. Harding, eds. 1962. *The Life of Sir Thomas More*, by Sir William Roper. In *Two Early Tudor Lives*. New Haven, CT: Yale University Press, pp. 197–254.

Tanner, Tony. 1979. *Adultery in the Novel: Contract and Transgression*. Baltimore, MD: Johns Hopkins University Press, 1981.

Tax, Petrus. 1990. Wounds and Healings: Aspects of Salvation and Tragic Love in Gottfried's *Tristan*. In Stevens and Wisbey, 1990, pp. 223–33.

Tayler, Edward W. 1979. *Milton's Poetry: Its Development in Time*. Pittsburgh, PA: Duquesne University Press.

Taylor, Gary. 1980. The War in *King Lear*. *Shakespeare Survey*, 33:27–33.

Tillyard, E. M. W. 1951. *Studies on Milton*. London: Chatto and Windus.

Trilling, Lionel. 1963. The Fate of Pleasure. In *Beyond Culture*. New York: Viking, 1968, pp. 57–87.

Troncarelli, Fabio. 1993. *Il ricordo della sofferenza: Le "Confessioni" di Sant' Agostino e la psicoanalisi*. Naples: Edizione Scientifiche Italiane.

Turner, James Grantham. 2024. Milton, Lucretius, and the "Womb of Nature." *Milton Studies*, 66:1–41.

Vitkus, Daniel. 2003. *Turning Turk: English Theater and the Multicultural Mediterranean, 1570–1630*. New York: Palgrave Macmillan.

Vitkus, Daniel. 2019. *Othello*, Islam, and the Noble Moor: Spiritual Identity and the Performance of Blackness on the Early Modern Stage. In *The Cambridge Companion to Shakespeare and Religion*. Ed. Hannibal Hamlin. Cambridge: Cambridge University Press, 2019, pp. 218–33.

Waldock, A. J. A. 1947. Paradise Lost *and Its Critics*. Cambridge: Cambridge University Press.

Wangh, Martin. 1950. *Othello*, the Tragedy of Iago. *Psychoanalytic Quarterly*, 19:202–12.

Ward, C. Macauley Jr. 2011. Of Milton's First Disobedience and the Fruit of the Tree: "Ad Patrem" as Prologue to *Paradise Lost*. Master's thesis, University of Massachusetts, Boston. 36 pp.

Weatherly, Caitlin. 2020. Innocence Lost: The Consequences of Extramarital Affairs. Unpublished manuscript, ENL 4221, University of Florida.

Webber, Joan M. 1980. The Politics of Poetry: Feminism and *Paradise Lost*. *Milton Studies*, 14:3–24.

Weisinger, Herbert. 1943. The Self-Awareness of the Renaissance as a Criterion of the Renaissance. *Papers of the Michigan Academy of Science, Arts, and Letters*, 29:561–7.

Weiskel, Thomas. 1976. *The Romantic Sublime: Studies in the Structure and Psychology of Transcendence*. Baltimore, MD: Johns Hopkins University Press.

West, Rebecca. 1933. *St. Augustine*. New York: Appleton.

Wharton, Janet. 1990. "Das lebende Paradis"?: A Consideration of the Love of Tristan and Isot in the Light of the "huote" [Surveillance] Discourse. In Stevens and Wisbey, 1990, pp. 143–54.

Whigham, Frank. 1996. *Seizures of the Will in Early Modern English Drama*. Cambridge: Cambridge University Press.

Whitney, Lois. 1922. Did Shakespeare Know Leo Africanus? *PMLA*, 37:470–83.

Wilde, Oscar. 1891. *The Picture of Dorian Gray*. Ed. Peter Ackroyd. Harmondsworth, Eng.: Penguin Books, 1985.

Willbern, David. 1980. Shakespeare's Nothing. In *Representing Shakespeare: New Psychoanalytic Essays*. Ed. Murray Schwartz and Coppélia Kahn. Baltimore, MD: Johns Hopkins University Press, 1982, pp. 244–63.

Willbern, David. 1997. *Poetic Will: Shakespeare and the Play of Language.* Philadelphia, PA: University of Pennsylvania Press.

Wills, Garry. 1999. *Saint Augustine.* New York: Viking.

Winnicott, D. W. 1953. Transitional Objects and Transitional Phenomena. In Winnicott 1971, pp. 1–25.

Winnicott, D. W. 1964. *The Child, the Family, and the Outside World.* Harmondsworth, Eng.: Penguin Books.

Winnicott, D. W. 1971. *Playing and Reality.* London: Tavistock Publications, 1984.

Wittreich, Joseph. 1987. *Feminist Milton.* Ithaca, NY: Cornell University Press.

Woodhouse, A. S. P. 1949. *Samson Agonistes* and Milton's Experience. *Transactions of the Royal Society of Canada,* 43:157–75.

Worden, Blair. 1987. Andrew Marvell, Oliver Cromwell, and the Horatian Ode. In Sharpe and Zwicker 1987, pp. 147–80.

Worden, Blair. 1995. Milton, *Samson Agonistes,* and the Restoration. In *Culture and Society in the Stuart Restoration.* Ed. Gerald MacLean. Cambridge: Cambridge University Press, 1995, pp. 111–36.

Worden, Blair. 1998. John Milton and Oliver Cromwell. In *Soldiers, Writers and Statesmen of the English Revolution.* Ed. Ian Gentles, John Morrill, and Blair Worden. Cambridge: Cambridge University Press, 1998, pp. 243–64.

Wordsworth, William. 1850. *The Prelude, 1799, 1805, 1850.* Ed. Jonathan Wordsworth, M. H. Abrams, and Stephen Gill. New York: Norton, 1979.

Wulff, Mosche. 1946. Fetishism and Object Choice in Early Childhood. *Psychoanalytic Quarterly,* 15:450–71.

Index

Volumes in the Series

Mourning Freud
by Madelon Sprengnether

Does the Internet Have an Unconscious?: Slavoj Žižek and Digital Culture
by Clint Burnham

In the Event of Laughter: Psychoanalysis, Literature and Comedy
by Alfie Bown

On Dangerous Ground: Freud's Visual Cultures of the Unconscious
by Diane O'Donoghue

For Want of Ambiguity: Order and Chaos in Art, Psychoanalysis, and Neuroscience
by Ludovica Lumer and Lois Oppenheim

Life Itself Is an Art: The Life and Work of Erich Fromm
by Rainer Funk

Born After: Reckoning with the German Past
by Angelika Bammer

Critical Theory Between Klein and Lacan: A Dialogue
by Amy Allen and Mari Ruti

Transferences: The Aesthetics and Poetics of the Therapeutic Relationship
by Maren Scheurer

At the Risk of Thinking: An Intellectual Biography of Julia Kristeva
by Alice Jardine, edited by Mari Ruti

The Writing Cure
by Emma Lieber

The Analyst's Desire: The Ethical Foundation of Clinical Practice
by Mitchell Wilson